Divided Lives

Divided Lives

Dreams of a Mother and Daughter

LYNDALL GORDON

virago

VIRAGO

First published in Great Britain in 2014 by Virago Press

Copyright © Lyndall Gordon 2014

A CIP catalogue record for this book
is available from the British Library.

Hardback ISBN 978-1-84408-889-8
C Format ISBN 978-1-84408-890-4

Typeset in Bembo by M Rules
Printed and bound in Great Britain by
Clays Ltd, St Ives plc

Papers used by Virago are from well-managed forests
and other responsible sources.

MIX
Paper from
responsible sources
FSC® C104740

Virago Press
An imprint of
Little, Brown Book Group
100 Victoria Embankment
London EC4Y 0DY

An Hachette UK Company
www.hachette.co.uk

www.virago.co.uk

For Pip

Contents

1

'Sister'

I'm to be my mother's sister because she wants one so. My part is to be there if she's ill. At four years old, it's a privilege to have this responsibility instead of trotting off to nursery school like other children.

My mother looks back to the wide-open dawns of her

childhood because these days she has to be drugged as soon as she wakes. The powders dull her, she explains, a temptation not to take them, and no one knows if she does or not. Morning is the darkest time of her day.

Suddenly she calls in her danger-voice, 'Help, oh-h, help me. Quickly!'

It's a test she might fail; if she does she might go mad, or worse. I fly to her side and find her on her knees or crouched on all fours. I grab the glass jug on her bedside table and toss water in her face. It doesn't matter if it splashes the bed or spills over the floor. If she doesn't revive I must dig in her handbag for the large blue Mason Pearson hairbrush and push its bristles into her wrists. I never do this hard enough. Is this because I don't have the strength or can't bear to hurt her? She wrenches the brush from my hand and drives the bristles back and forth across her wrists – until she comes round. Sooner or later she will come round. Then she pulls herself up from the floor and lies on her bed, moaning. Lenie, the cook, hears the commotion, and comes pitter-patter on small feet. I'm relieved to see her, and ashamed too for Lenie to see Madam so. Lenie sucks her tongue in dismay and brings a cup of sweet, milky tea. Lenie never says a word, but has her share in our helplessness. None of us say a word. It happens, and we go on till the next time.

My mother is slow to get up, slow to dress. She runs the tap and splashes her face, on and on to the measure of slap, slap, drip, slap, slap, drip to counteract the miasma of the powders. Then she draws seamed stockings over her feet and hooks them on to the four straps dangling from the belt around her waist. All her underwear, including the silky petticoat, is purest white. Her smalls are washed separately every day; nothing unclean touches her skin. I'm waiting for her to finish, but her dreamy slowness makes me restless. I go off to the nursery to dig into the toy cupboard behind the ruched green curtain patterned with a thin red thread. Across the passage I hear her dialling the telephone, her finger in the hole, a whirr to the number then the varied slide of the returning dial; and then her housewife voice, wearily dutiful as she gives Mr Romm the grocer or Mrs Bass the fishmonger an order to be delivered to Lenie (since my mother rarely visits the kitchen). Mrs Bass, leaning over her counter with her gap-toothed smile, has the ready-to-please manner of South African service. She spares the time to answer my mother's many questions as to quality and freshness.

In the forties and fifties, husbands of housewives have a right to complain. My father Harry is easygoing and enjoys (as my mother puts it) 'fullness of life', but he does grumble if breakfast does not appear as he ties his shoelaces, putting one foot and then the other on the *riempies* of his dining-room chair. The grumble isn't made to Lenie but to his wife, who has nothing to do but take charge of the servants and yet, at this moment, is reading Wordsworth and reaching out to a girl who 'dwelt among the untrodden ways'.

Harry's grumble is routine; he's looking forward to a lawyer's day, ready for his next case as in youth he'd stood ready, swinging his arms in his one-piece racing costume: the first whistle took him to the brink of the pool, toes curled around the edge; at the second blast his arms swung back, knees bent, tensing his shoulders for the dive; and then – GO. Other whistles blew him about the pool in games of water polo. The secret of water polo, he tells me, is to tackle an opponent under the water where the referee can't see.

In childhood my mother, as Rhoda Press, lived in a different world, a barely populated place called Klaver (more commonly called Klawer) on the border of Namaqualand, which stretches along the *Weskus*, the harsh west coast of the southern tip of Africa. It has low rainfall, and at that time, before irrigation schemes, looked like the parched landscapes of the Bible. She recalls how 'I opened my eyes on a shepherd's world with flocks of bushes stretching to the curve of the veld.'

The horizons of Namaqualand are often so cloudless you can see line upon blue line of mountains and, looking up at night, a river of stars. In 1917, when Rhoda was born, Klaver was little more than far-flung farms at the end of the railway line that ran more or less parallel to the coast. By the time I'm born, in the forties, the railway has been extended some way beyond Klaver, but it never reaches what is now Namibia to the north.

I am to be a channel for my mother's life and writings. It's impossible to remember at what age this emerges into consciousness. All that can be said with certainty is that a sisterhood of child-carer changes during my schooldays into a sisterhood of poems and stories. She reads Emily Dickinson to me over and over. There seems no divide between the 'Colossal substance of Immortality' in the visionary poets she loves – Dickinson and Emily Brontë – and her own desk-drawer poems. These she reads aloud with modest disclaimers.

Let me be clear: my role has less to do with love than reliance. I am not lovely; I am heavily freckled; not a light spray, but splotched all over despite the floppy-brimmed hat on my head. When the sun is at its zenith each December, impeccable Aunt Berjulie, who was brought up by her own impeccable aunts in Northern Rhodesia, comes down to the Cape. In well-matched outfits from John Orr's in Johannesburg, Aunt Berjulie never fails to alert my mother to my uneven teeth and ruined face. My mother, whose darker skin is unmarked by sun, never thinks much about looks. This makes it comfortable to be with her. I'm a conscientious child, not winning, not brainy, but exercising an earnest intelligence – not the most attractive of qualities, yet it includes attention to phrases like 'the river of stars' and 'the curve of the veld' that fountain from my mother. And I am there; she feels close to those who have shared what she calls her 'attacks'. There are others she loves more: my brother Pip belting out 'Great Balls of Fire'; her Pooh-Bear brother Basil, with a healthy appetite and is inclined, his sister teases, to think it 'time for a little something'; and then there are her schoolfriends, maternal Auntie Monica and practical Auntie Lilian. All charm her as different while I am like, and in that sense an extension of herself.

A channel, then. My mother never explains how this channel is to be dug between her shut-off invalid existence and some far-off future when her voice will emerge.

Nor, given our reversal of roles, does she foresee a divide. It never occurs to her that separation will ever be necessary. In fact, it's part of her appeal for me that the common course of existence plays no part in her dreams.

Mothering may be the strongest bond most creatures experience, and the acts of separation from that bond shape our lives. For me, a daughter caught up in the crises of illness, this divide must be deferred.

2

Mothers

My name is an embarrassment. If only my mother had called me Linda, or any other common name.

'Stand up and spell it,' teachers will say on the first day of the school year.

They never recognise the name of the singular woman in Olive Schreiner's novel, *The Story of an African Farm*. Nor can any teacher know that it marks me as my mother's creature. My name comes from Rhoda's other life, called up more fully in the memory-dream she inhabits. The Lyndall of the novel is a curiosity of the veld: a woman shaped by unstoried spaces where the curve of the earth can be seen on the encircling horizon. I pull the book from the shelf and glance at its opening line: 'The full African moon poured down its light from the blue sky into the wide, lonely plain.' Vaguely I take in an embrace of nature and solitude. Rhoda is not particularly drawn to the politics of the heroine's turn to the feminist cause. What matters is her authentic nature: a woman without a mask, rising from a bedrock of stone and bush.

Later, when I read the novel, I recognise my mother in the perceptive girl, a rarity amongst the farming people about her, and echo my mother's empathy for the solitary shepherd boy Waldo – with his philosopher's name – a dreamer too innocent for this world.

Rhoda's secret self is partly open to detection, through not-so-buried signals like my name. A poem she reads aloud remembers 'children's voices chipped out of silence' when her brothers, Basil and Sydney, dared her to tread the single track of the railway bridge above the Olifants River. There are only three trains a week, night trains due at dawn, but the children work up their dread of an engine, a dark face looming around a curve on the approach to the bridge. They imagine far-off, then near, the puff and clank of a piston. Safety, she tells me, is possible in the form of three, square bays at intervals along the bridge, each just big enough for a person to stand back from a train thundering along the track, and Rhoda makes her advance from one to the next; then leans over the rail to gaze at the drop to the river below.

This scene fills out Rhoda's courage to go on in the face of oncoming attacks. Her fear is my fear for her precariousness. Yet, as a dreamer, she can dissolve fear and, in a poem she writes, can hear 'in the hollows of space / where the wind scoops bliss / the eternal ocean of the universe.'

A timeless landscape, pulsating with import, means more to her than the present where she performs as she must from day to day. It's as though she's protected from what her beloved Wordsworth called 'the prison house' of grown-ups. He too believed the soul must be sustained by memory's allegiance to the child who comes trailing memories of pre-life.

'One morning in school,' she says in her story-voice, 'I saw a crowd of children round the tin lavatory whose door stood open. As I approached there was laughter. On the high wooden seat sat a little girl with her legs dangling and her drawers round her ankles, half way from the ground. Her eyes were helpless before the mocking crowd. This was my first acquaintance with cruelty, and though it remained with me I did nothing about it.'

My mother bathes such scenes in reminiscent tolerance but now and then memory does throw up brutal scenes, which she does not hesitate to reveal to me. If we listeners were not colluding in the dream of Klaver we'd say this: it was a place of violence. Violence against the weak. Mr Biebek, who called his wife 'Girlie', beat her – but, people said, that was a husband's right. At one of the gangers' cottages along the line, a railway worker chased his son round and round the house with a whip, the boy's thin neck-bones straining as he ran. This boy died young, and that is all people recalled in after years: the fact that his father whipped him, and that he died before he grew up. It was, they said, a father's right. 'What can you do?'

But cruelty can't explain why this woman says 'Klaver . . . Klaver . . . Klaver' all her life. She hadn't seen a bald dorp under the glare of the sun; she had seen the source of all life. Once, there was mystery here. The wind in the gum tree, the snake in the lucerne patch, the twofold *mielie* shoot in the saffron earth, the swallows' mud-nests under the corrugated roof of the stoep, the air of winter mornings (so cold and pure it burns the nostrils), the nursery by candlelight, their father's tales and Yiddish lullabies, will hold for Rhoda – and for her more worldly brothers – the source of some power that propels their lives, as though the God of the Hebrew Bible walked with them in that wilderness when they were young.

'An impress of the everlasting' came to her first when she was six. She repeats the story to me in her memory-voice, throbbing with import when she's not reading or jotting down a poem and wants a listener, and I'm standing there next to her bed, looking down at her to check if she's all right. She won't simplify her words, as other mothers might. A poet expects her listener to catch on, so phrases like 'impress of the everlasting' come my way. Her memory-voice sounds so inward, she's almost murmuring to herself.

Six years old, in Namaqualand, she was sweeping the silky brown sand off the stoep in the early morning. 'I looked across flocks of bushes to where, in the far distance, sun-shafts, like pillars of gold-smoke, moved on the face of the veld. The light and its smoky breath flooded my being.'

For all Rhoda's readiness to share these memories, she shuts the door on others.

'I can't tell you . . .' she stops short at the onset of illness or what she understands about its nature. And she never follows on from hints of a sad love affair before she married my father.

Why can't she tell, I wonder. Are there things in her past too bad for a child to hear? Am I lucky to be spared a fuller sisterhood? Like a sponge I sop up these hints of suffering, then turn away to do a puzzle on the round nursery table or open a jokey picture in *Winnie-the-Pooh*: the motherly Kanga inflicting a bath on Piglet, who has dared to take the place of baby Roo in her pouch. It's a relief not to read my mother's downcast face.

My brother Pip recalls 'our lying-down mother'. She leaves hands-on care to servants, harassed by her mother who, as Rhoda protests, 'interferes', disrupting the household when she tidies the pantry till one in the morning. Annie Press, our grandmother, is on the watch as the housemaid turns out the rooms every morning. Has the maid swept every particle of dust blowing into the open windows from Lion's Head, the mountain above us? Has the washerwoman fetched the sheets from the top room? The washerwoman's lips are pressed together as she kneels over the tub and pegs sheets out in white swathes, flapping in the wind with gunshot sounds until they stiffen in the sun.

Granny knows that you can't leave running a home to the maids, as she tells Harry her son-in-law, whom the servants call Master (as all South African servants call the man of the house). Our father, too breezy to notice what anyone can see, that Rhoda's respect for servants is more effective, backs Granny's reign. There's audible bustle when guests arrive and tea is not served at once. Lenie mutters '*gits*' quietly over the oven as she takes out her Lenie-cake, to be iced with deft pats and strokes into delectable peaks. Lenie is a church-going, single woman in a starched white cap and apron, whose modesty is not lost on my mother. She has read the New Testament as well as the Hebrew Bible, and sides with Christ's defiance of worldly might: the meek shall inherit the earth.

'Lenie is a saint,' my mother declares.

For all their differences of faith and occupation, as well as the colour bar, Lenie and my mother are suited as moral beings. So Lenie puts up with Granny 'for Madam's sake', and one or other servant agrees out of the corner of their mouths.

Granny whips the cups off the tray Lenie has prepared so that she can replace the tray cloth with one she's embroidered in green stem stitch with pink lazy-daisy loops for the petals. I trace the petals with my forefinger and ask Granny, 'Will you show me how?' I want to touch her skeins of silky embroidery thread, confident that Granny will let me choose the loveliest colours.

Granny's interference seems to me mere fuss, a bit of a joke. Less so to her daughter.

'You see her as she is now,' Rhoda confides behind her closed door. 'You don't know how powerful she was when my father was alive. He never called her anything but "darling", and let her have her way.'

Rhoda idolises her father, a 'sensitive man, a Press'. His character as a Press is another clue to who she is. She is decidedly not a creature of her mother, wholly an issue of her father, a reading, thinking man with an intelligent capacity for suffering. He came from Lithuania, like almost all of the hundred thousand Jews who migrated to South Africa. At thirty-six, after twenty years in the back veld, he visited Cape Town and fell in love with auburn-haired Annie, aged twenty-two, who kept house for her widowed Papa (pronounced 'Pupper') and in her fondly insensitive way bossed four younger brothers and sisters.

When Rhoda tells the story of her parents' courtship she defends her father's superiority, even though, as an immigrant, he'd driven about the veld in a mule cart.

'There are no class distinctions amongst Jews. We are equals in the sight of God.'

She speaks to a child as to an adult, yet I'm aware of things elided from her stories of the past. When I'm older this unease can surface as words that I keep to myself, knowing by then how deftly she translates her preference for her father into myth and principle.

Annie and Philip Press married in December 1914, and for some time Annie continued to preside over Papa's comfortable house on Maynard Street in town while her husband continued up country. It was only after the births of a son, Basil, in 1915 and a daughter, Rhoda, in 1917 that Annie joined her husband at the end of the railway line.

This was the setting for Rhoda's romance with her father – dubbed 'Sir Philip' by farmers in the region, as she asserts too insistently to be convincing. So, as 'our lying-down mother', she fills out the memory-dream into which she wanders away from household routine. On the edge of Namaqualand her father sings by candlelight to four children. Her mother holds dances in the cleared dining room of the hotel; she hangs cheeses from the ceiling of her separate kosher kitchen; and

Engagement photo, *c.* 1914, of Philip Press from Lithuania
and Annie Hoffman, born in Johannesburg, 1892

receives a gift of home-grown tomatoes from 'the Giantess'
who farms in the *kloof* in the Matzikamma Mountains behind
Klaver. Rhoda remembers the gloaming light on the oranges
deep in the *kloof*, a waterfall and the stinkwood furniture: a long
black table, so polished it reflects three bowls of violets.

But Annie damped this down with calls to the nanny to
smarten up her daughter and brush her hair. Annie's crassness
knew no bounds. Rhoda likes to repeat her mother's put-down
of the Parthenon during a tour of Europe: 'I'm sure to *crich*

[toil] up there to see a *Goi-ish-ke* cathedral.' Granny's Yiddish is limited to a few dismissive words, and distorted by the vehemence of a South African accent.

'You're only a *pfefferil* [peppercorn]': her emphatic fs blow me away if I offer an unwelcome opinion.

Granny has no idea what others think or feel, and this makes her a very happy person. A child can nest in this easy insensitivity. There are no undercurrents of need. Her chat has the confidence of a woman at home in her life.

When Annie reaches her eighties her daughter asks her, 'What was the best time in your life?'

'Now, of course,' is her answer.

Basil (left), Sydney and Rhoda, *c.* 1920, in front of the hotel built by their father when the railway was extended to Klaver. 'Three Little Pigs' is Sydney's caption in Rhoda's album

This absence of reflection comes to me as comfort. I associate it with the plumped-up pillows and puffy eiderdown of my grandmother's high double bed, which I share during her long stays with us. She's soft when she unsnaps her corset, warm and round with long breasts from feeding children. I lie at rest, released from the tension of my mother's face, her fear of that beast lurking in the corners of her room, the blue brush with its strong bristles, the jug of water waiting at her elbow, the glass and pills that she may or may not take.

Granny's domain is the large front bedroom, which for some reason we call the top room, though there's no upstairs. The top room is furnished in Rhoda's feminine style. A white muslin bedspread with gathers at the side over a pale pink under-slip covers what was Granny's marriage bed, and where she gave birth four times, tugging (she will tell me when I'm old enough to hear) on a sheet tied to the post at the foot of the bed. There's a rose carpet, and above hangs a curly chandelier painted a faint white.

For a brief spell, it had been our parents' room, before an attack happened there. It was prompted, Rhoda hints, by an unwilling move from Rhodean, her family home since they left Namaqualand. In 1945 she was taken from shady, old-fashioned Oranjezicht and stuck in the glare of Sea Point, with coloured lights strung up on a sea-front hotel and cocktail parties in its palm-filled garden. It suits Harry to be close to the beaches, where bodies stretch out under the sun, turning from back to front or front to back as on a spit. Displaced amidst housewives who invite her to morning cards, Rhoda withdraws into Wordsworth's 'bliss of solitude', fortified by *The Bible Designed to be Read as Literature*.

Harry is cock-a-hoop because he's acquired a house for five thousand pounds. It doesn't occur to him that it's not such a scoop if his wife dislikes it. Too ill to view the house in time, she's dismayed to find herself planted in a thirties box with little natural light, darkened further by a hideous red curtain at the end of a passage. Our house, 11 Avenue Normandie, is in an area of Sea Point called Fresnaye. The avenues, named in the seventeenth century by Huguenot refugees, rise perpendicularly up the increasingly steep slope of Lion's Head. My mother confides that her secret name for our house is 'Upwards'. Secret it has to be, because a way-station on an allegorical climb would be out of place in a suburb where houses and streets have European names like Bellevue and King's Road.

After the top-room attack, our parents move to a back room opposite the nursery. One night in the nursery, I wake to sounds never heard before. Not, this time, a call for help, but almost inhuman cries, coming from my mother. I know at once this is the thing she's feared: the full-on, unstoppable thing. Between the cries, there's our father's courtroom voice. This time I don't run to her, but lie petrified. Am I a coward to leave it to our father, who can't console her? No one can. No doctor is called; Harry is handling this on his own, trying to quiet her. The cries die down and the next day my mother is sunk in a half-daze. She can barely speak, and escapes from time to time into sleep. I tiptoe to see if she's all right. If I don't open the door softly she will stir and cry, 'Oh, NO-O-O.' The feminine touches to her room, the white moonflowers in a dainty vase, the rose lamp-shade and the pale pink bed-jacket knitted in a lacy pattern, are futile against the attack of the beast.

After our parents vacate the top room, Granny installs her glass-topped dressing table with an oval, swinging mirror and her massive three-door wardrobe packed with hats, sunshades and a fox fur with paws, bead eyes and snout. It has a strange, chemical smell when I put my nose to it to feel its softness.

On summer nights, with windows open to the murmur of the sea and the salt-smell of seaweed, moths and brown, hard-winged Christmas beetles fly towards the lamp. When I hear the click as one knocks blindly against the wall or wardrobe, or see the flutter of a moth, I cry and duck.

'It can't hurt you,' I'm told, but I flee all the same.

'Wait, I'll catch it,' Rhoda says, cupping her hands. Gently, she carries the fluttering creature to the window, opens her palms and frees it into the night.

She takes seriously the Commandment: Thou shalt not kill. Her respect for creatures is in keeping with a creative spirit that rolls through all things. She draws out what she expects to find in all small children: a moral sense, untrammelled as yet by the prison house.

Her absolutes are as striking as the poems and psalms she reads aloud, and I puzzle over certain contradictions: the sticky fly-papers, for instance, dangling from the kitchen ceiling, stuck about with the black spots of dead flies. Though the kitchen is not my mother's scene, she must have seen them. Or does she block from her line of vision what she doesn't care to see? And although we are by no means rich, and although too my mother, cherishing books and memorabilia, scorns 'shop-bought' – mass-produced – goods, she does buy the best when it comes to quality of clothing or linen or food. Money, I slowly realise, can't be as irrelevant as it seems in a house filled with women – grandmother, wife, daughter, female servants – where the man of the house leaves for the office. Rhoda's three brothers are 'in business': they have a growing chain of clothing and houseware stores called Edgars, yet Rhoda exempts them from her abhorrence of getting and spending. For she loves them, and more: she's proud of their enterprise, and overrides her contempt for commerce with praise for her brothers' probity.

As a girl of my generation, from whom little is expected, I'm imbued with my mother's liberating counter-commerce ideals, reinforced by her younger brothers' veneration of books. For many active men in our provincial society, books mean little:

snippets in the *Reader's Digest* for white males like my father or, for black youths in the townships, the *skiet en donder* routines in high-rise cities across the ocean. Aspiring men choose to be doctors or lawyers or accountants, hardly ever scholars or editors or writers.

My father is the son of a dairyman. His school, the South African College School, is lucky enough to have its own Rhodes scholarship to Oxford. Sport is a condition of this scholarship, and since the top boy in his class plays no sport Harry, who comes second, is in line to win it. He has no regrets for deciding not to apply. Bright enough, confident, articulate, yet with no taste for superfluous learning, he shares the view of his mother that Oxford is a luxury he can't afford. For Thekla, a British university is off the map. She comes from Latvia. Small, pretty, her white hair neatly combed away from her face and secured with hairpins, she admires three grandsons, Peter, Gerald and Neville, who greet her with smiles and good-natured ease.

'Good boys, well brought up,' Thekla nods over their heads to their mothers who are her twin daughters.

I'm a little dashed not to be included in Thekla's favour, and have no hope of a share in the neat features of my father's family. To my uneasy feelers, Thekla appears on the lookout for lapses when it comes to Ps and Qs.

Gerald, Peter and Neville are the handsomest boys I've ever seen. My father has that same kind of masculinity, born of the beach, sun, jokes, normality. Gerald is two years older than I. At his house, 21 Avenue Protea, higher up on Lion's Head, he asks, 'Shall we play rude doctor-doctor?' and introduces a twist of plasticine to my bottom. My mother is appalled and reproachful when she discovers it at bath-time. All the same, I'm ready to play again. One summer afternoon we cool off in the sprinkler on Gerald's back lawn. I haven't brought a bather, so wear one of his. He invites neighbouring boys to inspect a naked girl. I'm game to show off in a hollow of the hedge where no one else can see.

Gerald is with my mother and me when we go on a ten-day holiday to Monica's vineyard. It's on a hill in the wine region of Stellenbosch. We play in the long, sun-stroked grass on the summit of the hill, but one morning wake to find an infestation of moths all over the farmhouse.

'Would you rather die or have fifty moths on you?' Gerald asks.

It's hard to choose. 'I want to go home,' I beg my mother.

She gets up and encloses a moth in her palms, then slowly opens them to show how beautiful the creature is with its folded wings. When it's still, I concede its beauty, but when it grows frightened and flutters, I scream and run.

Back home I hear on the wireless a different tale from the domestic or orphan's stories my mother tells. 'The Adventure of the Speckled Band' by Conan Doyle is my first horror story, enhanced by sinister sound effects. They tune up my fears of insects with a new fear of poisonous snakes. Might a snake, like the one in the tale, slide through the high-up ventilator leading into the top room from the stoep where, in summer, lizards cling like scaly hyphens to the walls? This becomes my pet fear; Lenie has to check under the bed to make sure no snake lurks there. A nightmare sends me rushing to my parents' room. It's dangerous for my mother to be jolted awake so I am told to wake my father very quietly, to say, 'It's me' and to get into his bed. After a while his arm feels like iron under my head, and I slide out and return to the top room. The worst that can happen is to hear my mother groan, 'Oh NO!' It means I've woken her to an actual nightmare: fear of an attack. Her terror is lodged in me.

There's a different dread on Sundays when I'm taken for a

stroll with my father along the bustling seafront. Here I'm exposed to comment on my face when my cheery father turns away, every so often, to greet people who listen in to his Saturday radio broadcast on *Sports Roundup*. As soon as I'm idling on my own, children, from a safe distance, yell 'freckle face'. Is that me? It has to be, for who else − certainly no one in sight − is so splotched with brown marks? These children assure me of a disfigurement others pretend not to notice.

Afterwards we visit Thekla in her flat in Gloucester Court, on the beach front at Three Anchor Bay. I sit on the edge of a stuffed chair, wary of touching the white crocheted covers protecting the headrests and arms of the lounge suite. Chopped herring is offered. It gives off a sour smell. I can't put the fishy mush in my mouth, so a wish to please compels me to accept one of Thekla's *taiglach*, though it looks like poo: a sticky brown kind of doughnut cooked so hard that milk teeth can only scratch at the surface. I lick it tentatively. Sugar. Unmelted crystals rasp my tongue. It's like licking a sugared rock.

Thekla has an air of no nonsense, a kind of not listening − different from my mother, who may be dreamy but can be relied on to take note of real trouble. Some years before, Thekla's daughter had a row with her husband when they were new to marriage. I picture his blazing red face as he shoves Aunt Lena out of the house and locks the door. No answer when she rings the bell and calls to be let in.

'What could I do?' Aunt Lena relays this scene to my mother, who feels for the wrongs of women. 'I ran home to my parents. My mother didn't want to hear: "Go straight back," she said. "That's your home now." That taught me a lesson.'

To manage on a modest income from the dairy, Thekla had trained her five children to switch off unnecessary lights and limit hot water in baths. Harry calls Rhoda's attention to waste. She listens patiently to Thekla's grumbles, and explains to me afterwards that surviving, for Thekla and her like, has been too hard to take a wider view. She means a wider view of all she herself cares for: the arts, nature, horizons to be crossed – the travel now closed to her.

Lying in bed with her windows wide open and whenever she ventures outside the house, she opens my senses to what is time-less: the roll of the sea; the rocky crag of Lion's Head rearing above the avenues bumping up its lower slope. Rhoda is awake to the stir of thoughts and feelings in the smallest child. It isn't instinctual or textbook or imitative mothering, and nor is it the busy nurture of mothers today. Mothers of her generation aren't busy, and Rhoda's invalidism allows her to be less busy than most. Contact is not a matter of quality time; there's quiet, a readiness on hold so that a spark can fire spontaneously. Then Rhoda's blue eyes glow, she sits up, looks intently at the child and stills the child's attention as she switches into narrative mode. Family stories pour out. This telling is a ritual: it's not the biographical search for authenticity that I learn later; it's a re-telling, shoring up family myths that declare where we come from and who she is.

Rhoda mythologises the past of her father's family, helped by its distance in the Old Country. 'My father sometimes lamented that his children lived in a different world from his.' Philip Press (in Lithuania the name was Pres) came from a town called Plunge or, in the form he used, Plungian. 'Plum Jam', his children would joke. Rhoda pictures the inhabitants of Plum Jam as rare and gentle beings singing Yiddish lullabies. She sings her father's lullaby about raisins and almonds – *rozhinkes mit mand-len* – in such plaintive strains that we indulge in rather pleasurable sadness.

The facts, discovered later, are that in 1941 the Nazis rounded them up with the help of Lithuanian neighbours, shut the entire community of eighteen hundred Jews in their wooden synagogue for two weeks without air, food or water, and then shot the survivors into three great pits they'd had to dig for themselves in Kausanai forest. It's only one of numerous killing fields. Three generations later my journalist daughter Olivia, sent by a magazine to trace her family, will visit the pits surrounded by silver birches. Olivia, weeping, will light candles there and keep the matches to this day.

Philip Press, an immigrant, felt that his children lived in a different world. Surrounded here by his South African wife and children, from left: Hubert, Annie, Basil, Rhoda and Sydney

Olivia, right, lights a candle, accompanied by Jacob Bunka (left) and
his wife (standing). The only Plunge Jew to survive, Bunka
was away in 1941, fighting in the Russian army

In the absence of facts, Rhoda retells her father's memories.
Even Press poverty is romantic in her eyes: her father's mother,
dropping her hands in her lap when she's unable to afford more
thread to sew caps for country fairs. As a boy, when he was ill,
his father brought him one grape.

'One?' I ask, thinking of a mound of golden *hanepoot* grapes
on the autumn table. Amongst the vineyards of the Cape such
deprivation is strange.

'In that cold, northern world one grape was luxury,' Rhoda
says gravely. I see the scene but can't get inside it. She believes
the intensity of her otherness comes from those far-away people
with expansive souls.

Her mother's family, the Hoffmans, are decidedly not soulful. They sing together at the piano, 'ta-ra-ra-*boom*-de-jay'; they rollick through songs of the Anglo-Boer War ('We are marching to Pretoria'). As children, they and their parents took off in the reverse direction: they caught what they claim to have been the last civilian train out of Johannesburg bound for Cape Town, a thousand miles to the south, where British troops were landing. Their father, Jacob Hoffman, imported British woollens, suitable for the rainy winters and windy nights at the Cape.

The three Hoffman sisters in Cape Town:
Annie (top), Minnie (left) and Betsie

His jolliest daughter is the youngest, Auntie Betsie, whose fingers perform extra trills on the keys; her bracelets tinkle as she
bounces up from the final chord. Rhoda loves her aunts but
thinks their eldest sister, her mother Annie, small-minded.

'Why are you reading?' her mother asks. 'You're not in
school.'

Little is said of Betsie's eldest daughter, my mother's cousin
Cynthia, who lives in England. Photos show her to be in the
Hoffman mould, and yet she doesn't entirely fit that mould.
Buxom, tightly packed into a uniform during the war, Cynthia
married an Englishman and now writes stories – romances set
in the Namaqualand of her childhood – that are broadcast the
radio. Because Cynthia's stories are read on the BBC's Light
Programme, Rhoda dismisses them as light-weight. I don't
know if she read them or not. I think not, because Rhoda,
along with the rest of the family, shuns Cynthia for marrying
out of the faith.

When her name comes up, they say in told-you-so tones,
'Poor Cynthia has to scrub her floors.' Servants' work, that's
what comes of marrying an Englishman like tall Mr Hind.
Photos of him in army uniform had revealed little – or little
satisfactory to Cynthia's family back home who assume that she
writes for pocket money, which this husband can't provide.

Her parents relent when Cynthia produces a baby. I'm eight
years old when she's invited to bring little Michael Hind home
on a visit. He's adorable, with a round moon face and fluffs of
white hair. I want to seize and squeeze him in my arms, but he's
glued to his mother's lap, wary of strangers inspecting him,
Cynthia's English-looking child. Grown-ups' talk of scrubbing
floors in straitened, post-war England has led me to expect a
downcast Cynthia, but she's sturdy and humorous. To her, I'm
neither a child-confidante, as with my mother, nor a *pfefferil*, as

with Granny Annie, nor plain and awkward as with Granny Thekla. Cynthia talks to me like a motherly friend.

In after years, when I'm grown-up and a writer too, Cynthia makes a low aside at a family party on a stoep one starry night at Basil's house: writing, she says, has been her delight, though none of them, including Rhoda, take any notice. This isn't an instance of jealousy, because that's not part of Rhoda's character. I think it has more to do with her myth-making. Cynthia won't fit Rhoda's bifurcation of hereditary traits to prove how exercise of the mind derives exclusively from her father's side. Of course, it's common enough for people to define family in this divided way, but Rhoda's stories are repeated with so much conviction that her myth has prevailed.

As a child I'm filled with my mother's barely veiled boredom when men jabber about business, the same boredom that deadens the air around my father when he and swimming cronies put heads together over stopwatches. I will never settle for such a man, I promise myself. And then I glance in the mirror and see that I may have even less choice in the matter than my mother did.

I watch her put on make-up, as she stands short-sightedly peering at her serious blue eyes and high nose in the mirror of the three-corner cupboard in the bathroom. There's rouge in a small round pot and a tube of red lipstick. Too red. It's like putting on a mask before she can be seen by a visitor, who might at any moment pop in, or even by the gardener or the women who come to the door seeking work.

'Are you reliable?' she asks. 'Do you have a reference?'

And then the woman fumbles in her bag and holds out a battered bit of paper. If it's a man, it's shaming to see the excessive humility of his hunched shoulders as he cups both hands to receive the ten-shilling note my mother offers. Before the bell starts ringing, my mother parts her hair on the side and puts a finger along the unruly bits to make them wavy not wiry. She pats down and scrunches her brown curls, and if not in a hurry, rolls up a lock in a bendy brown curler to make it behave.

If favoured friends arrive, my mother exerts herself. She gets up and rather tiredly slips on a dress. Her thinness looks frail but passes for feminine delicacy in the turquoise muslins or shades of tea-rose she likes to wear. I trail along as she carefully clicks open the side door of my grandmother's Edwardian tea trolley, with its brass trim and rounded glass, which stands in our dining room. And gently, one by one, she lifts out a set of fragile teacups, thin porcelain with pink and mauve sweet peas on a faintly blushing background. My mother prizes this design for dispensing with the vulgarity of gold rims. Her word for over-decoration is something like 'berahtig' – sounding the 'g' with friction at the back of the throat, as in the Afrikaans of her early schoolroom. I think she's inventing her version of a Yiddish word without knowing Yiddish. Once she'd make a word her own, I and other listeners must lend our ears as best we can.

She relishes words that are expressive, pausing over them, rolling them around her tongue, including the humorously rude or pithy words in the tales of Chaucer's fourteenth-century pilgrims – 'likerous', more expressive than 'wanton', in the portrait of the eighteen-year-old wife in the Miller's tale, who has a 'likerous' eye. It charms me when my mother, telling a story, takes on a character unlike her own: the lasciviousness of the Miller's wife or the punitive hatred of Jane Eyre's guardian, Mrs Reed.

No one outside the house would know that she's ill. I watch a brave performance, her role as wife and mother and what goes with it: household, nursery, guests, servants. Concealed in this casing, along with illness, is a many-shaded freakishness that co-exists with her visions.

With Rhoda on the windy shore at Muizenberg

I partake of the freakish aspect, am shaped by it, yet have no access, as yet, to its secrets. Meanwhile, I lean on the insensibility of Granny Annie and my sporting father who provide a cast-iron armour of normality. The daily marvel of their oblivion is the ease with which they don't see what they don't have to see. I'm less adept at concealment than my mother. The deception of normality – barely convincing as I know it to be – makes me ill at ease with Granny Thekla and other members of my father's family.

My mother broods darkly, in a way that can provoke an

attack. Although it's not possible to press her with questions, the extremes of her self-portrait leave a gap between the other-world illumination of her childhood and what she terms, in her cryptic way, 'suffering' and 'illness'. Each word comes freighted with explosive: the danger of what actually took place. It's her way to hint – a nightmare journey to Europe; misguided doctors; a young man who died – so that I peer ineffectually through a fog of unfocused feeling made up of pity with a pinch of alarm. If only I could calm her; give her pleasure. In a small way it contents her that I fall in love with *A Child's Garden of Verses*: I know by heart 'how do you like to go up in a swing', and 'on goes the river', bearing the child's paper boats to 'other little children' who'll 'bring my boats ashore', and the invalid child who lives in his imaginary 'Land of Counterpane'. My mother is drawn to writers like Robert Louis Stevenson, who contend with illness.

All she will say about the onset of her own illness was that it 'befell' her at the age of seventeen, and that it was bound up with a bereavement. Who was it she had lost? There is an air of things that happened before I was born, an air that her real life is over – as though her lips are kissing her hand to a person I can't see.

3

'Illness Was My Teacher'

The first week of July 1944: I'm told a baby is due. At the age of two and a half, I accompany my mother to a one-storey nursing home in the Gardens. On a glassed-in stoep there's a row of prams. In each lies a newborn, and while Rhoda talks to Matron I skip from pram to pram, in love with the babies whose eyes squint up as I loom above them and bend to look. It's hard to choose, but at length I settle on the one for me. When Rhoda emerges, I too am ready to go, my hands curled round the handle of the pram.

Matron's determined fingers are prising mine off the handle, and then I'm crying because she won't let me take my baby. The cries gain in volume along Upper Orange Street, as the bus climbs the lower slope of Table Mountain. All the way I'm wailing 'Where's the baby?' to my shushing mother, who's seated with a cauliflower atop her pregnant mound.

At this time, before our move to Sea Point, we live with my grandmother, Annie Press, at Rhodean, in the mountain suburb of Oranjezicht above the town. While Rhoda is away at the nursing home, I trot beside Granny down Forest Road, which falls steeply towards the Reservoir. Granny, her pale auburn hair neatly waved, wears a mauve linen dress, buttoned down the front. It has padded shoulders, like the outfit Granny wears when she marches in Adderley Street with the WAAFS.

'I was the only one in step,' Granny reports proudly.

Rhoda often repeats this, laughing. She has a hoard of stories pointing up her mother's blithe oblivion.

I'm content next to the confident swell of Granny's chest and her purposefulness, for she's carrying a jar of home-made chicken soup, the panacea of Jewish mothers. It's to build up her daughter's strength after the birth of my brother Pip. Granny exudes bounty and optimism. But soon after Rhoda returns to Rhodean with the baby, she's beyond the reach of comfort. There's a hush around her.

My grandmother tells me not – *not*, her forefinger raised – to go into my mother's room in the mornings. I stand in the passage outside her door, afraid that something is being done to her – too awful for a child to know. One morning the silence is so heavy that I manage to turn the handle with both hands and burst into darkness. The curtains are drawn against the invading sun. As my eyes adjust, I see my mother prone on the bed, face down, and a stranger leaning over her. What's going on turns out to be massage. Relief runs down my open throat and dangling arms, the first of many occasions when a hush around Rhoda is scarier than fact.

My father, wearing trousers with a funny name, white ducks, reports to Granny that Rhoda 'gave way' in the doctor's office. She fell down. The doctor says she might get well if she goes away; the hushed word 'Valkenberg' crosses the air between the grown-ups. I wonder anxiously if my mother will go far away and not come back. 'If she can't control herself,' they say.

When I'm older she will tell me a lot more about that day in

November 1944 when my brother was four months old: the day she believed that she was mad.

She speaks eloquently, as though she's told this to herself many times. 'Hope died. I lay on the bare boards of the back-bedroom floor. To lift myself seemed as impossible as lifting one's dead body from under the earth. But I forced myself up, and saw a hooded moon through the window above the back door.

'I went out and looked at the grass, the phlox growing in the garden and the contour of Table Mountain against the sky. Then I walked into my bedroom where Auntie Betsie was drying Pip after his bath. I lifted my baby, and walked up and down singing to him a farewell tune. And during that song, "It" passed away and I was released. To be free of terror was strange as a dream.'

So she didn't have to go away.

Our rented house in Cromer Road, Muizenberg, where we spend the summer, is called Sun Blest. It has a trellis with a creeper over the front, which shades the stoep and keeps it cool. The stoep runs round the house to one side, where the nursery I share with Pip opens on to it through folding doors and shutters. Sunlight slants through half-open shutters onto the floor. Two years later I watch the play of light from my bed, because Pip, aged two and a half, and I, turned five, have temperatures.

The local doctor, interrupts the dreamy haze. He orders my mother to take off my pyjama bottoms and put me on a pink potty. 'Make a weh-wee,' he commands in a funny accent, bending down and fixing his eyes on me. I feel stripped, and hate him too much to produce what he wants.

After he goes away, my mother comes back to the nursery with a fat book under her arm, the book she's reading all summer: *Joseph and his Brothers* by Thomas Mann. Sitting on my bed, she tells the story of Joseph and his coat of many colours. In the first

volume, she says, Joseph is thrown into a pit. A shaft of sun pen-
etrates the shutter, and I can see from the cast of Rhoda's face that
she's in a pit of her own. Joseph is lying at the bottom, thrown
down and left to die by jealous half-brothers. It would have been
the end of him had not God brought him up out of the pit.

The narrative goes on, a serial, day by day: how traders find
Joseph and sell him into slavery, and how Joseph, as prophetic
dreamer in the house of Potiphar, rises to become a power in
the land of Egypt. My mother looks tired but I beg her not to
stop. As she yields and takes a fresh breath, 'and then ... ' –
breath – 'and that's not all ... ', she looks intently into her listener's eyes, and yes I'm listening all right. Pity, which includes
pity for the teller, carries the story through my veins: the darkness of the pit, the horror of Joseph to find himself there (he,
his father's adored child), and the power of dreaming.

With each additional 'and' of biblical narrative, the story rises
to crisis, and behind it beats the ancient family tension of two
mothers: wives of the patriarch Jacob, who happen to be sisters.

I'm troubled by the fate of Leah, the elder of the two and
mother of the murderous brothers. Knowing that Joseph is des-
tined to be saved, I'm sorrier for Leah, who wasn't chosen
because she wasn't pretty. Plain, unwanted Leah with her weak
eyes – a handicap in the ancient world where there's no such
thing as spectacles. Jacob worked seven years for Leah's pretty
younger sister Rachel, and when, as he thought, Rachel was
given to him in marriage, he removes the bridal veil and discovers Leah. Tricked, Jacob has to work another seven years for
the bride he really wants.

Rhoda's sympathies lean to Rachel: her sensitivity and physical fragility, making childbirth difficult, and leading to an early
death as Jacob and his retainers travel with their flocks through
the desert. Jacob grieves for Rachel and dotes on her two sons,
Joseph and Benjamin, stirring hatred in Joseph's brethren.

'But Leah . . . ?' I remind my mother, who allows and sometimes invites a child to reach into the story.

She stops to think. What she sees is a wife who tries to win
Jacob through her fertility: many strong sons, the preferred
gender. The name for Leah's first baby, Reuben, is a call to her
husband: 'Re-u! Ben! See, a son!'

Rhoda is matter-of-fact about the fecund Leah. She hastens
on with the chosen son: Joseph guided in his dreams by the
hand of God. It's a story of the innocent victim and his ulti-
mate transcendence. The crease between her brows, the
intentness of her inward eye, tells me there's more to the story
than the story. Her voice resonates with private import.
Dreaming is prophecy, and prophecy is power. Political power
for Joseph; inner power for Rhoda, a compensation of sorts for
the blight of illness and the constraints of an existence between
Rhoda's mother and husband who are temperamentally
untroubled, content to manage around this dark space they will
not attempt to understand.

At Sun Blest my mother stands at the front door with her
husband's parents, his twin sisters and their handsome boys.
Civil too. They need no prompting to thank Auntie Rhoda for
tea. Neither mannered nor careless, they carry themselves
already with a manly ease that makes me shy. The sheen of their
future popularity daunts me and I try to look away, expecting
to remain unchosen. It's enough that such boys should grace
our garden: I see them from an inner space, which I'd die rather
than reveal, and look to my mother for the conviction she
brings to this space by way of poems and tales. As a reader, she's
at liberty to live all over the place, and I follow where she goes.
She takes me to places where females long in vain for love, sacrifice themselves and find themselves defeated: Hans Christian
Andersen's little mermaid and his little match girl, or the far

At Sun Blest. Rhoda (on right), ill, made an effort with
visitors Granny Thekla and Grandfather Louis (back).
In the centre is Granny Annie, holding Pip

north where Gerda must travel to melt the ice in the eye of her
beloved with her warm tears.

Our visitors are not in the know about Rhoda's illness, nor
could they have told from looking at her. She wears a cotton
frock, striped blue to match her eyes, with a wide collar.
Tendrils of curly hair blow about her head and, as the camera
clicks, she's putting up a hand to smooth her flapping collar.
That's what others see, but I've learnt to detect the effort she
must make to appear normal.

On the stoep Pip is reading *Tootle* upside down: the story of a merry little engine with a top hat of a funnel who goes off the rails. Like Pip himself, later, when he's running in a little boys' race at Clovelly, our father's golf club. Pip's so braced against the wind, ribs lifted and face back, arms pumping from side to side, that he will veer off course into watching clumps of parents.

I'm jealous of Pip because he's smiling and lovable in his miniature-man pullover designed by Auntie Betsie's daughters, Berry and Garda, who have knitted the letters PIP in white wool into a blue front. The letters stretch over his swelling pigeon chest, and as we walk along the promenade strangers call out 'Hullo, Pip!'

That summer when I'm five, I run away. Without a plan, I set forth one afternoon past the faded, peeling bathing boxes, past Tubby's hot-dog stand, under the raised booms and past Muizenberg station, in the direction of St James with its tidal

Pip and me on the seesaw at Tubby's beach,
near the railway station at Muizenberg

pool, appealing to children because it's tamer than the open sea. The narrow coastal road at the foot of the mountains runs so close to the sea that my route is simple to follow: the waves to the left; grand houses to the right (including, tucked amongst them, Rhodes's thatched cottage, preserved as a museum – a landmark on drives but hardly visited by summer visitors who come down in droves from Johannesburg). I whiz along in a mood of adventure, exhilarated to be on my own. Another little girl is playing on a swing in the garden of a big house. I cross the road, open the gate and call out, 'Can I come and play?' And then, happily, I swing up and down to lines my mother has read aloud so often I know them by heart:

> How do you like to go up in a swing,
> Up in the air so blue . . .
> Up in the air and over the wall,
> Till I can see so wide . . .

Flying on the upward beat, pumping higher with bent knees, what I'm seeing is not the quiet countryside observed by Robert Louis Stevenson. I see the heaving ocean, its curling waves with exquisitely menacing undersides of palest green as they rise to their crest and crash back into troughs of dark blue. Our father was out there on long-distance swims when he was young. Women swimmers must have outdistanced him because he's still peeved at women for an unfair advantage: a layer of fat under the skin that keeps them warm.

I swing until John, the Xhosa gardener, finds me and carries me home on his high shoulders.

The rituals of Muizenberg are fixed. In the afternoon the wind comes up and blows the sand about, so it's a morning place. In the morning we swim in the sea, and at lunchtime I throw on my sundress over a damp costume and forget to rinse it. Salty costumes, gritty with sand, hang over the rails of the stoep and dry in half an hour. We stamp the sand off our feet outside the front door, or, if it's caked on our calves, rinse them under the garden tap. The sea makes us hungry, and Lenie serves the main meal of the day at lunchtime: grilled chops and peas, followed by fruit salad. After lunch my mother breaks off an oblong of Fry's chocolate and nibbles delicately.

'Eat slowly,' she says, handing over a piece, 'and if you wait ten minutes the urge for more will pass.'

On weekends, if Rhoda is too ill to get up in the morning, our father, barefoot, his knobby toes slightly turned in (he claims this helps in swimming races), leads the way to the beach, stopping for ice-creams. Pip and I lick them under our white

Our father, Harry, went barefoot whenever he could.
On summer weekends he often took care of us

hats, held in place with elastic under our dripping chins. Granny, in her wrap-around beach gown, drapes towels across our chests. When the door closes on my mother, there's this support system, carrying me from that secret space of trial to the norms of the seaside.

During the summer months of December and January, Jews congregate at Muizenberg: the fortunate descendants of refugees from Lithuania, and more recent refugees – the last to escape before South Africa blocked immigration in 1933 – who come together to shake heads over nightmare rumours from Europe and sing yearning songs like 'My Yiddishe Mamma'.

The hot breath of sentiment makes me squirm. I can't admit that 'My Yiddishe Mamma' leaves me cold, since my mother and others accept that sentiment is called for, if only as respect for refugees. But to take it in feels like manipulation, something I will never manage to tolerate, whether it be these plaintive strains or the words of ads or pop songs. My body seizes up against their insistent, hypnotic beat. It feels as instinctual as a different rhythm in the blood. Generally, for my mother, the sounds of untruth jar more, as though nerve endings detecting what's false stand to attention.

In the privacy of her room she tells me what she can't say to others: how fiercely she rejects false authorities, doctors who don't admit their ignorance of her condition and professors who say what critics say. Once, she relates, she made the effort to sit in on a professor's class on T. S. Eliot, because she loves the poems so; and he, the head of English at the university, said there, in front of the class: this woman is not schooled in the New Criticism, ergo, she's reading wrongly. If you are a house-wife in the forties, if you live where she does, there's no place to say what you think. Only in your own room; only to a lis-tening child.

Was it solitude that developed her sensitivity to truth? This question comes only later when I read Virginia Woolf's essay 'On Being Ill': 'what ancient and obdurate oaks are uprooted in us by the act of sickness'. She makes bold to seize one gain of long illness, its potent subversiveness.

On rare afternoons when my mother is up to it, she takes Pip and me to one or other of the three shelly beaches between Muizenberg and St James. This is a treat because you descend into a white tunnel under the train line that winds around the inlets along the False Bay coast, all the way to the British naval base at Simonstown. The tunnel echoes and magnifies the sound of the ocean; at its far end is a vision of the blue rim of the sea melting into a clear blue sky, and then, as you emerge, there are rocks interspersed with pools big and small, covered with fronds of green seaweed. It's a water-baby paradise.

When she reads aloud from *The Water Babies*, published in grimy Victorian London, I stare at the colour plate of the sooty little sweep, Tom, descending through the chimney into Ellie's gauzy bedroom: the astonishing sight of middle-class comfort. We follow Tom's transformation into a water-baby, along with other fantasy babies in their snug home pools.

My mother suggests that we prepare a water-baby pool for the likes of Tom to discover. I imagine his delight to find a cradle (a rocking shell) waiting for him and inside it a lump of smoothed green glass for a pillow, a silvery 'Venus ear' for a looking glass and curtains made of frilly fronds of green sea-weed.

One afternoon my mother collects a party of children play-ing on the beach and sets up a competition to see who can create the loveliest water-baby pool. I can't now recall who won because winning didn't matter, only an intense absorption, when you become what you make. You hear it in a child's hum – my mother called it a 'cosmic hum'. It's a kind of bliss that has visited me again two or three times in an adult life as a writer – once, tuned to the surges of Eliot's sea-quartet, *The Dry Salvages*.

The shelly beaches are afternoon beaches: no swimming here; the rocks lie close together and sometimes, at high tide, there's almost no sand. The wonder of these beaches lies in their secrecy, smallness and tidal obliteration: no names; no signs; simply steps down to the damp, rather smelly tunnel and a rising anticipation if the tide is low: the chance to hunt the rarest treasures: an anemone waving its salmon tendrils in a rock pool and sucking your finger; a shell with the roar of the sea when you put it to your ear; the Venus ear with its dotted curve and, on the inside, a pearly sheen of silver-grey-pink; and the round green shell of the sea urchin, so fragile it's a triumph to find one intact.

'Close your eyes,' Rhoda says, 'and count how many sounds you can hear.' Concentrating on sound alone, I hear more than one might with eyes open: the gulls of course; the whirr of a fishing rod as a solitary fisherman on a rock reels in his catch; footsteps along the cement floor of the tunnel; the whine of a dog tugging on its leash; the tickety-tack of a passing train and cries coming my way that make me open my eyes to look up at black children in the third-class tail of the train, who are waving from the window as they sweep by.

4

Orphans and Stories

Early readers. Some of Rhoda's library children at the Jewish Orphanage
in Oranjezicht in the forties. At the back of the orphanage grounds,
with Table Mountain behind them

A short walk from Rhodean is the Cape Jewish Orphanage,
filled to capacity during the war. Not all the children are
orphans; some have parents who can't keep them; some were
evacuees during the Blitz. They are housed in a three-storey
building backing on to Table Mountain, and in its shadow. Each

floor is in a different architectural style: arches below; columns for the entrance floor, up flight upon flight of steps; and Dutch gables ornamenting the dormitory floor. This melange of designs manages to shut off sunlight from the main hall. Two branching stairways lead to separate wings for girls and boys. There's a largely deserted playing field on one side, which has the look of a space that exists to show what's provided.

No fun to play here, I think as we pass, because it's exposed like a vast, empty tray plonked on a grass slope, a strip of man- icured mountain sheering down to Montrose Avenue – too steep for rolling.

Inside, the orphanage is very clean with an odour of polish. The salty, seaweed tang of peninsula air, tossed about by winds, can't blow through small, out-of-reach windows. In my sister role, I accompany my mother who goes twice a week to run the library.

'Librar-ee ... librar-ee ... ' she sings up and down the long corridors, putting her head into dormitories with rows of whitewashed iron bedsteads and uniform white bedspreads. Her heels tap-tap along the polished floor.

Children come running, books under their arms. They clus- ter around as she asks them what books they like. *Biggles*, say the boys. *Pollyanna* or *Anne of Green Gables*, say the girls, who like to read about orphan girls whose opinions disconcert their elders. My mother fires up with eagerness to introduce them to the spark Jane Eyre keeps alive throughout her chilling and starving at Lowood charity school, and to another favourite, David Copperfield, the orphaned victim of Mr Murdstone.

'Mr Murdstone,' she says, drawing out the fearful first sylla- ble, alarm in the cast of her face.

The children's eyes fix in reflected alarm as the bully torments the child; then, from deep within, questions well up. Questions about adult cruelty. Impossible questions because, towards the end of the war in Europe, the Allies come upon the Nazis' extermination camps, and there are no answers for Jewish children. It's enough that Rhoda takes up each question with attentive seriousness. A child who comes to this library has its beak open, ready. Each child gets a kiss when they line up to check books out.

It's not sentimental; more a ritual. 'Have you had your kiss?' Rhoda asks as though it's a right. Some return with a second book, to receive another kiss.

She also asks each one, 'Did you wash your hands?' Books are precious, to be handled with care.

The library is a musty room, long shut up, at the back of a disused wing. This wing, higher on the mountain, is set apart from the rest of the orphanage, and reached by a covered walkway from the dormitory floor. Here are empty classrooms with piles of Bibles, for this back wing had once served as a Hebrew school, and here boys approaching thirteen are prepared for bar mitzvah, undistracted by any outlook on an African mountain three thousand feet high with sunbeams playing across its woods and crest.

My mother, in purposeful mode, trailing children, tap-taps through a dank classroom with a key in her hand. As she unlocks the library the children crowd closer, and help to push open the reluctant door. All at once we're enfolded by what I've thought of ever since as the library smell – print and paper – with its promise of worlds to enter. I associate the enticing smell with books for my mother's generation: all the sequels to *Anne of Green Gables*, running to Anne's children in *Rilla of Ingleside*, where spoilt, lisping Rilla has to grow up when she adopts a baby with croup.

I run my finger over old-fashioned bindings, which have images tooled on them in gold or silver: the intrepid bull terrier from *Jock of the Bushveld* or chums wearing gym tunics in school

With Rhoda in town, *c.* 1945–6, on her way to the library.
She kept records of what the children read in her case

stories by Angela Brazil. Away at boarding school, English girls
appear not to miss their mothers because they are level-headed
and have their minds on midnight feasts and helping those in
trouble. These self-sufficient chums in books I can't yet read and
absorb at first through illustration will come back to me at the
end of one Hilary term in Oxford in the late seventies, when a
student brings a humorous present to his last tutorial: it's an old
title by Angela Brazil, *The Jolliest Term On Record*.

*

Colonial settings abound in the old-time books of the orphan-age library. I pore over pictures of the paddock at Misrule in *Seven Little Australians*. These motherless children more or less look after themselves, especially Judy, a creature of the wild who runs away from boarding school. In the books I pull from the shelves, colo-nial girls in nowhere places, with no prospects and disempowered as the weaker sex, dare to aspire. Their hopeful stories often start with orphaning: in *Emily of New Moon*, Emily Byrd Starr is taken in by maiden aunts living on Canada's Atlantic coast: Prince Edward Island. Emily herself feels like an island, placed as she is with people who lock away books as lifeless possessions. Or there's Marie in *That Girl*, by Ethel Turner, who's orphaned and then treated as a servant by the Australian couple who adopt her. Marie is determined to be an actress. The novel ends with her sailing away to fulfil her dream in the mother country. Katherine Mansfield, sailing from Wellington to London in 1903, and Olive Schreiner, sailing from Cape Town twenty years earlier, are real-life versions of a colonial dream.

At the outset, this dream must have looked improbable, which made their stories all the more telling for a girl like my mother sprouting on the veld, to be asked – that unforgettable question – why she's reading when she's not in school. *The Story of an African Farm* was written in a leaking, lean-to room assigned to the governess on an isolated farm. Feminist elo-quence was not expected in such a place. Nor was it expected that, under an umbrella, the governess would be writing a work of literature that would leap provincial and colonial barriers. This novel proved a sensation when it came out in London in 1883. Such were the narratives that shaped my mother as a girl, and make her their natural custodian.

She isn't only a guide to reading; the stories she holds out are also offerings of intimacy with her secret self. At the same time as *The Little Locksmith* invites me into another world – the New

England of Katharine Butler Hathaway – I can't but see my mother's closeness to the autobiography of a writer whose imagination is sharpened by disability. This new book lies in its plain blue cover next to my mother's bed, and she unveils the mystery that surrounds the condition of the author as an invalid child. The little girl is strapped flat to a stretcher for twenty-four hours a day, and her neck is stretched upwards by a pulley. Turning her head to one side, she sees a little locksmith at work, and she feels kin to him because his deformity is what her regimen is intended to prevent.

'He's a hunchback,' Rhoda explains.

The word is never uttered in the author's home or in her story, but when, at fifteen, she's allowed to get up, she looks in the mirror and finds that she is, after all, the 'terrible word'. At the time my mother reads this aloud, her own condition is still unrevealed to her and a mystery to me. I delight in the bed-life of this little American girl long ago: her cut-outs; the doll's clothes she sews, edged with ruffles; her painting hair brown by gaslight, then discovering by daylight it's purple. I try the experiment but electric light permits no mistake.

Katharine Butler resolves to give her life to writing: she's in love with what she writes, as well as with her piled-up notes and peerings into others' faces. None of this can be taken away because she will not attempt publication. After her hunger for experience is thwarted by her deformity, she can never again risk disappointment. To enclose her writing life more securely, she looks for a place of her own and finds the house of her dreams in Castine, Maine. My mother partakes of this dream, with a singing uplift on the second syllable when she says 'Castine'. Though she never sets eyes on the coast of Maine, it's alive in her as a place where a quirky creature can dwell in possibility. In a similar way Emily, in *Emily of New Moon*, is open to 'the flash'. My mother recalls her excitement to find a girl in a book who'd had the same intimation that came to her as gold-smoke across the veld when she'd been a child of six sweeping the sand off the stoep.

I listen as one who's not up to 'the flash'. People remark how I look like my father, a sun-baked, outdoor look of readiness that's common at the Cape. I'm not rare, moonlike and fragile with large, glowing eyes like Emily who means to be a poet and is climbing 'the Alpine path' – taking her gift to its heights – in a sequel, *Emily Climbs*. This has been a model for my mother who, like Emily, 'scribbles' in secret and is suitably delicate with pale cheeks and crisp, dark curls.

From the start, in 1943, Rhoda prompts her library children to write by bringing out a magazine, *Oranjia*.* The idea grows out of Saturday afternoons at Rhodean, where children from the orphanage gather for debates, competitions, jokes, riddles and readings. Rhoda's first editorial declares her belief 'that to cultivate a taste for good literature by reading in youth is to invest in happiness: to provide ourselves with never-failing friends who open their hearts to us, teach us, entertain us, comfort us in loneliness and sorrow, and inspire and encourage us to realise our highest ideals'. She types up the contributions on her home typewriter, and includes her own triptych of orphanage scenes.

'Rachel' is about new arrivals, a thin, agitated girl and her younger brothers and sisters, holding on to one another's baggy garments. The 'big sister' Rachel wails in an exasperated-mother voice that the younger ones never leave her alone. Yet it becomes apparent that Rachel's duties are self-imposed; it's Rachel who follows them about, wiping noses, slapping, settling disputes. In the library, she won't join the other children looking at books and turning the pages of the *National Geographic*. Instead, she starts howling. The librarian promises her 'this will pass' by the

---

* Though everyone spoke of 'the orphanage', Oranjia was the official name.

time of her next visit, and Rachel licks up a tear. Sure enough, when next she appears in the library her unkempt bush of hair has been washed and tied back, and she's wearing a new dress, which she spreads out to sit. In an artificially polite voice to go with the dress, she returns to 'Miss' a book she'd taken on the quiet – a story of children going off on a ship. It has entranced her, and gradually, as Rachel's cheeks fill out to look like a child, a more natural voice emerges.

The second scene takes place in the orphanage nursery when the littlest ones are going to bed. Routines are disrupted by the excitement of a visitor from whom the children demand 'Story! Story!' The third scene is about a group of dreamy girls in their early teens who adore their dance teacher, Mrs S, and are thrilled to be invited to spend the day with her at her home. One of them, Lottie, is in a fever of expectation – Mrs S might come to know her awakening self – as their train winds to its dreamt-of destination along the ocean. Each of these scenes conveys deprivation through a child's imaginative longing to be seen, recognised, wanted.

One contribution to *Oranjia* is by a boy of ten, Louis Franks. The Jewish community in Worcester, a country town, has invited Louis, along with other children, for a holiday. Elated at the prospect of staying in a family home, Louis gazes out of the train window: 'I followed rivers with my eye until they disappeared ... At one part of the journey we went through a mountain pass.' Then the time comes to return to the orphanage. 'I did not look out of the window coming back,' Louis writes. 'I was too sad.'

On the cover of a 1946 issue is a photograph of Esther, a girl of six with a sprinkle of freckles across her nose and black hair cut in a straight fringe. My mother calls Esther 'a story-book girl', a phrase for her favourites.

What does it mean to be a story-book girl, I wonder jealously.

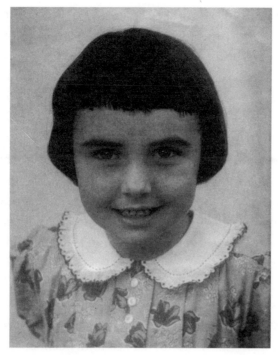

Esther on the cover of *Oranjia*

I'm never one, however keen on stories. Is it because I have a different role as a sister? Introducing me to strangers, my mother calls me 'a long John', a girl too tall for her age. I decide not to grow any more than can be helped. She explains that deprecation is her way of concealing maternal pride.

Two of my mother's special girls impress me because, in their early teens, they discuss the sayings of blind and deaf Helen Keller, which my mother proclaims in the library: 'The world is moved along, not only by the mighty shoves of its heroes, but also by . . . the tiny pushes of each honest worker.'

Rosalind, aptly named with her rosy cheeks, has a lift to the corners of her mouth when she concurs in a smiley manner; if her life has been vulnerable, there's no sign of it. Amongst my mother's notes on each reader is praise for Rosalind's 'enthusiastic spirit in seeking new fields, which has improved the quality of her reading'.

Fay Lipschitz, paler, has a waiflike appeal. She's definitely a reader of good books, 'with a taste for humour'. From under heavy lids, Fay fixes her eyes on my mother and chooses her words in a way that suggests her need for a discerning mentor, someone unlike the members of the council who run the orphanage.

Molly Nochemowitz is a childless, older woman on the council, and often about the orphanage. Her affection is on offer, but it comes out so loudly and fiercely that I shrink from her. The boom of her voice announces her presence as she limps up the steps to the hall, looming into view like a monster. In a fairy tale her reddened skin, loose throat and bulgy eyes would warn you to beware. If only we could run away. But my mother stops to commend her. As we walk off, my mother assures me that the orphans do love her. I both trust this and wonder if it's a measure of how bereft they must be. Rhoda sees my hesitation.

'She's a winner of hearts.' Rhoda's pace quickens when she's energised by a point to be made. 'Most evenings, when there's an exodus from the dining room, a ring of children pushes close to Molly. They follow her as the children did the Pied Piper. She charms the older ones with her original opinions, and she can express herself on practically every subject. She charms the younger children by her understanding. "Books-smooks! Dancing-smancing!" she waves me and other visitors off. "Awright we like reading story books, awright we have fun dancing, yet who but Auntie Molly is there every night?" She's there when they need her to stroke their hair and ask, "Your cold is better today?"'

Dancing lessons are conducted by Ren Stodel (the adored Mrs S) who has an upright carriage and wears her hair in crossed-over plaits on top of her head. She teaches the Madge

Atkinson Method of Natural Movement to girls in orange tunics with glossy brown cords about their waists. Barefoot, toes pointed, the girls skip to the rhythm of Dvořák's well-known 'Humoresque', played on the dining-room piano with thumping beats – dah, de dah, de dah, de dah . . . – on a rising scale.

'The dancer listens with her inner hearing,' Ren explains to the girls. 'She feels the rhythm and mood of the music in order to stir in others the depth of emotion awakened in herself.'

After Ren's class, she and my mother, who is well whenever she's with Ren, stride arm in arm down Adderley Street. We go to visit Ren in her thatched cottage, Peace and Quiet, hidden away amongst bush and foliage along a road winding inland

Rhoda and Ren

from the seaside station at Clovelly. It's disconcerting to come upon a husband who is anything but quiet: a grinning, cigar-chomping impresario, Sonny Stodel, who strums his ukulele with head cocked to one side, as though listening to himself while he performs.

Sonny and Ren, who have two boys and wish – so I'm told – they had a daughter, invite me to stay a night at Peace and Quiet. Would my mother have let me stay had she known they would take me out that night to a show at the Alhambra, followed by late-night dinner with the performers at a fashionable nightclub called the Del Monaco? Ren has plaited my hair and pinned the plaits on top of my head in her own style. Only my hair is skimpy and the plaits don't cross to make a crown; they barely meet, but Ren hides this with a bow. I'm amazed by the lavish gestures and kisses of the performers, which spill over onto me, Sonny's newest acquisition. Next morning I'm set to perform on the lawn. He takes off my dress and makes me lie on the grass, toes pointed with hands under my chin. In the photo he takes my face is full of unease: I don't want to be posed in my vest and panties. I want my father to come and fetch me. It's a relief to spy our old Chevrolet flashing into sunlight along the twisty road.

My mother doesn't have to state that she finds Sonny coarse. It's implied when she holds up Ren as a model of wifely forbearance. Wives of that generation don't expect to be known in the ways brothers or friends know them. Their voices are warm with fun in the company of women. But what transforms Rhoda most is to emerge like a mermaid from the waves at Muizenberg on the Indian Ocean or from those on the colder, Atlantic side of the peninsula. For Rhoda, the colder the waters, the more they heal. She's at one with grey days thick with sea mist and great breakers rising, frothing and racing towards her.

*

Photographed by Sonny on the lawn of his house

Back home, at bedtime, she goes on with the water-babies, who are children liberated from the deathly conditions of nineteenth-century child labour. They live together in the chambers of the sea. It's a kind of fantasy orphanage. Water-babies are freer than the children at Oranjia, but like them are subject to visitors. These visitors are moral teachers whom I don't much care for. Mrs Doasyouwouldbedoneby hands out sweets to well-behaved children. Next comes Mrs Bedonebyasyoudid, who pops a pebble into Tom's mouth when he opens it to receive the sweet he expects. The shock and physical hardness of that pebble, as I

take it in, is fixed in memory once and for all. In after years it
will come back, when I'm seventeen and trying out dreams of
love (shaped by thrilled replaying of arias from *La Traviata*). It's
late one summer night, January 1959, and I'm kissing a boy of
twenty on our stoep, semi-curtained by vine leaves and unripe
grapes. Startlingly, he passes a peach pip into my mouth. His
green eyes glimmer through the dark, inviting me to share the
joke, but I'm taken aback, and literally step back.

Unlike our father, Rhoda lives almost entirely in books, an
inner life she keeps intact, separate from her outward identity as
Harry's wife. In her housewife aspect, she often appears defeated
and in need of awareness – even a child's awareness. If she
absolutely has to go into town – to the dentist, say – she takes
me. I hold her hand as much as she holds mine. Dressed for
town, she's made-up with red lipstick and walks rather hurriedly
in a Swiss Hanro suit and a mannish felt hat; at her side I'm
ridiculous in a green tweed bonnet with curled-up brim to
match a double-breasted coat. It would suit a doll-child, not
one sprouting freckles. If only we don't meet anyone we know.

During the appointment, she leaves me in a nearby bookshop.
In the children's corner, I sit on the floor, pulling out a book with
pop-up pictures of castles in fairy tales, and another with tags to
waggle so that a lion's mouth opens, his teeth gleam and a red
tongue comes out as he roars. I feel safe there with the books.

When we return home, my mother opens A. A. Milne and
reads aloud about James James Morrison Morrison Weatherby
George Dupree, who warns his mother, 'never go down to the
end of the town / without consulting me'. I'm invited to laugh
at the imperiousness of this little English boy.

But however much I yield to my mother's intonations as she
reads aloud from *When We Were Very Young* and *The Water Babies*,
longings continue to circle around the two bookshop books –
not the kind my mother would buy. As my birthday approaches

I dream that, magically, someone will divine and grant what I want. When Granny Annie tells me to make a wish, her hand guiding mine in cutting Lenie's home-made birthday cake, I close my eyes and choose the toy-books, dwelling on the lion because there's more chance of the wish coming true. I want the pop-up castles even more, but sense that those tiers, wobbling as the page opens, are too wondrous to own.

Another longing is for a baby doll in the window of a toyshop along Main Road at Three Anchor Bay. She's made of rubber, and dangling from her hand there's a miniature bottle to fill with water and feed into the hollow of her open mouth, with an outlet below. I don't like fanciful, dressed-up Raggedy Anns; what appeals is a doll who looks like a real baby. I gaze entranced at the baby on the other side of the glass whenever we pass on visits to my father's parents. And then, one day, my tall, sombre grandfather, an old man of few words, announces, 'You can choose a present.' As he shuffles along Main Road, desire intensifies. Inside the toyshop the darling doll, retrieved from the window, turns out to cost ten and six. Instead, my grandfather buys a tiny one – too tiny to have an inside – for sixpence. Embarrassed by my extravagant choice, I pretend to like the substitute.

Truth be told, I'd known that the life-like doll cost too much before that visit to the toyshop. When I pointed it out to my grandfather I was playing ignorant: the simple child who can't tell the difference between what's affordable and what's not. My pretences fail to match my mother's instinctive sensitivity, for she's told me how, as a child, she'd drawn back from greed.

'Everything lived for me in the light of my father's love,' she says during one of her reminiscences. 'It was just because he gave all that I developed the conscience not to take all. I remember reluctantly returning a gold sovereign, which he pressed out of the spring of the sovereign case men wore on a chain across the chest in those days. I returned it because I felt instinctively it was too much to take.'

It's all too clear that others' instincts, including mine, are grosser. However compelled I am by the rarity of my mother, and by her reading, writing, taste and judgement, my secret self has to acknowledge how much comes from my father: appetite and energy and wanting ordinary things. Above all there's the fascination of what's difficult: I want to be lovable, like my brother Pip who's a laughing baby with a cute nose, pointy tongue and a fluff of fairish hair against my mother's shoulder. In her striped dressing gown, her face lights up as she turns towards him; how tenderly she's brushing his hair upwards into a little curl on top of his head.

In 1989, when St Hilda's College, in Oxford, is about to elect a new principal, the tutor in Roman history, Barbara Levick, suggests that we ask candidates for an adjective or noun describing how they'd wish to be remembered. We elected Elizabeth Llewellyn Smith, who said 'integrity'.

I was old enough by then to admit to a friend, the writer Gillian Avery, that my dream adjective is less high-minded. 'It's "lovable",' I confessed ruefully, as one who knows the time for hope has passed.

'Mine too,' Gill offered, 'but it would never do to admit it at an interview.'

I felt a surge of fondness for her. As a writer, she might have wished to be successful or to be remembered, as my mother (for all her modesty) wished to be remembered after her death. The whole edifice of my mother's married life was alien to the writer my mother felt herself to be. Through writing she escaped to her first world, 'roots clasping native stone'. In a poem she read aloud, the word stone rhymes with home, and home to her was elsewhere, not with us, not with our father.

Rhoda, aged seventeen

Like a tree born in dawn's dark crystal stillness
Roots clasping native stone
My spine, my staff
For I am home.

I understood that home was the timeless face of Creation, and that she felt interfused with the veld, that stark terrain of her primal landscape, as (I'd later learn) Clym Yeobright blends into Egdon Heath in *The Return of the Native*, or as the Brontës blend into the Yorkshire moor. These inhabitants of my mother's bookcase are amongst her intimates.

Her other lifeline is memory: her pre-illness past. She's in her late twenties, and then thirty, and still she doesn't know, or dreads to know, what is wrong with her. In so far as she's beset with uncertainty and mentally alone, she does cross the borderland of deep depression.

5

The Silent Past

It would be untrue to say that, back then, I had no ideas about my mother's illness.

As I grew up, the fog around it did block questions in a way that must have become habitual: the absence of words closed off thoughts, and that would have been all too easy in a house where talk flowed about public issues — racial oppression and legal cases and the declaration of the State of Israel in 1948. A closed-off channel pre-empted questions, even to myself, and I realise now how convenient it became to ease the discomfort of awareness by closing the valves of my attention.

Pip has no recollection of threatened attacks when we were small. Where I have the sister role to stay at her side, Pip's role is to delight. She's charmed and amused by the swelling maleness of his chest, his readiness to sing and even his glee when, bored by our obligatory after-lunch rests, he stands up in the cage of his cot in order to smear poo on the nursery wall. Unlike me, he trots off to nursery school. Our father drives away to his law office in town, so he too is not a witness, or not by day; nor is he told on his return. Nor is my grandmother present in my memory of these times. I'm alone with my mother as she falls on her knees next to her bed or on a rug in the dining room.

Curious to me, looking back, is that my father and grandmother must have known that these emergencies would occur from time to time. Why did they say nothing? Might they have hoped she'd exert more control in the presence of a child? More likely, I think, was their reluctance to imagine what might happen when they weren't there — what George Eliot meant when she says that most of us go about well-wadded with oblivion. She actually says 'stupidity', but that's too dismissive, and her link of herself with 'us' doesn't ring true. It tells us more about the frustrations of George Eliot herself as an intellectual in a provincial society. Harry and Annie were certainly not stupid. Their extrovert high spirits simply overrode the intrusion of troubling thoughts. Their wadding may even have been of benefit. It ensured a cover for anything out of the ordinary.

It will happen quite casually when I'm fourteen that my eye falls on words my mother has set down at the age of thirty-eight.

Mid-afternoon, the house is quiet. The servants, having cleared up after lunch, have gone to their rooms off the yard at the back. Wearing uniform, a white panama hat and a green cotton dress that looks creased and rumpled by the end of the school day, I'm returning home, through the gate, across the stoep festooned with heavy boughs of vine, and quietly pushing open the front door. To the left of the hall is a black, stinkwood bench with three *riempie* seats, which came from one of the farmhouses in the *kloof* behind Klaver. In the corner next to it is a round pedestal table, and on it is 'Love and the Soul', a long body enfolded by a winged angel by Lippy Lipshitz, the Cape Town sculptor born in Plungian. Next to it are three lavishly illustrated books between carved wooden bookends: *The Happy Prince and Other Tales* by Oscar Wilde, *The Bells* by Edgar Allan Poe and the plays of Shakespeare. I often stop at that table to look at Millais' painting of Ophelia singing as she drowns with 'clothes spread wide, / And mermaid-like, awhile they bore her up'. This time, I notice that my mother, in her absent-minded way, has left a half-finished poem there before she closed her door for her after-noon rest. It's usual for her to be sleeping, or trying to and easily disturbed, when I tiptoe back from school.

As I glance at the poem a word leaps out. The word is 'epilepsy'. Instantly, it hits me: That's what it is.

Until that moment the problems besetting my mother seemed various: tension, fatigue, anxiety, falling, jerking awake, sleeplessness and 'dry-sickness' (the last a made-up word that she associated with *The Waste Land*, and familiar long before I read that poem). It has never before occurred to me that one symp-tom could take precedence. My next thought is surprise that there might be a word for it after all. Something definite; some-thing by then made known to my mother.

I never mention this discovery to her, but it will linger at the back of my mind as a possibility not to be communicated or explored. Why not look up the word in a dictionary? I can't explain my incuriosity.

Branded on memory, the scene will present itself, two years on, in another scene that will open up the rest of my life. A student invites me to see a French film. I have just turned seventeen, and the student's name is Siamon Gordon. Afterwards he walks me home and asks about my family. His directness – more than I'm used to – invites direct answers, and impulsively, because medicine is his subject, I blurt out – swinging back and forth on the gate – the secret in our family, and what I suspect might explain it. To utter that word aloud is, for me, more intimate than touch, an exposure of fears for my mother going back to the age of two and a half.

'It's probably correct,' he says. 'There's an irritable focus in the brain. It can spread from one area to another.'

As facts dispel uncertainty, I feel grateful. Jokey though he is most of the time, he takes this seriously.

'Have you witnessed a seizure?'

'No. Only threatened attacks.'

'If a full attack happens,' he warns, 'it could look like your mother is dying, but that won't happen. Sit tight. However desperate she looks, she will eventually come round.' I lock this promise away, to be called upon in time to come. 'Hold her hand,' he advises, 'and comfort her when she comes round, because there is often an after-effect, a miasma.'

Long after, I will find assorted statements amongst my mother's papers: '*Through epilepsy I was stripped down to the foundation-rock from which I was able to strike new sparks. For on the edge of that precipice, any weakness in thought, word, or deed could plunge one into the bottomless pit, there where all vanities and falsities are expunged.*'

Where does the history of an illness begin? A history told to a doctor would begin with a symptom in the sense of malfunction. It's well known that visions can be associated with epilepsy, yet for Rhoda visions were not a sign of disease. No medical term, no ordinary words, only poetic language could reach towards this inexpressible thing, like Wordsworth's 'sense sublime' or the wandering airs that closed in on Emily Brontë when, she said, 'visions rise and change that kill me with desire'. Dostoevsky, himself epileptic, records the exhilaration of this visionary state in his portrait of the epileptic Myshkin in *The Idiot*: a breakthrough into 'a higher existence' when 'there shall be time no longer'. To take in this is to see how far any medical explanation of visions as symptoms must fall short of leaps in imaginative minds.

The diary, written when Rhoda was seventeen, eighteen and nineteen, was found after her death. Pip did the first sifting of her papers: poems, autobiographical fragments, copies of *Oranjia*, stories, letters, notes on the Bible, scribbles on the thin, almost transparent blue paper – you could write only on one side – that our father used to bring home from the office. Pip sorted identifiable batches into large brown envelopes, which he handed over when I came from England, to be kept in my flat perched over the ocean at Saunders Rocks.

A separate, small room on the floor below comes with the flat. It's dark there, cave-like, behind the blinds that close it off from a walkway. Here I unpacked Rhoda's papers and books. In the envelope containing the diary is Rhoda's list of books she was reading during the first two years after she left school. In a separate envelope is an exchange of letters with a young man, starting in the same period, 1935, and extending to the end of 1937. I took the diary and letters upstairs and lay on the window seat to read them, with the waves pounding on the rocks below. Here was my mother as a girl whose life gets rocked by two successive blows.

*

A stranger appeared at her birthday dance when she turned fifteen. A new neighbour, befriended by Rhoda's brother Basil. His name was Lou Freedberg, a tall youth, blowing moodily on the short end of a cigarette as he let fall contrary remarks in the manner of an atheist. His eyes crinkled and he folded his arms, not a twist but one hand clasping an elbow, as he withered an optimistic view of progress. 'Human nature is what it was five thousand years ago.' Rhoda was struck by the sound of cynicism, unheard amongst the men around her: Basil, as benign as Pooh Bear; his friends the Bradlow twins from Johannesburg, mildly humorous; while her father, as an immigrant, could not afford futility. Lou was an intellectual, impressive to a reading girl.

As a corrective to her taste for Romantic poets, Lou gave her one of the books on her reading list: *The Mysterious Universe* by an astrophysicist, Sir James Jeans. Predictably, what she took away from it were philosophical questions where physics touched infinities. For these were not incompatible with the focus on infinity in the poems of her favourite, Emily Brontë.

She respected Lou as a reader, and twice was drawn to him physically; both times at night when she was caught up in the pulse of sea or wind: once while playing a ball game with a group of friends on a beach, the other time when she was pressed against him in the dicky of a car, while the wind 'blew the stars about the sky'.

It was unprecedented for Rhoda to acknowledge physical attraction. I remembered how she brought up the Virgin Queen in one of what she calls our 'lying-on-beds' conversations in her room. She imagined that Elizabeth's withdrawals when it came to marriage were not primarily a matter of caution or sexual coldness. Nor was Elizabeth exercising her power, rather her desire for expressiveness, which would be terminated by an act as conclusive as marriage. Her idea of Elizabeth's desire

came from her understanding of a fuller kind of desire prompted
by emotional intimacy, drama and the play of character, which,
she implied, the blocked-off husbands of her milieu (their reading confined largely to law reports, finance, sport, war and
politics) did not entertain.

Rhoda would have discussed this only with a trusting daughter untouched as yet by the social agendas that accompany
reproduction. What my mother never discussed was her attraction to Lou and her conviction that he preferred another.

One Wednesday 7 March 1935, a week before Rhoda turned
eighteen, she woke to hear Basil start the engine of his car, the
Ashcan, to rattle off to medical school. She sat up in bed and
told her schoolfriend Monica, who had stayed the night, to
throw open the shutters so that they might call goodbye. And
then – suddenly, with no warning – she fell back in a faint.

Fainting took her over all that day. Knowing this and also the
fact that she was due to sail for Italy the following day, it is to
me bizarre that on Wednesday a girl is fainting all day and on
Thursday her mother waves her away at Cape Town docks. My
grandmother's oblivion wouldn't have extended to a physical ill.
But if she thought a love-crisis had brought her daughter to the
point of breakdown, then it would have been reasonable to
consider it best for Rhoda to go away. In that case, the voyage
would not have been conceived as a jaunt, rather as a cure. As
this idea came to me, another fact I've always known seemed to
confirm it: Rhoda's travelling companion was not a girl of her
own age or someone close to her; it was middle-aged Aunt
Tilly from Rhodesia, who was a hospital nurse.

Why was it not seen to be epilepsy, I wondered, turning the
pages of the journey. Could it be that the jerking of arms and
legs accompanying the worst form of the condition did not
manifest initially? 'Faint', the word she uses in her diary, means

that she lost consciousness, but there may have been no readily identifiable symptoms when she had that first seizure in 1935. It's easy to blame a victim, and Rhoda would become complicit with a view of herself – implied if not stated – as 'failing'.

Two days out to sea, she remained dazed.

10 March 1935: All the strangeness of a poem by Edgar Allan Poe, all the loneliness of a solitary gull skimming the waves, all the terror of eternity grips me as I look upon this watery waste . . . grey sea and grey sky and a grey dawn breaking . . . utter desolation.

Was this one form of the wasteland experience she'd often lamented to me as a child? Or does desolation often follow an attack? She went in fear of another, and her diary records tight-lipped that this did happen on deck.

Wrapped in a rug as the ship ploughed through the Bay of Biscay, she was reading keenly, dismissing ephemeral publications. Noel Coward was 'disappointing'; A. A. Milne's *Two People* 'too nonsensical'. The emotional nourishment Rhoda craved came from *Othello*. The Moor's suffering and downfall, and his self-punishing death left her 'greatly moved'. Vera Brittain's *Testament of Youth* offered a more resilient answer to the cruelty of existence when a woman loses the man she's loved, and finds the courage to make service to others – Brittain's work as battlefield nurse – a way to go on. 'Slowly absorbed every page from first to last – vivid account of woman's side of wartime.'

Rhoda was away for nearly a year. Aunt Tilly returned to Rhodesia and in July, Rhoda moved to England. There, responsibility for her care fell on her mother's closest sister, Minnie Ross, at 3 Alvanley Gardens, a pleasant house in Hampstead.

This is where Rhoda stayed all through the second half of

1935. Her aunt welcomed Rhoda like a daughter. They looked alike with dark hair and narrow, dignified faces. Solicitous as her aunt was, Rhoda's condition – the attack on deck had been followed by another in Jerusalem and then one in London – was beyond her.

She took Rhoda to three doctors. The fact that they went from one to another suggests that either no satisfactory diagnosis was made, or treatments proved ineffective.

First was a seasoned, somewhat old-fashioned neurologist of sixty-six, Wilfred Harris of Wimpole Street. Included in the history Rhoda gave to Dr Harris was her infection with the love-germ.

'Never mind, Chicken,' he told her kindly, 'we all get that disease.'

In late September Rhoda accompanied her aunt, uncle and their younger daughter Phillis to Het Zoute, a chic resort on the north Belgian coast. Close to the Dutch border, Zoute boasted blond sands, golf, luxury cars, a casino and appearances by Maurice Chevalier and Marlene Dietrich. What happened during that fortnight was silenced until Phillis, now in her mid-nineties, told me. Phillis, aged fourteen, shared a room with Rhoda in a separate wing of the hotel, far from her parents. She had been told nothing of her cousin's illness. One night she witnessed a seizure – the worst yet. Thinking Rhoda was dying, Phillis rang desperately for help. No one came for what seemed ages, and when a waiter did eventually appear he spoke only Flemish.

This instance of failed translation lights up the nightmare Europe would remain in Rhoda's memory: the strains of travelling, the constant fear of public exposure and the blight of helplessness reinforced by the self-blame induced by doctors' talk of hysteria, that diagnosis reserved for women.

A final try, in November, was to consult a Dr Leaky, who

Rhoda looks drawn between her London cousins,
Phillis and Rita Ross. Seated: Auntie Minnie

treated Rhoda through hypnosis. He meant to prove to his patient that she could train her subconscious to control her faints, and provided a notice to this effect. Rhoda was to put it above her bed. The implied diagnosis was self-induced hysteria, a womanish excess, which she must resolve to control. The onus of a potential cure therefore fell on her. She was persuaded to believe that if she did not manage to control her attacks she could go mad.

Two months later Rhoda, supposedly cured, left for Cape Town. As she drove for the last time through London, to catch the boat train at Waterloo, she was terrified at the prospect of travelling alone, with no one to help if she went under.

January 9th, 1936: . . . These months have seemed dreams; dreams that followed close, one upon another . . . dreams filled with an hysterical horror passing that of hell – nightmares of insanity . . .

We passed Westminster, and I saw Wordsworth leaning over
the bridge.

. . . silent, bare,
Ships, towers, domes, theatres and temples lie
All bright and glittering in the smokeless air.

The Thames flowed quietly by.
Waterloo Station . . . Farewell London . . . I am going home.

When she went to her cabin after dinner, panic and melancholia crept upon her 'like a Thug'. During the night she woke sharply, wanting to scream yet knowing no one would come. She felt herself ascending 'a pinnacle of insanity', her body shaking violently with repressed fear. She prayed and recited poetry, and the panic gradually subsided.

Leaky. Wilfred Harris. Here are names I could look up. Harris was prominent in the field of epilepsy. Could Leaky be Dr J. E. A. Leakey, who advocated a 'ketogenic' diet for epileptics in the thirties? Until these names surfaced in the diary, I'd believed that doctors had been in the dark. This is what my mother told me, and probably also what she'd told herself because she, certainly, remained in the dark. But these doctors' associations with epilepsy, coming up on the computer screen, suggest that the nature of Rhoda's illness was not wholly a mystery. If Auntie Minnie took her to these respected physicians, then the possibility of some form of epilepsy was aired. There must have been a decision amongst the older generation to conceal it from anyone outside the family, and from Rhoda herself. The secrecy makes it clear that the illness continued to carry a stigma, particularly for a young woman. It could have spoilt her chances of marriage. And since the illness carries a genetic element, there might have been a question whether she should have children. All this would have been mulled over, I imagine, behind closed doors.

Fourteen days out of Southampton, Rhoda woke at six to find the ship gliding past Robben Island wrapped in morning mist. As they docked in Cape Town her parents and her dear schoolfriend Lilian were waiting on the quay. Then she saw Monica, the other member of their schoolgirl trio, getting out of a car and knew all at once, 'I love her.' It was as though some

Rhoda and Monica (left) on holiday at Hermanus.
The last illness-free summer, 1934–5

fount of feeling, sealed for ten months by the artifice of normality, was suddenly unstopped.

Monica was astonished by Rhoda's grown-up look in a green
Tyrolean hat and fox (as though she were still in wintry
London). 'You've changed,' Monica told her. Rhoda thought
how surprised they would be to know that the change was due
to illness.

It was high summer, hot, dusty. Her distanced ear picked up
'uncouth accents'. These sounds, she knew, would grow dear
and familiar again. Her father took her and her mother for tea
at Markham's in Adderley Street. There was a family quarrel,
and for a moment Rhoda felt about to faint, but managed to
control herself. Then they drove fifteen miles to a house on the
dunes at Muizenberg, which her parents had taken for the six
weeks of beach life known as the season. As they neared the
ocean the air grew cooler. There were gold coins of sunlight
on the grey-brown carpet, and the sea, she thought, sounded
for twenty miles along the shore like the roll of eternity.

After lunch, Basil, large, trusty, sprawled across her bed and
she told him how she'd loved Lou, and all she'd had to endure
with her illness. Basil was 'shocked and upset', and wished she
had confided in him before. His presence was balm. She could
lean on him from now on, and he would help her get well.

In her nightie, before she went to sleep, she leant out of
her bedroom window, listening to the 'rhythmic purr' of the
sea across the dunes. And looking up 'at the arch of the stars',
she felt the wind blow the constraints of London away. Here,
at home, she would be free to say what she thought. She
would heal the strained ties with her parents, though as far as
dependence went, Basil had replaced them as a father-
brother.

Basil now brought about the next drama in Rhoda's young
life. First, he relayed Lou's identity to their father, who duly

Rhoda and her eldest brother Basil were close throughout their lives.
Clockwise, from top left: Klaver days; Rhodean days; Muizenberg days, 1940,
with Basil on leave from Pretoria Hospital; Muizenberg again in the early fifties

Low tide at Muizenberg in the thirties. Back: Phillis, Monica, Rita, Rhoda. Basil second from right, Lou far right. Front: Hubert

invited Rhoda for a walk to St James. There, over tea, he assured her that he and her mother would favour a future attachment. He even suggested that Lou might have been in love with her all along. Then, on the first Saturday night after her return, Lou – whom she still believed to be the prime cause of her breakdown – drove out from town to see her.

Rhoda heard a car come to a stop at the dunes across the road. Entering the house, Lou's eyes behind his glasses creased at the corners as he smiled on a girl to all appearance metamorphosed at nearly nineteen: slim and delicately beautiful in her well-cut London dress, shorn of ringlets, her bubbly hair smoothed and short. He fell in love at that moment.

Rhoda decided that she liked him, but was not in love. He had the watchful half-smile of someone who's not entirely well. Lou was thin and carried a shadow of paleness under the usual layer of sunburn. Though land-surveying took him out of doors, his shoulders were a little hunched and his chest a little concave, rather like immigrants from Lithuania, raised on a poor diet, whose frames had not spread and hardened in sufficient sunlight.

Returning at last to Rhodean and her little room with the shutters, which she'd left as in a dream the year before, Rhoda felt 'like a ghost revisiting some vaguely familiar place'.

She and Monica visited Good Hope Seminary, a school founded in the 1870s along the lines of the Girls' Public Day School Trust in England to provide equal education for women. They went to see Miss Krige (their literature teacher, related to the Afrikaans poet Uys Krige) and Miss Stevenson ('Stevie')

Friendships formed at Good Hope were lasting. The top girl, Monica, is second from left, back row. Rhoda second from right, middle row. Lilian second from left, front row. Third from right, front row, is Thelma, who was to illustrate Rhoda's children's book, *Jonah*

who taught Latin. Stevie had birdlike bright eyes and a face like a wrinkled apple. Their teachers kissed them and the girls' 'untainted lips' were 'besmirched' with lipstick. Miss Krige almost wept when she told Rhoda that their literature class had been the happiest she'd ever had. Teachers then (and into my time at the school in the fifties) were not models for their pupils. They were single women, whose professional lives seemed unenviable, unthinkable. Although some found fulfilment in work, motherhood tethered to home was still a pervasive norm. In my mother's time, a girl might earn a bit or she might travel and go out with well-conducted men (it was considered fast to flirt or kiss on a first date) before she settled down to home-making in her early twenties.

So it was that Rhoda's parents could think of nothing better than to start her on a course of shorthand and typing at Underwoods, a secretarial college in town. It was a dusty, crowded place full of silly girls with little to offer in the way of friendship.

Later, my mother will say how she'd longed for higher education at a time when her father, after his losses during the Great Depression, could not afford it. Her parents, though, had managed to send her overseas for almost a year. Restoring her health would have been a priority; not a daughter's education, and in this they were not unusual. None of Rhoda's set went to university.

Why, Rhoda asked herself, did she not find with Lou Freedberg the intimacy that she had with Monica and Lilian? 'His absolute worship seemed strange. I was unaccustomed to being loved, and not a little worried because I believed ... I was not being quite honest – and yet I could not force myself to break.'

Rhoda's father, mindful of her breakdown and unaware of the doubts she confided to her diary, invited Lou to accompany

The trio. From left: Rhoda, Monica, Lilian,
in front of Muizenberg Pavilion

the family on their winter holiday, in July, to Graafwater, in the
rough terrain of the *Weskus*, near Klaver.

On Lou's birthday she gave him an illustrated copy of *The
Happy Prince and Other Tales* by Oscar Wilde, 'to begin your
education in the importance of unimportant things. They prove
that cynics write the loveliest fairy stories.' The title tale is about
a statue of a happy prince, who in truth never experienced happiness. Viewing misery from his plinth, he asks a swallow to
strip the gold leaf covering his body, to give it to the poor. The
statue is then torn down, but the lead heart, all that's left when
he's melted down, is taken to heaven.

Rhoda and Lou took long walks, not entirely agreeable to

With Lou, *c.* 1936–7, on Clifton Beach (left) and with a river picnic party

Rhoda because they found 'so few points of contact mentally'. Lou's ominous perspective on human history, reinforced by a film they'd seen, H. G. Wells's *Things to Come*, alerted her to Europe's rearmament. To acknowledge what was to come changed her inner landscape. '*The buoyancy of mind I had been building up since my return to Africa sunk as he talked … The inexorableness of the distant blue hills which had cleansed me, the beautiful silences of the veld which had uplifted me, now overpowered me with a terrible sense of futility.*'

In September 1937 a streptococcal infection found its way into the weak left ventricle of Lou's heart. He was admitted for observation to Somerset Hospital, near Cape Town docks. And then, ominously, he was moved to the main hospital, Groote Schuur. Lilian recalled holding his hand in the ambulance rocking around the mountain curves of De Waal Drive. Later she stood with Rhoda in the corridor outside his ward and heard him scream in pain.

Each day during visiting hours, Rhoda watched Campbell, the night nurse, as she bent over temperature charts under the lamp at the centre of the ward. It was she to whom Lou turned. 'I will never marry,' he told her while Rhoda was there. To Rhoda, he spoke harshly.

Nurse Campbell cared so much for 'dear old Freedie' that Matron, Miss Pike, had to tick her off for favouritism. Miss Pike then moved Campbell to another ward and forbade her to see Lou. Campbell had to glean news of him from other nurses and resort to smuggled letters.

On 15 March 1938 Rhoda turned twenty-one. A birthday letter from her brother Sydney in Johannesburg invited her to join him, promising to look after her. The invitation may have been prompted by awareness of what was coming. On 31 March Lou died, aged twenty-three.

On the day of the funeral, Rhoda sat with Lilian in her father's car. Her mother had forgotten her hatpin, and held up the party because a well-dressed mother couldn't set out for the cemetery without it. When Lilian is old, she will remember how the two girls, in fits of mirth, rolled together on the back seat.

During the burial, Rhoda blamed herself for failing Lou. Listening to the strong whistle of a bird, she felt 'deeply ashamed', but apart from this, no emotion:

I knew positively that Lou was not in the box covered with a black cloth. I felt no emotion whatever. Why should I? I knew this was an unreal conventional ceremony & Lou would have hated it if he had been there and yet I deliberately squeezed out a tear. Inside I felt quite dead & yet I did this because I felt it was expected of me!

I am afraid I am full of what K[atherine] M[ansfield] calls 'sediment'. Examined in the clear light of what has happened I know I was tinkling & vain and grasping at shadows. That is why I failed him so terribly. And yet for the rare moments when I 'broke through' and was 'real' he loved me.

My mother never spoke of Lou, but she did tell me that she went to live with her brother in Johannesburg 'after a bereavement', and that she was wretched there.

Although Rhoda and Sydney felt and appeared polar opposites – Sydney, at nineteen, at the start of a high-flying business career, Rhoda opposed to 'getting and spending' – they were temperamentally the most alike in the family, with a vein of originality entwined with moodiness that could make them, for all their charm and courtesy, difficult. There was a lurking vehemence, a sense when you were with them of having to tread lightly on top of tremors in the earth.

Sydney intended to be helpful after Lou's death but an ill and grieving sister would have burdened a young man who was working every moment and often returned to his workplace at night. Rhoda would then be alone in his flat, in a city dominated by mine dumps. In the allegorised landscape of her imagination, Johannesburg was a place of hollow men groping for gold.

In the winter of 1938, three months after Lou's death, she sank very low during a bout of flu. *'People say grief goes over. Right. Perhaps it does. But what has one left?'* Basil came a thousand miles – two days by train – to fetch her home.

I understand now why *The Happy Prince* stood to attention beside my mother's much-thumbed volume of Shakespeare on the pedestal table at the entrance to our family home.

6

'Only a Housewife'

They meet, of course, on Muizenberg beach. In 1939 Harry, at thirty, is an attorney, handling traffic accidents and divorce. Traffic is the last thing Rhoda cares to notice. As for divorce, it's off the map for orthodox Jewish women. Orthodox women are observant, attentive to the community, and they look on marriage less as a private story than a ritual of communal perpetuation. If a bride has a poetic bent, it's nice enough as a pastime, but irrelevant to what's expected of a wife. And if marriage makes a Jewish wife unhappy, she learns to put up with it.

As Harry breezes about the beach in his swimming trunks and the cream and blue striped blazer of the South African Swimming Union, divorcées, hair in clenched blonde ridges, wave to him with toothy smiles. He raises a hand and winks back. Winking is almost a reflex as his light green eyes scan the crowd for his numerous acquaintance. Now and then, exuding health, muscles shifting in his shoulders, he bends down or crouches to shake hands with one-time rivals. He has firm views on sporting behaviour. Swimmers sprout up around him.

University of Cape Town Swimming Club, winners of intervarsity 1930.
Harry is second from right, middle row

His passion is sport: swimming, water polo, soccer and baseball. In the past he'd raced in pools around the country, intervarsity contests like the annual Currie Cup, and now he manages teams, sorts out disputes and does running commentaries on the wireless.

He first spots Rhoda sitting on the sand under a sea-coloured sunshade, which matches the blue-green sundress spread over slim legs tucked to one side. Her dark skin doesn't have the sultry olive tint of the Mediterranean; it's a serious darkness. Her large blue eyes and a high-bridged nose lend her face a thoughtful cast. Though she holds a poor opinion of her appearance, it has dignity, the kind of face that gains distinction with age. Her poor opinion probably has its origin in her mother's pride in Sydney, the favourite and the only one of the four to look like her. He has her fair skin and what my mother calls, a little enviously, 'a chiselled nose'.

Harry is good looking in the sunburnt, South African way,

with hair parted off-centre. His legal office displays photos of Western Province teams, rows of solemn men with arms folded over their one-piece racing costumes, and at their feet the Currie Cup.

Men like Harry play around with floozies as a matter of course and marry virgins – manliness demands no less. In the meantime they slip in and out of divorcées and, satisfied, go their way. In male company they joke about needing the know-how, as though they're Boy Scouts obedient to the motto Be Prepared and in training for their next badge. 'Marie Stopes showed us the ropes' is the jingle of those prepared enough to pack condoms when a team sets off.

Born in 1909, Harry is eight years older than Rhoda, and by the time they meet a veteran in the sheikh role. At fancy-dress parties he would appear in Arab robes, layers of exotic stripes topped with a flowing headdress. In addition, he sports a prickly brown moustache, the current badge of masculinity, and hard knots of muscle bulge in his calves and arms from long-distance swims in rough seas. In his youth, girls hummed an old hit in his vicinity: 'I'm Just Wild About Harry'.

None of this, of course, impresses a high-minded girl like Rhoda Press. Harry, who knows loads of pretty women, has never encountered any as serious as Rhoda. He doesn't quite know what to make of her. Though Rhoda needs a man to protect her, she's unsure if she wants to marry someone so on the go, calling to her to 'shake a leg' if she isn't ready – and she's never ready – when he comes to take her out.

When Rhoda stalls over his proposal Harry picks up the phone and dictates an ultimatum to Lilian, now a legal secretary, who is to pass this on. Either Rhoda says yes, or the offer is off.

This is Lilian's story, and it rings true, yet Rhoda has a different story.

It can happen that some trivial pressure drives a life-changing

Harry meets Rhoda on Muizenberg beach

decision, as in the case of a friend of mine who didn't want to
go through with her wedding. She went to my Aunt Berjulie
for advice, and my aunt, an arbiter of rectitude, told her it was
too late.

'You can't do that to Krafchik.'

Krafchik was the caterer and since then, 'Krafchik' has been
our family code for an absurd obligation. What really drove
Rhoda to accept the proposal, she told me, was an invitation from
Harry's sister Lena, who had given birth to a son. Lena, always
friendly to my mother, asked her to be Gerald's godmother. It was
not easy to refuse. Yet, since Harry was to be godfather, to agree
was to appear a couple. So it happens that Rhoda, unwilling to
cross Lena's overture, finds herself engaged.

As a bachelor, Harry has been a habitué of cocktail parties and so at ease, waving, winking, engaged in confabs on the latest scores, that no one noticed he didn't drink. He actually had no taste for alcohol, and I will inherit this – though coming to Oxford in the seventies will compel me to touch a glass of sherry to my lips from time to time. The result of Harry's visibility at cocktails means that my parents receive no fewer than eight cocktail sets as wedding presents. Rhoda will consign them to a cabinet in the dining room from which they never emerge.

The night before the wedding the family tells the bridegroom ... something. It remains confidential, and my guess is that they didn't say too much. Certainly, whatever they told him came too late for a bridegroom to retreat. So then, the intermittently visible illness and the invisible shadow of Lou behind this union.

How much did Harry know? As their first child, I both know and don't know, and the weight of suffering, unspoken but present, makes it nicer not to know as I grow up. I think it's nicer for my father not to know, or not fully, what it's like to live as what Katherine Mansfield calls 'an exile from health', and naturally it's easier not to know whether his wife did or did not continue to grieve for her lost love. And I see now how readily I took on my father's unknowing.

So it is that, for years, I turn away and put off the task to be her channel. Was it cowardice? Does emotional cowardice block me even now? 'Winter kept us warm,' Eliot says. It's tempting to wrap ourselves in a blanket of unknowing, for life-writing demands that we come to know ourselves through our subject.

The two are married on 9 April 1940. Rhoda looks dreamy in white satin embossed with hearts. The dress has a plain round neck and girly puffed sleeves. Lilian and another schoolfriend, Marjorie, are bridesmaids, both engaged to marry in June. Monica is not

present because her new husband, Bill, an accountant, is going up north, and Monica has gone to Johannesburg to be near him while he trains in the army. The senior partner of Harry's law firm, Bertie Stern, went up north in 1939. They agreed that Harry should remain in Cape Town to man the office.

After the wedding, Rhoda decides not to go on honeymoon. She stands in her shuttered room at Rhodean, her wedding dress on the bed, as Lilian helps her into her going-away suit, and watches as Rhoda bends to the mirror to put on a little pointed hat with a veil dipping over one eye. She says to Lilian that she's gone through with the wedding, and that's as far as she's prepared to go.

Lilian, another virgin told nothing by her mother, looks forward to marriage with keener anticipation, and assures Rhoda that marriage will do her good. Lil will be waiting when Rho gets back, and they will love each other dearly as before. Rhoda allows Lilian to persuade her to go away.

They go off to the Wilderness, a five-hour drive up the east coast to a honeymoon place on the Indian Ocean. There's a wide white beach, steadily rolling waves and thatched rooms strung out along the shore. Granny had prepared her daughter with a satin nightie and matching gown, and when Rhoda, suitably arrayed, attempts an entrance, she trips over the flowing gown. She often, regretfully, called herself 'excitable', meaning nervy.

In my teens, my mother will relay something of her wedding night as one of her arguments in favour of virginity. She said that her purity so moved her bridegroom that he, a man not given to tears, shed a few when she gave herself to him. She looks on the body as a temple, not to be cheapened by casual use. She never utters the word 'sex', always 'love-making' because, I take it, she includes what she herself may not experience, delicacy of feeling.

My grandmother's own story is calmer and sweeter. Her honeymoon was at Caledon, an inland spa with hot springs that was fashionable in 1914 – Granny was always fashionable. After the wedding, she likes to recall, 'My husband said to me, "Now we'll enjoy the fruits of our love."'

He wasn't a native English speaker, yet found the perfect words. Annie is not attentive to language, yet these words remain with her all her life. The feeling is active, as she repeats it to me lolling in her room at the Balmoral Hotel in the centre of Muizenberg. In her eighties she's still vigorous enough to cross the Beach Road to dip in the sea before breakfast, bending over first to splash her freckled arms.

Her husband was a good man, she wants me to know. He was so good that when he heard that Annie's sister Minnie was pining for their mother (who had recently died), he insisted that

Minnie should join them on honeymoon. Granny was teased when it came out that the sisters had shared the bed (as they'd shared a bed at home) and my grandfather had slept on his own behind a screen. Granny sees fit to confide that she was observing the Jewish law that forbids a couple to share a bed during menstruation.

It's impossible to be accurate about the past. Reports conflict. In a photograph, Rhoda dances along the sand in a bathing costume, arms flung wide. There is also the 'amazing' fact she reports to Basil, 'that after rigorous daily tuition from a determined husband I got my Driver's Licence on Honeymoon!' She rarely succumbs to the vulgarity of an exclamation mark; it is a measure of her surprise. On her return she looks radiant in the expected bridal way, to the noticing eye of a teenage cousin (Auntie Betsie's youngest daughter, Garda). She thinks that Rhoda was happy on honeymoon.

The family's precaution in not divulging Rhoda's history until the last moment does Harry an injustice: he never loves Rhoda any less on account of her illness; he may, in fact, love her more, though it isn't in him to know her as a reflective man might. A more sensitive man, on the other hand, might cope less well than Harry, with his ready optimism. If Rhoda is unwell, he's content to leave her in bed with a book – he rarely requires her company. Her invalidism and his unquestioning acceptance of a condition that neither he nor anyone fully understands frees her to read and write. In no time he's on to the next case, the next match. Leaving the house, he calls in his happy going-away voice, 'I'm off like a dirty shirt.'

Rhoda has no interest whatever in sport, though she does like to plunge in the breakers. The sea is 'pristine', while swimming pools are decidedly not her scene. I watch her after her bath, parting each of her toes carefully, one by one, and patting the crevices with her fluffy white towel in her battle against athlete's foot, which Harry, she complains, picks up in public swimming baths.

Like many outdoorsy South Africans, he likes to walk barefoot. Pip and I patter barefoot at his side, careful to step over the lines of pavement slabs. In our heads is the sing-song of a superior English boy, Christopher Robin, who warns not to step on the lines because, if we do, *bears* will emerge: burly, shaggy bears hungry for the flesh of little children. Although there are no bears in Africa – no bears in the zoo with its monkeys and lions on the hump of Devil's Peak above De Waal Drive – we've stared in willing suspension of disbelief at these grim, other-world bears in Shepard's illustration for *When We Were Very Young*, before our mother turns the page to the poem we like best because it makes us see ourselves in a humorous light: Mary Jane is 'crying with all her might and main' and refuses her food, though it's *lovely* rice pudding again.

Pip and I side with Mary Jane; we detest puddings second only to stringy rhubarb, and marvel at the steady spooning-up on the part of our visiting cousins out from London, the well-behaved grandchildren of Auntie Minnie. Their no-nonsense English nanny ('a white nurse', in our mother's mock-awed tones) sets out wobbling gobs of pudding on the nursery table at the flat they have taken on Beach Road.

If the cream slabs of Muizenberg pavement get too hot, you can cool your soles by balancing along the stone edging or, better still, walk in the invitingly cool stone gutter, dry in summer. At noon, the tar of the road sears a child's tender feet: to cross the road, we reluctantly put on brown leather sandals with difficult buckles. Our father good-naturedly crouches down in shorts over his dampish swimming trunks (catching cold doesn't concern him as it does our mother) to do them up.

His sheikh costume, meanwhile, is relegated to the top of a cupboard in our nursery. I climb on a chair to fetch it down and

try it on, the layers of thin, striped garments, this outfit being
the offshoot of a torrid novel and silent movie, in which a girl
is carried off into the desert by Rudolph Valentino. I will dip
into this novel later, in adolescence – a few pages are enough to
explain why my mother dismissed it, along with other sex-
hungry fiction of the twenties, which she sees as a response to
the lost generation of men killed in the First World War.

Rhoda's letters to Basil during the forties challenge my memory
of a suffering semi-invalid who lives through books and poems.
With Basil she continues to be the outgoing girl she'd been
before her illness. In May 1940, after her return from honey-

Rhoda posing on honeymoon at the Wilderness

moon, she hastens to assure Basil that she's well and happy in the marriage, 'since you played such a big part in engineering it'. I picture her bored by Harry's sporting chums, yet it's through him that she meets the dancer Ren Stodel, who invites her to watch her Monday class – this then is Rhoda's introduction to the orphanage – and she also meets an advocate, Gerald Gordon, a left-wing intellectual with whom she shares books. They take long, heads-together walks. He's active against racial oppression, and after the National Party comes to power in the late forties he brings out a novel, *Let the Day Perish*, about two brothers who live apart on separate sides of the colour bar. The cover has two Henry Moore-like figures, side by side with hands touching but divided by a line down the centre.

When we're alone, my mother calls it, somewhat disparagingly, 'a social service novel'. This is her phrase for a novel written primarily to protest a wrong, as distinct from literature, even though she shares the author's political views. Later, when I gave tutorials on the poetry of the First World War, I asked students whether propaganda – in that case, against war and war-makers – can be literature? Oxford undergraduates invariably argued that most great writing contains propaganda of one sort or another: a famous instance would be Levin's philosophy in *Anna Karenina*; another would be George Eliot's humanism. All the same, my mother had a point, I think, in her distinction between the primacy of a current issue and lasting art.

My parents stay, at first, in the Mimosa Hotel. It's opposite the Sea Point Pavilion, spread out between the rocks, where Harry swims every day after work. It's a complex of open-air, sea water pools of differing depths – including a sixteen-foot pool with diving boards mounting to a perilous height.

The plan has been to look for a place of their own, but war defers this. In May 1940 Rhoda sees seven giant British ships move 'silently and mysteriously' into Table Bay, escorted by the South African Air Force. Twenty to fifty thousand soldiers from Australia and New Zealand wake up Cape Town. This is their 'last fling'. The future to Rhoda looks 'nebulous', and to act for herself alone seems wrong. For the duration of the war she prefers to stay in her old home in Oranjezicht.

Her high-minded reasons often take precedence over mundane ones, and I suspect that my father's frugality played some part in this decision. They rent a flat near Saunders Rocks for a while, but Rhoda is 'ill' and takes against the setting where it happened. She becomes averse to the sight and smell of the sea, and finds herself happier back on Table Mountain amidst the pines and oaks.

Beloved Monica is there too, staying in her father's house while her husband is up north. Each morning at a quarter past eight the two friends take a long walk through the Avenue lining the Gardens and into town. Rhoda's state of health veers according to her company. Mood plays so large a part, it's a little disheartening, when I come on the scene, to find that I can't cheer her – not in the way of Basil or Monica. They don't have to do more than walk into her room. She loves them so intensely, her spirits soar.

Reading between the lines of my mother's letters, I see a return to Monica as the prime reason for settling back at Rhodean after her marriage. The death of her father in 1941, and my birth later that year, may be further reasons to return to her family home. Her practical mother is there to help, assisted by jolly Auntie Betsie, who comes to town from Namaqualand. In those days, a live-in nursing sister accompanied a newborn home in order to establish its routines and allow a new mother to lie down for the protracted period then thought necessary. With the prospect of three women to nurse her, as well as the support of Basil, on leave from Pretoria Hospital, Rhoda appears content. She remains so for the next two years, despite my 'feeding problems'.

At the time, mothers are still tyrannised by the childcare guru Truby King, who rules against demand feeding, as practised by African women. My mother would have seen those African babies easy at the breast, but like other mothers of her ilk obediently mashes together five vegetables for every meal, to be given on the dot, and denied if a baby is so ill-regulated as to cry at the wrong hour. I don't take to this regimen or to the stuffing, and my mother pictures herself rather comically circling my cot with a spoon while I edge around it, holding on to the rails. My mother has more success with a blue dog, who meets another blue dog in the mirror, and when my mouth opens in wonder she pops in the spoon.

The other tyrant is the paediatrician. The nervous voices of young mothers echo his rulings to one another: 'Dr Rabkin said ... ' and 'Dr Rabkin thinks ... ', and one day, when I'm about two, my weary mother is forcing herself to take me to him. There are called-out instructions to Lenie as my hair is brushed into a sausage curl on top of my head and I'm put into my tucked dress. I can remember Dr Rabkin's pallor and long-faced solemnity; my mother's deferential intentness.

When both my grandmother and father are away, she's content to be alone with me at Rhodean. There's 'conversation' and we go for walks. She's safe at night because John, the gardener, sleeps on the stoep outside her room. (Like many Xhosas he's taken a 'white' name as his working identity, a common habit to this day – the assumption being that employers can't get their tongues around a variety of clicks made by the tongue against the teeth or palate.)

It's not until early in 1944 that Rhoda's morale appears to crack. The hormonal run-up to my brother's birth is inextricable from 'illness'. During the summer of 1943–4 Basil was on holiday in Muizenberg and stayed with Rhoda. The letter she writes to him on 19 March 1944 attempts to cover up signs of illness that Basil has seen. 'I must ask you to believe that those nervous explosions you witnessed are by no means normal to me and have completely disappeared . . . ' She takes the onus on herself: the explosions will be under control if she's sufficiently occupied.

'I feel very distressed that I should have allowed you to acquire such a very distorted version of our married life, and especially of Harry,' she goes on. 'I can assure you we have never been so out of harmony before or since . . . I am happy to say that Harry does much good in his own way through little personal acts in which he takes pleasure.'

Basil must have noticed Harry's frugality, for Rhoda defends this: 'As for money, luxurious living is particularly abhorrent to me in Wartime, and . . . I have never personally suffered a single want since my marriage.'

Marriage, as the ideal arrangement for life, is unquestioned. Basil and his friend Frank Bradlow (both in the army and out of contact with women, except for leaves) have told Rhoda that they feel their married friends are one up on them. In warning Basil against his easygoing propensity to fall for any girl who is amiable, Rhoda envies a man's freedom. 'Unlike our sex you have the advantage . . . of being able to Wait and Choose.' Despite all she's said to contradict Basil's impression that her husband has proved ill-suited, that sentence might seem to confirm it.

Housewives like my mother are assumed to be at home, and other wives pop in on impulse. The front door bell can ring at any moment, and Lenie brings tea, a 'cool-drink' (a granadilla cordial) and home-made iced cake. Wives speak detachedly, though not disloyally, of men as needy pets whose antics amuse them. Lilian's husband Bertie Henry, it's said, has never worn pyjama bottoms. Twin beds (as seen in the film *The Red Shoes*) are currently in fashion for couples. Monica, it's said, marks the deliberation with which her husband has to cross from his bed to hers.

Listening to them, I wonder at their accommodation of such husbands as they have chosen: dependable men respected in the community. Is this what the future will hold? Do they expect less than I will want, for I'm under the spell of books with dreaming girls. They too had been under that spell, and lived in those books. What had happened to make them accepting? My mother tells me that she married to have children. That's what wives of the forties say. The romances and desires of their teenage years seem to be left behind in favour of home, family and community. At best they take the position articulated perfectly by Jane Austen when she relates how a mother 'had humoured, or softened, or concealed [her husband's] failings, and promoted his real respectability for seventeen years; and though not the very happiest being in the world herself, she had found enough in her duties, her friends, and her children, to attach her to life'.

This is Lilian's solution as a farmer's wife. At dawn she lays out great tureens of porridge and steaming mugs of coffee for the labourers; come autumn, she's shoulder to shoulder in the apple-packing shed; in summer, when a mountain fire breaks out, she's out there with the men. The farm flourishes; in time they are no longer poor.

After the birth of their second son, a fretting baby who leaves Lilian depleted, Bertie's mother arrives from Edinburgh. An antiques dealer in a kaftan and Moroccan shoes with turned-up toes descends from the plane. Mother, as Lilian dutifully calls this apparition, has brought her daughter-in-law a silver belt and an antique sugar shaker – neither of use on a farm – but then proceeds to ignore her. Each evening mother and son sit down to dinner on their own (Mother's favourite meatballs), and it does not occur to Bertie to draw in his wife.

After Mother departs, Lilian finds herself inert. She loses weight and her well-spring of feeling dries to nothing. Bertie takes her to a doctor in Cape Town. Women like Lilian don't speak readily of their trials. Not many town women would have adapted to a farmer offering rough and barely furnished quarters. And there'd been more to be borne, I learn later, when Lilian gives me a copy of her memoirs. For when, as a bride, she came to Pomona, at large in the kitchen she found the foreman's wife who, Lilian guessed, had served her husband's needs during his years as a bachelor. The most Lilian could do was get rid of that brooding presence; it was not possible to run home from the top of Piketberg Mountain; she didn't for one moment consider it. The only way forward was not to pursue the facts.

Is Lilian's doctor aware of things to know beyond physical symptoms? A consultation that fails to enter into the buried cause of distress can be dangerous, as when Rhoda fell to the floor in a doctor's office and went home to end her life. So it happens that when Lilian turns her head to the doctor's open window on the sixth floor, she wants to throw herself out.

Instead, she takes refuge with her grandmother in Muizenberg. Only unstinting love, the same as Lilian herself has scattered like seeds falling in the furrows in fertile abundance, can extract her from what my mother calls 'dry-sickness' – what medicine might, in Lilian's case, label post-partum depression. It's out of character to abandon her two boys, one a continuously wailing baby, to her brusque husband. After two weeks he asks her to return, and she resolves to do so. What eventually brings her back to life is another pregnancy. She is sure this time it will be a girl. She will grow a creature of her kind who will be a companion.

Where Lilian's maternal nature brims and flows into practical altruism, Monica's maternity is more consuming: it emerges in her twenties as the bedrock of her being, filling the vacant space left by a mother who was put away in an asylum after Monica was born. While Bill, her husband, is up north in 1944, Monica gives birth to Michael. My mother goes to see her, and never forgets the scene that meets her eyes. Monica is standing in a shuttered room with a baby in her arms: as she carries the baby out of the shadow, my mother sees that Michael has Down's syndrome. Monica wraps her maternal nature around Michael, ready to give him her life. Though she goes on to have three more sons, Michael's need for protection takes precedence. As he grows up, he will become my father's most faithful listener to sports broadcasts – a consolation to Harry for my mother's habit of switching off his happy voice.

During the forties, these three friends struggle to come to terms with difficult lots: Lilian off on the farm with a rough man; Monica brooding over Michael; and Rhoda sunk in depression after Pip's birth. They don't meet much, and their twenties go by minus the balm of their friendship. Yet it's during these hard years that each constructs something of her own.

In her unassuming way Monica creates a garden in tiers on the mountain slope high above Bantry Bay. It's a secret garden, invisible behind a suburban house, Bayhead, on Kloof Road. My mother, recovering, breathes in the fragrant tea roses blooming in abundance.

By the time I come to know Auntie Monica there's no sign of the winner my mother pictures in their schooldays: the girl who came first in every subject, the best at games and the lead in a Good Hope production of *Peter Pan*. She's mild with that slightly cut-off look of women feeding babies, and I can't fathom the depth of my mother's attachment. Books are still part of it, and they reminisce about *Testament of Youth* and *South*

Riding not so much now for their portraits of independent women as because they were read in friendship – read by the girls Mon and Rho had been. Nowadays, Auntie Monica is less ambitious than my mother, and quieter than Auntie Lilian. Auntie Monica appears contained in her matronly skirt and cardigan, the unobtrusive, covered-up clothing I associate with Englishwomen in magazines from overseas. No sundress flaunts her flesh; nor does she choose the floaty muslins and organdies that suit my mother's slender form; nor of course the boots and overalls Lilian dons on the farm.

'Mon,' my mother greets her with a joy no one else can give. Mists clear. The curtain rises and her friend flies out of the window as Peter Pan.

Monica's mouth curves into a slow, charming smile as she says softly, 'Rho.'

While Monica cultivates her garden, and Lilian her farm, my mother is 'scribbling'. When she pulls herself together to leave the house, she carries her small wire-bound notebook in her handbag, and sometimes stops in the street to set down a character she's noticed or a line of a poem that comes as she sniffs the sour-sweet tang of the *fynbos* with face uplifted. The challenge is to voice what has been voiceless.

Where are words for extremes of experience? A glimpse of pre-existence or plunges into what was once called the falling sickness co-exist with the veld awaiting a poet's voice. Sealed in a car, cut off from her first world in her suburban marriage, Rhoda spies a gazelle. Native of the veld, its eye meets hers. No language, she intimates, for what that creature feels of terror and bliss:

> *The veld is voiceless*
> *Africa is dumb;*

flat and far as space can reach
mountains that bless
await in the sun
a poet's speech.

In steel machine
and glass we glide;
metallic void and sterile cell
from Great Africa divide.
While a Gazelle —
eye tendrils long —
sucks from sourbush and scent of clod
a poet's song.

I feel privileged to be her sole listener, though my attention does wander: 'gazelle' has a lovely sound but I've never seen one. My mother tells me she has another, secret name, like Upwards for our house. She's Tsviah, meaning 'gazelle' in Hebrew. 'It sounds like my middle name, Stella,' she justifies the choice, 'and I prefer Stella to Rhoda.'

Not to hurt her feelings, I don't admit my indifference to a more ordinary poem she's written, designed for us children: 'Story of a Tree for my children, Lyndall and Pip'. A tree without its leaves, stilled by 'Winter's breath', waits 'secretly and faithfully' for the 'tremor' in the earth that brings on spring. This seasonal story of renewal doesn't touch me like the word 'suffering' (an ominous word on her lips), and again 'suffering'.

Her models come from books beside her bed. One is the journal of Katherine Mansfield who, my mother says, was ill in the south of France, away from home and unsupported by her husband. And yet, for her, illness was a 'privilege' because it opened her eyes as a writer.

This is the challenge Rhoda undertakes: to transmute fear
into sight and to find words to unlock those words that 'lie
beyond the mouth / locked in the mountain's chest'. Her
metaphor is prompted not only by the difficulty of expression
but also by modesty. For Katherine Mansfield had genius.
Rhoda, laid low at the bottom of Africa, can make no such
claim, not even to the child at her side. All the same, I understand in some fashion how sightings along the way come as
compensation.

August – late winter 1946. I have something the doctor calls
'trench mouth'. Before penicillin becomes available in general
practice, temperatures run high and infections don't heal that
fast. I'm in bed for some time, not in the nursery but in my
mother's room. I'm impatient for my mother finally to finish
splashing her face and giving the orders on the phone. She sits
down on my bed with the finality of a down movement mingled with an air of expectancy. Whenever she lends herself to
the drama on the page she becomes these characters: bungling
Pooh Bear hunting a heffalump; the naughty look in the corner
of Peter Rabbit's eye when Mother Rabbit warns him not to go
into Mr McGregor's garden; and Betsey Trotwood calling on
laughably simple Mr Dick for his opinion as to what to do with
her runaway nephew Davy Copperfield.

When I get up and am helped into navy blue woollen dun-
garees, I wobble. I take a few steps to the open window and see
the sea in the distance and smell its salty sharpness mingled with
ripening loquats. I'm uncertain whether or not to believe my
mother's story that I once spat a loquat pip out of the window,
and it grew itself into a tree in the soil below.

A glad day to be up again, and my mother celebrates by reading aloud a new story, 'The Doll's House'. It's about an
awakening to snobbery. This could be any suburb, it could be

Sea Point, but it's based, my mother's explains, on Katherine Mansfield's colonial home in Wellington, New Zealand. Here, Aunt Beryl rebuffs two children in ragged dresses, the Kelveys, who are hanging about after hearing boasts at school that Aunt Beryl's nieces have acquired a doll's house complete with furniture. Kezia, the Katherine Mansfield child, smuggles the ragged Kelveys into her middle-class home. Proudly she shows off the doll's house, before Aunt Beryl shoos the children out. Lil Kelvey's cheeks burn, but the smaller girl, filled with wonder, says, 'I seen the little lamp.'

These words of 'our Else' come back to me in my mother's plangent tones, resonant with that child's undamped wonder.

At the end of the war in Europe my mother posts food parcels to an orphaned girl in France. I'm fascinated by my mother's letters to this motherless girl, and decide to write to her myself. My letter is pencilled on the invitingly blank margins of *Winnie-the-Pooh*, covering many of its pages. It's puzzling that my mother should say with a line crossing her forehead, 'You must not scribble in books.' Scribble? To me it looks like a faithful imitation of adults' joined-up writing, and each page is filled with thoughts and feelings.

My mother picks up a stick and draws the letters of the alphabet in the gravel of the Sea Point beachfront. In her poem 'Her Girl' she's laughing with me as we lie, 'close-huddled', drawing faces on the hot, white sand, 'the wind threading our hair / Filled with the voices of the waves'.

A companion poem, 'Her Boy', is more humorous. It starts:

Better than poetry
Are your buttocks

and pictures her boy 'standing so donkeymeek / To let me

peer/ Into your ear.' She records Pip's comment at the end of
'The Doll's House':

> 'That story's sad'
> You ruminate
> 'Until the end —
> 'But the tip-end's glad.'

Her scribbles in pencil have rhythm marks to one side. Then
she types a fair copy. She says to Pip and me, 'If the house was
on fire, I'd save first my children, then my typewriter.' It tells me
how much poems count.

7

School versus Home

Little as Pip is, he's a fighter, and he has the courage to act against Nurse (as we call her) from St Helena. Unlike indulgent local nannies, Nurse declares that nowhere has she come across such bad children. How we hate her with her cross face and oily hair under the prim, white headgear of a hospital nurse. Once, when we are seated at our round table, Pip hears our parents' voices in the next-door bathroom and on an impulse breaks out of the nursery to tell them. It's a wild risk. Though they listen

patiently to what Pip has to say, they lead him back to her hard-
ening control.

Two years later Pip will come home from his boys' school,
Sea Point Junior, with two red lines across his small bottom.
Caning, I'm shocked to hear, is to be expected. Once again, it's
not a matter for parental protest.

My mother decides that the time has come for our morning
companionship to end. I too must go to school, and her choice
falls on FPS (Fresnaye Preparatory School) – Mrs de Korte's
school, as it's known. My father demurs at the expense, six
pounds a term, twenty-four pounds a year, but he's overruled.

Sighing, because it's difficult for Rhoda to rouse herself for
an interview with Mrs de Korte, she walks me along Avenue le
Soeur, where the High Level bus to town sits, chugging, at its
terminus, and then up the steep, cobbled slope of Avenue des
Huguenots. It's only ten minutes from our house in Avenue
Normandie. There's the resinous smell of the mountain pines –
we children pounce on fallen cones and, sitting on the kerb,
crack the nutcases with a stone. Nothing is so delectable as
chewing a newly extracted *dennepit*, mashed by the stone.
Ranged over low walls are the pointed beaks of orange poin-
settias or, reaching towards the blue sky, the blue shock-heads
of agapanthus. Above looms the rocky crest of Lion's Head.

Sorry though I am for my mother's forced steps, I'm ready to
go, eager to belong with other children. Mrs de Korte, with a
dark bun, talks gravely to my mother, who is ill at ease. I'm given
a tray of shapes to fit into holes and an inviting new box of
Crayola crayons: I pick green, and draw a house like the houses
I've drawn many times on the sand. My mother tells her friends
afterwards in a rather sad, self-mocking voice that she's surprised
by my alacrity, as though she'd expected more reluctance to leave
our retreat. At such times she comments how much I resemble
my father.

That hint of reproach is not only about defecting too willingly to my father's active mode. The retreat she and I shared had offered a pirate's cave of treasures, what might be called an alternative education, but now her secret sharer is to be recast in the standard mould.

At school we are asked to recite a rhyme, and one child after the other picks 'Baa Baa Black Sheep'. I vary this with 'Little Miss Muffet', thinking of the scary spiders from Lion's Head, who pop up on our walls. When I report the choice at home my mother lets loose a displeased 'ohhh'.

In the back garden, ready to leave my mother for the first day at FPS

She shakes her head at so mundane a choice.

'Why not "The Swing"? You know it by heart.'

I can't explain about conformity, and a sense that to choose this poem would appear as showing off.

Almost every other child carries a school suitcase. A satchel is better for posture, my mother argues, but I don't care about posture. Only Denise Sagov has a satchel like mine and, even so, her walk is ungainly. Denise is 'unpopular' – that's the word children use. It's not discussed; it's a fact. And it will stick when we go on to King's Road Junior School at the age of eight, and then, at twelve, to Good Hope Seminary. Denise compensates by bringing to school a giant box of Crayola with enticing half-shades of greys, blues and greens, and though we besiege Denise to try these out, she's no more popular than before.

Truth be told, I don't much like Denise because she boasts, even though there's something pathetic as well as intransigent in such bravado. My mother, who'd been at school with her mother, urges me to befriend Denise, but I prefer the party in power, all the while recognising another kind of outsider in my secret self, to be preserved in silence. My mother's retreat or some instinct warns that it must fade to nothing in public. I'm too sorry for Denise to join the bullies, yet too craven to risk protest.

In our early teens I shy away from parties, but at one or two where I'm an onlooker there is Denise, uninhibited as ever, bopping (my diary says) 'with her mouth open'. Then, at fifteen, Denise comes into her own in the art room. Her boldness takes shape in strongly coloured figures in local scenes, barrow-boys and street musicians slapped onto canvas with lavish strokes, like the paintings of Irma Stern. (I'm familiar with the style because my mother has an Irma Stern: two Xhosa women, one in yellow, the other in orange, leaning towards each other to share a pipe.) Miss Lust, the American art teacher, who tears around in a jeep, cheers Denise on: the bolder the better.

Later, when I return on a visit from New York, Denise invites my daughter Anna, aged four, to her child's birthday party at her old Fresnaye home. The party is too big and too much entertainment is laid on. While I mill about with other mothers, it shames me to hear Denise blasting out above the noise that I'd been her only friend at school.

Still later, Denise (re-named Dunya) emigrates to New York. I hear from anti-apartheid activists Rusty and Hilda Bernstein that she opens her home to them and other refugees during the Struggle. They like her wholeheartedly, and look puzzled – as well they might – to hear how it was at school.

Jane and Dick pat the cat in our reader. The cat sat on a mat. Jane and Dick toss a red ball. My mother says that there were no books on the veld except the reader in her one-room school, and that her imagination 'irradiated' the equivalent of Jane and Dick. I'm less imaginative, bored, and yet content to line up after break and pencil a row of wavery Os.

Away from school, the houses I draw on the sand are for dream-families with lots of children who act in a world of their own. There's always one girl amongst them, the Judy or Jo March girl, who clashes with adult expectations. These dreams are prompted by *Seven Little Australians* or *Little Women* – orphanage library books whose stories my mother reads aloud, like the humiliating scene where Amy March secretes pickled limes in her school desk, is found out, and has to offer her hand to be caned.

A generation later, when my second daughter, Olivia, starts school in 1984, I recall a scene of humiliation in mid-January 1947. I write it down for her in an exercise book entitled 'Old Stories', which she edits and illustrates.

The First Day at School

Miss Grey, who was small with a red face and grey hair, was our teacher. When we were seated in rows at our desks, and Miss Grey had asked us our names and checked them in the register, she suddenly did something odd. She turned to the blackboard. On it she drew

Two big, round circles.

'What is this?' Miss Grey asked the class.

No one put up a hand. There was a long silence.

'This,' said Miss Grey, 'is what Charlie's nose will look like when he grows up, if he goes on picking it.'

Humiliation. How it dominates memory. 'What is the worst thing in life for you?' Virginia Woolf once asked T. S. Eliot in the early twenties. It was night-time. They were in a taxi, passing through the damp market gardens of London. 'Humiliation,' Eliot said unhesitatingly. As I call up that first-day scene for Olivia, my second biography, on Virginia Woolf, is due for publication, and I'm struck by her innovative idea of Lives, questioning her father's necessary focus on Lives in their public aspects, as the first editor of the *Dictionary of National Biography*. Looking back over six lives, the passage of one generation, in her masterpiece *The Waves*, she perceives that all our stories of birth, marriage and death aren't true, only the 'moments of humiliation and triumph that come now and then undeniably'. This fits my mother's sense of the unseen, her focus on the inwardness of existence.

To go to school is to switch from my mother's expansive story of suffering and transcendence to narrow rituals of obedience versus disobedience. It's simply a matter of learning the rules. One rule is to put up your hand and say, 'May I leave the room?' if you need the lavatory. Unable to utter these words, I postpone the need so unbearably long during drill that, very quietly, I wet the floor and leave the puddle there, pretending it can't be me. Cowardice adds to my shame.

When we can read for ourselves we devour *The Naughtiest Girl in the School* by Enid Blyton. Here, allegiance to school replaces home, and an obliterated mother appears solely to wave her daughter away. Farewell to nurture through the domestic affections. Whatever the reasons – custom, class, empire (still intact in 1940, when the book came out) – those affections are distanced at an early age, to be replaced by head girls who enforce rules. Elizabeth Allen is a hot-headed girl prone to forget the rules but well up to spelling them out to a new girl, a scorned Mother's-precious-darling, in *The Naughtiest Girl is a Monitor*. Central to this ethos is the disempowering and exclusion of Mother.

At the bottom of a colonised Africa, we're fascinated by school stories from England – that far-away, superior civilisation we look up to and try to copy, so far as our noisy voices and flat vowels will take us. Mrs de Korte employs an elocution teacher who makes us recite with rounded, elongated vowels. Some mothers affect this pseudo-English manner, a sign how posh they want to be.

There are few Jewish children. One called Gilda Myers, with brown eyes and a lovely bloom, is chosen to be the princess in a school production of *The Sleeping Beauty*. She's tearful when she proves just a little too plump for the princess costume and the part goes to a thin, Afrikaans girl called Welien. Of course I long to be the princess, but am cast as the ugly fairy, who has to cackle evilly from the folds of her black cloak. My mother tries to comfort me that it's a more active part than that of the princess who has little more to do than lie back and be kissed. She bestirs herself to make me a wand, and this effort is some- how more effective comfort. Laboriously, she draws its star with a ruler on cardboard, and then carefully cuts it out and covers it with silver paper.

I can't be jealous of Welien because she isn't proud. She and her straight-backed older brother Hendrik say what they mean. Inevitably, they are seen less for themselves, but as Afrikaners whose parents, it's assumed, vote for the party in power. Even before the Nationalists come to power in 1948 and put their policy of apartheid into law, separate groups exist beyond racial divides. School is a microcosm of the white group with its sep- arate sub-groups, divided by class, language and religion. Jewish children stay in an empty classroom during morning prayers, as does the sole Roman Catholic, a rosy child called Linda Prest with straight blonde hair behind her ears. We call her *Padda Kwaak*, Afrikaans for 'a frog croaks', because she has a wide mouth stretched in smiles.

Conformity has always held for me an intriguing otherness, like theatre, shaped as I am by an apart and questioning mother. Can I play this unlikely role, I ask myself en route to school, and later as I approach unlikely roles as wife and mother. Those who confer normality, daughters especially, are dear, not only for what they are in their home selves but also as playmates on the public stage. In this spirit of play, script in hand, I skip down the slope of the playground, unprepared for unscripted scenes.

The elocution teacher runs every side-show at Mrs de Korte's. It's she who casts me as the ugly fairy and burdens my mother with having to produce a costume to her satisfaction. Her next venture is to audition us for a children's sequence in a mannequin parade. This is another of the stories I will pass on to Olivia when she goes to school.

The Mannequin Parade

In Sub B, the second year at Mrs de Korte's school, our speech teacher, Miss Lurie, wanted the six-year-olds to join in a mannequin parade at the Sea Point Town Hall. 'The audition,' she said, 'will be held at Marion's house.'

Now Marion lived in a very grand house and, to tell you the truth, she was a very proud girl who never invited me to play. So when Miss Lurie asked 'Who can't come to the audition?' I, together with Gilda, put up my hand.

'Why can't you come, Gilda?'

'I have Hebrew every afternoon,' said Gilda.

'And why can't you come, Lyndall?' asked Miss Lurie.

'I – don't know,' I faltered.

'What a silly you are,' said Miss Lurie. 'You must come.'

Unwillingly, I made my way there when the day came. Close up, the grandeur looked gloomy. The house stood back from Kloof Road in the shadow of Lion's Head. At the long windows, shutters hung half-closed. In the dark lounge amongst strangers, I was told to look through a blue hoop, then to roll it, chase it, and pretend to slip. Miss Lurie thought up this act. 'It's not hard, is it?' she said. 'See how silly you were.'

When the day came for the parade, I was put into a sweet heart dress, blue, covered with love letters sealed with red hearts. The act went to plan but next day – oh dear – there was a photograph in the gossip section of the *Cape Times*, headed GIRL FALLS IN PARADE. There I was, pictured for all to see, with legs in the air.

During our last year at Mrs de Korte's each seven-year-old has a turn to be head girl or boy. I'm paired with Frank Guthrie, who'd been a wooden soldier in *The Sleeping Beauty*. He'd mastered an eye-catching turn: his body stiff, to attention, would

rock back and forth on his toes and heels, more and more violently, until he fell over – still rigid – for the hundred-year sleep.

Head-girl responsibilities are delightfully trivial. Puffed up
with temporary importance, I repeat to myself a line from the
Naughtiest Girl – 'the tall head girl walked up the steps' – as I
mount the steps from the playground to Mrs de Korte's stoep
to report a nosebleed. Mrs de Korte comes with a brass key to
put down the back of the bleeder. I can't see how this can help;
it belongs with adults' inexplicable rituals, like sticking
Elastoplast behind a child's ears to prevent car-sickness.

My mother takes me to see Alicia Markova in *The Dying Swan*
at the Alhambra. At the end the audience is too rapt to clap, not
for almost a minute. My mother says, 'Silence is a higher trib-
ute to perfection.' From this moment I want to learn ballet.
Unfortunately, my toes won't turn out and my point is poor.
Still, I love bending to music at the barre, the beats of the *bat-
tements frappés* and *entrechats*, and the rhythms of *grands jêtés*,
soaring and turning across the studio. Behind the closed door
of the top room I practise the leaps with more abandon. In the
same way, I respond to the abandon and decorum of prose that
comes down with its feet on the ground. Though I'm no good
at ballet it remains as a rhythm in the blood. When I prepare a
talk, I pace it with my feet, moving to the rhythms of prose
with its leaps and turns.

King's Road Junior School is bigger and stricter than Mrs
de Korte's. All the classes are assembled and the head, Miss
Goodchild (not a made-up name), tells us to sit cross-legged
on the floor.

'Hands on heads. Hands down. Hands on heads. Hands
down.'

When we are still, Miss Goodchild calls for Jill Habberley to step forward, and in a solemn voice accuses her of forgetting what sounds like a trivial rule. Then Miss Goodchild, gripping the culprit's arm, whacks Jill Habberley, who looks like a stumbling spider with long limbs around a closed rose mouth.

In those days, every school has its feared teacher. At the age of nine we enter Standard Three (fifth grade), taught by the school's terror, Mrs Thatcher (again, not a made-up name). We sit in our double desks with dipping pens poised above inkwells. In unison we repeat a multiplication table. We are baa-ing, not thinking. At ten each morning a hush falls and all eyes swivel as the door to the classroom opens. A girl called Isabel with a high, polished forehead is carried like a doll to her seat in the front row. Her legs are stiff. Her face is closed against stares. We suppose she comes late because she has to have daily treatments, perhaps for polio, but we don't know because nothing is said. No one ever speaks to her because speaking is not allowed.

Uncle Sydney, who lives in America, has sent me a book called *Seatmates*, and I'm friends with my seatmate Marcia. She says 'Gah!', growling the 'G' as in Afrikaans, with a jerk of the head like play-play English gentlemen who throw back their heads to say 'Pah!' It's irresistible to cheer on Marcia mouthing 'Gah' when Mrs Thatcher turns her back to chalk a sum on the board.

'Who was speaking?' Her fierce ears catch the sound. Reluctantly, I have to own up.

'Don't let me catch you again.'

She turns again to the blackboard and in a lowered, almost inaudible whisper I mouth something to Marcia.

Mrs Thatcher whirls around. 'Go – out – of the room,' her voice stabs. 'No – go – to the Office.'

The Office means Miss Goodchild. My legs take me down the stairs and along the corridor towards the Office, and then they carry me past it to the row of lavatories at the back of the

school. I hide there for what seems an age, and then, heart beating, I run away from school.

At the time, my parents are away and I'm staying with the top
girl in the class, Jasmine. Her mother says firmly, not unkindly,
that I'm to go back to school next day. It's a relief to find Mrs
Thatcher says nothing. Not so the children. Nesta, arm in arm
with a chum, comes up to where I'm sitting on a bench in the
playground.

'Why did you run away from school?'

I lie. 'I felt sick.' It sounds lame.

Once each term we are bussed to the botanical gardens at
Kirstenbosch to learn about plants with the curator, Miss Johns.

'Gather round,' says Miss Johns as she examines an indigenous
flower in its bed. We crowd about her, and because the flower
is so small and the crowd so tight, I edge this way and that in
order to peer.

'Did you step on a plant?' Miss Johns's iron hand clamps my
arm. Dismayed, I look down and see that I probably did.

'I'll have to give you a paddy whack,' nods Miss Johns archly
and slaps my shin, while the girls watch in silence.

'What's your name?'

I force it out.

'Are you Harry's daughter?'

'Yes, Miss Johns.' I'm sorry he's brought into this.

'I know your father,' says Miss Johns, her voice softening,
'and he wouldn't like his daughter to be disobedient.'

This disgrace follows me back to King's Road. Mrs Thatcher,
grim of face, says, 'I hear you were disobedient.' It confirms her
opinion, and nothing can change it. For years to come, my eyes
are shut to Kirstenbosch – until, at seventeen, I went there with
Siamon. In a glade, under overhanging trees, we threw pennies
in Lady Anne Barnard's pool, and wished.

'What did you wish?' I pressed him, thinking he might want to kiss me.

'I wished for peace of mind,' Siamon said, looking away. Somehow this dispelled the blight of Miss Johns.

Rhoda's room seems a far cry from what goes on at school, yet all the while its books and dramas echo in my mind. Jo March, obliged to keep Aunt March company, shades into my mother's urge to write, blocked by a woman's duty. Sun and Moon, children thrust aside by partying parents in Katherine Mansfield's story, call up yapping voices at Granny's tea parties, jarring to Rhoda's finer feelings. Her own voice, resonant with import, impersonates the monotone of Dr Manette, holed up in the Bastille. And then comes bloodthirsty Madame Defarge, one of the knitting women counting the heads severed by the guillotine: I hear even now the dire 'aaah' of Defarge, as my mother pronounced the name. I've never read *A Tale of Two Cities*. It's a book heard in childhood, not overlaid with an adult response. I lie spotted with measles in my mother's darkened room as emotions rise like a wave: my mother reads right through the day – a marathon read – until she comes to the famous ending: 'It's a far, far better thing . . . ' Far better for a man to give up his life than continue to degrade his body. I'm all for the moral imperative of sacrifice that emanates from my mother as much as from Dickens.

On top of Katherine Mansfield, or sometimes under her, is the Bible. My mother relates the parable of David and Goliath, the simple shepherd boy versus a giant warrior – she is partial to the innocent, the obscure, the weak and pure of heart. But more significant for her than David on the battlefield or David the King, is David the poet whose psalms walk him through 'the valley of the shadow', certain not to be abandoned by his heavenly Father.

Familiar too is the story of Jacob on the road to his destiny
as one of the Chosen, who wrestles all night with a divine force.
In the morning he limps away, his hip out of joint. His injury
is proof that it's not a dream. 'I have seen God face to face,' he
claims. Two women, each secluded at home in complete obscu-
rity, venture to make like claims. As day breaks, Emily
Dickinson's astonished Wrestler finds that she has actually
'worsted God'. Her spirit is that strong.

My mother's wrestler is less of a winner. There's 'no Jacob's
dawn, limping triumphant'. The sign from on high is rather like
a seizure, an encounter so fraught it nearly wrecks the wrestler.
During the course of the night, 'the desperate soul is nearly torn
from its socket'. Come dawn, and it's not over. 'Starved for
light, in abbadon we grope at noon . . .'

I see now that there's no given word for the dislocation of her
being in the wasteland that follows the seizure. 'Abba' is
Hebrew for 'father', so 'abbadon' suggests abandon by a divine
Father. It's fear, not the actuality of abandon. For in the end the
wrestler does survive by holding on to Psalm XXIII:

> . . . *Turn*
> *on the edge of death and walk on the tightrope psalm*
> *steadfast to the end: 'surely goodness*
> *and mercy shall dwell'*
> *till the clayhouse body knows*
> *the Inrush of the Spirit*
> *and the fountaining of love.*

As a child I can't fathom what she's saying beyond an
unspeakable horror I'm reluctant to know. Clearer to me is her
tenacity, and I'm somewhat relieved when she moves on to love.
And of course I'm glad that she's making me into a person who,
she says, 'will one day understand'.

So it happens that while my mother scribbles in her wire-bound notebook, I become a watcher of her chrysalis. Rhoda elevates this role of watcher, through her feeling for Dorothy Wordsworth, who watched and often prompted the creative fount of her brother. Wordsworth catches 'gleams of past existence' in his sister's eyes. Years later, as a biographer, this will put me in sympathy with others who watched at the side of writers and seers: Emily Hale, who watched T. S. Eliot, and waited for him; and 'Fenimore' (great-niece to James Fenimore Cooper), who watched Henry James; and Charlotte Brontë, watching her sister Emily, who was herself a watcher of the night, awaiting the 'wandering airs' at her window – reminding me how Rhoda each night opens her window to the roar from the ocean's throat.

Lives I will watch years later turn on the inner life of that room, its moral character, its sufferings and resilience, above all the 'fountaining' of a writer's voice.

*

Rhoda after her marriage, with her three bachelor brothers.
Left to right: Hubert, Sydney and Basil

Rhoda brightens when Wordsworth calls Dorothy his 'dear, dear sister'. In her late twenties, when her friends are unavailable, she's missing her brothers, especially Basil.

As a doctor in the army during the war, Basil has been posted to Walvis Bay in the former German colony of South West Africa. After the First World War the colony was taken over as a South African mandate (with red stripes on maps, not as entirely red as fully British colonies). The German inhabitants of SWA are so pro-Nazi and the anti-Semitism of South African troops so blatant that Basil, usually unperturbed, finds it disturbing to be there.

Once, in the officers' mess, they ask him to leave so that they can joke about Jews without of the constraint of his presence. Another time, he's summoned by a German woman to examine her sick boy. No sooner does Basil enter the house than he walks slap into a poster of Hitler. The boy, shivering with malaria, leaps out of bed and kisses the doctor's hand – unaware that he's kissing a Jew.

After the war, Basil joins his brothers, Sydney and Hubert, at Edgars, the family's chain of clothing stores. Basil had intended to move on to specialist medical training, which meant going to England or America, but Sydney asked him to postpone this because help was needed with the mail-order side of Edgars. Basil began travelling to small towns around Southern Africa, and when there were sufficient customers the Presses would open new branches. In time there were hundreds, and Basil never went back to medicine. His sister lamented this often; she felt he had the caring nature of a born doctor.

The three brothers settle on a farm called Evermore in Morningside, now swallowed up by Johannesburg but then on the outskirts where it's still country. In 1946 my mother decides on a visit. It's a two-day journey by steam train, and at one stage a second steam engine puffs up behind the train to push it to six thousand feet above sea level. I'm given a Little Golden

Book to read on my own, the story of the Three Little Pigs and the Big Bad Wolf who says, 'I'll huff and I'll puff and I'll blow your house down.' Pip clutches his own Little Golden Book, *Tootle*.

The train stops at Matjiesfontein in the Karoo. My mother recalls that Olive Schreiner lived here. Rising from this bare landscape, as isolated as Klaver, came her feminist *Dreams*. In 1891 she sent them to London. Reprinted twenty times, and translated into eight languages, they sold eighty thousand copies. Lady Constance Lytton read aloud one of the *Dreams* to fasting suffragettes in Holloway Prison. My mother writes a poem for Olive Schreiner; it's about the longing to write in a landscape where the distant horizon stands to attention.

Lenie, who accompanies us because no white woman can manage without a servant, alights from the 'coloured' coach, to see if help is needed. The train has barely stopped before our restless father is racing along the platform, reaching up to other carriages to shake hands with travellers who listen in to his broadcasts. I'm scared he'll be left behind, and in fact the engine steams up and belches tremendous hoots before Harry, sportingly, leaps onto the last carriage as it leaves the platform to wind its way around the koppies of the Karoo.

Towards evening, a rather tired engine is rolling slowly through the long grass of the Highveld. The sun, which had been white-hot at its zenith, is now a red ball on the horizon. We jerk the wooden shutters so that they fall into their bottom slot, and put our heads out of the windows to sniff the acrid smoke wafting back from the engine's funnel, rub the occasional bit of grit out of our eyes and turn our heads to the carriages behind us in the curving tail of the train. Behind the coloureds in second class is the sole, packed third class carriage for 'natives', who sleep on bare ledges, not on bunks with fresh bedding made up for the night.

My mother points out how 'each tree has a shadow like a wing outstretched'. The swiftly fading light 'silvers the auburn grass'. Then she's scribbling 'High Veld Time Exposure' in her notebook.

> *. . . The veld to velvet glows;*
> *Dark moles the anthills seem*
> *And bushes have a gentle look.*
> *In the sunsucked grass*
> *Africans stand*
> *With legs loose-lagged*
> *Talking slow . . .*

At Evermore two thickly grown hillocks promise secret places. To the right is a tennis court where our uncles entertain. A Zulu got up in white with a tasselled red sash serves drinks to visitors reclining under their hats after a game. Fenced off at the bottom of the garden are horses, cows, hens and bales of straw. Granny Annie, presiding in the home of her three bachelor sons, orders a male cook to boil new-laid eggs 'for the children's supper'. Here, in the interior, there's more vigilance against infection; here, our great-great-grandfather, fresh from Europe, unprepared for what was alien in Africa, soon died of dysentery. He was forty-five. Malaria is still rife, and we are put to sleep under mosquito nets hanging from hooks.

My mother doesn't figure in my memory of Evermore. Was she re-absorbed into her family? Certainly, she resisted a mercenary Johannesburg in a poem, 'The Great City of Goli' (with an epigraph from a Zulu song: 'Over the banks of the Vaal lies the Great City of Goli [Gold]'), with its 'costly portals' and 'backdoor rapes'. Dominating the skyline, mine dumps testify to the exploitation of black miners who are paid a pittance, housed in barracks and separated for years from their

Granny Annie in Johannesburg with her younger sons
Hubert (left) and Sydney Press

rural families: 'Lords of the Rand sphinx-idols lie / The gold
dumps white in a black sky.'

It may seem strange that, until the age of thirty-one, Rhoda
doesn't ask what her illness is. In 1948, while Harry is away
at the Olympic Games in London, she has 'a bad attack', her
phrase for a full-on seizure. Afterwards she again consults
doctors who continue to prescribe powders she tries not to
take because these doctors, like the doctors she'd seen in
London, treat her as an hysteric who brings illness on herself.
But this time she resolves to articulate her suspicion that

there's something more to know. She puts this to her brother, the only doctor she can trust.

My Dear Basil,

I'm writing to ask you to come down [from Johannesburg] during the next long weekend. Besides the pleasure of seeing you again, I urgently wish to discuss with you matters concerning my health.

While you are away I always determine to speak to you when next you come down & always fail to do so while you are here. Recently I had another of my attacks. For many years now I've striven for health of spirit by trying to strengthen my character, to purify my thoughts, to perfect my life. I have forged precious weapons wherewith I continually fight off attacks[,] which are especially valuable in conquering the ensuing depression & fears after an attack. But I am beginning to fear that I cannot under all circumstances prevent an attack. I seem to have wasted months, even years fighting this illness. I long to be a free normal human being at last.

As I've imagined & expected the worst for long periods of my life nothing you know or fear can terrify me & I think as an intelligent person & at my time of life, I've a right to know all that is within your power to tell me of my illness. Only the truth can help me . . .

Much love from

Rhoda

Basil does come, and he breaks it to her that she has the severe kind of epilepsy known as grand mal. How he puts it I don't know, yet at last she understands that her illness is physiological. It's a huge relief. For Basil's words release her from the obligation to control her illness through acts of will. From then on she accepts the necessity for daily and nightly doses of anti-convulsant pills, Epanutin and barbiturate, even though they dull her imagination. At last she can get up and go out with a degree of confidence.

Four years later, freed from attacks, she makes up her mind to leave her refuge.

8

'Lapp Heights'

On 10 June 1952 Rhoda leaves home, bound for Finland. Why Finland? If anything were simple in her intentions, the answer should be the Olympic Games, where her husband will offici-ate in the swimming. But Rhoda has no eye to any competitive event. For her, the tug of Finland is its proximity to Lithuania. Guided by her dream life, her imagination calls up 'Chagallian villages', her father's memories and the luftmensch aloft in northern skies. To go to Finland is to reconnect with her 'father-root'. Her dream is not only fantastical; it's allegoric in the way she assigns people to moral compartments: a poetic father-root to be claimed; a mundane South African mother, well intentioned but alien.

Rhoda is thirty-five years old, with two children, aged ten and eight. We will remain with our grandmother, Annie, who's hap-pily down-to-earth. We three visit the well-appointed cabin on board the Holland-Afrika liner, the *Klipfontein*. When my father travels alone he cuts corners, but first-class comfort is considered necessary for Rhoda's better health, and her brothers would expect no less. The cabin is full of farewell bouquets from friends, and the orphanage has sent a basket of fruit for the long voyage. The siren blasts a warning of departure and we tread carefully down the ridges of the gangplank, turning to wave to our parents on deck.

I'm relieved to see our mother elated, and ease into Granny's hands. Unstoppably, she surges forward in the main thoroughfare of Adderley Street, holding up the traffic with the point of her sunshade. She loves to shop, and we spend hours matching a ribbon to furbish her newest hat. In the shoe department at Stuttafords we choose warm winter slippers in preparation for a holiday up country. Schools shut for three weeks in July, and Granny is taking us to Vredendal, four stations north of Klaver. Throughout the night the train stops at sidings, lanterns swing, '*Maak gou, Meneer*' drifts by the windows, footsteps quicken and milk cans clank. At dawn, an arid landscape of bush unrolls in shafts of sunlight, and a rather sleepy engine puffs and subsides as the train's long tail winds across the veld.

Granny has no time to look at the veld because she's rummaging in suitcases. Her fuss leaves me free to dream my way into books; rolled in her puffy pink eiderdown, I join far-away Canadian children in *Rainbow Valley*. It's one of my mother's childhood favourites, an old hardback with the inviting smell of thick, rough-edged pages and printer's ink, acquired for the orphanage. Strictly speaking, I have no right to it, but no one objects. Part of that library's appeal is its smallness; the books are selected to mend a child's heart and invigorate courage. In the gravel outside Eisenberg's Hotel on the corner of the wide main street of Vredendal I play hopscotch with a girl called Hereen van Zyl. Her English vocabulary is small, my Afrikaans likewise, but the game is all, and we understand each other better by the day.

Then Granny spoils it. She sends something from her stylish wardrobe to Hereen's mother. When I go with Hereen to her house, I find Mevrou van Zyl furious.

'Tell your grandmother I'm not in need of cast-offs!' she says, and shuts the door against my open mouth.

I see now what my mother means about her mother's shaming ways.

Meanwhile, the *Klipfontein* is sailing on into the northern hemisphere. Rhoda's deckchair companion turns out to be Laurens van der Post, with whom she can share her feeling for the *vlaktes*, the untrammelled spaces of her early childhood. En route to Stockholm a poem, 'Midnight at Malmö', rises as her train streaks through the night. This hurtling speed is strange, like taking off into a fairy tale.

Swedes appear 'glassy', unlike the 'simple friendliness' aboard a Finnish boat plying between Stockholm and Helsinki. Her impression is coloured by Sweden's neutrality during the Holocaust, in contrast to Finland's protection of its minute Jewish population. For Marshal Mannerheim refused to hand Jews over to the Nazis, even though, in 1941, Finland entered the war on the German side – a consequence of Finland's struggles with Russia. It was an unprecedented situation where Germans found themselves encamped, one Saturday, near Jewish soldiers in a field synagogue.

Rhoda's letters home invite us to travel with a semi-invalid as she wakes to a new life out in the great world. The decks are packed with comers from every country. They huddle in sleeping bags, exposing children's 'carved eyebrows and lids like pointed buds'. A man lies with 'a water-lily hand in his gloved one'.

I can't go to bed, Rhoda thinks. She moves from group to group, talking, a little touch of nearness in the night, and crossing paths with children 'sleepwalking' in red woollen caps.

Above this knot of peace hangs 'a single fringed star'. Throbbing, the boat slides past dark islands 'asleep on the ocean'. Rhoda's knees are beginning to freeze.

They stay in a white wooden manor on a lake. On the opposite side lives the composer Sibelius. The building itself is a bit decrepit, but it's well run by staff in national dress. There's an interpreter, an elderly Russian-French intellectual, who is half-Jewish and calls Rhoda 'dearest', and whom Rhoda suspects is deeply corrupt. She wears grand, ancient clothes and is fond of the bottle, like the madam of a brothel, and in fact there are 'goings on' in the manor.

Rhoda steps out in navy organza and a silver-grey stole to a party in a semi-circular restaurant on a more distant lake. She's animated between Harry and a tanned South African water-polo player, Solly Yach. Both have participated in the Maccabiah Games and know almost everyone at this largely Israeli party. Rhoda ventures to stumble through a few Hebrew phrases. Her

gameness is welcome; an American judge kisses her hands. She and Harry drive back 'as dawn was almost breaking into silvern lakes in the dark foliage of the sky', and walk up an avenue 'of honey-scented lime trees' towards the manor.

During the swimming finals, my father is broadcasting for the BBC and other Anglophone stations when, suddenly, he spots that the grandstand opposite is swaying. It's overloaded with about four hundred visitors, and might collapse at any moment. Stopping his running commentary in mid-flow, he addresses the crowd through the microphone. 'The stand is unstable. Please follow instructions. Sit still. Stay calm. Top row, come down.' He talks them down, one row at a time. This is Harry in his element, with a quick eye and ready to act.

One night Rhoda and Harry go down a long white jetty to a sauna. They stand in the steam and beat each other with birch twigs, as an extra tonic. Three times, as instructed, they sweat up their bodies and then, each time, dive into the lake.

'You feel as good as after a bathe at Muizenberg,' Rhoda decides, 'only much cleaner.'

It's half-past ten, but scarcely dark. Rimming this scene of silver air and water are dark clumps of 'porcupine earth'. On closer inspection these turn out to be 'tree-dark islands like children's heads asleep'. As she looks out over the lake, there rises in her mind a half-formed prayer to share Finland with someone.

While others go daily to the Games, she goes to the Ateneum, the national art museum, in a square with linden trees in the centre of the city. One Wednesday in late July, the guide is an art critic, Sirkka Anttila. Her long black hair is drawn back in a casual bun, baring high cheekbones, and her slanting black eyes snap and flash as she points to soulful paintings, punctuated by 'Hey ... hey ...' when she draws back from a conclusion. Rhoda warms to Finland's best-known woman painter, Helene

Schjerfbeck, an invalid who withdrew into seclusion in the provinces. Her self-portrait of 1915 bares a face pared down to intense inwardness. She has the unwavering gaze of an observer, similar to the gaze of Katherine Mansfield when she's fine-drawn and alone, arms folded over her tubercular chest, in a photograph my mother has on her desk.

A viewer amongst the visiting party asks why a sculptor has made a woman's legs absurdly thick. Sirkka hears behind her 'a small, small voice' explaining – 'so marvellous, intelligent', she records that night in her diary – the deliberate disproportions of modernist art.

Slowly, she turns a hundred and eighty degrees to see who this is. It's a woman of her own age, mid-thirties, with dark hair, in thick glasses with pale-blue rims around attentive blue eyes. After the viewing Rhoda asks for Sirkka's address at the very moment that Sirkka asks for hers. Sirkka lives in one room, teaching art in a high school, reviewing exhibitions and editing art books.

She feels, she remarks to Rhoda, 'rich each flash of time when there is a moment to glance up from work'. Flash. She knows. Their eyes lock.

When they meet for lunch the next day Sirkka plunges into the kind of inward utterance Rhoda has ventured only in poems.

Rhoda shows Sirkka two poems on Finland that she's written. Sirkka seizes them to translate into Finnish. I think Rhoda wrote 'Sallinen – Finland' overnight because the first of its two stanzas responds to one of the museum's paintings by Tyko Sallinen, *April Evening*. It's the rough-hewn landscape of the north:

Patient under the wind lies land
Stripped to the rocks.

One bony tree spreads a jointed hand.
Since Creation this sky knows this land,
This land this sky.
Loose clouds above, knit rocks below,
Only the blizzard between.

This pre-human land takes the observer close to Creation, and the second stanza re-explores this proximity through a seascape where sky, rocks and sea give and receive 'Familiarly / No human voice divides them'.

Two days later, on 26 July, Sirkka writes the following letter to Rhoda:

My dear, dear Near-One,

I began to translate your poem ... I'm out of wits being touched so deeply by the pure strength, perfectly the stern ... Dear You, it is after all a surprising present to get you thus, although from the first flash of the intuitive contact with you I know what you are. It is amazing in you the silent ascetic strength, clear & pure – spontaneously sure as ever a archaic soil. Impossible to express myself in English. I hope I do it better in Finnish – in my article.

Sirkka will include 'Sallinen – Finland' in an article on foreigners at the gallery, which *Finlandia Pictorial* magazine is to publish, illustrated by the painting. She singles out 'Rhoda Stella Press from Cape Town' as a visitor whose feeling for Finnish art and nature 'gave birth to a group of sensitive poems. In their rhythm and words she has captured the mystic spirit of the desolate back woods of the north.'

Sirkka's family, Rhoda hears, comes from Karelia, a setting of white birch trees on the fought-over border with the Soviet

← **Self-portrait:** Helena Schjerfbeck, the greatest of Finnish women artists, as she saw herself in 1915. Many consider her the best of modern Finnish artists. She created her subtle style while an invalid, lonely and withdrawn into seclusion in the countryside.
→**April Evening:** In T. K. Sallinen's works, the gray colors of Finland's barren and rocky land reflect the rugged rapture of northern nature. With his primitive strength and closeness to nature, Sallinen is the most noted artist among Finnish expressionists.

the combination of these qualities is born the mystical twilight, the feeling of the destiny of the northlands, which is revealed so well in Wäinö Aaltonen's »Maid in Black Granite» and in the work of expressionists such as T. K. Sallinen, Alvar Cawén, and Marcus Collin. In young Aimo Kanerva many saw a guarantee that the qualities that make Finnish art what it is still are inexhaustible.

D. Los Baños, a teacher from Hawaii, was struck by the intensity of Finnish works, even those in which the grayness of lichen and peatbogs predominate.

»Strange,» he said, »that these artists surrounded by winter and darkness do not feel the need for brilliant colors and light.»

»Yet,» he added, »it is just that which shows how close they are to nature itself.» He said Finnish artists seem to gain strength from harsh surroundings in which other artists would be lost.

Many visitors ranked the monumental works of Juho Rissanen and the intimate and symbolic works of Hugo Simberg among the top treasures of Finnish art.

Italians often compared Rissanen's works to frescoes of their own country. Rissanen also got the vote of J. Methuen, a Rhodesian architect, who was asked to name the greatest Finnish artist after having viewed the entire collection.

J. K. Weckl, a Vienna art critic, rushed out of the Atheneum after viewing the works of Simberg. The exper-

SALLINEN – FINLAND

Patient under the wind lies land
Stripped to the rocks.
One bony tree spreads a jointed hand.
Since Creation this sky knows this land,
The land this sky.
Loose clouds above, knit rocks below,
Only the blizzard between.
— — —
Grey green sea
Relaxes on rocks.
Sky lowers a pale mustard mist.
Wind whips a flare of white.
Sky rocks sea
Each give and receive
Familiarly.
No human voice divides them.

By *Rhoda Stella Press*

Rhoda's poem is published, fittingly, on the same page as two paintings she particularly admired in Helsinki's Ateneum

Union. This is a region of folk craft and the oral tales collected in the national epic, the *Kalevala*. In 1939–40 the Red Army had invaded Karelia: the brief Winter War. Sirkka, then an art student aged twenty, had swum by night across a lake, behind the Russian lines, to retrieve – of all things – three painted spindles as objects of Finnish folk art. She went to 'steal' is the way she puts it, laughing triumphantly.

Rhoda's part is to talk of the apartheid regime, and she dashes out to find Sirkka a copy of *Cry, the Beloved Country*.

Sirkka tells Rhoda that her real destination is the far north – her poem has already marked it out for her own. Lapland will meet her need; it will transform her; it's her destiny to go.

She hands Rhoda her boots.

'Be clear, be open my Rhoda,' she urges. 'My strength is yours, Rhoda, you, who have the transparent and human eyes.'

So Rhoda postpones her departure. 'A tremendous power of urgency to go to Lapland' seems to be taking her there. To do this in the past, to travel to a far-off place on her own, would have seemed 'insuperable' to the semi-invalid she's been. Now, she tells herself, 'If one wishes to be an observer, one must be alone.'

She boards an overnight train to Rovaniemi, seven hundred kilometres north of Helsinki, and then a bus takes her to the outpost of an arctic wilderness more than three hundred kilometres farther north. The terminus is Muonio on Finland's western border with Sweden. From there she will enter the lonely fells of Pallastunturi in the Pallas-Yllästunturi national park. On 8 August she looks back on this journey.

Lapland freed me from the last of my prisons. The 10 hours with Finns and Lapps in the bus going to Muonio ... ended in a burst of laughter ... At a kiosk on the roadside I am deciding with a Swiss girl whether to take a taxi to Pallastunturi – Suddenly I hear a rumble – our bus has started off. But my luggage! It's on the bus careering down the road – back to Rovaniemi. 'My luggage!' I run, shouting. There is a man on a motorcycle outside the kiosk. A Finnish woman mutters swiftly to him. She tells me to get on the pillion behind him. 'But what of my coat?' She takes it, a tall American my hat, and a British girl my book of Scandinavian poetry. Away I fly. Hair streaming, clutching the shoulders of an unknown man. I have never even seen his face. I don't know where my legs are, and I don't seem to care about them. I am fine, loving it – and laughing, but laughing!

When we reached the bus & got my luggage I . . . emptied my purse of small coins into the reluctant palm of the 'motorcycle man'. He phoned for a taxi but before mine could arrive, another turned up – & inside I am astonished to see – my coat, my hat, and my book of poems! The Finnish woman had sent this taxi . . . Back at the kiosk they laughed at my 'Charlie Chaplin technique'. I waited with them for the bus to Pallastunturi. At a quarter to eleven we climbed among the bare blue hills – never, except in pre-human vision, have I known a blue like that. In summer there is no night over those glowing coal-blue fells but now the horizon was ringed with pink fires.

Early next morning she climbs Pallas fell. After about two and a half hours she reaches the wooden tower at the summit, from where she looks out on 'blue hills streaked with silver lakes'. It's like 'the round top of the world', a place close enough to Creation to see 'God's shadow'.

Harry follows her. He arrives that evening and climbs Pallas fell until three in the morning. Up there, more than a month past midsummer, he sees the sun set on one side and rise on the other within an hour. So it is that this gregarious sport joins, for a space, Rhoda's lone pilgrimage. He finds her alight with a resolve to remain in Europe, and here, at Pallastunturi, Harry is persuaded to agree. For Rhoda invites him to lend himself to what she sees now as her future. It's a proposal of sorts, a passionate sequel to the legal business of getting married. What she offers her husband at this moment is the chance to bond with her real self.

For the rest, I don't know exactly, but can guess. She's been imprisoned since the age of seventeen, she would have said, and now Lapland is conferring on her the blessing of recovery. She must carry recovery through with a further lease of life. To do this she must go to London and nourish her mind and poetry with a year of higher education. This is the basis of a pact with her husband: the Pact of Pallastunturi, we might say.

Needless perhaps to say is that in 1952 a pact of this sort is unheard of for an obscure housewife and mother, with no profession, no visible talent.

Sirkka's farewell gift is a book called *Voices of Finland*; opening it, Sirkka intones lines from the *Kalevala*, and its pulsing rhythm takes over their bus to the docks. Finns listen with grave attention.

Thirty years later, Rhoda will affirm: 'Finland was my soul's window through which there fell on me exquisite blessings.'

9

Free in London

As her train passes through Germany, Rhoda averts her eyes. In 1952, Germany is still 'the poisoned stomach' of a Europe that degenerated into the Holocaust. Happiness returns when her eyes open to works of art. In Florence, Giotto and Filippo Lippi, she finds, 'lift me out of the decay that is Europe into the purity of their vision'.

She drafts a letter to Sirkka, who will understand that though she has to cope on her own, 'loneliness is what I have chosen'.

Sirkka commends her breakout. 'You are a lonely one too, so different & so perfectly like me.'

How miraculously 'our two souls leapt together', Rhoda replies. It was 'one of those strange things that happen once or twice in a lifetime'.

Harry, who has been in Spain, joins her for a day in Rome, and then, on 30 August, flies home to us. Pip and I are leaping about at the gate to welcome him.

Rhoda is now really alone. Her stagnation for so many years has not accustomed her to plan ahead in practical ways. What exactly will she do in London? Until she gets there it's a dream: in part the colonial dream of a great civilisation across the sea, in part the dream of lone writers who long for guidance.

Uneasy about money, dependent on a husband whose optimistic investments often prove shaky, she roughs it in Rome and Paris, where she sleeps one night in a bathroom. She lingers too long in Paris, entranced by art, and reaches London 'dog-tired' at six in the evening of 9 September.

That night, at 250 Elgin Avenue in Maida Vale, she finds herself in one of those unwanted rooms that Reception can foist on a woman travelling on her own. It's at the back on the third floor: small, with dirty bits of carpet, stained walls and mice.

There are two letters from home: one from her husband and the other from Monica. Her friend's advice is to stay no more than two months, and return for the school holidays in December.

There's no need for a mother to organise school holidays, nor is Rhoda one to do it. Her illness meant that we'd never depended on her physical attendance. Yet it's clear from Monica's letter that within three days of our father's return to Cape Town he is talking over his children's deprivations with Rhoda's most influential friend, more than ready to concur.

Monica may not know that Rhoda has never been the kind of mother who packs her children's days with educational outings. Monica herself is the epitome of the selfless maternal woman who finds complete fulfilment in tending her babies. She carries no shade of regret for other gifts – for learning and games – nature bestowed on her as a girl. This shadowless maternity, and the force of it despite the mildness, is shaped by the absence of Monica's own mother, Rose, throughout Monica's childhood and that of her sister Zelda.

According to my mother, no one knew exactly how Rose (born in 1889) came to disappear. Rumour had it that this mother was 'mental' and had been sent away overseas to a British asylum, which was only possible because the sisters' father was wealthy. Rose never emerged, and her daughters never saw her again. My mother remarked that Isabella Shaw, wife of the novelist Thackeray, had suffered a similar fate after the birth of her second daughter. My mother would speak darkly of those wasted and unreachable lives, and – though she may not have said as much – I conceived them as victims of medical practice who shut away young mothers who could not perform as mothers. When Rhoda came to know Monica at the age of nine there was a substitute for a mother in the form of 'Nurse'. The large house on Belvedere Avenue, opposite the Reservoir, was dark with the gloom of Monica's father, aged forty-five, who sat eating in his braces, and behind him, the brooding presence of Nurse Eppie Howes. She may have served her employer's sexual needs, so my mother will hint when I'm older. As girls, both Rhoda and Lilian sensed something awry in that home with Nurse as dominant figure. Small, forbidding, Nurse Howes vetted who might or might not visit. Rhoda and Lilian detested her, but dared not show it.

So behind Monica's mildness was a desire to fill that vacant maternal space. In 1952, when Monica spells out the duties of motherhood, Rhoda calls this 'gentle' advice, but Monica's tone is firm, risking (she articulates the risk) intrusion. Her firmness is surprising, because neither Monica nor anyone at home asked if we missed our mother. If they had, I could have assured them that we felt cocooned. There's Lenie dabbing icing (flavoured with orange juice and grated rind) on a Lenie-cake, and Granny who allows me to choose a red sundress – my mother would think it garish – for the sake of its elasticised bodice. And there's an outer layer of security provided by our father.

As always, I walk to school, about half an hour up Kloof Road, and then cut across the 'coloured' area of Tramway

Road, to the slope of King's Road, sheering steeply downwards towards the Main Road with its trams. Often, King's Road girls in brown uniforms and panama hats stop to stare at a lamed tram, while its grim-faced driver manoeuvres a long implement to fish for a lost feeler from the top of the tram and re-attach it to the line overhead.

Every Saturday morning, as always, I take the High Level Road bus to a studio in town, carrying ballet shoes, folded inwards with soles on the outside. Uncle Sydney sends me one of the new black leotards from America, which schoolgirl conformity forbids me to wear.

'Harry tells me you spoke about sending the children over to England,' Monica writes. 'Well, Rhoda, as a very old friend I think it is a rather hare-brained idea. Uprooting children of their age really does not do them any good, and they are too young to benefit from a stay in England.'

How can motherhood not come first? Five weeks earlier, Monica has given birth to a third boy, who is proving a champion at the breast. And there is Lilian, who also has given birth to a third child, the longed-for girl to be a companion on the farm. Monica has taken Lilian and the baby into her home, for Lilian, she says in her mild, caring voice, is 'het up'. Lilian herself is matter-of-fact when she speaks of her husband. 'Bertie is busy with water-boring and putting in pumps.' The silence around this statement resonates with marital loyalty in the face of the farmer's incomprehension.

'I can't write to you with my usual buoyancy. I think I must be suffering from that period of deep depression that sometimes sets in after childbirth,' Lilian confides to Rhoda. 'At night, when one's thoughts are so wild, I think of you and a calmness comes over me when I realise that you have conquered that turmoil.'

Can it be, I wonder now, that my mother was less of an

oddity than she appeared? Was she, after all, not far off from other women who entered into a dark night of depletion?

Into this maternal scene at Monica's, with yards of hand-washed nappies flapping as they dry in the wind, steps our father. He's dressed in his after-office shorts, and his muscled calves flash down the steps to Bayhead. His forehead, touched by a slanting ray of sun, is creased, for it's disconcerting to come back to a wifeless home. How did it happen that he gave way in Pallastunturi?

Far from solitary Lapp heights, local talk is closing around him: a gallivanting wife, a broken home, neglected children. For a divorce lawyer, these are common narratives. The raw meat of the courtroom obliterates the fountaining inner life Rhoda will attempt to release in London. Wives don't go off to be poets abroad; they are taken along by husbands to enjoy a tour. How is he to explain?

Unlike Lilian, who has transformed herself into a farmer's wife, Rhoda has shut the door on her husband's concerns. More than anyone knows, she has lived unhusbanded, not letting go the landscape of childhood. Her husband can rely on her attentions to his family, to servants and to the household, as well as the occasional favour of an appearance at a swimming gala, to present the cups, but beyond this, she does not pretend to enter into Harry's life, and of course illness has excused her. All along, though, she has made the divergence of their minds and purposes abundantly plain, and he knows that however confident he feels on radio or when he blows his whistle at the poolside, he cannot engage the wife he looks up to and loves in his exuberant way.

As a father, he likes to squeeze: 'Oochy-coochy-coo' he says, clasping me to him with three breathless hugs. He runs his rough cheek over mine and sometimes over my back, and though it scrapes on tender skin, that's his way of showing affection.

How far my mother yields something of her self, I can't say. They never quarrel. I assume that they are too far apart to strike that sort of spark. Yet until September 1952 she's been there, not fully present but physically in place. Suddenly she's not, and it occurs to him that she may have left in some more permanent way neither has foreseen. A whole year on his own stretches out; he wonders if she will meet another man more fitted to her tastes. This is what his family and others hint. What might Rhoda's friends think of her disappearance from the scene?

It's uncommon for him to feel at a loss, and being a man of action he doesn't waste time brooding. He's here at Bayhead to talk over his abandonment with his wife's closest friend, and not to put too fine a point on it, he's here to co-opt her influence. Monica, if anyone, can reel Rhoda in. As biddable wife, as gentle-voiced mother, Monica speaks for the womanhood of 1952 with the appeal of maternal intelligence.

So it is that Monica posted her letter on 3 September to await Rhoda's arrival in London. Don't overrate a university education, she counsels. Neither Nadine Gordimer nor Doris Lessing has a degree. It's irrelevant for a writer. What Rhoda needs is not to study overseas, but rather to exercise the discipline to work regularly at what she does.

'Your family is so thrilled by your new zest, they are prepared to indulge you to the utmost,' Monica says, 'even to a long stay away from Cape Town.'

But what does a long stay mean? Monica concurs with Rhoda's husband that December must be the limit. 'I have a feeling that by then you will want to be with the children.'

When I look at these letters from Rhoda's maternal friends, particularly Monica and Ren (who agrees with Monica), a question of jealousy occurs to me. These are reading women; they are very intelligent; and yet they disapprove of a woman who puts her head outside the home, except to perform what

their society sees as acts of charity like the orphanage library or
Ren's dance lessons for motherless girls. In a provincial town in
the fifties, it's peculiar for a mother to stay away for the sake of
a 'great opportunity'. As it happens, I feel no need of their protection. I was a child enjoying a more carefree life with father
and grandmother, relieved that my troubled mother was finding a way to be happy.

Alongside Monica's letter is Harry's, listing problems at home. His
mother-in-law, shaking her head over her daughter's hands-off
domestic management, is empowered by Rhoda's absence. Lenie
is put out by Granny's interference in the kitchen, while Granny
herself is put out by children who ha-ha at her raised forefinger.

'It's true Mom does not understand children at all,' Rhoda
replies, projecting her uneasiness with her mother onto me.
'*I* know how she must be reacting.' In truth, I'm the cause of

Rhoda (left) was dependent on her mother (centre), whose domestic
management jarred her. On the right is a rabbi's wife,
Mrs Kiwelowitz, who was Basil's mother-in-law

the trouble, for I take advantage of my mother's absence to tease
Granny.

'You're giving me aggravation,' Granny protests, but so calmly
that I annoy her all the more.

One day while I'm bent over the bathroom basin, holding a
facecloth over my eyes while she washes my hair, she tells me
about menstruation. Gleefully, I follow at Granny's heels, muttering 'drip, drip, drip', until she's cross.

My father duly reports this 'bathroom incident', and my
mother bats it back as a matter of no great moment. A spell of
'grannydom', she asserts, won't do the children any harm.

Harry's letters don't survive, but the replies register a barrage
of household complaints: Granny's friction with Pip over piano
practice and reverberations of the bathroom incident. Nothing
appears to deflect Rhoda's intention to stay in London; she deals
with complaints one by one. Her mother should stop supervising Pip's practice because he might lose his love of music.
Then, too, her mother should stop exhausting herself furbish-
ing up the house and bothering about the children's clothes. A
happy atmosphere is all that children need. Patiently, she
explains that if the children were ill she would return at once,
but kitchen and piano squabbles are not going to rush her back.
It's expensive to cross the sea, and an effort to establish herself
in London – not to be thrown up lightly.

'Naturally today & tomorrow will be difficult days,' she goes
on, 'not knowing what will happen or I if shall be able to
choose the correct path to follow.' She reminds her husband of
his agreement. 'It's good of you to fulfil the pact we made at
Pallastunturi. I know how difficult the next few months will be
for you but I feel what I am doing is Right however difficult it
proves. Even if this time does not bear fruit, it is still Right for
me to do this. It is not easy for me either. I think I shall need
some food parcels and warm pyjamas. It is very cold already.'

That day she trundles in buses across London to visit five universities. Wherever she goes, it's too late. Courses are already full.

A different sort of difficulty arises from her decision not to stay with Auntie Minnie or near other members of her family in Hampstead. This, she finds, has been misreported as a wish to have nothing to do with them. She does what she can to correct the mistake. Her aunt is, as ever, a hospitable darling, and there are three dinners at Auntie Minnie's during her first week in London and a visit to her cousin Rita in Buckinghamshire.

There's a worse misreading of her intentions. At lunch with Harry's cousins, Greta Brown from Manchester and her brother Benny, Rhoda fizzes with her burgeoning sense of freedom. Benny, a physician whom she's consulted from time to time, declares that he's never seen her looking better, yet he's strangely cool. Afterwards, Rhoda hears that Mrs Brown's schoolgirl daughter Laura does not want Rhoda to visit, 'because she's not a nice person, and won't go back to her family'.

'I thought I was amongst *friends*,' Rhoda reflects, astonished that Harry's cousin can have spoken in such a way to her daughter. However unworldly Rhoda may be, and entirely lacking in malice, she does recognise the danger of gossip.

'Please Harry,' she asks, 'don't discuss me with everybody & be very reserved ... about my absence because in a small place all sorts of false ideas start circulating in no time. Merely tell people the simple facts: after 10 years at Home with the children I'm taking advantage of being overseas and having a little extra holiday.'

It's politic, she finds, to call it a holiday. A decade or more earlier, Auntie Betsie had left her children with Granny, her eldest sister, for five months while she toured Europe with her husband. Their youngest daughter, Garda, was miserable to be left alone in the dark when Granny shut the door on her night fears. To this day Garda remembers lying on the floor next to

a crack of light coming from under that door. A letter she wrote
to her parents, asking them to come back, was intercepted. No
one asked Auntie Betsie to cut the tour short on account of a
child, because holidays abroad were highly prized.

While Rhoda is in London, Ren takes a holiday in Madeira
where she performs with 'unRen-ish' abandon before an all-male
crowd. Her account of this scene to Rhoda presents another face
of fifties womanhood. In an outdoor bar her husband Sonny,
squat, beaming, takes out his ukulele and belts out a song. Once
the drinkers join in he orchestrates a rollicking scene like a
Hollywood musical, like Marilyn Monroe strumming a ukulele
as she advances her hips down the aisle of the train. Ren, lifted
onto a table, does an African dance, then an undulating Spanish
one with alluring glances over her shoulder. What makes this virtuous is that her glance turns repeatedly to her 'adoring husband'
who's masterminding the sway of her body.

Dancing on a tabletop, holidaying, mothering: all are approved
in 1952. But for a mother to stay abroad with a serious purpose
of her own, for her to speak earnestly of poetry and long-term
study, is quite another thing: it puts my mother in a suspect
position.

Reading these letters as a daughter and a writer, and a mother
myself, knowing full well how much she gave of herself as a
mother and how much she needed to write, I feel for her situation. She conducted herself with admirable rationality when
people back home forced on her a conflict between aspiration and
children, opportunity and marital duty, London and Cape Town.
On the one side there was Sirkka, calling her out as 'my sister in
fate', emboldening her to unbury herself. 'My strength is yours,
Rhoda.' On the other side: Monica, who would draw a mother
back to the fold. And behind Monica stands our father the lawyer
who relies on Monica to make a better case than he can devise.

The Rhoda of the past would have acted on Monica's advice,

but this is a different Rhoda, whose hunger is such that she must feast now – not vicariously, like colonials, like Monica rewarming the events of *John O'London's Weekly* at a distance of six thousand miles – but here, at first hand, bathed in the abundance of London, 'an oasis in the middle of my life'.

The oasis turns out to be lectures on contemporary poetry, philosophy and Shakespeare at the City Literary Institute in Goldsmith's Street (now Stukeley Street), in the theatre district of Drury Lane. Its purpose is to offer a second chance to pupils in their thirties and forties, and the fee charged by the London County Council for a whole term is all of one pound, seventeen shillings and sixpence.

After failing to convince Rhoda how badly she's needed at home, my father simply demands her return. It comes as a bombshell. On 24 September, after only two weeks in London, Rhoda gives way. She books a passage on the *Jagersfontein*, due to sail on 19 December and reach Cape Town by 2 or 3 January. She has just three months to be in London.

'Harry,' she pleads, 'please bear my absence patiently. After all I had to be father & mother on all your trips away from home including England and Israel, during one of which the children and myself were continuously ill.'

For a mother to claim an equal right for herself in 1952 is unheard of. It's twenty years too early. Rhoda tries to assure her husband that she's not taking on anything too demanding, and yet her enthusiasm breaks out – together with what is bound to gall him, her separate tastes, compounded by minimising the household issues he's put forward.

I have only been to one lecture and found it most stimulating – unlike anything I could find in South Africa. I am not doing any courses. Only four evenings a week I go to these discussion-lectures at which I have an opportunity to meet people with the same interests as my own … Now that I am here I must not waste time. This is my opportunity … It would be silly to drop everything & rush home unless of course there is a serious reason to do so. I have been ill and stay-at-home for so many years that I would not like to have to cancel my plans unless it is necessary.

At this point the publication of her poem 'Finland' in the *Cape Times* plays into her hands. Here would seem some proof that her sense of herself as a poet may be justified. But Harry has been taken aback to find 'Rhoda Press' at the bottom of the poem.

Why not her married name, he asks.

'Whatever poetry is in me comes from the Press side,' she insists.

Monica is thrilled to see 'Finland' in print. She perceives an improvement on Rhoda's earlier poems, some of which might be publishable if she can bring herself to revise them. If she resolves to shut her door to visitors (it's usual for people to drop in), she might clear three hours for herself each morning.

Monica offers an idea that might console her friend for leaving London: why doesn't Rhoda approach one of *John O'London*'s poets and reviewers, Richard Church, for a one-off consultation – 'on a business basis of course' – on how to improve her poems.

Instead, Rhoda joins a craft of verse class at the City Lit. The first assignment is a poem on Charlie Chaplin, and she discovers that she can, if required, turn her hand to humour:

> *Crazy cooing eyes, a mimouthed smirk,*
> *Nidnodding missus, coquettish shoulder jerk*

before the little tramp vagabonds over the last hill.

The class goes on from year to year. Its members are all aspiring practitioners, discussing one another's poems. Rhoda makes friends with Edith Roseveare – Roseveare, as she always calls her – who has listened 'with pointed ears' to Edith Sitwell's 'quixotic eloquence' in a performance of *Façade* at the Festival Hall. She describes how Sitwell, in a flowing white mantle lined with black, strode boldly about the stage, taking a 'long breath' to deliver each of her lines. To Roseveare, seated far above 'with the five-shilling intellectual crowd', Sitwell's face had been a blur but her voice, riding Walton's music, reached them. This is the iconic woman poet of the day. Though Roseveare applauds this 'splendid old trout', she herself cultivates a cooler voice: 'Distrust the clouds. Turn your back on the view / From the ornamental tower of your hopes ...'

Roseveare's distrust of the blue haze of dreamscapes is bracing. Keep your eyes on the ruts and the traffic signals, Roseveare warns. 'Will nothing break you of sucking your dreams / Like sweets?' There are other things to observe, like 'the loud hard street' outside the City Lit. Stop, she orders in her no-flummery, English voice. Stop scanning the great horizons and unattainable peaks.

There's a reservation on Rhoda's part. Roseveare, she discovers, has German antecedents, and she repeats this to me after her return, as though she's entered into a surprising, almost forbidden relationship. Roseveare, she gives me to understand, is more contained and ironic, alien in a way Sirkka, the sister of the lit-up soul, is not – and, by extension, Finland is not. It escapes her notice – or she allows it to do so – that in the second phase of the war Finland did *not* join the Allies. In that post-war decade there are many, like Rhoda, who refuse contact with Germans as well as German goods, feeling that anything German is tainted with the stench of the gas ovens. At the same time as Rhoda nurses a

prejudice against Roseveare, the two will correspond for years
to come.

A male classmate observes Rhoda's 'almost biblical charm' as
she tiptoes into the room ten minutes late. What 'fascinates' him
(as he teases in a set of couplets, written out for her in an educated
hand) is 'something in her face / Of ancient, semitic grace / What
centuries of suffering lie / Covered by that velvet eye!' In her, a
woman of the Bible lives once more, coming through the door
with 'an invisible amphora on her head' – ten minutes late.

I recognise the lateness. It's hard to organise herself. The pills
she has to take fog her in trivial ways: she'll forget where she's
left her handkerchief or put down her glasses. Before leaving,
she will rummage distractedly through her bag, muttering 'I'm
im*poss*ible.'

Discussions go on after class in the café at the institute. One
of the lecturers is John Heath-Stubbs, whose verse is in a book
she owns. News is passed around about the Poetry Fellowship,
run by another lecturer, J. W. Reynolds, a small man with a
'sickle smile' and a 'big, resolute mind'. His aim is to 'bring
together in the spirit of fellowship all students at the Institute
who are interested in poetry'. Happily, fellowship is what
Rhoda finds at meetings and talks. 'Is there a new poetic
drama?' is the topic on 18 October. Ten days later she attends
a reading of poems on poets and poetry, including Richard
Church on Wordsworth, Siegfried Sassoon's 'To an Eighteenth
Century Poet' and Gerard Manley Hopkins' 'To R.B.'. The
only poem by a woman is 'Poetry' by Marianne Moore.

After much searching, Rhoda settles in a mansion block near
where she stayed in Elgin Avenue. It's a relief to be in a clean
room overlooking a stretch of garden with trees and lawn
behind this ground-floor flat. Her room has a Persian rug over
a fitted carpet, reading lamp, desk, armchair, eiderdown and

even flowers. There is an ample shelf for her books, a shelf in the kitchen cupboard and the bottom half of the fridge. All this for three guineas a week (the same as she'd paid for the squalid room near by) in a flat belonging to a refugee from Germany, Mrs Mannerheim, whose interests are art, music and literature.

'I don't see how you will survive going out to restaurants in all weathers,' Mrs Mannerheim says, eyeing this lodger who looks in need of nourishment. Might cooked lunches (for four-and-six or five shillings, considerably less than a restaurant) be welcome, as well as breakfasts? Yes, they would. Rhoda feels no need to own that she's never cooked a meal in her life.

For her breakfast, Mrs Mannerheim orders 'special milk' that is a quarter cream. Arriving back late from the City Lit, Rhoda finds her landlady ironing the undies Rhoda has washed in the bathroom they share. Rhoda decides that the way this woman has taken to her and goes on 'spoiling' her is 'of the same strange calibre of the magical things that happened to me in Finland and Lapland. I was "led" here.'

Afterwards, when she's back at home, my mother will act out a comic scene when her 'nudist' landlady opens the door to receive a basket with gefilte fish from Auntie Minnie's driver, the respectable Edward, startled into an eyes-front, glassy stare. How can I not believe in this nudist? I see her through the haze of a South African summer, little knowing how relentlessly damp England is, how people can't wait to put on their woollies. The point, though, gets through: how my mother's bohemian drama, playing off Maida Vale against Hampstead propriety, underpins the pleasure she took in independence.

In fact, the place is, and ever was, comfortably middle class: a row of dignified red-brick blocks in a tree-lined street. When they were built in 1897 it was a largely Jewish area, near to the Spanish and Portuguese Synagogue, the headquarters of the Sephardi community in Britain.

Since rationing is still in place, tighter in fact than during the war (one egg a week, one and a half ounces of cheese, meat limited to about 1/9d), Granny posts off parcels of supplements: tins of Silver Leaf peas, stewing steak, baked beans, soup, peaches, pineapple and, somehow, butter and eggs. In the fifties, flats are unheated, but kind Mrs Mannerheim moves her own heater into Rhoda's room when she's due back.

This is a make-do but culturally vibrant London. One Sunday evening, 16 November, Edith Sitwell recites 'The Shadow of Cain' together with Dylan Thomas, a cataclysmic atom-bomb poem, to a musical setting by Humphrey Searle played by the London Symphony Orchestra and described by *The Times* as 'shattering noise, dead silence and instrumental monotone or held chords'. Emlyn Williams performs as Dickens; Claire Bloom, with her black hair and pointed chin, is an 'exquisite' Juliet; and Alec Guinness has the lead in a comedy, *Under the Sycamore*. Mrs Mannerheim takes Rhoda to a preview of an Epstein exhibition at the Tate; Rhoda returns next day to a greater delight in Blake; she sits in the institute café with members of the poetry class and is quickened when they applaud a poem she submits, anonymously and trembling, to a workshop.

It must be 'Sing Heart', for that poem (as well as 'Charlie Chaplin') is included in a City Lit anthology for 1951–3. Like many of Rhoda's poems, it's about utterance: the struggle to articulate the dark night of the soul. This big subject, central to the lives of Jeremiah and Jesus, makes utterance daunting, particularly for a woman in an orthodox tradition that reserved the higher reaches of the devotional life for men.

'Sing Heart' takes us into the terror of 'a dark pit', the biblical scene of spiritual trial. A parallel trial from her own life is to cross an abyss, based on the childhood scene when her brothers dared her to cross the one-track railway bridge above the

Olifants River. In 'Sing Heart' the crossing is made on an untried, spider-like thread 'spun from the entrails'. But unlike the unending ordeal in other of her poems, and unlike the female avatar of Jacob wrestling to no good with the angel, here, in the finale, comes an exulting release, couched in the seascape of the Cape:

> *Sing heart*
> *of the Sea*
> *that bursts from sunrise*
> *with a rush of foam vision white,*
> *(O silverflitting bees*
> *Sunmantling the seas)*
> *Sing heart.*
>
> *Sing joy-shot heart*
> *Dune-high*
> *Catching the wind in my throat*
> *I wave the veil of the sky.*

After years of writing surreptitiously and alone, it's heady to be in this great city where others care for poetry as she does. What she used to term 'attacks' are now no more than 'flaps'. They happen, but she can 'manage 'em'. Not for years has she been so well as in this chilly, rainy autumn. In the parks, skeleton trees wade in evening mist, 'serene silk of sky and water'. In the noisy Strand she sits 'dream-lidded' among packed and grubby tables in a crowded café. A band plays and, in a poem, 'Café Music', music 'spreads a space'. This space is Europe, she tells herself — a Europe distilled as architecture of a grandeur inconceivable in Africa — and she muses 'how far I've come / from tunnelling underground / to this world's peak alone . . .'

Throughout the autumn of 1952, Rhoda feels nourished by

all the arts, with poetry at the centre of her life, as it was meant to be. The real issue is about what is central to a woman's life. Her poetry group is 'a great opportunity', she repeats. Though Monica hears these words, she can't hear their import. Why do you keep saying this, Monica asks. You can go overseas again in a few years.

However plainly Rhoda makes her case, she's unable to penetrate the mindset of time and place. She cannot communicate the urgency to her husband and mother and the like-minded people behind them, including Ren, who signal a simple message: think of your children. She's closer to arguing with Monica than she's ever come, diverting her protest through the ready-dug channel of exasperation with her mother. 'May I point out that it is not my absence, it is *what I am doing* she disapproves of.'

Rhoda blames her mother for her husband's opposition. She can hear her mother's voice all through his letters. 'You must realise,' she warns him, 'Mom understands me and my purposes even less than she does the children. She simply has no idea whatsoever what my life's about.'

Since Rhoda is easily moved to anxiety over obligations to others and any signal of displeasure, I imagine my father's surprise to find her so resolute. I suspect he's more alarmed by this composed character – this changed wife – than he can admit, even to himself. She's detached from the perspective of Cape Town, not rebelliously but with a courteous dutifulness that is actually more challenging.

'When I return I shall devote myself to the rest of the children's holiday,' she promises. 'As for ourselves, we have fitted our lives together for the past twelve years in the face of illness and disparity of interests, and will, I hope, with the help of God, and the exercise of our best qualities, adjust ourselves in the Future.'

It's one thing to look up to the wife you possess as a superior being; quite another to find that wife exercising her superiority in this distant way. Since Harry is 'woebegone', Rhoda hastens to say that all she wants is to prove she's 'no longer a cripple' and 'to water the seed that has lain for so many years in drought-stricken earth'. As always, her train of thought turns back to her own drama. The comedy of the woebegone husband – in line with her friends' humorous accommodation to oppositeness of 'the opposite sex' – does not look into a possibility of something more disturbing: a widening of the divide already between them.

Each letter reminds her husband to send ten pounds to an American artist in Amsterdam, Mike Pedulke, from whom she's acquired an etching called *The Prophet*. He's yet another stranger for whom she felt affinity. Back in July, when she and Harry were travelling together, he had wanted to give her this work for her birthday, but in the end she has to pay the artist herself. Is the non-appearance of the ten pounds mere carelessness on Harry's part? Is it tightfistedness? Can it be that the artist reciprocated the warmth which Rhoda had felt for his work and a husband had felt left out? Or may it be a signal of his displeasure? It's common enough to be displeased with those we block. Harry feels uneasy, if not guilty, at going back on the Pact of Pallastunturi; all the more reason then to take a tough line. He stops writing.

Fourteen days before Rhoda's ship is due to sail she makes a last plea that her London life should not be 'thrown away'.

... As in Finland my pangs grow greater as the time draws near for me to leave the rich full life I have made here. This time however there is an equal urge towards you and the children. At times I fiercely regret feebly relinquishing (during the first trying two weeks in London) our original

plans forged at Pallastunturi that you should bring the
children over for a year. But as soon as you slipped back
into Cape Town's conforming garment you were aided and
abetted in your desire to have me back by parochial hands
raised in horror at such a 'new' idea . . .

My Verse Class cannot believe that I am leaving just at
this critical juncture when someone is undertaking to
publish a poetry magazine which will be fed by our class.
We all met in a Pub the other evening to discuss this new
and thrilling development. And both my lecturers have
expressed extreme regret at losing me and my poetry. One
said: 'We just won't let you go.' And another – 'I'd like to
sabotage your ship!' Quite another lecturer has invited our
class to spend Christmas at his house where he has
arranged (between parties) some Poetry Lectures by
famous people. In January I am also missing a University
Residential Weekend on Poetry held at a lovely old Manor
House on the Downs.

It is not easy to throw away the Cup towards which I
have been fumbling in the dark from earliest childhood.
Because I am so happy I know at last that this is my life-
blood. Is there perhaps still a chance of your flying over
here with the children? <u>Please answer at once.</u>

Eddie* was here for tea (and to fetch his groceries)
yesterday. He was surprised to find how frugally I live. I
live on less than half of what he does per week . . . My
landlady took me to 'Claridges' for lunch the other day for
a treat and I sat right next to the Duchess of Kent's
daughter who was with her governess, dressed in a shabby
school jersey. We had a fine time and then I went on to a

---

* Harry's feckless youngest brother, who depended on him, and perhaps others, for
handouts.

French film which made me laugh and weep together, then to the British Museum and on to my Lectures in the evening. I also saw the opera 'Figaro' and was charmed, charmed ... On Saturday afternoon I am going with my Theatre Club to 'Porgy and Bess', and then on to our Poetry Society in the evening ... If I must return on the 19th there is scarcely time. I have a sort of suffocated feeling at the moment.

As it happens, at this very moment, millions of Londoners are feeling suffocated physically, by the yellow-brown smog spreading across the city. Coal is rationed, but the government has given a go-ahead to small lumps of inferior, peculiarly filthy coal. Chimneys pour polluted smoke into the air, thickening the smog. A performance of *La Traviata* is halted because the figures on stage are barely visible. Spectral figures, heads down, cover their mouths with scarves as they struggle home through the murk. The environmental disaster lasts five days, from 5 to 9 December, with deaths rising to four thousand, a number comparable to the cholera epidemic of 1866 and the Spanish flu of 1918.

Is my mother too absorbed in her private drama to notice? Pressure and silence are tugging her away at the moment when her life-blood has started to flow. As I read her plea to my father, I can't help thinking how like her it was to ignore what's happening. And yet, all the while she's speaking, I remember my mother's excitement over poetry, art and theatre. Was there, I wonder, a heightening of the arts that was concurrent with the physical gloom, in some sense called out by it?

Sirkka comforts her friend. 'I am not too sad that you must leave your valuable loneliness in London so soon.' Fertilisation, she says, will suffice, for Rhoda to 'develop and create' by herself.

Once more, Sirkka sends Rhoda on her way. 'My boots' –

lent to her for walking in Lapland – 'are always there for you, Rhoda. Know that I am smiling with secret triumphant happiness all the time you are trotting around in them.'

I've turned eleven by the time my mother comes back. During her six-month absence, the mental space she'd occupied has been filled with try-outs of normality. It has been easy to lay down the freight of my mother's alertness. Courtesy of Granny and my father, daily doings have filled out, untrammelled by insights: the automatism of long division in Standard Four (sixth grade), games of snap and Monopoly, and the commotions Granny sets up – starched napkins, polished cake forks, a spread of triangular cucumber sandwiches, soft cheesecake and sticky meringues – when her friends came for tea. Her friends, these brides of 1914, have sweet-pet names like Girlie and Toffee, and they are sweet in the way they say 'shame', the South African endearment for babies, little girls, puppies and kittens; or '*Ag*, shame' in commiseration when Granny fusses over a missing teaspoon. Little is required as I hang around the edges of Granny's teas; it's enough to be her granddaughter in a freshly ironed dress, hair neatly parted on the side and combed around Granny's finger into sausage curls, as though I were as sweet as they.

My mother deplored the way aspiring parents loaded children with extra lessons. For some schoolmates, afternoons are so packed with music, ballet and elocution that little time is left to read and dream. As a child, my mother had not enjoyed her piano lessons; she resolved to spare her children if they weren't talented. My brother is; I'm not. All the same, I was alight when Granny, seated on the piano stool one autumn evening while my mother was away, taught me to read music so that I can look at the sheet and finger the opening notes of 'The Blue Danube'.

On weekends my father took me to the Union Swimming

Club at the Long Street Baths. You were given a pink card, folded over, and when you opened the two cardboard sides there were the names of the worthies of the club, including my father. As a favour to him, patient old Mr Mitchell taught me to breathe out bubbles in the water. At King's Road the ten- and eleven-year-olds exchanged brown lace-ups for white tackies before we ran on to the netball court. Blonde Miss Eales, feet apart and bouncing lightly on her toes, coached us for a match against Ellerton, the junior school in the neighbouring suburb of Green Point.

'When I blow my whistle, I want you to run as fast as you can towards the circle,' she said, as though this were of the utmost importance.

I loved this instruction as I turned with the ball at my shoulder in the centre of the court. It wasn't only sport; it was the first efflorescence of a lifelong love affair with normality. And so, it's a routinely occupied daughter, less dreamy, less watchful, who awaits, quite matter-of-factly, her mother's return.

'Loneliness is what I have chosen,' our mother said.
Our father looks after Pip and me while she's away

10

Mother to Daughter

A healthy mother with a spring in her step descends the gang-plank to embrace her children and our father. He is beaming with triumph to have brought her back, to his way of thinking, in record time. Excitedly, she turns to draw forward two unknown young women coming ashore at her heels.

On the voyage home in the Dutch liner, the *Jagersfontein*, Rhoda has befriended Dorrie and Astrid, sisters who appear to be on their own. With a distant father and no mother, they are all-in-all to each other. Rhoda tells us how she came upon them in the ship's library. They were conversing in French, and it was all about books.

Speaking with ready aplomb, they confirm the delight of this encounter and enthuse over Rhoda's readiness to read (in translation) their favourite French authors, Colette and de Beauvoir and the tales of Balzac and de Maupassant. For young women still in their teens, they have an astonishing intellectual confidence and an almost voluble flow of words. They enunciate each English word with the perfection of cosmopolitans, rarely seen in Cape Town at the time. Mainly sporting and sailing people visit, or naval officers bound for the British base at Simonstown. After the ship docks, my mother adopts Dorrie and Astrid, as if she were a kind of older sister.

As a girl of their age, my mother's hair had fallen into ringlets, and it had been her habit to wind my hair into similar curls – even though ringlets look old-fashioned and silly surrounding a face marked like mine. How tactfully Dorrie alters that in front of the bathroom mirror, alternately brushing and pulling my hair straight back from the forehead; 'Like a Swiss girl,' she says, banishing absurdity. Dorrie, who has been to finishing school in Paris, is elegant, unlike anyone I've seen in South Africa where stylishness often seems contrived – a studied imitation of 'overseas'. 'Overseas . . . overseas' resonates in our uncertain colonial world.

My mother brings back an aura of belonging in a London circle – no longer the outsider she had been during her invalid years. Her participation over there, across the ocean, comes through obliquely in comic scenes: the motorcycle chase in Lapland with Rhoda clinging to the back of a stranger whose face she hadn't seen, and the bohemian eccentricity of a nudist in London opening her door to Auntie Minnie's driver. All this sounds fantastical and far away. But Dorrie and Astrid are here, an authentic sample of overseas, chosen, as it were, by my mother to bring home to us. They laugh a lot in their vibrantly alert manner, amused at our ways, like sophisticated older sisters a girl can look up to. Being with them is like an introduction to cultivated, foreign forms of life I've known only vaguely and at a distance.

Contact with my mother reignites over two new books from England: *A Dream of Sadlers Wells* and *Veronica at the Wells* by Lorna Hill. Veronica is an orphan with a talent for ballet, but as the *Dream* opens she's forced to leave her classes in London, as well as the comfy Cockney landlady, Mrs Crapper, who has looked after her. She's on a train to Northumberland to live with county relations she's never met. Apprehensive and displaced, she confides her longing to be a dancer to a stranger on the train, a humorous boy called Sebastian, who confides, in turn, his dream to be a conductor. Their secret dedication and dread of obstructive provincialism reclaim me for my mother's narrative. Normality subsides to the status of diversion, and once more the outsider holds sway.

Lying on my back in the dark, I'm ready for one of her talks after she switches off my light. Sometimes she tells me things in the palm of my hand, like the drama of the French Revolution: she pictures the rage of the women marching on Versailles to demand bread; the oblivion of Marie Antoinette, asking why they don't eat cake – a curling question in my palm; the uprightness of the queen's bearing when she stands in a tumbrel on her way to the guillotine; and the knitting women – a sinister tap, tap on my palm – placidly occupied as heads fall into a basket. Then there's Sarah, the wife of Abraham, eavesdropping in her tent – my mother closes my palm around her Sarah-finger – when an angel announces to her husband that she will bear a child. And Sarah, barren and ageing, laughs in disbelief. Women long gone laugh, speak, feel, unlike history at school narrowed to rulers, colonies and wars, the fighters of the Great Trek, surprised by the *impis* of the Zulu king Dingaan at the battle of Blood River, when the river ran red.

'Marriage is the proper ground for men and women to come together,' my mother is saying. 'Otherwise you degrade the body. Men are always ready, but they despise girls who offer themselves.'

I think of my father's divorcées with raised cocktails, who flirt gamely as he buzzes from group to group at sports parties. Though my mother is no longer an invalid, she does not join him for these events and they resume their separate ways. Perhaps because they lived in different milieux, an exception stands out in my memory: an evening when they went out as a couple to a ball. Dressed, our father in black tie and our mother in silver-grey scalloped tiers from her slender waist and pearl-drop earrings, like an exquisite doll, they appeared before Pip and me to show themselves off before leaving. We were entranced by this image, like a film about a romantic pair about to waltz away into the mist.

She has hastened back – my mother adds – to tell me that, hallowed by marriage, 'intercourse is beautiful'.

Until now I've trusted what my mother says as coming from the soul of truth. For the first time, I don't quite believe her. The words are flat; they call up no scene. Then too it seems unlikely for a mother to travel from the northern to the southern hemisphere in order to spell this out.

Though I don't ask, she wants to explain. Her haste has been to counteract Granny, who has usurped a mother's role and provoked laughter over the serious facts of life. Once my mother reclaims me, the female body is not to be demeaned with hilarity. Her tone forbids it. Though I'm aware how rude I'd been, and how annoying, I let well-meaning Granny take the blame. Sex now takes a back seat; we've shifted to familiar territory: the scarred ground between Rhoda and her mother. I listen with the solemnity her concern invites.

What's definitely unbeautiful is the prospect of becoming 'unwell' each month. Joking had served to dismiss this fact of life; taking it in, I foresee mishaps: blood seeping onto a dress. Others will find out. Nice girls don't speak about the body. We are adept at keeping beach towels tucked under our arms as we step into a bather. Am I about to be different again, and embarrassed? My newly acquired normality fades before the prospect of bodily change.

A few months after my mother's return, I do start to be 'unwell'.

I show my mother the stains. Is this what Granny told me about?

'So soon,' my mother sighs.

She'd started at thirteen – the better age, she intimates. Her sigh carries a vibration of reproach, as though I'm not like her after all. My body is too ready, too forward by two whole years. I'm wailing at the wrongness of it. In Standard Five, the last year of junior school, I'm still officially a child. I dread going to school with an unaccustomed bulk between my legs; they stiffen with potential embarrassment in gym and netball. Those lessons become a test of secrecy, for no girl, bar one, ever admits this happens. I remember the only exception, some years later in high school, when a girl called Pam will rise from her desk after a long Latin class and hint at the sensation – unexpectedly pleasurable – of a swelling flow. There's an instant of complicity as I smile back.

Otherwise the only acknowledgement appears in American magazines like *Mademoiselle*, commercials for 'feminine fresh-ness' nudging girl-consumers to be worried enough to persuade mothers to buy a particular brand of sanitary napkin. Mothers bought a supply for daughters; it was unthinkable, then, for a girl to ask for herself over the counter at the chemist.

An added embarrassment is daily swimming, since my mother believes females are too 'unwell' for that during the first three days of a period. Awkwardly, I summon a lie to my lips – 'I have a cold' – and detect suspicion in the eye of Jasmine, the cleverest girl in the class.

To prove what a child I still am, I join a chase after Valerie, who has the biggest breasts in King's Road Junior School. We are after her to 'feel if she's wearing a bra', and she's made to flee into the bushes at the bottom of the sloping playground, below the netball court. I race after her with the others, thankful that my breasts don't yet merit attention.

Dorrie's sister Astrid is only fifteen, and my mother persuades her to finish school. She's sent to my mother's old school, Good Hope Seminary, where a year later I follow. At assembly the incoming twelve-year-olds in Standard Six file into the front row of the school hall. We are singing the school song, 'Between the mountain and the sea / Our alma mater stands . . . *constantia et virtute*'.

The principal, Miss Tyfield, stands gravely on the stage, like a small hawk in a black academic gown sliding back from her shoulders. My mother has told me that Miss Tyfield is uncommonly clever and has published a set book for schools called *The Living Language*. I'm agog, looking back over my shoulder, to see Astrid, with straight hair and a strong, intelligent face, standing on the balcony amongst other full-breasted girls in the top class, 10A, who have the privilege of Miss Tyfield as teacher.

Next day, Miss Tyfield enters our classroom along an outdoor passage to the boarding school. As she pushes open the door a gust of the south-easter roars and blows out her gown like a shadow behind her. Twenty-five girls, some menstruating for the first time and dazed with afternoon heat, wake up from daydreams and shuffle to their feet. A scripture lesson is in progress and Miss Tyfield walks up and down the aisles inspecting notebooks. She stoops to peer at my drawing of Jacob's wedding night when the couple is left together in a tent. I'd pasted over Leah a removable striped flap for the veil covering the bride's face; opened, it reveals an ugly girl with a reddish, bulbous nose and thick eyelids. Miss Tyfield chortles as she lifts the flap. It isn't meant to amuse, but one could never explain.

*

In consultation with an architect, Dorrie helps Rhoda build and furnish a room of her own, the sunroom, on top of our garage, with rough-textured 'kaffir-sheeting' curtains and bookshelves constructed from bricks and planks – a novel idea then. Two divans at right angles, forming a seating corner, are covered with striped, goat-hair fabric made by Africans who use natural dyes.

Dorrie, who likes simplicity, accomplishes this with astonishing assurance for a young woman of nineteen, venting her neighing laugh, head back, showing all her handsome teeth. Quite soon Dorrie marries the architect, Sam Abramson. I'm disappointed because he's shorter than tall, lithe Dorrie, and not handsome.

'Not a romantic choice,' I say to my mother, thinking of the Scarlet Pimpernel.

She disagrees. 'Better a good man who's interesting.' She takes a poor view of handsome men who drink too much and gad about. Privately I note that my father is handsome and gads about – though not a drinker.

As Sirkka predicted, Rhoda is not thwarted by leaving London. Sirkka's translations into Finnish and the unexpected acceptance of her poems by fellow poets in London initiate a fertile period when her return to her sea-girt landscape extends the breakthrough mood of 'Sing Heart'. As David the Psalmist lifts up his eyes unto the hills from whence cometh his help, Rhoda looks to the sea, and not only for help in healing; her beat lends itself to the tug of eternity in the ebb and rise of the waves.

> *Ocean throat, well of peace,*
> *Draw me back like a wave*
> *Into your being's bliss*
> *My sky-blue childhood.*

Draw me back
From the seething edge of teeth,
The roaring that feeds
On the soul's food,
Into the deep heart of sleep
Home of my healing.

Crowned I will rise, and unfurl
Over the curve of the earth
My white sea wings, with songs
I will arise – with praise –
And hold the earth firm in my embrace.

A double glass door opens from the sunroom, down a spiral stair into the garden, and around the balustrade Rhoda plants honeysuckle to bring back the scent trailing a visionary moment in her youth. The glass door is her 'prayer door', where she stands absolutely still at night before bed. Her fingers spread as her spirit swells out like waves that reach into a hot, blue sky, and then stay there – stilling that swell into permanence

as mountain-waves
lifted to blue fire,
static forever
in a gesture of desire.

Affirmed from afar by letters from Sirkka, Roseveare and her circle in London who assure her she's still 'one of us', Rhoda longs to find some kind of public task, a counter to all those years of enforced seclusion.

In the course of 1953, as Rhoda remakes her life back home, a new friendship ripens with an Israeli Hebrew teacher called

Cille. She's a short woman with hair clipped in no particular style. Like other professional women of her generation she makes no play of femininity, though unlike her local counterparts, who depend on servants, she's a hands-on homemaker. Born in Germany, she has an intellectual energy that galvanises the women around her who are readers of Olive Schreiner's letters and Marie Bashkirtseff's diary, and have not concerned themselves with masculine opinion short of Shakespeare, Chekhov and other classics. Cille is up on the latest heavyweight controversies in biblical scholarship. Her small eyes are keen behind her glasses, focused fully on her listener, and from her wide, plushy mouth comes a flutelike voice. Her lips are mobile as she flutes in her instructive manner. It's a charismatic manner because it's so direct, so certain in her opinion and also so convincing as she holds your gaze, even a child's. Although my mother's friends are mothers above all, none sees me as Cille does, in her teacherly way. She's not concerned with dreaming. What she perceives is some reflection of herself, a more purposeful character who shouldn't be encouraged to dream her life away, but should think of work to do.

Not long ago, Cille married an engineer called Albie – an appropriate name, I think, because there's something a bit albino in his appearance, a fragile skin overlaid by unhealthy patches of sunburn. He's patient, faintly humorous, puffing a large pipe in the corner of his mouth. His air of refraining from comment is too mild to be critical. Like Dorrie's Sam, this is the type of good Jewish husband – the kind, family man – whom my mother never fails to commend.

Cille's verve is a lesson to plain or ugly women who fear to be left single, my mother says. 'If you don't think about looks, others won't think about looks.'

It's indirect advice to a daughter who's not pretty. One of my dreams is to be transformed when I grow up, so that I might be worthy of romance. My model of manhood is a discerning hero, Mr Darcy or Mr Rochester, who can fall in love with an intelligent woman even if she's not a beauty. Their historical distance helps my dreams. The current heroes of the beach, my older cousins Gerald and Peter, often stay with us for the summer at Kilve, on Wherry Road in Muizenberg, around the corner from Sun Blest, where we used to stay during my mother's blighted years. Peter and Gerald never forget to thank Auntie Rhoda for breakfast, but they've hardly downed their toast before they sling beach towels around their necks and push off to the Snake Pit. This is a triangle of hot sand between the pavilion and the bathing boxes where teenagers slither side by side, oiling their bodies and eyeing one another. Heavy-shouldered swimmers, talking about times to my father, seem even more remote: they never look at a girl who isn't a 'doll'.

I see Cille through my mother's eyes, a plain woman with the wisdom to make the most of the tame man who comes her way. In any case, that's the model for women in the fifties: a man who returns from an office in the evening to find an orderly home. In a small, Lakeside flat Cille takes pleasure in home-making. While my mother was abroad, Cille nearly died giving birth to a son, but she brushes this aside as nothing beside the love that fills her for this vulnerable creature. Her joy gives my mother pause. Can Cille's radiance reach back to marital contentment?

My mother confides one of those startlingly intimate facts she sometimes relays to me in my sister capacity. The fact is this: Cille had her hymen surgically removed, with the practical forethought of a mature virgin who wants to enjoy her wedding night. Unwittingly, my mother is revealing that a first sexual experience is unlikely to be enjoyed – or it may be much worse. I mull over this for a long time, along with a question too intimate to ask:

how does a bride, if she has her period, convey this to a bride-groom? What words would she use?

Another startling confidence from my mother is a question about frequency. How often should a couple make love? This question concerned her enough to consult a doctor who gave it on his highest authority, as it were, that once a week should satisfy a man. It happens that this particular doctor is a wom-aniser not known for his restraint, yet my mother, though aware of this fact, chose to exercise the peculiarly deferential mindset women of her generation cultivated for male doctors. Though my mother is usually reticent, she doesn't hesitate to proclaim this once-a-week ruling not only to me, but to other women, as a kind of defiance of husbands who expect too much of their wives. It justifies a wife who holds her husband off. The private issue is barely veiled, and I don't much want to hear it.

What I don't know is that my father consulted Basil's wife, Naomi, on how to stimulate a wife's desire. According to Naomi, he preferred to complain rather than hear what she could tell him. A twenties manual of *Ideal Marriage* laid it down that a wife 'must be *taught*, not only how to behave in coitus, but above all, how and what to feel'. A wife must adapt to a model a husband offers: an array of positions. When, as a curi-ous teen, I discover this manual at the back of my mother's cupboard, it's disappointingly mechanical, full of tricky dia-grams. Meanwhile, Pip reports something I'd also rather not hear: he's spied condoms in our father's suitcase. Lilian thought the satisfactions he took on his travels didn't matter. So Lilian said when I brought this up in 2004. She sided with Harry, and said that Rhoda should have surrendered more, and lent herself to her husband's concerns. 'Harry longed for her to come with him to swimming galas.' I too feel for him because he was hurt by the detached reserve of a wife he loved.

*

Cille is filled with initiatives animating to the dutiful housewives of Cape Town. She's a born teacher who brings pupils on, and she has a proposal for Rhoda: if she will produce a story every fortnight, Cille will undertake to produce a story as well. They will then discuss their work – an attempt to restore the stimulus Rhoda enjoyed in London. One of Rhoda's stories, 'If Only I Can Say "Peep"', is a comic monologue of a young Jewish mother – her age, accent and fairly recent immigration suggest a Holocaust survivor – in the next bed to mine when I'm in a nursing home to have my tonsils out. This survivor is about to undergo a dangerous operation, and all she wants, she tells my mother, is to wake afterwards. To say one word, 'peep', is all she asks. In the event, her resilient voice cuts out with shocking abruptness. At Cille's urging, Rhoda sends this to the *Jewish Chronicle*, which publishes it, accompanied by an author photograph.

My mother reads me 'Early Spring', a daughter and mother story. Emily, about my age, has a small-minded mother, preoccupied with appearance.

In the final scene, the gong goes for dinner and Emily goes into her mother's room:

> *Before the mirror her mother was fixing a Spanish comb into her coil of hair . . . Emily nuzzled her head against her corseted stomach: 'Mommy . . . ' she lisped.*
>
> *But her mother told her to stop being a baby. 'What you look like!' she exclaimed. And she told nurse to tidy her up for supper at once. She wouldn't have Emily going around neglected.*

She's like the bustling mothers around us. One day, when we girls are mothers, will we grow impervious in turn to our daughters' tastes and feelings? I am lucky to have a mother who's not like that. I go with her to the City Hall for a

An author photograph was published with
'If Only I Can Say "Peep"'

performance of *La Traviata* by the Eoan Group, a 'coloured'
company. She writes to Sirkka, 'I have always shared books
with my children but now for the first time, I have tasted the
pleasure of sharing concerts and ballet with Lyndall – and to
one who has no sister, who is an island in an alien but affectionate family, what a surprise, what a delight, to discover in
one's own child the close companion one has learned to lack.
The ballet has never seemed so enchanted with such a youth-
fresh dreamer beside me.'

At twelve, I'm allowed to read the stories she's turning out.
One is about a young man who is dying in hospital. To give
me this story is a gesture more intimate than maternal hugs.
For it reveals, as my mother must know it will, why her loss

before I was born had a painful twist to it, when the young
man turns towards the night nurse who tends him and away
from his girl. Recalling the fractured, imperfect days with Lou,
she thought 'Now you would have loved me.' Our closeness is
based on her writing and suffering. I'm proud to be her chosen
reader.

My mother's 'blessed years' last from the age of thirty-six to
thirty-nine, 1953 to 1956. When, later, I approach Emily
Dickinson's extraordinary fertility over the years 1859 to 1863,
my mother's *anni mirabiles* will come back to me. Both women
with thin, delicate bodies speak of an almost annihilating
'Bolt'. Both know the horror of a soul wrenched from the
body and put back askew. Yet I'm not thinking of sickness as
such, rather the way both use and transform sickness as part of
a visionary life: 'My Loss by sickness – Was it Loss', Emily
Dickinson asks, or was it 'Ethereal Gain'? My mother has a
similar compulsion to tell her unmentionable secret (what
Dickinson tantalisingly calls 'it'), but where Dickinson tells it
'slant', through metaphor, my mother tells it as a transform-
ing episode in a lifelong allegorical journey – the traditional
journey through the wilderness that originates in Exodus and
is re-enacted in the life of Jesus Christ, in the grail quests of
the Middle Ages, in Dante, in *Pilgrim's Progress*, and in the
poets Herbert, Hopkins and Eliot. My mother's metaphor
comes repeatedly from an actual scene: the abyss into which
a child can plummet as she edges, terrified, along the narrow
track over the Olifants River.

On the second night of Passover in late March 1955 my
mother has a full-on 'Bolt'. Next morning she relates the events
of that night. 'Avalanches of mental horror' descended on her
as she lay asleep in the sunroom. It's six years since the last
attack, and she'd come to believe herself safe from all but minor

The railway track over the Olifants River became
an imaginary scene of moral trial

flaps – so much so that she had neglected to take her bedtime
pills. That's one way of seeing it. What she actually says is that,
at Cille's during the Passover Seder, she felt her 'emptiness', neither a poet nor a person with work to do.

A second Bolt hits her the next night, and again, 'like shrap-
nel stuns / plunges to precipice edge'. A poem in three stanzas,
which she types and hands me to read, takes me with her into
this horror, stage by stage. At first there's no bridge; then, from
her entrails, she spins once more 'prayer's tightrope walk /
Slippery as panic'. Walk, she repeats to herself, 'with rod and
staff / through the death-edged psalm'.

Precarious after the attack, she plays a game with Pip that
evening, hoping to soothe herself. Then she turns on her side
and feels about to faint. It's warded off by holding, again, as in
a vice, to Psalm XXIII. Never, it seems to her, has she come so
near to the Shepherd who restoreth the soul. She holds to the

words, she says, 'with the intensity of deathbed prayer'. And this time something different happens, recorded on a torn scrap of paper. '*The aftermath of this attack seemed different because of the "Presence" I sensed near my glass prayer door as the soul was restored to the body.*' Instead of the usual miasma, she's pierced by three waves of 'Light'. The first enters her body; the second fills her body from end to end; and the third takes her into a Dickinson-dash on the frontier of consciousness, beyond what words can record.

My father, woken by her groans, came into the room, she recalls, and she thinks he must have sensed her state of grace without knowing it, for he said to her, 'Never have I loved you more than at this moment.'

A day or two later my father, mother, Pip and I are walking on the pipe-track at the back of Table Mountain, a high-up but level path along a series of peaks called the Twelve Apostles. It's late summer turning to autumn, when sunlight strikes the *fynbos* in gold shafts. Rhoda lingers behind, looking up at the still peaks looming above the ocean that is and was from the beginning, and there, at that moment, it seems as though a 'visionwhite fountain of Love' rushes upwards from her head.

Early that April an Israeli called Nahum Levin arrives in Cape Town. He's director of the Educational and Cultural Department in Jerusalem, and his mission is to forward study of the Hebrew language in the wider world.

It's seven years since the Declaration of the State of Israel in May 1948, and ever since, the country has called for the Return to a homeland for survivors of the Holocaust. At the same time, it's more than a refuge; it's a dream of recreating the Promised Land in Exodus, at source a dream rising out of a book, and part of the appeal of this dream lies in recovering the language of the Bible as living speech. Jews who may be thriving in countries like America, Canada, England and South Africa are invited to recast themselves as exiles – exiled two thousand years ago from the land of the Bible. After the displaced persons camps, in the wake of the war, the 'ingathering of the exiles' carries an immense imaginative charge, fortified by the even stronger tug of a socialist utopia. In the fifties Israel's political elite (including the first Prime Minister, David Ben-Gurion) comes from communal farms, the kibbutzim, committed to an ethical code of selflessness. This opens up a compelling biographical drama for the young and especially for young women: to turn our backs on a materialistic society based on 'getting and spending' and to shun its model of 'dolled-up and dependent femininity'. Mr Levin delivers a summation of this at the anniversary of independence celebration.

What is he *not* saying? This is a question for after years. It's not a question my mother and her friends ask in 1955. What they aren't told is that certain people are denied entry to Israel: returning Arabs with Palestinian passports; gentile wives of Jews; and their uncircumcised sons. This policy will relent to the latter two categories: wives can enter if they convert, and their sons if they submit to circumcision.

That May, when Mr Levin delivers another address, my mother is caught in a press photo, in the forefront of the listeners, beside Cille. She wears a round hat on her crisp, brown curls. How much is she taking in? For Levin, whose English is limited, is speaking in Yiddish, a language unknown to Rhoda.

Love shapes a life, Levin insists. Two kisses had quickened him. The first kiss had been high-minded: the metaphorical kiss of *shechinah* or enlightenment, an understanding of Jewish history, which had led him to the Promised Land. In 1922, as a young man, he had gone on *Aliyah*, gone 'up' to settle in what was then Palestine under the British Mandate. He appeals to his listeners to commit themselves to this redemptive journey and ensure that the next generation will follow. The other had been a farewell kiss from his mother in the Soviet Union, the sacrifice of 'a true Jewish mother' who expected, he says, never to see her son again.

What is a true mother? As a mother myself, looking back, I'm not too sure, except that a mother is bound to go wrong one way or another. That's what my generation of guilty mothers, the women's lib generation, will say ruefully to one another when our children question our determination to work outside the home. How can I judge Mr Levin's mother, two generations before mine, and far off amidst the Persian architecture of Bukhara? What did such a woman say to herself? Did she sacrifice maternal closeness for the sake of her son, as he declares a true mother would? Or was there some consolation in an offspring who would be in a position to rescue members of the family? Call it prudence, call it calculation, when my turn comes to go my mother (and others in apartheid South Africa) will be explicit about the obligation to go away as insurance against an unsafe future for loved ones who remain at home.

There's a photo of Mr Levin, one hand neatly in his pocket held in place by a thumb, the other palm open towards his mouth as though it were a microphone. Children should have twelve hours of Hebrew a week, he is saying. Mothers should encourage them go, when they take off to settle in the homeland. Expatriation will be hard – the climate, he concedes, will be enervating – yet this is the path to a rooted and genuine self, the only safe way into their future.

'It may be that this is difficult for the child, but it is best to let her go the hard way to happiness.'

Rhoda's chin is lifted towards the speaker, eyes keen yet half-covered by their lids as she enters this dream. Her rapt gaze can't

Rhoda (with hat) and friend Cille behind her take in the message
of Mr Levin, May 1955

be a response to words, which she can't translate. What she's responding to is rather the look and tone of a messenger, who appears to have walked out of the Bible, beckoning her to a further transformation.

11

At the Crossroad

In the mid-to-late fifties my mother changed, changed permanently, and with it, our tie. What I didn't know then was that my mother, at thirty-eight, was 'in love' with Levin, 'an elderly man of fifty-four'. So she confides to Sirkka. Only two other people know about Rhoda and Levin: one is Levin's friend and emissary, the Israeli Hebrew teacher Cille, twinkling, enthusing, who brings them together and acts as go-between for two people who lack a common language; the other is Harry, my father, as my mother will tell me years later, after he died. Even then she spoke in her tight, secrets voice – 'I can't tell you . . .' – and I continued to know too little until I came upon their letters amongst Rhoda's papers. And even then, what they say to each other feels far off, like voices coming from the Bible.

How is it that a man I saw only three times, and hardly to know, could – through his tie with my dreaming mother – mould my life? The first sighting happened on 13 December 1956, when I spotted a distinguished, white-haired man head and shoulders above a crowd. This was in HaYarkon Street,

parallel to the seafront in Tel Aviv. I was leaving the Gat
Rimon Hotel and he was making his way towards it.

That's him, I thought.

Not that my mother had said much, but I was used to significant silences, and understood in a casual way – I had just
turned fifteen – that we were here for him. We'd landed only
the night before.

The second and third times I saw him, during a year abroad
in 1959, were longer and somehow less memorable. In March
1959 I called on him in Jerusalem – at my mother's insistence.
I was seventeen, newly arrived, this time on my own, and too
miserable to feel anything but a reluctant sense of duty. He lived
in Jabotinsky Street (named after the Irgun militant whose ter-
rorists blew up the King David Hotel during the British
Mandate). It was a quiet area, with flats of pink-grey stone, near
the Prime Minister's residence.

Mr Levin had the weary air of a man who's recovering too
slowly from an operation. He intended to return to work as
Director of the World Hebrew Union; his aim, he said, was 'to
build a lasting edifice to the Hebrew language'.

His wife was short of delighted to see me, and why indeed
should she welcome someone's daughter come to tire her husband? In those days, eleven years after the state was declared, the
first question of every newcomer was 'Have you come to stay?'
The only acceptable answer was yes, and I couldn't say yes
because all I wanted was to fly back home. In minimal Hebrew,
I stumbled through evasions, not meeting his eye.

Afterwards he wrote to my mother, 'Your daughter's visit
made me very happy, because she has a spark of your soul in
hers.' He tells her what she would wish to hear, for I had no
sense of being 'seen' and nor, to be honest, did I try to answer
my mother's need by 'seeing' him.

To me, he didn't look like a lover, more a foreign admirer, to whom my mother referred in a deliberate way as a 'friend'. I did understand that Mr Levin, with his grave, reserved, rather aloof face, was a very special friend and, as a high-minded educator, fitted my mother's cast of mind, but I made little of it since she was given to Meetings with strangers. In case this sounds peculiar, which of course in a way it was, it's fair to add that in the late forties and fifties friendships did seem 'predestined'. That's Muriel Spark's word for the manner of friendship then. It wasn't a matter of liking or not, she said; even if liking fell away, the friendship went on.

Even so, my mother meant something more momentous. She adopted 'Meeting' from the philosopher Martin Buber, who says, 'all real living is meeting'.

It's an April night when Rhoda meets this stranger at Cille's new house in Golf Links Estate in Plumstead. (Cille sheds her light from this unlikely spot, a suburban housing development.) A mild night in early autumn. The window is open. Through it, Rhoda hears strains of Mozart as she leaves, walking down the path to wait for her lift at the gate. And as she steps into deepening shadow the stranger follows and says, 'Why are you so beautiful to me?'

'Well, you see I am blessed.'

Since 1952 Rhoda has had signs of the grace bestowed on her as 'God's child'. The stranger's awareness of this secret self and the drama of their exchange come like 'a bolt of confirmation' that she's singled out for some purpose. Levin is a 'messenger'; his coming carries the authority of 'annunciation'. Afterwards, she aligns it with the destiny Isaac confers on Jacob when he grants him his blessing. It troubles her not at all to reconfigure the Patriarchs' drama, reserved for father and son, as a scene where a chosen woman can be centre stage.

In the Bible, the chosen are re-named. Accordingly, Rhoda

brings out her identity as Tsviah, the gazelle. That's how she signs her letters to Levin, while he calls her 'my sister, my bride' from the Song of Songs.

During the remaining weeks of his stay Levin and Rhoda meet seven times. When he's taken to visit the orphanage Rhoda diverts the tour to the backroom library, and there points to the shelf of Judaica, wanting him to know her as a reader digging into these books in his field.

At Cape Point, where the currents of the icy Atlantic and warmer Indian Ocean meet, they commit themselves to an all-time bond. Levin speaks of 'the two oceans which witnessed the covenant that was made between us forever'. His eye casts back into pre-history; he's not seeing Rhoda's sea, the seething element where I watch her frolic and run out, radiant, dripping, unfastening her cap. He uses the biblical word, *brit*, the Covenant the Lord enters into with humankind after the Deluge.* Bonded to an old-new People embodied in Levin (who declares he is hers '*ve'ad olam*', for all eternity) she is swept by a purpose to her existence for which she has prayed.

Her first step along Levin's route, while he's still in town, is to attend a debate on a recent law to ban secular marriage, proposed in the Knesset. Her protest is published a week later in the *Jewish Chronicle*, drawing on the Bible to pose her argument against what we now call fundamentalism. 'Are we to sow … the vision of the Prophet or the Scribe?'

This catches the eye of a women's charitable organisation. The Bnoth Zion, the Daughters of Zion, whose focus is on nurseries and vocational training, resolve to try out one of Levin's recommendations: a study group for women. My

* *Brit* is also the word for male circumcision, signalling the maleness of the Covenant made with Abraham.

mother is invited to run it and accepts with alacrity, though in the past she's had no part in communal activity. Harry, Pip and I are proud of her move into the public eye. She's keen to start with the prophets.

After Levin leaves, his many letters to Rhoda never mention his wife or son. I notice something else missing: his home address. My mother's replies are sent to a post office box in Jerusalem. Levin's Hebrew is graceful, and accessible in Cille's translations, yet in a curious way it's distant, the language of a luftmensch who has dreamt himself into an ancient frame of mind where men, with souls in the making, are on easy terms with their Maker. The language of my mother is indeed 'turned' to her Maker, yet she's planted on the earth, and she speaks (as do her favourite Bible tales) from within the net of family ties.

Reading these letters now, I'm puzzled by my inability to know Levin through the written word. Why is he so unknowable? And then it occurs to me: all his letters are the same. An oddly unvarying voice comes from a stratosphere of eternal love, too elevated to notice who my mother is and what she's like at home. In fact, home, the whole edifice of domestic existence with a mother at the centre, does not appear to exist.

It does not surprise me to discover that Levin's mother, that 'true Jewish mother' kissing him goodbye for ever, settled in America. She preferred America to being near her son. Whether she migrated before or after Levin's pictured scene of maternal sacrifice doesn't matter; he floats too high to know her.

Was Levin like a guru, drawing my impressionable mother into a tie that can eventually distance family if they don't yield to where his master-dream is taking her? Can Levin, in fact, be that most dangerous kind of enemy who sees himself as God's instrument? For the correspondent Levin reflects is not the person I know as a daughter; to him my mother exists as a pure and beautiful soul – no more. Nor does he lend his attention to the study and work she takes up as his devotee, which she mentions sparingly.

'I too – although I have not spoken to you of this – have Work to do.'

Only the capital letter indicates how crucial Work is to her, how excited she is at the prospect of teaching. There are no capital letters in Hebrew. In translation* this would have vanished for a man who is anyway too far off to see, as her family do, how carefully she prepares her classes, how they absorb her and how mystical poems have shaped her, above all Emily Brontë declaring if suns and universes ceased to be, 'Every Existence would exist in thee'.

Like Emily Brontë baking bread and Emily Dickinson kneeling on a rug as she digs her garden, Rhoda's visionary existence does not detach her from domestic life. A month after Levin's departure she writes humorously of our school holidays in Knysna, a rainy town on the Indian Ocean favoured by British expats:

We are living on a lonely island in the midst of a silver-finned lagoon which flows between cliff-heads into the furling waves of the sea. At first it seemed inhabited only by Colonels and 'she-Colonels' but as I expected, these walking-sticks soon grew human and these umbrellas unfolded! Indeed I am already heart-to-heart with one of the she-Colonels, a salty old darling.

I remember that the she-Colonel thought me odd, at thirteen, to be carrying around a volume of Wordsworth. In the inviting bookshop, well placed next to the tearoom in

---

* Levin translates Rhoda's letters in English, while he writes to her in Hebrew.

Stuttafords department store in the centre of town, where mothers treat daughters to anchovy toast, my mother had encouraged me to use book tokens for my birthday to buy this volume of poems. She thinks one should buy books for life.

How much Wordsworth I read, if any, I can't now recall, but imprinted on memory is a childbirth scene I come upon in another book my mother recommended on the strength of my childhood fascination for the French Revolution: a biography of Marie Antoinette by Stefan Zweig. I'm appalled by her wedding night at fourteen, only a year older than I, put into bed with a clumsy bridegroom, the future Louis XVI. But far worse was giving birth in public, before the assembled nobility at Versailles. The girl had to keep up appearances in the midst of birth pains while onlookers chatted and sipped champagne. This is what stays with me from that biography: a girl exposed and fainting from her effort to preserve decorum.

I plead with my mother to let me join a Good Hope classmate on holiday with her mother at the Wilderness, the honeymoon resort, not far from Knysna. Scampering along a corridor we glimpse, through an open door, the bedding rolled back, and I wonder how it is for the pretty blonde bride with a husband who looks like he's made to kick a rugby ball. At thirteen I have no hope of real life outside the books in which I live.

Later that year, spring comes 'in puffs of morning air'. Enclosed in a letter of 5 September is a flower from the mountain where, Rhoda tells Levin, 'I drove my daughter yesterday. All day we lay among the daisies which have snowed over Signal Hill – sleeping, eating, reading good (and writing bad!) poetry, while the sea below shone motionless as the sky.'

My mother is so awakened by teaching the Book that in February 1956 she embarks on three years of university study with a view to reading the Hebrew Bible in the original language. In February–March 1956, in a drafted report to Levin, she marks the date when the Bible venture takes over her life.

> *I seem to have come to the crossroads between my writing life and a life of service – between my creative and my missionary self . . . Unknowingly, you have been the apostle of the missionary in me, and during the past year this side has taken precedence over me – who ever since I could read have struggled to express myself in writing.*

I'm shaken to come upon this dilemma because it shows how consciously my mother surrendered her very self, as if Jane Eyre were to surrender to the missionary St John Rivers and subdue herself to his call.

So it happened that my mother remade herself to fit a cause. Not that she hadn't always cared for that cause, but until Levin came into her life her sensitive feelers led her. The combined call of Cille and Levin broke into Rhoda's poetry life, broke with a somewhat insensitive force, carrying a vein of oblivion amidst the appeal of personal claims. Promoting their language, they did not pause to consider what English meant to Rhoda as a writer. Patriots both, they did not question their claims.

This alters her. No longer an obscure watcher of obscure drama, she's planted on a public highway where great oaks can't be uprooted.

At times my mother sweeps me along; at other times I argue. When she praises the virtuous woman of the Bible, whose price is above rubies, I squirm for my sex. Price. Rubies. How can my mother endorse that estimate?

At night, when she's splashed her face – slap, slap, drip; slap, slap, drip – she reverts to her old self. She'll look up from the basin, wet and fresh. In her powder blue, tucked Barbizon nightie, washed clean of make-up, she's seen at her best in bed, where she lies, propped on pillows, wrapped in silence, reading. Moonflowers, long, creamy funnels in the Finnish vase on the bedside table, send out their scent at night.

I sit on her bed, as she'd once sat on mine, and she talks in the old way with all her feelers waving. Why, I wonder, has she relegated discrimination to the margins of her daytime life: the kind of judgement she can still relish in Jane Austen ('A lucky contraction of the brow had rescued Mrs Ferrars' face from the disgrace of insipidity by giving it the strong character of pride and ill-nature'). According to her revised moral grounds, it's wrong to speak ill of anyone.

I prod her newly anodyne comments about individuals, and question her retreat from judgement. What does she really think of the headmaster of an unruly afternoon school for plodding through the Hebrew of the Bible as a set of grammatical issues? (The headmaster has renamed me Leah – that weak-eyed, unwanted bride. Leah is stupid at Hebrew, crawling from letter to letter, unable to see a word as a whole.)

And what does my mother think of Uncle Eddie, my father's sponging brother who fancies himself a singer? But my mother will not be drawn

That's a way of putting it, not very satisfactory. I should perhaps say that grace gives her access to universal love. Yet I don't want her to rise above the way she's shaped me as her companion. Nor do I want her to surrender her judgement to the claims of a community. To my gaping teenage gaze, she seems to disappear into consensus and close the door.

Rhoda plans to take me with her to Israel after her end-of-year examinations in November 1956. A reunion with Levin is 'intended to strengthen and renew us in our separate lives'.

What she hopes for most is a renewal of grace, which she
fears to have lost. I see that this is bound up with a fear of putting herself in a culpable position with a married man. At just
that time, the Suez Crisis starts. As she hesitates about going, she
reverts to being ill. This adds to the ordeal of sitting her exam
in the vast Jameson Hall of the university. Everyone around her
bending over their papers is about nineteen. She is thirty-nine,
in an era before mature students. Perhaps she should wear
puffed sleeves to disguise her age, she jokes. As a precaution (her
illness is not disclosed), she asks for a glass of water, not to sip
but to splash her face if needed. Under these circumstances it's
a feat to get a first, though in her deprecating way she dismisses
it as 'baby Hebrew'.

My mother has sent me to the Movement, as it's called, a
youth group of idealistic intellectuals, and I'm agog about the
alternative it offers to a girl who's what the fifties call 'a social
misfit'. My face is still wall-to-wall freckles, hardly improved by
adolescent spots. Relieved from the false cheer of a wallflower
at parties, I take to folk dancing and socialism. The aim of the
Movement is to send people to Israel, and my mother's plan
plays into my wish to show willing and gain credibility. Though
she's plainly ill, I press her to go. We fly to Tel Aviv on 11
December 1956.

Her reunion with Levin takes place the night after we arrive. It
appears a coincidence that a dashing South African, serving in
the elite Nahal division of the Israeli army, asks me to come
with him that very night to a Sephardi wedding. Since I've
never had a date, I take this to be the miracle of Israel. I see only
now that this date was orchestrated by my mother with the help
of a former Good Hope schoolfriend called Isabella, who ran
a South African club. Isabella's thin, square mouth is all smiles
as she greets us and introduces Barry, the soldier, as soon as we

The first morning in Tel Aviv, December 1956

arrive. Although my mother needs me as her travelling companion, it's essential to have me out of the way when Levin arrives.

It's when Barry collects me at the door of the Gat Rimon Hotel that I catch that glimpse of Levin coming like a comet through the crowd. My eyes turn back to Barry who is affable, ready to please, a familiar manner of men at home, yet in this foreign scene feels protective. He lifts me above the milling wedding guests to see the bridegroom circle the bride seven times. My body zings to the touch of his hands around my waist. The firmness of his hold is reassuringly casual.

Barry does not ask me out again. Did I do something wrong?

I change from stovepipe slacks and a sweater to a pleated skirt, socks and lace-ups. It consoles me to be a schoolgirl after all, as plain as plain can be. In the same kind of clothes, a straight grey skirt with a pink thread and a pink buttoned-up jersey, I fly to Athens. My unworldly mother waves me off, unconcerned about a girl barely fifteen travelling alone, and perhaps my prim clothes protect me, for nothing happens to jar my innocence. I jaunt off to climb the Acropolis, and late at night catch a plane crossing Africa. This Greek plane is not in great shape. At dawn next morning we are grounded at one of the stops, Nairobi. Feeling rather grown-up to be coping in Kenya, I lunch out-doors alongside matronly colonials – who enquire, as well they might, about a lone schoolgirl – at a British club in town, and then there's another plane to Johannesburg, and the puffing, two-day train across the Karoo to Cape Town, in time for the new school year.

January 1957. Miss Tyfield, her academic gown slipping back off her narrow shoulders, enters the Standard Nine classroom. I open my mother's copy of *Wuthering Heights* – illustrated with haunting woodcuts – and meet the ghost of Catherine Earnshaw putting her hand through the window; we meet the untamed Heathcliff who's calling to her; and we revel in the dream of deathless love.

'Their affinity,' Miss Tyfield explains to nice girls who loll on Clifton Beach, angling for a date. She writes 'affinity' on the blackboard. Meanwhile, my mother is staying on, meeting Levin from time to time, eventually in his stronghold, Jerusalem. There's a gap here. What happened with Levin? Was she 'crowned' after all on 'the throne of Jerusalem'? That's how she speaks, secrets furled in allegory. All I know is that, after two months away, she flies home. She comes back in a bad way.

*

It's the old illness, shuddering, it seems to her, on the brink of insanity.

A poem, 'Undine', written a month after Rhoda's return and sent to Levin, makes it clear that a relationship between a 'sea-bride' and a dreaming man is bound to go awry because embodiment, much as the sea-bride longs for it, proves impossible. It's a poem haunted by loss, as an opportunity ebbs away.

Levin misreads the poem. Instead of seeing the elegiac gesture of a sea-bride retreating towards her own element, Levin reads what he expects and wants the poem to be: an affirmation of 'the eternity of our love'. His reply comes in the same rather monotonously elevated tone. A more alert lover, reading 'Undine', might have realised how delicately ready she was to be embodied, but the grace for this – the grace he was to confer – did not come.

For this, she blames only herself. 'There was no excuse for going,' she mutters. 'I have no excuse.'

While she resists further invitations from Levin to join him in England and America, she continues to pursue the nationalist dream. Rhoda is not alone in living more fully in this dreamland than in the place where we actually are.

Assorted Israelis – the teachers and *shlihot* recommended by Nahum Levin in the memorandum he left behind – descend on South Africa during the later fifties.

These men have been through the military; they are forceful; their speech comes in brief bursts. Movement girls are taught a form of self-defence with sticks, called *kepap*. When Yoav Tibon, the *shaliah*, rushes at me with a lifted stick I quail. Unless I hold up my stick crossways to block his, he'll see I'm a coward. Yoav's wife keeps in the background, confined to household tasks. I wouldn't wish to be in her place.

Yoav has a solution for everyone: to settle on kibbutz. It's the best life. To make this choice takes a special resolve, he warns, daring us to take the risk. By risk, Yoav means that students should drop their professional training. Yoav's words come out as imperatives without nuance. 'Burn your bridges.' 'Crystallise your aims.' His foreignness, not so much his accent as this unblinking directness, is unnerving. Can you take it, this manner seems to ask, can you nerve yourself to leave home for ever? Have you the courage to make a choice, right now, at sixteen or twenty, that will determine the rest of your life? What we enthusiastically call indoctrination has the appeal of a challenge. Will we defy parents' expectations that we'll live the same bourgeois lives?

It's almost disappointing when my mother dissipates this challenge because she ardently favours emigration to the Promised Land – wants it as much if not more than I. Sharing this national dream, as I'd shared her solitary dreams, I think little of the divide to come, and welcome too blithely the test it presents.

12

Dividing Dreams

As school ends, I go out with the jokey student, Siamon, the night when I blurt out what has never been said aloud before. To utter the taboo word for my mother's illness feels more sudden and reckless than to have declared how much I like him. At sixteen I'd seen his green eyes light up when he spoke or smiled. For the last six months I'd thought of him in tandem with Movement dreams. My disclosure, binding him to my secret, and his serious response, lasts till three in the morning, while I swing back and forth on our gate. Far from the romantic fantasies I've let loose in the course of the crush, here is sense and understanding.

Siamon comes from the dairy-farming region of the west coast, where his father, a rabbi, who'd died some years before, had served a scattered community. Siamon's first language was Afrikaans, until he went to boarding school at the age of fifteen. His speech sounds blunt to my ear, infused with Afrikaans phrases, like the language of other up-country folk when they speak English. There's a directness to Afrikaans, an energy in the breath behind its consonants, that had appealed to my mother from her early days amidst Afrikaners at Klaver, and I pick up this appeal.

My mother takes me shopping to fit me out with clothes for settling in Israel. During the last year at school I've been saying that I want to go, and my mother supports me. In truth, she's more active than I when it comes to specific plans. It's increasingly unthinkable to let down my schoolmate and fellow member of the Movement, Jasmine, who's going too. We are to learn Hebrew; then work on a kibbutz; then join an American programme over the summer at the Hebrew University; and then take the Hebrew entrance examination for the university later in the year.

What incentive there was fades in January 1959 after I 'go steady' with Siamon, six weeks before Jasmine and I are due to depart. He's at the start of the fourth year at medical school, the first hands-on year in the hospital, and like most Movement students he hasn't succumbed to Yoav's urging to drop out. Kissing for hours on the rocks with the Atlantic breakers pounding about us, I don't think about leaving. It's my mother who dictates my letter of application to the organiser of the American programme. It's she who packs my suitcase. It's filled with modish

shortie pyjamas, wool sweaters, sensible shoes and a jar of Nescafé (unobtainable where I'm going), 'To equip you,' my mother says, 'for the future.'

What it means for her to send her daughter away, perhaps for good, she confides to Sirkka. 'For me it would be a happiness to continue my burgeoning friendship with her in close companionship. Nevertheless if she wins a way into the Hebrew University or takes root in the soil of Israel that too will be a joy to me.'

She commends my 'contribution to family life'. Her words convey a tone of ending, as though I'm leaving with the finality of her father leaving home. The linking narrative of Jewish history, a subject she now teaches alongside the Bible, is an obligatory migration from one country to another.

As she packs neatly in folds of tissue paper, her voice advises me to be patient with the hurdles ahead. I hardly hear, much less imagine any hurdles because I'm dreaming about the sweet sorrow of parting from Siamon.

'I'm looking forward to a sad love affair,' I tell him, and it isn't wholly a joke. Nothing in my experience so far can match up to the romantic drama of my mother's youth: the loss of Lou. The sadness impresses me as all the more poignant since she doesn't speak of it. All I know are hints and guesses from her hospital story. I'd page through her photograph albums of the thirties, wondering which young man he was.

My sadness explodes on the night of 18 February after the train pulls out of the station. That night I can't sleep, and at four in the morning leave the compartment to get a drink of water at the end of the swaying corridor. Only I am awake, I and the train, rushing together through the darkness. The low bush of the veld stretches to an infinity of solitude. The rhythm of the wheels, soothing on previous journeys, seems (I write to Siamon) 'like the "deliberate speed" of God's footsteps in "The Hound of Heaven", driving me against my will along a certain path'.

International flights leave from Johannesburg, and at this first stop en route Jasmine and I are to stay at Evermore, where Basil continues to live with his sculptor wife Naomi, another of my mother's sisters. Almost the last words of advice from my mother were a reminder to be 'cheerful and helpful' with her family 'who are helping you with their affection'.

I sense uncomfortably that she's intimating something about gratitude, and see now that she was trying to tell me – not too bluntly – that my venture abroad, and all she'd bought to equip it, depended indirectly on the largesse of my uncles. In other words she, not my father, is funding all this. It's not something my father would have pushed, he who had given up study abroad because he took a frugal – we might say, short-sighted – view of education. I leave replete with gifts, scented bath powder and coloured soaps, and with pats on the back for doing the right thing.

Everyone we know talks up the approved narrative: a latter-day exodus from our own Egypt, the decadent luxury of wealthy whites who thrive off the backs of impoverished blacks, often migrants parted from their own families, in apartheid South Africa. Entering into the Promised Land is to be a kind of moral cure.

I want to pause at take-off to hear once more a phrase my mother repeats: I am, she says, 'an extension' of herself. This may be a truism of universal motherhood and daughterhood, yet given the glowing eye of my mother's narrative and my tie to her imagination I'm about to experience a new birth. At this moment my life is energised and reprogrammed by my mother to enact and fulfil the Return. Her weekly letters over the next year will attempt to reset the programme when, at a distance, I deviate. At issue between us is her denial that I'm to enter an alien environment. It's an article of faith that the Holy Land will not be alien.

My mother embraces Israelis as 'bone of my bone', and speaks not of 'them' but of 'we'. The same identification prevails in the Movement. Neither they nor my dreamy mother has prepared me for predators on the prowl. Within hours of landing at Lydda airport, I allow myself to be picked up by an Iraqi. I think it's fine because he's Jewish and will see, as boys at home can, that I'm a nice girl, unavailable for casual romps. In fact, I'm keen to cross the colour bar in a country where races are not divided by law.

The Iraqi offers to fetch me that very night to see the sights of Natanya, a sleepy seaside town north of Tel Aviv, and a bus ride away from the suburban straggle ('pretty villages', my mother had imagined) where we have come to learn Hebrew at an ulpan. I think this grown-up man is giving me the welcome with open arms all newcomers are said to receive. In his taxi, parked in the woods, I fight him off and wrench open the door of his car. Bellows of obscenity – without understanding much Hebrew, I do know his language is vile – reach my ears as I flee through the trees, uncertain what direction to take. Next day in the dining room at the hostel an English girl, the head-girl type with a fair plait down her back and fresh from

Roedean School, makes an audible aside. It's about girls who go out with taxi drivers.

What happened is too humiliating to mention, certainly not in letters home. They would think me stupidly naive to bring this on myself.

Ulpan Akiva is run by Shulamit Katznelson, whom my mother fancies a friend. There's no sign of friendship beyond a courtesy cup of coffee in her house. She does not trouble herself unduly about individuals. We belong with the flotsam: displaced Romanians with whom, at first, I share a room; sturdy Polish housewives who live locally and have been here long enough to grasp the language; and gallant single women who need suitable husbands – sadly, there's no one suitable on the present course.

I admire a Lebanese girl called Vered, aged about nineteen, who has left her mother in Beirut and come via Cyprus because the border between Israel and the Lebanon is closed: no phone connection, no postal service. Cut off in this way, Vered speaks of her mother with mature concern, adores her, yet is too promising to linger in the Lebanon – Vered also plans to learn the language and go on to the Hebrew University.

As we sit in one another's rooms, stirring our precious Nescafé with sugar to make a rim of foam, we joke that middle-aged Shulamit is out to find her man, and it comes as no surprise that she does later marry a twenty-something Argentinian.

Holding herself apart amidst her divans and Arab tat, the directress appears now and then in the communal dining room to talk up the Return. Her rousing speeches are disconcertingly close to those of my mother.

'However tumultuous & bewildering the existence of the everyday,' my mother writes, 'be awake to the realisation that you are participating in this ingathering of the Exiles and this unfolding in history of a Divine plan which the prophets have envisioned. I did not expect you to find this easy.'

I can't take this in for two reasons. One is that it doesn't take long to notice the hostile apartness of Arab inhabitants whose past has to be obliterated by the ideology of the Return. At the same time the ideology of the new state compels immigrants to surrender their children to remaking according to the hardy, pioneering model shaped by school and army.

It comes to my ears that some time earlier Levin, then close to the centre of power as Director for the Cutural Absorption of Immigrants, had been involved in an incident that almost brought down Ben Gurion's government. The 'Magic Carpet' migration of a million Yemenites took place in 1951. Crowded in immigrant camps called Ma'abarot, the Yemenites protested against the removal of their children to secular schools. This policy, masterminded by Levin, had enforced a divide from parents, who'd brought their past with them. Levin's 'nation-building' generation had believed they were justified in doing whatever it took to compel adaptation to the model they themselves represented.

The other reason I can't take in my mother's dream of the land the prophets envisioned is that I'm not in the place she thinks. A fantasist myself, as adept as she at being somewhere else, I dream my way back, the train rolling into the station and Siamon on the platform, his varsity blazer slung over a shoulder – even though he too, a stalwart of the Movement, wants me to adapt. At the same time he lets me say what I feel, and that freedom to admit what would be inadmissible to everyone else proves a lifeline. The letters I write to him all the time (for when I'm not putting pen to paper, I'm saving up details and running up the scale of emotion) hold the kernel of a different life.

One of my first assignments, in March 1959, is to visit Nahum Levin in Jerusalem and deliver a book from my mother. She has alerted him that I will bring what she has pored over, 'sharing (in imagination) certain poems and pictures, as I do share all loveliness & all harmony with you my dear brother being ... In this book I visit you.'

I'm to report on Mr Levin, but though my mother is waiting to hear, I neglect to write. Meanwhile, four letters arrive from her, questioning my silence.

Jasmine's mother, she tells me, has word of our 'dream-weekend' in Jerusalem. When her friends enquire, my mother has to have recourse to what Jasmine's mother relays every time she phones my mother to proclaim 'fabulous' news from her daughter.

In fact, Jasmine is almost as miserable as I, and in one way worse off: she's detaching from her Movement boyfriend, and my backward longings hold up her ultimately successful effort to keep the future in sight.

My mother wants details. Testing if our sisterhood will prevail on her to hear the truth – how far will she draw in her feelers? – I make bold to offer the unheated dorm in winter, the glee of a matronly Romanian as she tries on my clothes, and idling men with oiled hair who eye up girls when we get off the bus in Natanya.

This is the wrong script. Any gesturing towards lacklustre reality reflects badly on the non-dreamer. As it is, I refrain from confessing more serious non-dreams: the rudeness of men in military uniform shoving other hitch-hikers out of their way as they clamber onto a passing truck; their talk that doesn't lend itself to other points of view; and a close-up of an Israeli woman at home, the wife of Jasmine's uncle. His wife's existence seems bounded by washing nappies and sterilising bottles. Motherhood, it appears, turns a woman into an *ozeret*.

I know in advance that *ozeret* will displease my mother – displease her with me. It's hard now to convey the disgrace of these observations, as much as if a Christian daughter were to cast a cold eye on Bethlehem, or a Muslim daughter on Mecca.

'Being catapulted suddenly from a luxurious life has darkened your vision of things,' my mother decides. 'I am troubled that this inevitable "desert journey" should be associated in your mind with Israel. On the other hand for a mature being who has fought through to wholeness, Israel could become in retrospect the country of your growth.'

'Luxurious' stings. The mirror my mother holds up reflects a spoilt girl who can't put up with minor privations. Yet physical conditions are not really the problem, and her further conclusion that I crave a 'millionaire' existence comes as a puzzling reproach.

My mother enjoys her dream of how she'd manage: how, if she were 'allowed' to be here herself, she'd live 'in a little room' with a few books and nibble on blintzes in a modest dairy restaurant. This is unlike her usual life.

For the Sabbath dinner on Friday nights, my mother orders flowers to be delivered; gladioli come arranged stiffly in a bowl. She adds more graceful flowers from the garden: a silver vase of fragrant sweet peas and small posies of pansies with their upturned faces. Three courses – gefilte fish, soup and casserole – are prepared by Lenie, and a light cake, a variety of melktert, comes out of the oven when Lenie serves tea later in the evening. It's unthinkable for my mother to do all this herself. But I turn out to be unfit in other ways. My mother asks me to put a shoulder to the communal effort of making where I am a better place. I have to own that my unwillingness precedes any good reason, and has to do with the habit of living through dreams: my dream-narrative carries me back homewards. Divested of my mother's eye for the red lacquer beak of a bird, her ear for a baboon's 'bacchanalian cries', her decided tastes in literature, in fact, divested of my mother I hardly exist: 'a very ordinary girl', my diary admits.

In this stagnant place, I'm dormant. Nothing contradicts my sense of failure, an embarrassment to my mother and a burden to Jasmine. Dead days, alleviated by reading *Cry, the Beloved Country* and Alan Paton's later novel, which I like even more, *Too Late the Phalarope*, about a forbidden love affair between a black and a white. I curl up in the unwanted tomorrows of a mediocre boarding school. We will hibernate here.

In June my mother relents. This is occasioned by a German refugee, Miss Hirschberg, one of Cille's friends whom my mother wished me to visit. A retired teacher of great charm and empathy, she draws out my impressions.

I blurt out how crude boys appear; how lacking in self-respect to stare fixedly at girls passing in the street. 'Revolting!'

'It's the fault of poverty,' she explains. 'Parents here are in such a hurry to earn money that they cannot waste time on contemplation and learning.'

She takes my hand and closes her other hand over it – oh, the balm of affection – and then shakes her head. 'Seventeen is too young to start a new life alone. One is still too unsettled within oneself and the home atmosphere is too necessary.'

Unexpectedly, I receive a letter from my mother in a softened voice. Miss Hirschberg, it seems, has intervened in my favour, soothing my mother's disappointment.

'My dear, your own feelings and yours alone, must decide your future course,' she says. 'And whatever you decide will make me happy.'

Even so, I don't dare crawl home at once, as I long to do. Even Siamon warns that I wouldn't be able to hold up my head. The only face-saving plan is to stay out the year.

*

My mother visits in August. By this time, after a spell on kib-butz, I've joined a group of friendly Americans who have come to Jerusalem for their Junior year abroad. As my mother and I stroll about the ultra-orthodox quarter of Mea Shearim and the Bezalel Art Gallery, she tells me that Nahum Levin is ill. When she leaves in early September her last words are a request: 'Please go and see him for me.' So I see him for the third and last time, and have to write that he has a resurgence of cancer. Rhoda confides to Sirkka alone that things are going wrong in her home, 'as must happen when the roof-tree is innerly, secretly on the verge of collapse'.

In December, she writes him what she knows will be her last letter. 'I have been walking in your footsteps – far, far behind you, but in your footsteps . . .* I am speaking of your message in my classes and also in public talks. I wanted to be a writer, but since your coming I struck out on a new path.'

Levin dies on 16 December. I cable my mother. I know she expects it, and nothing further is said.

I'm staying for the first university term in Jerusalem, running until January 1960. In a preliminary English test in practical criticism (a test of analysis with the name of the author with-held), it's luck to find a poem by Emily Dickinson, one I've read with my mother: 'A Bird came down the Walk – '. I unroll my feathers like her bird whose flight 'rowed him softer Home – '. But now the Hebrew entrance exam looms, and I warn my mother I'm not up to it.

'I must confess that I shall be disappointed if you don't pass your Hebrew exam,' she replies. 'After all it is the only subject you have really studied this year, and has now become the "practical purpose" of your stay.'

---

* No omission.

I fail. My mother refrains from further comment.

Since I'm no longer eligible for the Hebrew University, my return is now definite. The prospect of our renewed companionship makes my mother miss me more. She doesn't say this; it's what Siamon relays after they discuss my failure. He too does not express disappointment; instead he spells out what he wants from me, 'an open, sympathetic mind and an eager will to learn'. Then he adds, 'if you have the ready mind I shall try and instil the eagerness (if that is not presumptuous on my part) and we shall look for certainty in this crazy mixed-up world together'.

Siamon's emotional intelligence provided an
influential complement to my mother as dreamer

These attainable aims come as relief from my mother's unful-
filled dream. Here is someone not given to dreaming – not in
my mother's intense way – who is opening up a different kind
of possibility if I will lend myself to his idea. I respect his intellectual confidence and, through our letters (three a week), have
come to see how understanding he is.

Siamon's offer of learning in place of dreaming is not meant
to supplant my mother. He assures me of her wish to have me
back, yet there's a changing sense of home, centred less on my
mother and more on a mentor of sorts. It's not that I can turn
from her poetic ways with words, but having tested the heat of
ideology I crave a cooler climate. Mine is a mother who put
ideology before a relationship, while Siamon has done the
reverse. His move to limit damage opens the gate to a shift of
allegiance.

13

The Way Down

All the while I was abroad, the dream that kept me going had been a variation on the return of the native. Back home, it's not quite the same. My mother, more successfully than I, had detached herself: her friendships, her groups, her recuperative bathes and walks along the sea had closed over my departure. It's incomprehensible to her that the daughter who returns remains unmoved by the privilege of living in the Promised Land, reclaimed by the people of the Book. While there, my longing to speak the truth, as I saw it, was blocked by her conclusion: a girl who didn't take to this storied place must be misguided. Safely home, I give way to an impulse to try out truth once more.

On the first Friday night, at a dinner with a white cloth, candles and *kiddush* in the garden, my mother's many relations, on holiday at the Cape, sit up expectantly when I'm asked to say a few words about my experience. Aware of the risk, I state what's wrong: the militarisation; the know-all bark; the eyes-front walk of students released from the army. If I'm specific

enough and others listen, will my mother hear? No. Her face
tenses with dismay at such a daughter.

When I register for the first-year English course, my mother
decides to do the same. We are to be a mother-and-daughter
duo for the three years of English at the University of Cape
Town, and in sharing daily occupations I feel embraced by her
once more, once more her helper.

She scoffs at herself as her daughter's dependant: 'I follow her
into classrooms,' she tells her own followers. I drive us in
Cherry, her Morris Minor, to the campus perched on the slope
of the mountain. English is her natural subject, bliss after the
challenge of Hebrew.

'I am happy to be in touch with poetry again,' she writes to
Roseveare in London. Emily Dickinson, she suggests, would be
a fertile subject for the City Lit poetry group.

In the early sixties, T. S. Eliot is the greatest living poet. A
few years before, he'd addressed an audience of twelve thousand

on the subject of literary criticism, in a football stadium in Minnesota. The media quote his dicta from on high.

Eliot's most celebrated dictum proclaims the idea of a poet's impersonality. Yet my mother perceives that the poems are not so impersonal as they appear. She convinces me that the poet's first marriage to nervy, distraught Vivienne bore on his private waste land. The Eliots' letters, still buried in archives at this point, will later bear out my mother's intuition.

For us two, lectures are futile, groping in obscure corners. Only through my mother can I escape the current mode of reading Eliot as a hunt for the sources of the literary allusions that stud the poems' surface – as though Eliot wrote poems to provide sport for academics.

No lecturer, no critic apart from my mother, appears to offer a coherent reading. Instead of a career divided between the sophisticated satirist, who suddenly, in 1927, turns pious, she sees a single trajectory of what Eliot himself termed 'the sequence that culminates in faith'. She spells out the alternatives of 'the way up', the poet's ephemeral moments of vision, and 'the way down', the dark night of the soul – a psychic ordeal designed to reshape the imperfect self as a vessel the divine spirit might fill.

Shared reading, especially Eliot, brings my mother and me close again. As in childhood, our relationship thrives on books – to my benefit. For her, there's the 'warm soil' of a daughter's companionship. On campus, she tells Sirkka, 'I no long walk by myself and wave my wild tail but live pleasantly in the warm company of L & her friends.' She's 'surprised & pleased' that I attend her Bible class for students.

While I'm relieved to fly again under the wing of her independent mind, I'm also aware of a new responsibility to protect her from feeling lost amongst the vast number of students who sign up for English. I'm never unaware how a dispirited mood can jump the barriers to an attack. If she's precarious in the morning before we leave or jittery over an essay, I worry. I try to help in practical ways like finding the recommended books and driving her car. She's a tense driver, and if her pills fog her she's vague and forgetful.

So I'm relieved in another way when it's time to dash off to Monica Wilson's lectures in social anthropology and Dr Davenport's lectures on South African history, courses chosen because they don't derive from 'overseas'. I delight in their focus on home ground, the implied anti-colonial stance that here, in our local setting, is something to find out, untwisting the bigoted version of colonisation that school texts had imposed.

In the Cape school-leaving examinations I had a poor C for English. That grade determines my tutorial group, and my marks for essays stick in the average B range while my mother gets a well-deserved A for an essay on the moral comedy of Jane Austen. I try repeatedly to drop English in favour of subjects where there's hope of doing better, but then miss literature so much that I switch back. This decision to stay with the subject I love invariably feels right.

Siamon still means to emigrate. So long as I remained in Israel, he'd steadied a lifeline to me – no tugs – but my mother's report of an exchange with him carries a discomforting challenge. When she discussed the local elections with Siamon, he remarked that he'd voted 'for the first and last time'.

'Why last?'

'Because by the next election, I'll be gone.'

I'm not unaware of what lies ahead, and it may contribute to a nightmare: it starts with a familiar scene. I'm coming out of the sea with Siamon, but the situation has reverted to what it was when I left home the year before: it's that I'm to stay abroad, and return only on visits. In my dream it's the first visit, and I'm due to return to Israel that night. It feels like a return to death-in-life. As this hits me, I wake with relief to find it's only a dream.

Not for me, then, that testing narrative, the migration story that's linked with the oldest poetry of the West, the *Odyssey* and the *Aeneid*. On paper, I'm awed by the staying power of Aeneas, who has carried his father on his back, and whose ship still carries the household objects that tell him who he was. I'm gripped, vicariously, by the dream that compels him, that moment when the gods instruct him to sail on, promising *imperium* without end. But what touches me is decidedly not the heroic story with its horrors of fight and bloodshed. It's the melancholy prospect of a stranger in the strange land.

By day, that prospect dissipates. One evening when my mother is washing her face – the time of day we talk most freely – I confide to her that Siamon found me reading a woman's magazine and made it clear he was less than impressed.

My mother has never opened a woman's magazine in her life, which is one reason she's free of the beauty myth and 'must have' mentality. She admires Siamon's mind, and he sometimes accompanies her to lectures by visiting scholars.

I'm adept at reading my mother's furrowed face. She doesn't think I'm brainy enough for him, and fears he may drop me, especially if I don't fit in with his plans.

In the silence that follows, I think: she's too pure to consider physical attraction, and reassure myself that kissing in the shadow of the vine on our stoep and lying between the sand dunes on a deserted Macassar Beach will sustain the tie.

My grandmother, less tactful than my mother, warns me outright that Siamon could take 'the best years of your life, then leave you'. Granny reflects the opinion of the wider family that, given my looks and lack of allure, it's surprising there should be a boyfriend at all.

My own explanation lies in Siamon's alacrity when it comes to helping others: my concern over my mother was the kind of thing to engage him, and medical issues would engage him even more. His previous girlfriend had diabetes. I'm not saying he chose her on that basis – she's pretty and gentle – but, shall we say, her condition did not deter him.

I don't refuse Siamon's plans; nor, privately, do I concur. My mother, though, assumes I'll come to accept this future, which is of course her own dream. When she tells Sirkka how glad she is to have me again her 'friend and companion', she adds, 'It may not be for long.'

Three years after my aborted attempt to emigrate, Siamon and I decide to marry. In the run-up to the wedding my mother and I quarrel. As part of a community, she wants the traditional kind of wedding where bride and groom become a focus for a re-affirmation of community bonds. It's not that she differs from me in wanting a small wedding; it's that she's granting priority to what others want. There are to be myriad guests whom we barely know.

'The wedding is not for you. It's for your parents.' My mother makes this explicit.

Am I to be an outsider at my own wedding?

Yes, I am. I break it to my mother I might not want to go through with this. For once, I have no wish to please her.

As tension mounts Siamon says matter-of-factly, 'The wedding doesn't matter.' It's the marriage that does, he means, and that makes sense. I'm still put out that he doesn't side with me in defying what's expected of us. Where he appears calm, maturely considerate of parents' wishes, I appear a tiresome rebel. Resentfully, I give in.

When the wedding day arrives, my mother, alert to women's experience, knows how an obedient daughter – and even more, a less obedient one – comes to be that unreal construct, the bride, fixed in the artifice of communal rite.

'Think that you are marrying Siamon Gordon,' my mother reminds me before walking down the aisle as she adjusts my wedding dress and puffs up my breasts to fill its contour. I've recently lost weight and am caked with unaccustomed make-up to cover an outbreak of pimples – the result of ill-advised facials with products that stung the skin.

And then, there's a band singing about a sweetheart called Tammy, and to the strains of 'Daisy, Daisy' a dessert trolley is pulled into the dinner by a tinsel bicycle-made-for-two. On it are mounted a stuffed man and woman. To do my mother justice, her eyes meet mine, appalled by the community's keen-to-please caterer, Krafchik of course, who has sprung this surprise. When people shake our hands they say this spectacle

Greeting my mother's friend Zelda at our wedding.
Siamon is behind, on left

has been the highlight of the wedding. It's the first and last time we set eyes on a lot of our wedding guests.

'You are a lucky, *lucky* girl,' are my mother's parting words. I am indeed lucky, but wish she wouldn't say it with solemn emphasis, as though I may not be sufficiently thankful.

My resistance will not be forgotten. Twenty-five years later, when we are living in Oxford with two daughters, my mother phones from Cape Town.

'Are you happily married?' she asks in a stricken voice. This is Rhoda's way: she's given to sudden compunction.

During the political upheaval of the year we marry, 1963, when Mandela and his underground comrades are caught and tried, and the country seems on course to perdition, our plan – common to our generation – is to leave. After the Rivonia Trial, with Mandela starting his imprisonment on Robben Island, there's no place for the likes of us in South Africa. Many Afrikaners tolerate other whites only as participants in a racial segregation invading every corner, from separate entrances to the post office to seats on buses.

In the meantime, until I finish my course, Siamon and I live at 22 Lisdale, on the rocks at Sea Point, with Robben Island in sight. My mother's walks pass Lisdale. She wants to press the buzzer, then refrains, she says.

'This is absurd,' I assure her from the heart.

'A couple needs to be alone,' she insists, quite unnecessarily to my mind. We'd both love to see her, but she's resolved not to be a possessive mother and I can't budge this act of renunciation.

On a balcony over the ocean with Lion's Head looming behind, I read *Middlemarch* for the first time. The high-minded Dorothea, a St Theresa of the Midlands, is said to like 'giving up'. Here is a woman's life in a provincial town, which constrains her aspirations and reflects them in small mirrors. Dorothea idealises scholarly Mr Casaubon as her superior tutor, much as my mother has idealised Mr Levin. Craving higher education, they defer to educated men. And then, like Dorothea, my mother finds 'work-in-the-world': the agency to give to others in the modest sphere open to her.

Siamon too reads *Middlemarch*, and pronounces it the greatest English novel. He's taken with the doctor, Lydgate, who, back in 1829, dreams of discovering the 'primitive tissue', which he rightly assumes underlies and connects the different organs of the body, with its powers of renewal and repair. This is a historical version of Siamon's own ambition to move into experimental pathology, and it's not lost on him that Dr Lydgate is thwarted in the end by a fantasy of doing his research, undisturbed, in a provincial backwater.

If you grow up in Cape Town, where sunlit mountains rise steeply out of the sea, you can never be anything but a creature of that place. Ours, though, is a generation who see '*net blankes*' ('whites only') on benches along the sea and know that we have to live elsewhere. People like us who are still here are either waiting to leave or casting themselves into what appears a futile Struggle against an entrenched regime.

Our immediate plan is to spend a year in London en route to New York, where Siamon has a post lined up at the Rockefeller University for two or so years with a view to gaining research experience in a laboratory. His hope is to become a scientist worthy of the Weizmann Institute in Israel. I'm excited at the prospect of a new life in an England never seen but imagined through books. And it's a comfort to go with Siamon.

He has an unpaid attachment to the Wright-Fleming Institute at St Mary's Hospital, where Alexander Fleming first observed the penicillin-producing fungus. I find work in the library of the Royal Society of Medicine. It's a grand building on the corner of Henrietta Place and Wimpole Street – not far

At UCT, outside Jameson Hall after graduation, with Yasmin Behardien.
On left, behind, is Granny Annie (in hat)

from the fashionable doctors of Harley Street – in the West End.
The salary is £750 a year, enough for us to rent an attic with a
chilly bathroom down a few stairs at ten pounds a week, the
going rate in 1964. The attic is at 31 Netherhall Gardens in
Hampstead, not far from Auntie Minnie.

My mother predicted rightly what a comfort Auntie Minnie
will be when we come to London, and how charming I'll find
the quiet voices and considerate manners of her English relations. I'm delighted with them and with the kindness of Auntie
Minnie's welcome. At the time of our departure my mother is
reliving her heady time in London twelve years earlier. The
City Lit, having played the starring role in my mother's history,
beckons: I join an evening ballet class. In 1964 Fonteyn and
Nureyev's partnership is at its height. We sit in the highest
gallery of the Royal Opera House and I hang so far over the rail

to take in Nureyev's leaps in *Le Corsaire* that Siamon laughs and
has to hold my ankles. In summer we travel to Finland to stay
with my mother's soul-sister, Sirkka.

My love of books and my mother's wartime role as orphanage librarian has encouraged me to work in a library.
Unfortunately, medical books turn out to be in a foreign language. My daily job is to shelve and file. We librarians have no
contact with members of the society, and at lunchtime eat our
sandwiches in the basement. Every afternoon the hours creep
at their petty pace. After eight months I sign up for typing lessons three evenings a week.

When I mention this, the eyes of the Assistant Librarian
gleam. Next day she offers an opportunity for useful practice.

From then on, I'm in the office to help Beryl, the secretary
to the society. She's very nice, as they say in England: a mild,
middle-aged woman with dark hair sculpted round the head in
an off-the-face fifties style. Beryl has the comfy femininity I'm
drawn to in my grandmother. Chat with Beryl, starting and
trailing off and picking up again at intervals throughout the day,
has the cosiness of knitting needles going click, click in an even
rhythm. No jolts of surprise; no confessions; no demands; no
tests of competence. Beryl seems unbothered by my slow fin-
gering of the typewriter

Am I to go on lying low in this bath of warm water? I think
of Eliot in his office at Lloyd's Bank in the City during his first
years in London: he did this job for the sake of the poetry he
wrote after hours, and yet he didn't dislike it. If anything, he
welcomed the peacefulness of sitting there, adding up figures.
I prefer Beryl to a senior librarian, Norma, on the watch for
shortcuts to the labyrinthine routines she's laid down. Her cold-
eyed questions are designed to trip up a subordinate. Aren't I
fortunate to be paid to practise typing in pleasant company?

I look over a letter of recommendation from the head of the

To the left is J. M. Coetzee, who did some lecturing, and
on the right a fellow student, Itamar Avin, at a party in
Professor Howarth's garden, December 1963

English Department in Cape Town, Professor Howarth (whose
yellowed lecture notes make an appearance in J. M. Coetzee's
Youth). He'd thought me diligent enough to assist a scholar, and
the idea is appealing. I want to be that kind of woman: a helper.
I'd liked the role of helper to a writing mother. Now, turning
the pages of the *New Statesman*, I come upon an advertisement
from Benjamin Waife in New York, who wants a research assistant (who can type) for a book on confessions. He agrees to pay
me the same salary as the library, though calculated on an
hourly basis. I resign from the library, say goodbye to Beryl and
turn to the lives of St Augustine and Rousseau.

*

As planned we move to New York a few months later, in April 1965. I meet Mr Waife, who turns out to be an affable journalist for Jewish papers, writing as Ben-Zion Goldberg, and his wife turns out to be the youngest daughter of the Yiddish writer Sholem Aleichem. She smiles gently as she brings tea and toast while her husband and I review the situation.

He's satisfied, he says, with my writing, but can't afford to pay a New York salary. This is why, he tells me proudly, he'd conceived the idea of a cheap researcher in England. If I go on as before he might let me collaborate on his next book. Might I collaborate on the present book, I'm emboldened to ask. No, is the answer, because he already has a contract. I consult my father as well as a New York lawyer, Victor Frankel, and am not surprised to be advised against an oral promise. Their warning is reinforced by a sense that Mr Waife is losing interest in the present book, and in fact it never appears. Then, when I tell him I can't go on, he pays half of what's due for ten weeks' work on Nietzsche, saying we must share the loss.

We find an apartment overlooking the Hudson River at 417 Riverside Drive, a block from Columbia University on the teeming Upper West Side. As a wife, I've come in tow to America without much thinking about it. When my mother travelled she approached a foreign country through its writers, and so accordingly I apply for a graduate programme in American studies at Columbia. It's a blind step because I've never encountered American literature, apart from T. S. Eliot, some poems by Emily Dickinson and an extract from *Tom Sawyer* in a children's anthology. When I visit the chair of the department, Lewis Leary, in his office on the top floor of Philosophy Hall he is reassuring and the seminar, run by Professor Hovde, a Thoreau scholar, is everything an ill-prepared newcomer could wish: friendly and stimulating.

I'm puzzled by the absence of Dickinson in the official guide to the nineteenth century, *Eight American Authors*. All eight are men. A Texan in the seminar explains that this is a literature of men without women until you come to Pilar in *For Whom the Bell Tolls*, 'and she's a man'. The focus is on Thoreau's solitude at Walden Pond; Ishmael with his savage bed-mate Queequeg; Huck with an escaped slave, Jim, floating down the Mississippi on Huck's raft; and the Deerslayer with his red brother Chingachgook tracking through the woods of the frontier. A typical exam question is 'Discuss the renegade from civilization.' I drink this in, entranced by a self-reliant freedom to escape a contaminating society. My first report is on Thoreau's influential essay 'Civil Disobedience', written in prison when he was jailed for refusing to pay a tax that could be used to fund an indefensible war.

In the free period before our seminar I have coffee and muffins with two women who are classmates. Sometimes it's dark-haired, insightful Pearl, at other times blonde, vivacious Louise with a stylish silver bangle on her arm. Louise has come straight from Sarah Lawrence, an advanced college for women, and reminds me, I tell my mother, 'of the American girls in *The Little Locksmith*: strongly intelligent, fresh, groomed, beautiful'.

It's demanding to make up the primary reading the others have done at school and college. 'I am always behind,' I write to my mother, 'but it is so much better than the dread "emptiness." I could never stretch out the "woman's role" to fill my entire life.'

I'm four months pregnant and so far haven't ventured to see a doctor. In England I'd picked up a manual, Grantly Dick-Read's *Childbirth without Fear: The Principles and Practice of Natural Childbirth*, and am converted to its promise that a woman can exercise control over her body. This matters all the more to me having witnessed my mother's involuntary loss of control. An obstetrician at New York Hospital waves this away impatiently. What's customary, he explains, is to tie down a woman's hands 'to keep a sterile field', and fathers aren't allowed to be present 'because they get in the way'. A second obstetrician says the same, while Siamon, who delivered ten babies while he was a medical student, warns me that 'natural' childbirth is a misnomer. 'What's "natural" is for women to die,' he tells me dryly, and tries to wake me up to the reality of labour pains. I don't of course want to hear this, and think he's siding with his profession against more innovative and humane forms of practice. He agrees to 'go along' with what I want to believe, and I find a Belgian doctor at the French Hospital who's prepared to go along too.

Natural childbirth prepares a woman to banish pain and fear by taking a positive attitude. This doesn't happen. The doctor is kind, but dead-eyed orderlies wheel me, panting, into a public lift where the Marie Antoinette nightmare – birth in public – becomes a reality. In the middle of an agonising contraction, as the orderlies dump me like a sack of potatoes on the delivery table, I hear my cry of pain – can this be me, giving way – and then it has to be a forceps delivery after all. My lovely baby is born but I feel a failure, and relive that moment of losing control. Handbooks say that women forget, but it's impossible to wipe out this scene.

Towards the end of 1965 a line in a letter to my mother and grandmother mentions depression: 'Although Anna is now three months, I haven't yet recovered.' My obstetrician wants me to see another doctor, but I hope to improve by going home to South Africa. We are due for a visit during the end-of-year vacation, and Siamon ventures to warn my mother that the depression is serious. 'Our friends and contacts here are quite ignorant of this, and to a certain extent surround us with an illusory idyllic vision which ignores reality. There is probably no one bar yourself that we can turn to for understanding.'

Back where I'd thought to belong, my weight gain, bitten nails and uncontained offensiveness do not go down well. At the end of the visit I travel alone with Anna on the return journey through Johannesburg. There, I'm shaken to hear a rumour of my family's opinion that I'm fat and spoilt. It's not said unkindly; it's a fact I should know.

Fat. Spoilt. I'm not. Yes, I am. For don't I have what women want: a lovely baby?

I look into this mirror on the long flight back to New York, and once there, go under. There's some relief in going under: no more struggle. At St Luke's, a hospital near by on Amsterdam Avenue, a woman doctor training to be a psychiatrist listens carefully, and makes a provisional diagnosis of post-partum depression. Nothing is said about my mother's post-partum crisis, because epilepsy is perceived as her overriding illness. I open Dr Spock's best-selling handbook on mothers and babies, and stare at the flip phrase 'baby blues'. This guru of anything goes has not a clue what's going on. I turn to my mother, who's been in dark places; she will understand, I think.

She says she does regret not talking when we were together, and assures me that what I'd heard was misreported. But she thinks it wrong to dwell on hurtful words rather than how benevolent her family has always been.

Why does this response come as a blow? What she says is not unexpected. She has always put family feeling first and expects me, as an extension of herself, not to indulge a disruptive state of mind. Her insistence that I suppress what happened for the sake of harmony comes as confirmation that she will not defend me. The blow is this confirmation that I matter less to her than others do. She evades a conflict of loyalties by stressing gratitude as the appropriate emotion. Yet, since my mother herself experienced a breakdown after childbirth, I'd continued to hope she'd lean my way. That hope is gone.

Early in March 1966 I'm admitted to Clark 8, the locked psychiatric ward on the eighth floor of St Luke's. My mother now comes from South Africa to look after Anna. I'm sceptical about psychotherapy, like my mother who has a different answer.

'Abraham, Isaac and Jacob are continually tested and tried,' my mother says, 'and through these trials they are taught how to live. God speaks to them in what befalls them, and what befalls them has the power to teach and transform them.'

She wishes to save me as she had saved herself, by turning to her Maker. For her, this accompanies visitations – she is 'never alone'. I, though, am alone in a mental enclosure, and no one, least of all myself, can spring the door. I'm shut off from everyone who upholds that all-time norm that a wife follows her husband, whose career must take precedence, even if it means moving to another country. I want to go home, but the people on whom I depend are bent on migration. I'm trapped in their narrative, real to them, unreal to me, with no prospect of escape. The less they see the falsity of expatriation, the more I deteriorate.

In Clark 8, this is the way I think: adaptation, even transformation, is a biological necessity, yet don't creatures do this at a cost? Does the caterpillar blowing back and forth in its chrysalis, metamorphosing into a thing of the air, not regret its home in the earth that kept it warm? In human terms, is it not false to mouth the politically correct mantra of our contemporaries – 'I never want to see South Africa again' – as they take on the colouring of other people? How is it that everyone I know is managing to become something else? Why do I lack the resilience to do this thing – turn my back on the landscape that made me? My mother says, 'Geography doesn't matter.' She means it won't matter if you open yourself to your Maker. I look up to her faith, but cannot elevate myself in that manner and become that sort of extension of what she is. As a creature of the earth I'm a failure who couldn't even carry through natural childbirth. Nor, having made this move, can I go home. There's no way out.

A cold-eyed man I shall call Dr Kay is brought in to replace the trainee whose empathy had opened a channel of communication. Instinct warns me off Dr Kay the moment we meet. I refuse to see him for three days. But institutional rules insist that the apparent caprice of a mental patient can't be allowed: he's the one assigned, and if I want to remain in St Luke's no one but Dr Kay will be allowed to take the case. My protest is an embarrassment to all concerned, and Siamon, as a doctor himself, thinks Dr Kay entitled to the courtesy of allowing him to practise his profession.

Dr Kay conducts interviews from the safe hollow of his citadel, and from there he diagnoses a hopeless case. I test him once by saying that someone distasteful had got inside me: metaphorically it has some truth, but a flare in his eye tells me he's thick enough to take this literally. Earnestly, he probes the likelihood of delusions. After that I have no respect for him as a doctor, though the continued need for St Luke's means that I have to accept him.

The nurses are distant, keeping to themselves in their glass office, but the inmates are kind to one another and this makes Clark 8 a refuge of sorts. At first it's relieving to be on neutral ground.

After I've been in hospital for eight weeks, Dr Kay urges a new plan, a long-term asylum. To avoid this, there's a trial week back in the apartment, from 8 to 16 May.

Two days in, my mother reports to my father, who has asked for details: 'I find I am on duty from eight in the morning till 10 at night. Nonetheless love makes all burdens light, and I am continually upheld & sustained, as I have been from the beginning. There is a 20% chance that she might have to go back into Hospital, but although she has had a tough time for the past 30 hours she is putting up a good fight controlling the deep depression. This is the real progress in my opinion, that she does not give way as she did, but realises that she has to endure, and control herself or worse will follow.' 'Control' is my mother's watchword. She imagines me better when I'm 'considerate' and 'affectionate', and advises against 'letting go'. If I do let go, she warns, 'worse' can happen. What is 'worse'? The Terrible Sonnets of the Jesuit poet Gerard Manley Hopkins, which my mother and I had studied together, claim there's no finite superlative to the comparative 'worse': 'No worst, there is none.'

The more I subscribe to civil conduct, the more untrue living appears. Under layers of obligatory lies, the divide from my mother widens. Undoubtedly, she is generous in coming to New York, leaving her classes and her ethics course at university, taking on domestic responsibilities she's never done, and not least in her care for little Anna. There's a maternal ardour, unreleased with us, her children who were born to a semi-invalid. Now she's on all fours hunting a lost earring. Has the baby swallowed it? Anna laughs at such antics. Her Gran adores her and is never too ill to pick her up. Yet these offerings and sacrifices don't touch me because she believes women must follow husbands. It's too self-evident to be aired. I'm up against the fact that I must stay in New York. But more divisive is the fact that she had impressed on me, as a child, the nightmare of doctors who had judged morally, had judged her illness as her failure to control herself. I had felt shoulder to shoulder with her outrage. And yet, now, it's abundantly plain that she reads

my illness as something that shouldn't have happened – a loss
of self-control.

She delays this letter home, hoping to report improvement.
In Riverside Park, where she continues her letter on Sunday
morning, I'm heavily drugged after six days of depression, while
Siamon looks after Anna. 'I shed a tear for both of them. We
thought everything was coming right but this past week at
home has put L back. She wants to return to hospital.'

Back at St Luke's the depression lifts a little, but Dr Kay repeats
his plan for the long-term 'home'. He allows me out the following weekend so that I, together with Siamon and my mother,
can view the home in western Massachusetts; we are expected
to be impressed with its landscaped grounds and we meet an
inmate. I don't find this place has anything to do with me, and
actually feel rather better. We stay that night in a charming inn
in Northampton, and next day I'm well enough to join my class
tour of Edith Wharton's home, The Mount, and the towns in
the Berkshires where Hawthorne and Melville lived and wrote
in the early 1850s. My spirits lift in the company of intelligent
classmates, and bathe in the bracing truths of literature – even
fantasy must be 'true to the human heart', Hawthorne insists in
his preface to *The House of the Seven Gables*. Melville, writing to
Hawthorne from Pittsfield in April 1851, commends him for his
'NO! in thunder . . . For all men who say *yes*, lie.' Melville's certainty brings a measure of relief. So does his character Bartleby,
with his passive resistance to the hollow-heartedness of commerce. And so does Hester Prynne's self-reliance as social outcast.
In their company, with books, I'm not alone. For here is what
Emerson calls the integrity of a private mind.

My letter to Granny on 26 May says something simple and
true: I'm homesick and have far to go to get over it. This is a
sane letter. Could the determination of Dr Kay to push me into
an asylum for the long-term insane have been a defence against

his inability to communicate, reinforced perhaps by my resistance to him? What I couldn't articulate then, but see now, is a conservative, who moves to lock away the rebellious element in mental disturbance. If he detected as yet unnamed women's issues (wanting a life of the mind, wanting a life outside of domesticity, wanting equal partnership) latent in me in 1966, he was bound to outlaw a state of mind rising against the status quo. Only a guess, of course, but Dr Kay certainly tried to persuade Siamon to institutionalise me. As such Dr Kay was a danger, masked as benign doctor.

My resistance was merely instinctive; it takes Virginia Woolf to see through an authority figure, as she does in her portrait of the 'obscurely evil' Dr Bradshaw in *Mrs Dalloway*. He's based, in part at least, on one of her consultants, the distinguished Sir Henry Head, who had sent another patient, Henry James, 'down into hell'.

Dr Kay asks me to see him immediately after we return from the Berkshires, and once I enter the shadow of this wooden fortress, the threat of the asylum begins to erode the incipient cure of our excursion into the world of literature, those congenial nineteenth-century Americans. If I feel cut off in New York, an asylum in western Massachusetts will be more cut off. It's a fate I can't bear to contemplate, but the rationale is plain enough. If I don't recover soon at St Luke's, this is the alternative on offer. The alternative that isn't on offer is what I want, but can't voice: to return to the roar of the breakers on the rocks and the gulls overhead beating their wings against the wind.

I'm 'frightened', my mother reports to my father. The conditions are indeed frightening, for if I'm 'sent away' it has to be for a long time – might it be for ever? The policy of this institution is to review a case only once a year.

My mother is a different matter. Here is a sensitive being, alert to doctors' shortcomings and sceptical, on principle, of psychiatric diagnosis. If horror of life is not a symptom of derangement but a fair judgement, then an obvious course – tested in her own experience – is to follow a narrative that culminates in faith. So, as well as feeling I should stay in New York with my husband, she believes in the well-tried path, based on Exodus, where there is always a dark period of trial, whether in a desert, or pit, or prison, or a slough of despond or illness, followed by the divine light.

I do comprehend that my unwillingness to follow this course, to see it in either of her ways, is the cause of the divide growing between mother and daughter. Up to a point I understand the inflexibility of the social norm to which my mother was forced to yield when she resigned her 'great opportunity' in London in 1952, but I'm put out to find her siding with the laws of conformity when it comes to her daughter. Decades on, having read my mother's love letters, I now see how much the influence of Levin gave her a missionary purpose. At the time, the priority she grants to that remains incomprehensible in view of the mother she'd been, and I continue to struggle with the longing for home versus the route – migration – that seems to have been prescribed for me and Siamon. In 1959 I'd coped with migration by imagining a future return; now in 1966 there's no future beyond New York, except the continued possibility of migrating to Israel.

That possibility will remain active, supported by my mother, until Siamon visits the Weizmann Institute in 1967 and the offhand manner of his interview dims that hope; he nearly faints in the heat when he leaves. So America is to be our home for now.

Knowing I can't stay indefinitely at St Luke's, I decide to leave before being discharged. By leaving, my mother reports to my father, 'she's burnt her bridges'. She means that there's now no alternative to a stark either/or: either adapt or else be sent away. My mother herself is valiant, and doesn't complain how hard it is for her to be with me every hour of the day. Nor, from the other side of our divide, is it easy to live every hour with a mother's poor opinion, unvoiced though apparent in pats on the back for trying to put a lid on disruptive thoughts; that is, not complaining.

What a woman of my mother's generation deplores as complaining will surface four years later as a political movement, Women's Liberation: a full-throated public refusal to subordinate women's lives to those of men. The divide between mother and daughter looks like an isolated case of mental illness in 1966, but I believe that illness has everything to do with women's role and non-communication between a mother who'd worked out a way to conform to the norms of her society and a daughter who's awakening to an obsolete gender code, and refuses.

Time has proved my mother right about South Africa: I see now we couldn't go back. There was the evil of apartheid so that, if you were there, you were participating, whether you wished to or not. For me to abandon migration (to New York or Israel or wherever it might be) never, so far as I know, occurred to her, and without her backing I could not go home. There seemed no solution – my mind circled the same hopeless track. Cut off from the light on the waves, the salt wind, the big sky, to me the towers of New York look like prison bars.

One Friday night in August she takes me to dine with a South African doctor, Renée Abt, who had attended my mother's student class on the Bible. Unable to cope with prayers and conversation at table, I lie in a darkened bedroom in a kind of stupor. Even to raise a limb feels futile. Kind Renée gives me a game of Scrabble to take back to the apartment. 'To pass the time,' she suggests.

Siamon has recently been accepted for the doctoral programme at Rockefeller University, one of the first foreign
students amongst the hundred or so best science graduates in
the US. To have spent the last eighteen months in this place is
to understand how much he has to learn, and this course makes
it more feasible to switch from medicine to a research career.
The programme, with a generous stipend, will extend our stay
in New York by five years, well beyond my one-year master's
programme at Columbia.

All these tomorrows stretch endlessly ahead. A 'confidential'
letter from my mother to my father and brother admits how bad
things are, and asks them to say nothing to anyone in Israel.
Why Israel? It can only be because that's where she expects me
to go. My father, in his neat, legal hand, underlines in red what
he wants to remember, and nowhere else does he underline so
thickly – his red pencil moves back and forth. This is serious:
it has to do with his daughter's reputation. The prohibition does
not extend to talk in our home town, because I'm not to live
there again.

Back at St Luke's, in a hospital wrap, I lie on the stretched white
sheet with the passivity of a vegetable on a kitchen table. The
vegetable will be made to have a fit. At the time I make no connection between my mother's epilepsy and this artificially
induced fit. Dr Udall, bending over me to administer an injec-
tion, says, 'Just a pin-stick.' A wave rushes over my head.

The first four treatments are administered while I'm an in-
patient in August. There's some improvement, but it doesn't last
beyond a week. As an outpatient, from late August into early
September, I have a second course of six treatments. Afterwards,
it jars to be fetched by my mother, who appears detached. For
her to perform this duty is to accept what's done by authorities
in white coats. Pushing Anna, aged one, in the stroller, she

walks us the short distance from Amsterdam Avenue across Broadway, because in the aftermath of the jolt I may not remember my way to Riverside Drive.

These treatments are on alternate days. After each one I'm low and then improve somewhat by the second night, just before the time comes for another shock. This hardly seems useful. So what next?

After Siamon leaves for work one morning, I catch a bus at 114th Street that will carry me down Broadway; then wait for a cross-town bus at the Lincoln Center. I feel reckless, courting the relief of what my mother has warned against: giving way. I'm about to do something that I've not done before, and that other wives don't do – all those wives of Rockefeller scientists who, it appears, exist to give themselves to their husbands' meteoric careers.

I mean to surprise Siamon at work. Instinct tells me to meet him where he really is. I have to meet a man in the setting of a world-class lab, preparing to complete his leap from village school into the scientific stratosphere.

So long as I continue to accept the help of an end-of-day husband who comes home to change the baby and haul her diapers to the machines in the basement of our apartment block, I can't speak from where I actually am, at the far end of a widening distance that has opened between us. Siamon's considerate acts – too matter-of-fact to care for my mother's praise – prop up the home front, but the side effect is to close off feeling. Practical needs fill the hours, in the manner of people who don't address the ways they've diverged. A surface civility has silenced outrage at my mother's solidarity with Siamon. This life has nothing to do with me. Nothing, that is, beyond the helper role ingrained since earliest childhood.

In the cut-off cavern of my mind, I'm incredulous over the

compliance of other wives, turned out in primary shades of pink and green, the smiling consorts. Does it suffice to bask in reflected glory? I imagine how each wife expects a Nobel Prize. It would compensate for the dedicated service she does her husband. Here, the Nobel Prize is no mere dream: Rockefeller has a number of winners amongst its faculty. As a student, Siamon will enter their labs; he will mull over the macrophage (his favourite cell, the big-eater that keeps our immune systems going) and try out ideas over the long lunch tables in the dining room in Founder's Hall. As part of his induction into this elite, Rockefeller's photographer has already produced a photo of Siamon, the like of which I've never seen: his chin has been tilted upwards as though he's heading for the stars.

As the bus winds through Central Park towards the East Side, I dwell on the glory of Rockefeller, this American beacon of bounty and expertise spanned by the Queensboro Bridge where Gatsby's car rode, fenders spread, into the greatest of cities.

I dwell too on dead spaces: the so-called meditation pool, a square of water with a bench, never occupied, on each of its four sides; the artifice of ramrod tulips, transported fully grown on 1 May and set out in precise rows; and the bland faces of the scientists above their white coats. Nothing matters to them very much apart from the next experiment. Their drive and absorption appear detached from domestic turmoil – the province of wives.

Back in our apartment, gratitude to my mother for all she's taken on prevents us from owning how difficult it's become to spend our days together. Adept as I am at hearing what she doesn't say, her resolute stopping-up of reproach speaks to me of my unwillingness to take on her solution to illness. It seems that I have come to the end of my existence as her creation.

What remains in question is Siamon: what my breakdown might do to us. For my part, the responses that came naturally are numbed. I've assumed that he expects me to recover, but

what if I don't? What if damage lurks too deep to heal? That's
the darker matter, as the bus turns at the end of its cross-town
run, passes Rockefeller on York Avenue, and halts at its terminus on 67th Street.

Of late, trust in Siamon has been shaken by his respect for a
fellow doctor, the wooden Kay, who set up this double course
of shocks. Each time, Siamon would leave me to submit to
them while he drove off to the lab. That act of climbing out of
the car was like forcing myself to enter a nightmare.

Turning into the gate of Rockefeller and climbing the slope
of the campus, I'm approaching Siamon from an estranged position. Some would think estrangement a definition of mental
illness, but what I'm seeing is not distorted. I am striving to be
a mother, that's clear to all, but to go on acting as a wife and
daughter should – civil, controlled – is not a sign of improvement; they are all wrong about that; the lie in this performance
corrodes ties. I am maintaining the thinnest semblance of
normal, all the while seeing through the façades that sustain that
fiction.

Mount the steps to Founder's Hall. Ask for Dr Gordon. 'I'm
his wife.'

The receptionist directs me downstairs to the empty dining
room while he's called

And now he's walking towards me in a jacket and tie, a lock
of hair falling on his forehead. What I'm not prepared for is
how attractive he is, his green eyes alert, looking at me with
unexpected intimacy.

'I can't go on,' is all I can say.

He sits down in front of me, takes my hands and says, 'First
of all, you *will* get well.' His optimism and the concern in his
gaze touch the numbness – a sign that it might not be the end,
after all. This is in character: he's a maker of plans.

'Do something with your life,' he says, and he's quick with

ideas: a doctorate for a start. 'I've always thought you could write biography,' he suggests. It's an offer to help me find a sense of purpose equal to his own, like the purpose my mother once nurtured for herself, a purpose it has never occurred to me that I warrant.

'I'm not up to that.' It's beyond me to contemplate flying that high. This is what he wants. He likes accomplished women – looks don't impress him so much as flair. His ambitions affect me like the skyscrapers of New York: can you measure up, they demand. No. Not now.

'For now,' he's considering in his practical way first steps first, 'since something must be done, I think you must leave Dr Kay.' He says he will draw on expertise at Rockefeller, investigate what might be the best treatment of a case like mine that the

In the late sixties it felt like an experiment to combine motherhood and full-time study

city can offer and will undertake to find an agreeable doctor to replace Dr Kay. It is a breakthrough for us – and for me.

On 10 September, I'm taken aback when the new doctor, Silvano Arieti, orders five more shocks. More?

He will see me when these are done, he says firmly in a book-lined midtown apartment, 103 East 75th, away from the fret of the hospital. 'A patient has to be out of deep depression for therapy to begin.'

Memory loss is a side effect of shock treatment. In the nineties, when I'm writing on Henry James, I will open my copy of *The Tragic Muse* and see marginalia from 1966. A blank. I don't know what that novel's about. I can't re-read it. Nor play Scrabble again.

Throughout these shocks and after, I'm covering Columbia's Latin requirement: a course on Virgil with a bright classicist, Steele Commager, son of the historian Henry Steele Commager, who has recently edited a collection of critical essays on the Roman poet. The Sybil's warning to Aeneas, which at school had carried a reverberation of my mother's underworld, now leaps to life: the meaning of the descent to the Dead. I can't better the translation by Miss Hulston, the Latin teacher at Good Hope, which I'd paced into my body in the school grounds. The words come: 'O Trojan son ... easy is the descent to Avernus, but to recall the step and pass out to the upper air, this is the undertaking, this the task – *hoc opus, hic labor est.*'

Another memory from an English class comes to join it: Conrad's narrator, Marlow, in *Heart of Darkness*: not his glimpse of savagery – heads on sticks – but that same difficulty of return from the underworld. Marlow struggles to make his way back along the Congo to so-called civilisation. He hopes to leave the heart of darkness yet carries it with him, lodged in the brain.

Eventually, Marlow finds himself back in 'the sepulchral city' amongst faces stupidly oblivious to the savagery beneath the skin of the urban order. To pierce the false façade of civilisation is to find yourself mentally alone, and to be thus alone is to be disturbed. Marlowe has to convince listeners of what he's seen, and at the same time he has to admit how far what he's seen unfits him for normal life: 'I daresay I was not very well at that time.' The 'horror' of this state of mind speaks directly to the urban phantasmagoria of *The Waste Land*. 'Shall I set my lands in order' is a critical question when Eliot was trying to recuperate from a breakdown at the sanatorium of Dr Vittoz in Lausanne.

In 1968, when I'm at last well again and the final sessions with Dr Arieti turn into discussions of Eliot's debt to Dante, I do an extended essay on Eliot. It's a springboard for a biography that I start writing as a doctoral dissertation between 1970 and 1973. And thanks to my mother's intuitive reading I'm prompted to ask a vital question of Eliot's early manuscripts in the Berg Collection at the New York Public Library: when did his religious life start? The answer is resounding; it negates the standard view that religion was a development of Eliot's middle years.

In 1973 the Rhodes Trust in Oxford is impelled by the impact of second-wave feminism to offer opportunities for women, and I apply for a fellowship. At an interview with the great Eliot scholar Helen Gardner I will subdue Eliot's biographical ordeals – his expatriate displacement, his surrender to marriage and subsequent breakdown – to my attempt at dating the fragments that become *The Waste Land*. Though Dame Helen is not entirely pleased with me – she disapproves of mothers in the workplace – she decides that I shall come to her college, St Hilda's, and in time, as a Delegate of Oxford University Press, she ensures publication.

After classes, picking up Anna at a sitter's apartment on
the Upper West Side in the late sixties

So I begin as a biographer. Though my mother's route to
faith is, for me, the road not taken, it's still her writing and taste
in writers that's opening up the path I choose to follow. When
Rhoda Press says, 'I shall rise, and unfurl / Over the curve of
the earth / My white sea wings', she speaks for a woman's
inward power, as did the Brontës and Dickinson. Where we
part is over public utterance.

For 1968, that year of recovery, is also the year of the uprising at Columbia, a catalyst for the first meeting of the Women's
Liberation movement in 1970. This takes place on campus. The
room is so packed that I'm standing on a bench along a wall. I've
heard vehement speeches against apartheid, but nothing like the
torrent of molten rage – white-hot hatred of patriarchy – spew-
ing from the lips of Kate Millett, author of *Sexual Politics*. She
asks women to challenge men's authority and control of the

home, education, law, employment and, above all, the very idea
of what a woman is. Fair enough, but what amazes me is the
naked hatred of men. No more grovelling, no more self-
suppression, no more domestic limitations, no more constricting
our bodies in the artifice of bras, no more chivalry disabling to
our sex. With each assertion, the audience shouts assent.

'Yeahhh ... Yeahhh ... Right on!' The time has come for
confrontation. It's them or us.

Is this rage too categoric? Not all men are the same – or are
they, as the dominant order? We're reading *Villette* in Carolyn
Heilbrun's proto-feminist seminar on nineteenth-century fiction, and I think of the tight-lipped schoolmistress Lucy Snowe
containing her fiery nature.

A decade later Emily Dickinson, an avid reader of the
Brontës, reveals 'a Vesuvian face'. Freed from the conventions
of print culture, her poem 'My Life had stood—a Loaded Gun'
marks her explosive power. And although this appears a lone
voice, lava and fire were political currency for activists of her
generation. One of the first French cartoons of feminists in
1848 shows armed women erupting from a volcano, while a
group of young women workers unfurls a banner naming themselves *Vésuviennes*.

Watching Millett perform to 'right on' cries from four hundred women, I hold back. I wouldn't speak in that way. Yet I
have – and at night still do. These cries around me bring back
my giving way in the approach to the underworld, and then,
following my emergence, a recurring dream. For years to come
it moves towards giving way with my mother, a mouth opening ever wider until what comes out of that dark, elongated
hole takes over existence.

When Persephone was carried off into the underworld, did
she cry out to her mother for rescue? Demeter was distraught
to lose her daughter, and devised a plan for her annual return.

What else can a mother do when a daughter is trapped in a dark place?

The head of Siamon's lab has a passing notion to send us to some place in Africa for a spell. That brings a leap of hope, but lasting balm comes from American studies. I do a report on Emily Dickinson's line 'Mine—here—in Vision—and in Veto' and another on the significance of her dashes: I argue against editions that regularise her punctuation, editing out the dashes. It seems to me that she's pushing the words apart, the language of the dominant group, to allow for a muted communication with a reader awakened to unstated experience. There's the visible life – 'I tie my hat, I crease my shawl / Life's little duties do . . .' – and there's the crucial hidden existence: 'And yet Existence—some way back / Stopped—struck—my ticking—through—'. How passionately I read that in the light of St Luke's. That's how we have to read Dickinson, each reader bringing to a poem her own unvoiced life so as to complete these diagrams of Existence.

Nowadays, at literary festivals, readers ask how long it takes to write this or that biography. How to explain? George Eliot puts it best: 'No retrospect will take us back to the true beginning.' A biography of Emily Dickinson, published in 2010, rose out of my mother's secrecy, seclusion and visionary susceptibilities, and then out of those ten-minute class reports amidst the uprisings at Columbia where, if you had to move on with work, you squeezed apologetically past barricades designed to shut down the university as part of a corrupt military-industrial complex.

I was, you understand, in accord with the anti-power, anti-corporate ethos of the time – you might say that I finally discovered some sort of home in protest: in Dickinson's 'Veto' and Melville's 'No! in thunder' and in the rise of women's voices out of the anti-war demonstrations of sixty-eight.

*

My need for truth was to find an outlet in biography, a genre committed to authenticity. This is what impelled me from the start, as a student in '71, turning over Eliot's unpublished papers in the archives. I had to find Eliot's reality – 'human kind / Cannot bear very much reality' – which he inferred from its antithesis: the 'Unreal city' in its shroud of brown fog. And I had to light up women who appeared in the shadow of solitary genius, and re-conceive them not as passive muses, more as collaborators of sorts. Eliot's first love, Emily Hale, and his first wife, Vivienne, both gifted, both vital to his poetry, had to give in to living – partly living – in his shadow.

If the Eliot biography was in a way my mother's book, the next biography was my own. While researching Eliot in the Berg Collection I looked into Virginia Woolf's diaries (as yet unpublished) for impressions of him in his early years in London. I was often so absorbed by the diary that I would forget my research and go on reading. Like other women in the seventies, I turned to Virginia Woolf as a guide to women, and what gripped me most was an unnoticed sentence at the start of *A Room of One's Own* where she declares her fascination for 'the great problem of the true nature of woman'. In my biography *A Writer's Life*, and in later biographies – including two women who were collaborators of sorts in the art of Henry James – the deep pursuit will be that question Woolf asked about what is obscured in our nature: the authenticity of unuttered thoughts, the pressure to communicate the incommunicable – to say directly, even awkwardly, what's in the mind.

With Anna in our apartment on the Upper West Side, about 1968.
Women's Lib was in the air

With Anna on holiday at Nantucket, summer 1970. I was starting
what became my first biography, *Eliot's Early Years*, and also preparing
to teach composition at Hunter College

14

Lives for Women

Long before the spread of book groups, my mother formed a women's group for reading Shakespeare. It was the same invited set of friends as came together in the sunroom for her private Bible class. Only, they didn't come in a routine way; they fore-gathered, as my mother liked to joke. The verb suggests distant heads of state who come to put their heads together, not Monica knitting booties in fluffy wool and Ren, upright, plaits crossed over her head, dancing through the door. These women were not conscious feminists, though they'd read their Vera Brittain and Olive Schreiner. It's not that they didn't take huge delight in Shakespeare's spirited women, like Beatrice and Rosalind with their quips and repartee, but led by my mother they were more deeply drawn to Desdemona and Cordelia, the wife and the daughter who sustain purity of feeling for a raging husband and a manipulative father.

As they read and discuss, I resist this model of how to be a woman. 'Isn't it self-defeating,' I challenge my mother's friends, 'the pathos of Cordelia, who offers King Lear the love a daughter owes to a father, but who is cast off because she does not play up to the self-importance of a king? And how can Desdemona be so pure as to love a husband who is about to kill her? This is to yield to the crime of violence against women.'

It infuriates me all the more to feel, myself, the appeal of purity, an ideal that transcends life.

'Lear and Othello invite us to pity them in their contrition, but shouldn't we pity their victims more? What Desdemona needed,' I insist, 'what other wives subject to violence need, is a women's refuge.'

My father, with no soupçon of the feminine in his make-up, is never violent. I recall only one slap, when I screamed at the thought of a mouse. It was five in the morning and our father was not amused to be woken by silly children, for Pip stood up in his cot and screamed too. Our father bounded into the nursery, dealt quick slaps all round and retreated back to bed. It didn't hurt.

Bertie Henry, though, the farmer who married my mother's friend Lilian, disciplined his sons. They were sent away to school at an early age, the one stoic, the other seething. Bertie's voice was harsh with a hoarse note at the base. Visiting the farm as a child, I'd hear him: bark, bark – an angry sound. He was uncomprehending when Lilian suffered post-partum depression. Each time she gave birth, Lilian found refuge away from home: her grandmother; her friend Monica. Bertie's logic – for hadn't Lilian pressed him into having children – could not work out why she lost heart, and grew, as she observed to my mother, 'rake-thin'. And yet Lilian is able to love her husband. Her memoir records that he knew how to please a woman, tender to 'the wee breasties', and he trod beside her to the outdoor lavatory at night, when she feared snakes. As a loyal wife she says not a word against him, though her candour allows for silence. I respect this Cordelian purity, 'Love, and be silent', surviving into my mother's generation at the bottom of Africa.

Lilian in her home-sewn, cotton dress has made it to the friends' group, all the way from the farm (two and a half hours by car), to be passed over by my mother when her turn comes to read a passage. 'It's all right, Lil,' she'd say, as though releasing Lilian from an effort that would be too much for her.

Of late, she's taken to calling Lilian 'my practical friend', as though ladling hot porridge at dawn into tin bowls for farm workers who hold out cupped hands precludes the life of the mind. For Lilian is disconcertingly at home in her body, alive to physical response. Children love her intimate motherliness, as I do; her daughters-in-law cleave to her because Lilian stands ready to empathise with whatever it takes to be a wife. Then, too, Lilian attends the Dutch Reformed Church at Piketberg to share her neighbours' occasions with flowers from her garden and fruit from her farm.

So these days of the divide between my mother and me, I'm put out when she praises 'my practical friend'. It comes to me as a sign of her semi-detachment from the individual. To her, we are part of a larger pattern.

As my mother's journey becomes more allegorical, people turn into types. She's travelling through a moral landscape, and encountering people who illustrate or equate with one or other trait. Her multi-sided son is 'fun-loving'. Pip's tendency to break out at the piano with 'Great Balls of Fire' worries our mother. She fears he might become an entertainer like Uncle Eddie, whose stage name is Eddie Gaye.

Pip redeems himself through a more concerted effort than mine to settle in the Promised Land, learn the language and take a graduate degree, after which he returns home as a clinical psychologist. In this he continues to bear the impress of our mother, in his discernments of character. His professional career proves how much she under-rated him when she'd decided, back in his teens, that he should channel his charm into a career

Be-Bop-a-Lula: Pip, fifteen, at the piano jamming with friends, 1960

in hotel management. Her one-time plan for me was to be a nursery-school teacher. This came to her when I took to visiting various cousins at their babies' bath-time. During the day, nannies took care of babies, but the evening bath was the time for hands-on mothering. It was delightful to watch, but this never amounted to an ambition.

Odd, these plans for her children. Can it be that a cultivated imagination becomes deliberate, closed off in certain directions, what Emily Dickinson may have meant by closing the valves of the attention, 'like Stone'? Dickinson's poetically charged letters, and later the long letters Henry James penned at the end of a writing day, hardly reflect their correspondents, who barely exist beyond their assigned roles: Dickinson's threatening 'Master' or her loyal 'Little Cousins'.

My mother writes often to me in New York, and is relieved to have letters telling her all is well. A doubt that all may not be well wakes her sometimes at night, she admits soon after returning home: she caricatures the jolt of waking, '*wakker skrik*', pithier in Afrikaans.

In April 1968, two years after the asylum visit, there's a pause in one of her letters. Day-to-day events switch off and she thinks back to two questions I'd asked during a visit in July–August 1967. What these questions were I no longer remember, but their delayed impact after nine months brought back for her the non-communication as I'd slid towards breakdown. This leads to an attempt to cross our divide.

> The externals of my life here are so well-known to you that they do not bear repetition. On the other hand journeyings, the 'jungle of the soul', turning and returning, retracing one's footsteps to find what is dear and precious – how can that be told? . . . I remember precious years; and time-together which for me were flawless . . .
>
> I'm sad that I did not answer some of your 'questions' when you were last here – the one on the beach, the one on the mountainside. Things, meanings, take time to sink into me – only long afterwards when I uncover the reality I am sad to find that my response missed the need. My timing has always been bad[,] for as you know, I am very slow and out-of-time generally.

I do know. 'Slow' is her code for the hated barbiturate, which inflicts this side effect. Even now, it dissipates the questions themselves in an offer to renew an empathy based in the past. In October 1968 my mother sits alone in her *succah* after a 'young marrieds' class there. Poppies glow against the dark pine branches, and she's pinned up a poster I'd painted in my teens: a copy of Nahum Levin's New Year card with its blessing in 1956. She writes, 'The distant knock of a building-hammer seemed to intensify the silence. Sunlight filtered through the pines and I was surprised by a visitation of the joy of former years. I thought much of you, and retraced my footsteps together with you.' She's missing our talks, 'really one long talk, isn't it, without beginning or end'.

That year she completes her last course towards her degree. Hebrew, ethics, classical culture had all been selected to serve her Bible teaching, but this course, *Nederlandskultuurgeskiedenis*, lectures in Afrikaans on Dutch art and architecture, is something of a spree. She gets a first in the November exam.

Soon after, she takes a room for a fortnight at 25 Arlington Court on the Beach Road at Muizenberg. She always swims at the Far Beach on the great stretches of sand away from the pavilion and promenade. After her first bathe at nine in the morning she starts a letter to me in her old vein. 'At this early hour the human beings are lone, Wordsworthian figures walking towards the horizon.' As she bathes again in the middle of a 'classic' Muizenberg day, warmed by sun and fanned by breezes, and for the third time at low tide in the 'slanting light' at six o'clock, her anticipation of my end-of-year visit quickens.

Wherever I am I think of sharing things with you. I feel you are spending the day with me here. A sort of 'I–Thou' day in which every half an hour or so I break our silence[,] speaking a thought to you. I'm picking every remembered happiness we have shared through the years and storing it for your coming.

Why do I not advance through this opened door? The anticipation of doing so recurs each time we meet, and then there's
a retreat on both sides.

'I've *failed*,' she says two or three days after we arrive, lifting
her head from the bathroom basin, where she's splashing her
face. Her disappointed look over her shoulder holds my gaze as
I lean in the doorway, waiting to be her sister once more. Then
she drops her head towards the tap again.

My mother cannot hold back her need to convert me – she
has become her mission. This means that she must lay before
me, again and again, not so much her faith in its visionary aspect
but Israel as the answer to the Holocaust, together with an
embrace of the community that, like all groups in South
Africa – not only racial groups – is closed upon itself. It's as
though the shtetl in Lithuania transplanted itself to this land of
'separate development'. Afrikaners keep to themselves; English-
speakers in the towns keep to themselves; and Jews likewise. I
can't be locked away from other people.

An alarm rings for my mother. This sounds like assimilation.

'The assimilated Jews of Germany, even those who were bap-
tised Christians, found they were categorised as Jews during the
Holocaust,' she reminds me. Assimilation is futile; intermarriage
a betrayal of who you are.

'Should I keep my feelings for you to myself?' she looks at
me worriedly, because she's torn between conviction and her
nervous care not to speak in a way she'll regret. 'Even though
you reject my feelings, should they never be spoken because
there's this risk?'

It is, she says, extraordinary that, all through centuries of per-
secution, the Jews retained their community through their
commitment to the written word – the Word. The scrolls of the
Torah and the sages who sifted holy writ in the Talmud provided the core for the community of the faithful clustering

about them. And that community was all the closer for threats
from outside: Cossacks. Thugs. Nazis. Her father's brother, Berl
Pres, his children including my mother's cousin Hannah, a
friendly girl aged thirteen (the same age as Anne Frank),
together with all the Jews of Plunge, shut up to rot for a fortnight, dead bodies amongst the living. Plunge neighbours
collaborating in the kill, and then scavenging the homes of the
dead. How can she forget?

Nor does she forget Levin. His presence in her thoughts
results in the kind of posthumous visitation she confides, in her
casual way, from time to time as I hang about her bedroom.

A fortnight after Levin's death his wife found out about the
love affair and shot off one question in the centre of an air-
letter, with a glaring space above and below: 'Rhoda, what is to
be done with your letters to Nahum? Dunia Levin.'

She could not trust herself to reply, my mother confided, but
for years afterwards she'd wished to ask forgiveness, both of
Dunia Levin and 'the Almighty'. In 1968, eight years after
Levin's death, when her guilt was at its sharpest on the eve of
the Day of Atonement, she'd set down an unsent note to Dunia
regretting the pain she had caused by 'that strange, exalted tie
to Nahum'. It then happened one day, in the course of a lunch
party, overlooking the sea, that Nahum himself 'reached out' to
her with 'a message from the afterlife'.

The message was an instruction to read Psalm XXXII, verses
5 and 10: 'Thou forgavest the iniquity of my sin.' She copies out
these words in the original Hebrew, with 'an inrush of thank-
fulness': 'He that trusteth in the Lord, mercy shall compass him
about.'

Improbable as it may seem, my father too visits Rhoda on
this matter after his death – or so she tells me. In 1969, at the
age of sixty, my father falls ill with Hodgkin's disease, a malig-
nant lymphoma which spread to the lungs. In June I fly with

Anna from New York to be with him, and we are there for three months. During this time he makes a valiant effort to go abroad and officiate as usual at the Maccabiah Games. It does give him a lift to be cheered as he moves, on Pip's arm, around the pool, but after that he collapses and the north-to-south flight home across Africa is a nightmare. My mother and I are shocked to see how wasted he looks in the wheelchair bringing him towards us at the terminal.

On the last Saturday of his life I visit him in Groote Schuur hospital, and as I walk into the oncology ward his face drops. He's sad that my mother hasn't come, even though he knows it's the Sabbath, when it's forbidden to drive. And yet my mother would be the first to say that the law is not inflexible: 'This is a humane faith,' she'd say, 'illness takes precedence over observance.'

I try to explain how heavy her workload is, so that she does need the day of rest, but my father is not consoled. She has been the love of his life and he feels at this moment how it's never been the same for her. To see my cheerful father drop is too much for me. I shed tears in the corridor outside his ward.

A few days later, 4 September, when he lies dying, a delegation from the South African Swimming Union arrives at his bedside, not so much to see him, rather to consult him, as their long-time President, about one of their wrangles. Amongst them is a rival who has tried to oust Harry. He's sporting enough to rise to the occasion and find answers, as though he were at a meeting.

At the last, his left lung fails to function. 'I'm going to roll over and try the other lung,' he tells my mother, who praises his 'incorrigible optimism'.

Siamon flies out for the funeral, and the family regroups at Houw Hoek on a mountain pass for a few quiet days. My mother must take over the reins from a husband who has always protected her, and she finds herself unexpectedly strong, supported by trust in her brothers and above all by her story-telling closeness to Anna, aged four, another in the line of dreamers.

One morning three years later, in 1972, she wakes in alarm, she tells me (and no one else) afterwards. Something brushed her lips. She cried out, and then unmoving lips close to her own reassured her: what she felt was my father's moustache – a famil-iar touch coming upon her from somewhere else. His kiss, she said to me and more than once, confirmed her belief that her love for Levin had quickened her marriage.

Was this a strange illusion, I ask my brother, and he reveals that our father had been upset enough to visit Cille to ask her to stop egging Rhoda on with Levin.

I point out to Pip that our father was practising the old double standard, a different morality for men and women, and Pip gives the usual answer: 'But he loved her alone.'

I think a bit and say to Pip, 'Her love for Levin may have stim-ulated the competitor in our father, and his surprise to find an unsuspected ardour in Rhoda may have stirred him. I think too that her elation in the early days with Levin, before guilt set in, let off sparks, which excited all of us at home. Do you remem-ber how all four of us would dance to records on the Deccalion?'

In 1973 I fly to England with Anna to take up a research fel-lowship at St Hilda's College. Siamon will remain in New York for a while.

Our move disappoints my mother. This is not the migration she'd hoped for. We will not go to Israel, and neither, except for visits, will we go home. Oxford is an unexpected solution.

My mother accompanies Anna and me in late August 1973, and stays for a few weeks in a hotel while I fix up a house we've rented. In 1952 London had been, for her, a 'great opportu-

nity', and she's still attached to Auntie Minnie and her family there. But Oxford is alien; we know no one; and allegiance to Israel has turned her against England – for her, now, England is less its literature more the ruler of Palestine, who turned back homeless survivors of the Holocaust when they tried to land illegally.

I'm relieved when my mother leaves. Her resistance makes it harder to adapt, and this time I'm determined after my retreat from Israel and breakdown in America. It's not only a 'great opportunity'; the welcome at St Hilda's and its green lawns sloping down to the river grow on me. It's astonishing to be planted here.

My mother's youngest brother, Hubert, shares her dim view of this move. After we settle in Oxford he asks with grave emphasis every time we meet, 'And how is *Siamon*?', as though I'd undermined a brilliant career.

Siamon has decided it's right for a couple to 'take turns'. He's urged me to leave behind a 'helper' view of the workplace and become more professional. In the face of uneasy questions from fellow scientists, almost all married men, he's proud to encourage a wife to take off on her own. He has a grant from the American Leukemia Society, which he can bring with him when he eventually joins Anna and me, but his arrangement in Oxford is temporary, and for the next three years he's still centred in his New York lab. For one of these years, we all return to New York. After this, he's appointed to a readership in Oxford's Sir William Dunn School of Pathology, and opens his own lab in 1976.

When my first book, *Eliot's Early Years*, is published by Oxford University Press – the first deeply researched biography of Eliot – with reviews everywhere, Uncle Hubert asks, 'How much did you make?'

'Next to nothing,' I admit. For though this biography still sells steadily, an advance from a university press in 1977 was bound to be small.

Long after, Uncle Hubert's question continues to puzzle me because he cared so for books. Our exchange took place in his library in Johannesburg. Books with fine bindings stood to attention along the shelves, guarding a principle of intrinsic value. It occurs to me only now that my uncle's question may have meant this: if a woman is not the provider for her family, what business has she to move them?

Though the disapproving tone of my uncle's question gets to me, it's distanced by the novelty of a first book and my mother's almost astonished response to the fuel she'd laid down over the years. She calls it 'a little gem'.

Publication seems all the more extraordinary, coming from where I did. A writer's life is hardly thought of at the bottom of Africa. Only someone as gifted as Alan Paton can venture to be a writer; *Cry, the Beloved Country* has the resonance to catch an 'overseas' ear – that magical 'overseas', arbiter of values we can't judge for ourselves. Others my mother used to read were Afrikaners developing a robust vernacular – the *Taal* – for a local readership. Writing also for a local readership are talented black poets and playwrights of the *Drum* generation, a politically defiant magazine coming out of the townships of Johannesburg. Builders on the roads improvise in Xhosa or Zulu, chanting in unison to the beat of the pickaxe; they lift, bend back, let fall – audible, but hardly in print.

Some reviewers are outraged though. These men own Eliot. Who is this female scurrying around, sifting papers? I try (though don't quite manage) to console myself with Virginia Woolf's comic portrait of the gentleman put out to find the housemaid turning over books in his library. But for all that, the change to the UK is working out for me.

It's harder for Anna, aged eight and taking in her grandmother's disturbing clichés: 'the English are cold'; 'their manners put you in your place'. After the stimulus of New York, Anna's bound to feel the regimen of school in North Oxford and the narrow-mindedness of her class teacher who says to me, 'When Anna came she was very American, but now she's all right.' One rule she can't accept is to eat braised liver and onions at school lunch. The headmaster is so determined that she *shall* eat this meat that he sits next to her, waiting for her to put it in her mouth. She can't. They sit there, while the rest of the children go out to play. To escape this punishment she informs the headmaster that she will go home for lunch, and without telling me she sits out each lunch hour near the dustbins at the back of our rented house on Hobson Road. It's a narrow road with no one around, unlike the teeming street life and ethnic mix of the Upper West Side. Poor Anna. Either I'm typing upstairs or away in College. Guilt, compunction about the cost to families, accompanied wives and mothers of my generation, as we dreamt of a new life and made our crossing into the workplace.

St Hilda's was one of the five women's colleges in Oxford. I assume the fellows will share the New York fury over suppression of women. But at lunch, when I speak in this vein, shutters seem to come down over the faces at High Table.

'We are not career women,' says the Principal, Mrs Bennett, evenly, 'we are women with careers.'

Here, the decorum is balm after the blatant misogyny of Columbia. A tutor relates the history of a confrontation in the Senior Common Room. It had been the custom for the younger dons to pour coffee for the senior fellows, 'the Ladies', as Dame Helen Gardner and her contemporaries are called. Until then, the Ladies had dictated how their colleagues should vote at meetings of the governing body. One evening, instead of pouring the coffee, the younger dons just *didn't*. It was a bloodless revolution. That simple breach of manners sufficed as a declaration of independence: an end to the tyranny of the Ladies.

As a newcomer I'm struck by relish of the language as the English turn it around their tongues. Long sentences unfold, each subordinate clause flinging out a consideration or limb of doubt, or advancing with a leap and then coming down with feet on the ground. The English of the Cape is different, its vigour infused with the freshness of Afrikaans. I've come to England as a native speaker, but somehow unprepared for a language played out with so much grace and nuance, such extended diphthongs, such undercurrents of irony. Such ways with words reconfigure the brain, what we take in or give out, inviting a newcomer to partake. This opens up possibilities for speaking and writing I'd not foreseen.

At the same time the English tutors at St Hilda's, Anne Elliott and Celia Sisam, impress me with their absolute integrity and wisdom. They suggest teaching. Eliot is prominent in the Oxford curriculum at this time, when Helen Gardner, the Eliot scholar and leading Lady at St Hilda's, is Merton Professor – the first woman to be appointed to this position.

Eliot's essays offer stimulating topics for discussion: in his essay on Shakespeare, he asks if Othello is *'cheering himself up'* after he strangles his wife, when he presents himself as 'one who loved not wisely but too well'. Eliot points out how Othello 'has ceased to think about Desdemona'.

I lay Eliot's idea of reading before students: 'We must know all of Shakespeare's work in order to know any of it.' The meaning of any one of Shakespeare's plays, Eliot is suggesting, 'is not in itself alone, but in that play in the order in which it was written'.

This resonates for a biographer. I'm bent on seeing the continuity of Eliot's own oeuvre. It comes easily because my mother has shown how single-minded Eliot is, so that if you get the point of any poem you get them all. Finalists doing Eliot as their special author have a growing sense of empowerment, as one poem builds on another. It's the same high-level reading experience as Henry James offers in 'The Figure in the Carpet', which dramatises what makes for a great writer: a pattern suffusing the whole. Eliot, in fact, followed Henry James in calling for an imaginative reader to make a reciprocal effort. Virginia Woolf invites reciprocity in a warmer voice: 'Let books be an equal creation between us.'

I like opening her essays and sharing that invitation with students. The Oxford tutorial seems continuous with a habit of sharing books that had been part of growing up. My mother's bookplate, devised for the many who borrow from the tempting bookshelves in the sunroom, reads: 'I enjoy sharing books as I do my friends, asking only that you treat them well and see them safely home.'

Virginia Woolf's essays offer a trove of rousing questions. Is it difficult to catch Jane Austen 'in the act of greatness'? She spots an instance at a ball in *The Watsons*. I prefer these essays by writers to the rising vogue for critical theory, a thicket of terminology that often turns out to be an elaborate way of stating the obvious. I don't want students to submit to pretentious verbiage; great writing is readable. The reciprocity of the tutorial system, with the individual care practised in Oxford, turns out to be a fulfilling way of life, and it's for real. No longer am I failing to live my mother's dream or trailing in tow.

It's not all easy, of course. At the outset I feel a fraud beside

the fellows with their comprehensive reading, but once a tutorial or class starts the students' beaks are open. Should novels
end conclusively? Is Dickens offering social documents or
something closer to fairy tale? Is *The Waste Land* in any sense
a unified poem? I like the close relationship that the tutorial
invites: searching for answers together. This fulfilment as a
teacher is not unconnected with the past. For all the helpful
models amongst tutors at thirty colleges – I learn from them,
for instance, to select pupils for their capacity to go on developing, rather than fix on the top marks that may prove a
ceiling – my prime model comes from my mother's intentness
as a reader and the eager voices and laughter swelling from her
sunroom.

Moses is her model of the prophet-teacher. In the early, luxurious part of his life (as an adopted son of Pharaoh's daughter),
'he does not know God' – my mother puts this bluntly. It
appeals to her that Moses is not born with spiritual power. Only
when he's alone in the wilderness and spies the burning bush
'everything', Rhoda says, 'becomes clear. A man has found his
vocation; he enters into a relationship with the Supreme Being;
henceforth his powers are not exercised in accordance with his
own passions but are shaped and guided by this over-mastering
relationship.'

For her too this relationship shapes other relations in taking
priority amongst emotional claims. It's for this reason that she
can't always 'hear'. To hear the divine voice, she has to protect
herself from certain kinds of distraction.

We drive from Kloof Road, winding around Lion's Head
toward Kloof Nek. At a gravel rest along the road we park per-
ilously on the edge with a sheer drop of mountain below.
Sunlight slants through the pines and their resin smell mingles
with the sour-sweet tang of protea and other *fynbos*. To return

to this landscape is to find myself too deeply interfused to belong elsewhere.

'I'd like to come back,' I say. Not that I will, but I know from her dream of Klaver that she has it in her to share the fancy.

She turns her head, away from the drop, towards Table Mountain at our back. The late afternoon sun makes its rocky crest glow as though from within. She says nothing. The silence between us lengthens until I start the car, back onto the road, and proceed on our way.

All through the eighties, during these annual end-of-year visits, I write in the dining room from four in the morning till nine, when my mother appears for breakfast. I love those early hours when ideas stir and the dawn rays burst about Lion's Head. I think of biographical leads: Virginia Woolf falling on lives 'like a roll of heavy waters ... laying bare the pebbles on the shore of the soul', and Charlotte Brontë's wish 'to walk invisible'.

Distance and solitude fill my sails as a biographer with Chaucer's uncompromising advice to shun the crowd in his poem 'Truth': 'Flee from the prees, and dwelle with sothfast-nesse, / Suffyce unto thy good, though it be smal.' Virginia Woolf pounced on this, and I can't resist quoting it in *A Writer's Life*. In this second biography I again ignore academics' non-sensical mantra about 'the death of the author'. Because current literary theory has cast biography into the outer wilderness, to pursue this private writing life feels pleasantly secret, never mentioned in tutorials or lectures. I also ignore the current fashion for doorstop compendia of fact. As in *Eliot's Early Years* I'm committed to narrative momentum: a particular story I want to follow. At the same time I'm committed to authenticity and believe that biography could become an art if it treads the tightrope between verifiable fact and the story. At this period of fulltime teaching, everything discussed with pupils – both my own pupils at St Hilda's and those sent from other colleges to 'do' women's writing or American literature or Yeats and Eliot – seems to feed into the private biographic enterprise. One guide is Yeats, who claims that there's an idea to every great life. Yet my sense of what is great, unlike that of Yeats, is anti-heroic: I'm drawn to the lives of the obscure, and think often of three friends who died young. I cherish Virginia Woolf for asking 'What is greatness? What is smallness?' in her essay 'The Art of Biography'.

When my mother called me 'a lucky girl' at my wedding, she saw me as I saw myself, a satellite to a person of distinction, whether it be her poetic or Siamon's scientific imagination. As it turns out, my real luck is to live with a person who urged me to give up the satellite role.

Siamon reminds me of the rational thinker, William Godwin, who wasn't drawn to Mary Wollstonecraft until he read one of her books in 1796. He said it was 'calculated to make a man fall in love with the author'. One of Siamon's undertakings is to be a participant-reader of what I write. All the same, my experience as satellite, rather than as one born to write, has led me to the stories of Vivienne Eliot, Minny Temple and Fenimore, women who lived in the shadow of Eliot and Henry James, cast as satellites to solitary genius yet in actuality central to their works of art. For it was Minny and Fenimore who more than anyone revealed to James what a woman is and what she wants. Such buried lives seem to me marvellously dramatised by James's strange story of drowning Fenimore's dresses in the Venetian lagoon after she committed suicide. This scene, I tell Siamon, will open a biography of these two women and Henry James.

But my mother is displeased to find me in her dining room surrounded by books and paper. 'Why are you working on holiday?' she cries, and later in the day she will report this to family and friends. 'She *never* stops working.'

I don't get the objection. Is aspiration reserved for her, I wonder, and should it be, like hers, under wraps? Privately I admire her silence and concede my limitations, and at the same time try to explain. Writing can't be done in term-time; it has to happen during vacations. But that's not the heart of it, for writing has come to be a lifeline. My mother's irritation when she catches me in the act of writing leaves me cold. There is no way now that she can shake my separate life in the making. It's time now to live and write as I feel I should, true to my own light, not hers.

My mother behaves quite differently when a book comes out. She is celebratory. Like any other mother, she presents copies to friends and dips into reviews. She basks in praise from Monica, the reader she respects above all others. It's as though she makes no connection between a published book and the discipline that goes into its making: the questions we frame for visits to archives, the narrative order, the drafts, notes and verifying of facts; and all along, an eye for likely illustrations. When a book is actually at hand Rhoda reads avidly, and she rereads with delight her own story-telling role in my memoir of three friends, *Shared Lives*, with its extract from her story 'Vignettes of Namaqualand'.

Yet I'm troubled by two private reservations. Am I not using my mother yet again for a book? And is it not, if I'm honest, an impertinence, given the quality of her poetic gift, to include her as sideshow of sorts in one chapter, where she offers her mentor-mothering to my schoolfriend Flora, who drinks in every word with her thirst for eloquence, for emotion, for life?

For all that, I'm elated to please my mother by acting in this small way as her channel. A test, a first step if you like, towards fulfilling my childhood destiny, and a pre-echo of the purpose behind the present memoir.

*

Can the figure in the carpet be applied to biography? Might
there be an underlying pattern to each life, more visible of
course in the lives of the great but discernible – if a biographer
has the wit to see it – in 'the lives of the obscure', those lives to
whom Virginia Woolf directs us with her feelers for what lies
in shadow. The practise of biography compels a biographer to
consider her own life and mine, I see, is bound up with my
mother's, even as our ways part.

A biographer might say in the last decades of the century, a
mother in Cape Town ran seven Bible classes while her daughter in Oxford lectured on women in Victorian fiction and
wrote about Charlotte Brontë. So much for fact. Roads not
taken beckon in the shadows of lives where purpose, in the routine sense, may be withdrawn and the future does not exist.
This mother continued to imagine an impossible migration to
a Promised Land embodied in the love of her life; her daughter continued to imagine an impossible return of the native to
the Cape of Good Hope. Are we the sum of our acts, or are we
our un-acted dreams?

'The story of Abraham in the Bible is the first great biography,' my mother remarks to me. A man called Abram takes a
new name, Abraham, the father of Am, people, not any old
tribe or nation but *the* People, who must carry his idea of one
ethical God – a moral revolution against the idols he smashes,
the multiple gods who invite the wanton or brutal acts of the
fertility faiths.

Abraham, my mother wants me to hear, is the first in a succession of the Chosen to migrate away from home as an act of
faith. She quotes the Hebrew to bring out the original impact
of the Lord's command with its insistent repetitions: '*Leh laha
m'arze'ha, m'moladit'ha, m'beit aviha*' (Get thee out of thy
country, from thy birthplace, from thy father's house).
Migration is central to the biographical pattern my mother has

dreamt herself into and made her own. This is the tried and tested way for an ordinary person to be transfigured.

Though I have disappointed my mother by refusing to fit my life to this pattern, she and I do cross our divide now and then. I'm in sympathy with her reading of Isaiah's end-of-days prophecy as the highest point in the Bible: an end to violence when arms shall be turned into ploughs and pruning hooks. 'Nation shall not lift up sword against nation neither shall they learn war any more.'

Our disgust with violence is interlinked with agreement on what women could contribute to civilisation in so far as women are biologically formed to nurture life.

'In the eighteenth century, Mary Wollstonecraft saw it as women's mission to outlaw war,' I tell my mother. '"Brutal force has hitherto governed the world,"' I quote her vital message. '"Man accustomed to bow down to power, can seldom divest himself of this barbarous prejudice." She takes up Isaiah's prophecy when she ends, "I sincerely wish to see the bayonet converted into the pruning hook."'

My mother and her group have never read *A Vindication of the Rights of Woman*, a book rediscovered by my generation. My contemporaries, though, are all for rights, and tend to overlook Wollstonecraft's domestic ethos because our current struggle is to escape its constraints. (Siamon has his finger on the political moment when, jokingly, he awards me marks for aspects of marriage, including a D for domesticity – a D was a pleasing badge for a politicised wife in the seventies, even if it wasn't exactly true.) But my mother's generation, I realise, would be in accord with Wollstonecraft's wish for women to draw on their domestic traditions rather than remake themselves as imitation men.

'I'd like to write Mary Wollstonecraft's life,' I confide to my mother. 'I want to stress her commitment to what she calls "the

domestic affections", tenderness, nurture, listening and compromise, qualities that the civilised of both sexes can share.'
Vindication will be more overtly political than my other biographies. A book that has nothing to do with my mother, I
might say – and then must concede how deeply she used to
concur with the domestic, anti-power, anti-greed values
Wollstonecraft put forward for a women's revolution.

My mother, for her part, concedes how unacceptable it is that
Jewish tradition from the Middle Ages closed theology to
women, and that the ultra-orthodox cut off girls, even now,
from higher education. She's excited by a challenge to this from
the American writer, Cynthia Ozick, deploring the loss of what
women might have contributed to Jewish studies, and books
that weren't burnt by the Nazis because they were never written.

My mother has cut out a report of this speech at Bar-Ilan, a
religious university in Tel Aviv. The cutting lies on her bedside
table, and reading it in full, I wonder what my mother makes of
Ozick's dismissal of women's groups. Segregation, she argues,
disables women. Putting them at a distance permits rabbis and
theologians not to hear what women say.

But why, then, do rabbis appear uncomfortable with my
mother, as my brother has noticed? Suitably deferential and
self-effacing, she does nothing to jar them. Ozick convinces
me that the rabbis' unease cannot be because my mother is a
woman speaking to women. Unease is more likely because she
does not practise the rabbinic mode of reading; the rabbis do
not attempt to seize an authoritative Truth. For them, to
engage with the text, the Word, is a religious experience in
itself. Reading is to lend the mind to the play of multiple
interpretations (some fanciful and even to do with numerol-
ogy). My mother is out of line, and ahead of her time by
several decades, in reading the Torah, the first five books of

the Bible, as 'family stories'. She feels the cumulative force of generations in the passage of beliefs and traits from one generation to the next, and she brings out the bonds of parent and child.

Can there be another cause of the rabbis' unease? Can it lie in the very timbre of her voice, even though she conceals her visionary exhilaration? Its source is at the opening of her prayer door to the garden, with a limitless ocean booming to the left, and looming to the right the dark shape of Signal Hill. To silence private visions defers to a religious tradition that gives pre-eminence to the communal over the personal. Within her routines of prayer, observance and teaching, day by day, year by year, her soul's saps pulse unseen.

In teaching, she takes care to offer her groups the scholars' voices: Rabbi Abraham Joshua Heschel at the Jewish Theological Seminary of America, and the German-Jewish philosophers Franz Rosenzweig and Martin Buber. She's a devotee of Buber, and quotes him in conversation. Excessively, to my mind. This rumble of cogitation seems to me to interrupt and dissipate my mother's voice, to alter its very character so that it becomes rather carefully scrupulous. When she speaks in her own voice, the encounters at her prayer door pulse below the surface. That pulse comes through a voice direct, intimate and a little strained − the strain deriving from the barbiturate, which slows her brain, and from a voice slowed deliberately to attend to scholarship. It's as though the speed of intuition races her voice ahead while words follow at a measured, almost formulaic, pace.

When I was a child, she often spoke of the blinded Samson ('O dark, dark, dark, amid the blaze of noon'), as though Milton's *Samson Agonistes* spoke to her own dark night of the soul. By night, when she looked up at the river of stars or surrendered to buffetings by Cape winds, she felt alive, awake, cleansed of dross. She gave me to understand at an early age that only those who undergo unmaking, who experience a kind of hiatus of non-being in their lives, can purify themselves as candidates for regeneration.

As a feminist, I hear her more readily when she trains her eye on the women in the Bible: above all, that promoter of the emotional tie, Ruth, the young widow who famously refuses to be divided from her widowed mother-in-law though they belong with different tribes. My mother exclaims over the moral beauty of this attachment between two women and across the generations.

She also reveres the biblical woman of valour who acts without violence. In Egypt, Pharaoh commands Hebrew midwives to kill male newborns. The midwives can't bring themselves to commit murder, and invent an excuse that Hebrew women give birth quickly, before a midwife arrives. For the midwives it's not a matter of faith ('fearing God', the scriptures say with pious insistence); it's got nothing to do with God. It's the midwife's natural and professional respect for life.

'The midwives can't know God yet,' I hear my mother say, 'not the God who will carry them out of slavery and deliver a code of law.'

But what women feel and do does not much concern the Bible's compilers and scribes when a hero in the making is squarely in their sights. My mother corrects for this wherever she can: 'Pharaoh's plans for the annihilation of the children are defeated by WOMEN.' Her teaching notes spell this out in capitals, and you can hear defiance in her voice.

When she feels her way into the oft-told story of Moses in the bulrushes, she fixes on the word 'placed': a mother placed her baby in her home-made boat-cradle, and then placed the boat among the reeds of the Nile. That act of placing suggests to my mother the 'profound anxiety in the mother's heart', and her care to put the boat down 'as gently and tenderly as she had placed the child in it'.

Then too, when the Egyptian princess decides to adopt the child, there's the valour of his sister Miriam, the little girl who's watching to see what happens and runs to the princess with her offer to find a Hebrew nurse 'for thee', as though she's acting on behalf of Pharaoh's daughter, while naturally she's acting for the baby and his mother. Rhoda admires the diplomacy of 'for thee'.

The bravest woman of valour is Esther, caught between dangerous men. Esther conceals her Hebrew background when the Persian king, Ahashverosh or Ahasuerus (thought to be Xerxes, who ruled in the fifth century BC) chooses her as his queen. It's politic to conceal her background because Haman, the king's vain, boastful functionary, is preparing to massacre her people. The king himself is unreliable, a spoilt show-off with a temper if crossed. In the opening scene of the story that comes down to us through the Bible, he kicks out his first wife, Vashti, when she refuses his summons to exhibit herself to his drunken court. 'Every man should bear rule in his own house,' the king justifies his caprice.

At work in my old top room, I hear an unprecedented din erupt from the sunroom. Rhoda and the quiet housewives in her group are shouting, so that none can be heard. I run along the passage to hear. It's about Vashti. They read her as a feminist rebel. Married young to wilful, unseeing husbands, these loyal, middle-aged wives find themselves at white heat, shoulder to shoulder with Vashti's refusal to be, in the current phrase, a sex object. They see Esther forced to replace her. To the king, she exists only as his choice from a round-up of Persian beauties – 'like men who manage beauty-queen parades', my mother says, trying to quell the shouts.

This is so 'relevant' (as we talk then) to my political passions that I must stay and listen as my mother tells Esther's story: how Esther devises a more effective form of action than Vashti's confrontation. A different kind of theatre, my mother proposes.

At that, we simmer down to lend ourselves to the artistry of Esther as she stages a humane drama of a higher order: an operatic petition of her ruler-husband, risking her life ('if I die, I die') in successive banquet scenes, playing to the king's luxurious taste, as Esther prepares to pit an exposure of her background against Haman's extermination programme. My mother follows the biblical narrator as 'a consummate artist' who paces Esther's story with pauses to quicken the suspense.

The women in Rhoda's home group, Monica and Lilian and Thelma and Mickey and Ida, who live to be mothers, feel in their fibres what Olive Schreiner meant when she said 'men's bodies are our women's works of art'. Rhoda attacks the killer code of heroism by way of Genesis: the Lord breathed into our nostrils 'the breath of life'. From this, she says, 'flows the Hebrew understanding of the sanctity of human life. This was a new value in the world. We know that even the cultured Greeks exposed newborn infants on the roof to test their strength for survival; and their slaves were termed by Aristotle mere "tools with life". Even in the greatest development of pagan culture, we find Plato suggesting that in his ideal city the incurably sick and the mentally ill should be neglected. This seems to show a lack of appreciation of the resources of the human spirit through suffering and affliction.'

Her Moses is decidedly not a hero; he's a man suffering with his people, and struggling to overcome their wickedness and loss of morale as they wander for forty years in the desert.

My mother adds, 'The test of faith is to be steadfast in the

face of worldly failure, because the life of faith is in large measure a struggle with the world.'

'Steadfast' sounds tame, yet it's what she's learnt by holding fast to the lifeline of Psalm XXIII as she teeters over the
abyss.

Given my mother's history of post-partum breakdown, and
mine, following Anna's birth, doctors have warned Siamon and
me that to have another child might be a risk. By the late seventies Anna is twelve and has always longed not to be an only
child. Anna isn't eating, and Siamon and I are of course very
worried about her. We decide that the risk of childbirth will be
worth it if it makes Anna happy – as it does. Then too we are
settled enough in Oxford, with Siamon's lab growing and a lec-
tureship for me at Jesus College, to believe that this time we will
cope better.

This time it happens immediately, at the start of pregnancy.
It's like being switched off. It's an ordeal to get up, and I'm only
thankful that this is happening during the university vacation,
in the spring, between Hilary and Trinity terms. I lie prone,
reading Sherlock Holmes simply to pass the hours. My GP asks
if I really want this baby. I really do, and this time I'm aware
how little content there is to the depression. Siamon says the
one helpful thing: what I'm experiencing, he says, is the impact
of pregnancy hormone, the dramatic change to the body at the
start of pregnancy and after childbirth, to which some women
will be susceptible. I hold on to his promise that the depression
will stop once the hormone has reached a certain level – and so
it does.

The first thing I do after the birth of Olivia, in November
1978, is to shuffle along the corridor at the John Radcliffe hospital in Oxford to a public phone. I can't wait to tell my mother
what a strong, alert child has come into our family. Flying out

to Cape Town three weeks later it's like crossing a fissure with an offering in my arms. This time I will share mothering with my mother. Can we push our divide aside?

She receives Olivia with delight, but though we enjoy the baby together it doesn't budge the divide. With Olivia, it's not

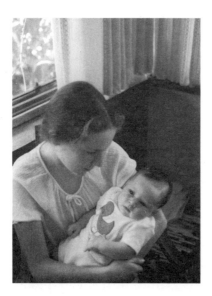

Anna holds her longed-for sister, Olivia. Clockwise from top right: in Oxford; coming to Cape Town – four generations at the gate; with Granny Annie; in the sunroom

the same for her as with Anna. With Anna, she'd replaced me
as a mother when I was away in hospital weeks on end.
Maternal protectiveness welled up in her for Anna as a baby, and
remained firm. She's older and established in her far-off working life when Olivia arrives. She's now a grandmother, and no
more. As Olivia grows up, a sturdy child, strong in mind and
will, she is not as entranced as Anna by her grandmother's Bible
stories. At her children's Bible class, Olivia looks forward most
to the butterscotch my mother hands out. When Olivia is a
healthy ten-year-old my mother says to her, with the unthinking insensitivity of her own mother, 'When I was your age, I
was a thin girl.'

Once, when my mother and I are talking intently during a
long car journey, Olivia bites me. She explains later, 'It was to
get your attention.' Anna is one of my mother's 'lovely girls';
Olivia (and I) are not, with the result that she can't quite see
us.

Rhoda's definition of mankind as 'a family of families' leads her
at the age of sixty-two to take action against apartheid. With her
woman's eye, she's long noticed that numerous women working in Sea Point have nowhere they can go on their Wednesday
or Thursday afternoons off. It's only an afternoon, so there's not
enough time to travel home to one of the townships, really a
sprawl of shacks, Windermere or Langa, which social engineering has relegated (without lighting, water or police
protection against rampant violence) to the periphery of the
city. There are men-only bars for blacks in Sea Point, reeking
of cheap liquor. When women are off they stay in their rooms:
dark, close rooms in back yards.

At length, my mother realises that no one will act on behalf
of women workers with no vote. She must act on her own. In
the winter of 1979, Rhoda and her cousin Garda, who has

recently moved to Sea Point, distribute leaflets inviting women
to tea one Thursday in July. They also accost 'madams' in the
street, asking them, 'Would you object if your maid is asked to
tea?' Katie Erasmus, my mother's able housekeeper, is in charge
of the food: she bakes delicious scones and cakes, and spreads
them out in her no-fuss manner on long trestle tables in the
Weizmann hall on the Main Road, which has been donated by
the synagogue.

To forestall a Special Branch raid on people crossing the
colour bar in a public hall, Rhoda pays a visit to the Sea Point
Police Station. In tea-rose and pearls, with lipstick, a neat, side
parting to her curly hair and a handbag over her arm, she performs her hesitant 'only a housewife' act – performed so often
that it's almost second nature. Afrikaner policemen, peremptory
and rough with blacks, are brought up to respect white, older
women. They listen politely to my mother assuring them that
all she has in mind is food provision for poor women. No need
to suspect trouble from this fragile lady.

To my mother's astonishment, over three hundred women
turn up. She'd assumed they'd want 'tea and *gesels*' (she uses the
Afrikaans word for chat because street Afrikaans, a local dialect
full of verve and slang, will be the home language for most who
come). It turns out that the women want to use their off time
for courses and activities.

Garda organises the most popular course, in nursing and first
aid. The training by St John Ambulance makes it possible to
find better jobs as carers for the elderly of Sea Point. By the
time the Friendship Club, as it comes to be known, celebrates
its sixth anniversary, two hundred and thirty members have
gained Home Nursing Certificates. Some are proud to be on
duty at rugby and soccer matches, as well as in theatres (as
required by law, wherever crowds gather). My mother offers
Bible study. Lilian sets up a sewing circle; there are knitting, cro-

chet and embroidery groups; cookery demonstrations; and my mother's neighbour, Anne Rabie, runs yoga and aerobics. Gymsuits discarded by the well-fed matrons of Sea Point hang oddly on the wiry frames of domestic workers.

The Friendship Club, meeting each Wednesday and Thursday, thrives from year to year. A statement to my mother from members at the start of 1980 suggests a motto: 'With Love we serve one another.' Helen Khun accompanies my mother to a concert at the City Hall, one place where races are not divided. Katie September and Betty Rhenoster say that the Club is 'home' to them, and they hope it will 'go on for ever'. Justina Fadana, a quiet, elderly woman with nowhere to live, becomes a permanent guest in Katie's one-time room at 11 Avenue Normandie (when a new room for Katie is built). My mother makes out that Justina is employed by her, since non-whites are not allowed to live in Sea Point, except as servants.

Members are required to pay twenty cents a time, to avoid an atmosphere of charity. All the same, my mother is not shy to elicit donations: one firm supplies cups and saucers; another, offcuts of fabric for the sewing group. Eventually, there's a choir and group excursions: a hired bus takes a party to Namaqualand each September to see the white, yellow and orange daisies that cover the veld. At an end of year party, my mother joins in a country jig called the *tickey draai* (literally, a three-penny turn: a hectic, breathy bobbing and turning to folk music, *boeremusiek*), familiar to Rhoda from the dances her mother had held at Klaver Hotel. My brother is there, and when he sits down at a piano to belt out his party piece, 'Great Balls of Fire', the women abandon their cups and saucers, leap to their feet and dance.

My mother's favourite of all her groups is a children's class each Saturday morning, in a separate room during the service at the Marais Road synagogue. She's especially fond of a little boy, whom she calls 'the professor'. He sucks his thumb while he listens; takes out his thumb to deliver 'a profound question'; and then, satisfied, returns the thumb to his mouth.

One day in 1983, Thelma, the artist in the private Friends' Group, sits in on the children's class. That day, Rhoda relates the 'wonder' story of Jonah, who is swallowed by a whale and spends three days and three nights in the whale's belly before he's spat up on a beach. Jonah has been a runaway from God's mission: to cry out for repentance in the wicked city of Ninevah. Thelma is excited at the way the children respond to the moral nuances, as when, in terror of a storm at sea, Jonah begs the sailors to cast him into the ocean because he's failed in his duty to God, and the sailors, who are heathens, do so unwillingly.

'They know how precious is a human life': Rhoda brings out the sailors' reluctance, implying that you don't have to have faith to be humane.

Jonah does then undertake the Ninevah mission, and the inhabitants do wake up to corruption. Rhoda's telling brings out Jonah's discontent: he's sulking because the Lord forgives Ninevah too readily. For all Jonah's effectiveness as divine agent, he hasn't grasped the higher good of mercy.

Thelma wants this to be a children's book. Rhoda brushes off the idea with her usual deprecation. Thelma insists: she tapes Rhoda telling the story, has it typed, illustrates it, and sends it to Oxford University Press Southern Africa, who publish the book with a commentary for parents and teachers. Having always shunned publication, Rhoda remains passive, at most compliant in the hands of her determined friend, but the press likes the narrative for its closeness to the tone and language of the Bible, and markets it as suitable for both Christian and Jewish readers, 'for in the story of Jonah the Bible reaches a peak of universalist teachings'.

*

The 'runaway basket' filled with unseen poems

In the mid-eighties my mother takes out what Katie calls her 'runaway basket' packed with her poems. At this point she selects seventy poems to put in order as a spiritual autobiography, 'Notes on a Journey'. Here she shows an initiative absent in the run-up to *Jonah*. Over the next few years she reconsiders her choices and reshuffles the order. And all the while her commitment to teaching goes on, thirty-four years in all, from the time Levin inspired her mission in 1955 until she retires from teaching at the age of seventy-two.

On a torn scrap of paper she scribbles: 'So she went on Teaching until her memory began to fail, and time short "to tell of all Thy Works".'

15

Lost and Living Memory

In New York Rhoda (front left) and Basil (centre) meet
Ben Miller (right). Back: Alma Miller, Naomi Press; front: Anna

When my mother is seventy, in 1987, she counts up the years
that separate us: 'Twenty-three years apart divide our lives. The
division between the generations is painful.'

She's confiding her pain about our divide to a cousin, Ben
Miller, a doctor in New York, who lost his family – that is, our
Pres family in Plunge – during the Holocaust. Worse than my

distance in miles, though, is my involvement in a foreign, Oxford world: 'the commitment to our bereft Jewish people is lost in their faraway lives'.

'Bereft.' It's a lament for Ben, who had been lost to sight for many years after the Holocaust until my mother's determined efforts to find a survivor had turned him up in America. It is a lament too for mothers and daughters. And I suppose, the generations passing.

It's also a private lament following Monica's sudden death from heart failure:

> ... my life-long sister-friend Monica, a 61-year friendship beginning at the age of 9 years when I came as a little 'backvelder' from Klaver and found this wonderful gifted child at the head of my class. We met in the Library and ever since we have shared books – indeed shared our lives in every aspect ... In spite of her many gifts, being bereft of a mother from babyhood she chose motherhood.

A mother's duty. A mother's duty was at issue when Monica pressed Rhoda to give up her poetry group in London in 1952. But we, Rhoda's children, were old enough to understand that her deferred longings to see beyond our provincial world did not conflict with her maternal bond. She came back to a town where she had no one to talk to about poetry; no one to guide her as in London. Her predicament, as she confided it to a sister-child, was to alert me ever after to women's un-acted aspirations.

As I write this in the summer of 2013, a one-time neighbour from New York arrives for lunch: Barbara Robey, who still lives on the tenth floor of our apartment block near Columbia University. She has with her a nine-year-old grandson, Sam, whom she's treating to a Harry Potter week in Oxford. As we recall our ways as young mothers, I remember how Barbara once thought to become a doctor. Yes, she confirms, she took pre-med courses at Smith College, where she was advised – this was the fifties, the era of Sylvia Plath – that, for women, such study should not be with a view to a professional career, merely as preparation for educated motherhood.

My mother's expectations were even more subdued in a place where, if a woman worked it was a sign of poverty – almost a stigma, lowering your class, in the way Charlotte Brontë discovered back in the later 1830s, when she went out to earn her living as a governess. I opened my biography of her with the scene of Charlotte left alone on the servants' floor by middle-class employers with whom she'd been accustomed to mix socially as a daughter of a minister. When I came to England in 1973 I was astonished to hear class-conscious remarks about Valerie Fletcher, who, before their marriage, had worked as Eliot's secretary in the fifties. These remarks hinted that the poet married beneath him: a young woman from Leeds who (said an owner of a fine old Cotswold house) drew on *nylon* gloves when a visit came to an end. None of these observers did justice to Mrs Eliot's feat in editing the manuscript of *The Waste Land*. Back in the fifties, my father meant to protect his secretary, Mrs Swan, from prejudice against working women when he'd say, 'highly intelligent, always a lady'. Attitudes to working women changed with the mass entry of middle-class women into the workplace since the seventies. This may make it hard now to fathom the intensity of my mother's longing for 'work-in-the-world' in the early fifties, and what a blessing such work appeared when it washed up at her feet on an after-wave of Levin's mission. So it was that fulfilment as a teacher displaced more unlikely fulfilment as a poet – a dream realised only briefly, with her escape to London.

Siamon was appointed Professor of Cellular Pathology.
He and Olivia visit me at St Hilda's College, Oxford

The twenty-one years between 1952 and 1973 made all the difference for women of the next generation. In 1973, it was unusual but not unthinkable to take off with a child and move on my own to another country when the chance came. Siamon agreed to this. He was ahead of his time in his belief that women should work, and after a while he found a way of joining us in England. Whether it was the right course for a daughter born in New York is another question. On our last night, bags packed, furniture sold, the apartment emptied, Anna, aged eight, stood silently at the window looking out at Riverside Drive and the Hudson River. It's fair to ask whether in that decisive act of migration I did to my daughter what my mother did to me.

Given that past, I hope to free my daughters to bear what fruit they were made to bear, without an obligation to be an extension or a channel. At the same time, I'm convinced that the home education my mother offered, reading aloud and books that awaken empathy, is vital to mothering, and more formative than formal learning.

Anna will grow up to be a teacher like her mother and grandmother before her. When I ask her now what mothering meant to her she reminds me how, at the age of three or four, she used to confiscate my pencil. She didn't want a mother to be preoccupied. She'd have liked a mother who baked cakes, and compensated by baking herself. Later on, she says, 'having a mother who was passionate about her own work' taught her 'to be immersed' in what she does. She thinks a mother should 'see and appreciate' who her daughter is.

Anna ruminates over what she witnessed as a small child: my criticisms of the lifestyle of liberal whites in the face of extreme poverty, aloft in the palaces they've built for themselves on out-crops of mountain, and my feminist anger at the inequalities of Columbia and the workplace. 'Your rebellious streak probably influenced me,' Anna says. 'I am not afraid to tread the path less travelled, to be internally daring. So many people have had mothers who never found their own light. Your family did not like you being outspoken and rebellious, but I did. It led me to feel free to speak out about injustice – to tell my truth plainly whatever the world might say.' I am relieved by these words.

As it turns out, my most memorable experience of mother-ing will have nothing to do with seeing and speaking out, the ways learnt from my own mother. In fact, it will have nothing to do with experience, but will be – like much mothering – instinctive. It comes about years later, when Olivia has grown up and married: she asks me to be with her when she gives birth.

As she approaches the seventh month of pregnancy there are signs that the baby can't deal with the fluid surrounding him: it's around his lungs and under his scalp. Excess fluid is drained by the foetal surgery unit at University College Hospital in London, and then over the next fortnight the fluid builds up once more. Suddenly, Olivia goes into labour, eight weeks early.

I'm apprehensive, because I'm no expert on childbirth and this is clearly a complicated one.

'I may not be able to help you,' I warn her.

'Just be there for me.'

When she asks for pain relief I leave her side to call the midwife, who takes one look and says, 'Too late. The baby's coming.'

As the contractions lengthen I urge Olivia to cry out if she wants. 'It's all right.'

'Don't waste your energy,' the midwife contradicts. 'Use your breath to push.'

Wrenched though I am by Olivia's pains, it's extraordinary to watch the midwife like a director of a drama. 'Wait – hold your breath. Now pant. Now! *Push.*'

To my surprise, she uses only two fingers to ease out the head, holding the fingers almost still, with minimum intervention. The delicacy of that handwork is exquisite. It could be a work of art: the pulsing of birth against that quiet hand. It's astonishingly quiet: only the concentrated breathing of Olivia, the low-voiced instruction of the midwife and the baby's steady heartbeat (amplified), reassuring us he's not distressed. The consultant, Dr Kendall, and two doctors in his team are ready, waiting at the foot of the bed. The moment the baby emerges, a wool cap is tucked over his head. I'm holding my breath for his cry, and it doesn't come. 'Fortunately, there's no immediate emergency,' Dr Kendall says, and places the small being on

Olivia's abdomen for the briefest look at each other before racing the newborn to intensive care for the ventilation his lungs need.

I feel a rush of delight in this tiny creature, who has held on to life despite the encroaching fluid.

'He's a serious chap,' I say to Olivia's husband Phil, a musician who has stood up to the sight of blood, which he'd thought might shake him.

There's a shower adjoining the delivery room, and as I help Olivia to wash herself down I feel washed clean of my own first childbirth, which had been part of my concern for Olivia. For that scene of uncaring orderlies with a heaving body, exposed to view in a public lift, gets expunged at last by my closeness to my daughter, and by her wanting me there, throughout this ordeal.

Now, when I ask Olivia what mothering means to her, she fixes on an awful night that preceded the birth. 'We had just had the news that our baby was seriously ill, and you stayed up all night watching over me in hospital. To me, on the cusp of motherhood yet feeling more than ever in need of mothering myself, what you did brought home to me what a mother does for her child – and the fact that as mothers, we crave and value our mothers even more.'

Olivia recalls also an exchange we had after Humphrey was born. 'I was afraid I wasn't a good enough mother, and you told me that you yourself didn't always feel selfless – like me, you wanted time for yourself. It relieved and strengthened me to hear this. As a child, I never noticed if your mind wasn't focused on being my mother. I felt that it was. Maybe we are "perfect" mothers already without trying to be perfect.'

As Rhoda enters her seventies, I bring up the question of publication. Her intention is set out in her papers, what she confided

Olivia with me at an interview when
Virginia Woolf: A Writer's Life came out, 1984

to me long ago: 'If this is ever worthy of publication it should be after my death.' But at this point a counter intention rises, encouraged perhaps by *Jonah*. She brings a typescript of the seventy poems with her when she visits England during the hot summer of 1986. We take her with us to the isle of Harris in the Outer Hebrides where, on impulse, she slips off the side of a boat in her petticoat to bathe in the icy ocean. On an empty beach we pick up the most delicate shells we've ever seen, faint transparent pinks, as though washed up by waters newly divided from dry land.

On our return to Oxford, I suggest we try my publisher, Oxford University Press, which has a strong poetry list built up

by Jon Stallworthy, a poet himself. He has been replaced by an
editor unknown to me. I write her a covering letter, explaining that my mother has accumulated an oeuvre of poems. We
submit them in August; in October, the editor sends a courteous rejection, saying that she finds the choice of words
'overwrought'.

Emily Dickinson too had a belated counter-intention when,
in 1883, three years before her death, she sent a sample of her
poems to the prestigious Boston publisher Thomas Niles. He
replied that he could not 'consume' them. He thought them
'devoid of the true poetical qualities'. She left no comment.

My mother leaves a midnight scribble, dated 28 February
1987, retreating into the modesty of a woman accustomed to
living in the shadow of rabbis and theologians. She permits herself to speak in public only as a disciple of Martin Buber. That
night, while reading a biography of Buber, she tells herself, 'I
have only a limited power of thought. My experience comes
from the "encounters" granted me through the epileptic deaths
and abysms of my life, and the visionary grace bestowed on me.'

To find her naming her illness is still strange to me. It's not a
word she ever says aloud. She has kept a tally of '22 deaths' in
all.

That year, 1987, she consults a doctor about lapses of
memory. As memory begins to fade, she forgets the ways I'd
disappointed her and we come close again.

It's a relief to revert to something like our original tie. The
early reversal of the protective mother-daughter relation in our
case was peculiar, though it had, for me, its gains. After the
independence of my mother's 'work-in-the-world' from the
fifties till near the nineties she's dependent on me once more,
and this time, to be a daughter tending her ageing mother is in
the normal cycle of things. Curiously, this is not a sad turn.
There are moments of delight in rediscovering what we share

and the deep comfort of closing our divide. I see in her taste and the quality of her mind what has shaped all that's mattered in my life. What's different in this later phase is that my protective feeling for her is not new; it's repetition. And it's this fact of repetition that's threading a pattern in the carpet of our lives.

Though my mother is prone to leave taps running and mislay her glasses more than ever, this appears at first no more than habitual forgetfulness. Some time after she retires from teaching, one morning in the early nineties, Katie finds a poem on the floor next to Rhoda's bed. It appears that retirement has released the poet in her.

> *Tired by the day*
> *The breezes of freedom*
> *blow all around me.*
> *My body like the harp*
> *left idle in the midst*
> *of the morning orchestra*
> *trembles quietly*
> *forgotten by the pains,*
> *by suffering, by necessity.*
> *I listen to the quiet*
> *resonator of the universe*
> *O miracle of love!*
> *Top of a high tree*
> *moved by the song of the birds.*

Her inward and poetic life continues after she's thought to have lost her mind to confusion. Her last poem in May 1993 lays out three possible passages through the lifespan:

> *Some step into the world*
> *stable, strong,*

Some go on long
slow journeyings
or ride on fiery serpents.
Some never seek
but stumbling go
they wade no-ways
until they blench
and fade in the numbering
of death

By 1993 she is, she knows, often 'stumbling', yet at times she's capable of keen enjoyment. In August she accompanies us to Edinburgh and attends the Festival, while I look at a manuscript memoir by Charlotte Brontë's publisher, George Smith, in the National Library of Scotland. We return to London by sleeper, which brings back the overnight trains of her childhood, puffing slowly to Namaqualand, so much so that when I help her out of her compartment on arrival at Euston she thinks we've reached Klaver.

One day in Oxford she wanders out on her own and we can't find her. A secretary at the Sir William Dunn School of Pathology, where Siamon works, spots her looking about vaguely in South Parks Road, and drives her home. She's not distressed. Should I smile at her old-fashioned femininity depending on, and warmed by, the kindness of strangers? So long as you treat her as normal, she's quite at ease, used to her own vagaries and to owning as of old in mildly amused tones: 'I'm impossible.' At some point, though, she's bound to notice how some are discomfited by oddity.

There is an unsent letter to her youngest brother, after he and his wife have been in Cape Town. When Hubert was little in their Klaver nursery Rhoda had offered him tickeys to kiss her. Now she foresees an oncoming divide.

Midnight
Wednesday May 19th 1993

My dear Hubert,

. . . When I was sitting and listening to you in the garden
of the Mount Nelson [Hotel] waiting to see you and
Berjulie off at the airport Berj called a taxi and sent me
away. Why?

   It's true my memory is impaired, perhaps by the
medication my life-long illness has necessitated – was this a
reason to turn from me even if such impairment was
irritating? Please help me . . . – to understand.

A misunderstanding is likely: her sister-in-law probably wished
to spare my mother a journey to the airport, not realising that,
for her, it was not a duty. And then too, undoubtedly, the hotel's
taxi company was safer than a random taxi at the airport. That
said, Berjulie does find muddle off-putting, so it's also likely that
Rhoda's feelers picked this up.

   Other unsent letters in 1993 show shifts in crucial relation-
ships. That year, her eldest brother almost dies of septicemia in
the intensive care ward at Groote Schuur Hospital. Her scribble to him is close to prayer:

How shall I thank you enough Basil my beloved brother.
You have blessed me and cared for me all my life long –
May you be helped and upheld and strengthened and
blessed and speedily healed.

Your loving
Sister

Basil recovers and my mother is soothed by his peacefulness as
they sit together on his stoep looking out over Danger Beach

between their old haunts at Muizenberg and the fishing village of Kalk Bay. They are full of the past. 'Klaver ... Klaver ...' The beat of hooves as Daddy gallops off to the farm at dawn. The pony and trap carrying them to their one-room school. Italian engineers arriving to build 'the furrow', and then, by night, when they play their records, the voices of Galli-Curci and Caruso filling the vast spaces of veld.

Another midnight scribble has to do with the shifting tie to her son. There are tensions between them: she has never approved of Pip's 'fun-loving' side, involving poker nights and 'jolling' – a local word for sprees. But now there's also his partner, a dancer with Dulcie Howes (whose fine ballet school

In the early nineties my mother and I revisit her early years when 'train days' – only three trains a week – brought excitement

trained the choreographer, John Cranko). It appalls Rhoda to discover that Kristin is 'German' – by which she means German antecedents. And yet she needs Pip. It is he who hires cleaners and carers, and who monitors her medication, since she's increasingly unreliable about taking it. He puts up notices around her room, even in her walk-in cupboard, to reassure her of his care, and remind her where she is and where to reach him. He takes her out two evenings a week. They quarrel; they make up. Their bond is more active than mine, with only inter-mittent visits from overseas. He's now the companion I'd been in our childhood. She scribbles worriedly after his heart attack. 'For some time I have been depending on Pip for all social pleasures . . . I have recently been conscious of the burden my needs & failing memory have loaded on him.'

Over the ten years of Rhoda's memory loss, the large circle of friends and family gradually falls away until, without Pip, she'd be alone with a succession of paid companions. Lilian now lives in Johannesburg with her daughter Joan. Lilian and Marjorie, my mother's two bridesmaids in 1940, visit when they come to the Cape each summer. I'm there, at home, at the end of the year, and talk turns to the plays of Athol Fugard and the stay-ing power of defiant, multi-racial drama during the bad old days of apartheid at Jo'burg's Market Theatre. We talk past Rhoda; she's left out.

Friday nights remain outwardly the same with the candles, white cloth and two loaves under the prayer cover; and there are guests, most often our father's humorous nephew Arthur and his warm-hearted wife Bernice; or it might be Monica's second son, Ronnie; or Gloria Sandak-Lewin, the top girl in the year ahead of mine at Good Hope, who later attended the Bible classes. Sadly, my mother no longer enjoys Friday nights: the talk is too fast, too full of the present, which is unreal to her, or too full of allusions she no longer recalls. Her manner is nervous, and she fills her gaps with her role as hostess. Arm shaking, she offers dishes repeatedly, cutting across conversation: wouldn't we have more peas, more pineapple pudding? A second later, she urges the same. It's hard to keep some semblance of a dinner party, with vacancy pressing itself upon it to the point of disruption.

'You've offered Pip more already,' I reproach her, as though she can take this in. I break out when she grumbles at Katie whose dinners are, as ever, perfection. Here I am, shouting about South African housewives who take service for granted – no more than a white woman's due. How can she have lost all sense of Katie's need for appreciation, I shout. There's glee in the kitchen, as though my loss of sympathy with my mother relieves the helpers.

I'm convinced that her deepest self is there, even while doctors and carers commiserate over her decline. A carer frets that when she takes Rhoda to the library, she has no interest. In fact, I find her reading all the time, though not newly published books in their bright covers, which the library displays; she's absorbed in *Pride and Prejudice* from her own shelves. Since she can't recall the plot, it's her infinite delight to read Jane Austen for, as it were, the first time.

One day she's walking along the passage at home talking half to herself, half to me. It sounds like a fantastic story of rebellion against her fate, and love for a married man, and running off to a solitary life. There are elements here of her own life but it sounds confused. And then, suddenly, I see.

'Why, you're Jane Eyre.'

She nods a bit impatiently, as though I should have known, and then wanders on in this character.

1994 is the last year she's fit to visit us. Pip arranges for a wheelchair, and we collect her at Heathrow. From Oxford we

Olivia (left) and Anna at their grandmother's, ready for Friday night prayers

take the train to Devon. She will like the track along the sea beyond Exeter and the steep hills at Totnes. We are on our way to the Dartington festival, where I'm to talk on Charlotte Brontë. My mother is in high spirits to be amongst writers, who sit at a communal table for lunch.

'And have you met Jane Austen?' she asks a puzzled novelist across the table.

In a sense, Austen is indeed a present companion to my mother who lives with her, the Brontës and other writers who confide in her across time: 'Reader, I married him' and 'There are not so many men of fortune in the world as there are pretty women to deserve them.'

My mother's visit to Oxford is an opportunity to have her memory investigated, and we ask a team in the university to include her in their research. A research assistant tests her on the days of the week, on which subject she's predictably blank. One day is much like another.

'Do you know who the Pope is?' the researcher persists.

'I'm Jewish,' Rhoda says politely.

If questions were to lend themselves to the patient, rather than expecting the patient to lend herself to the questions, the research might have revealed something worth knowing. If my mother were asked about the gold-smoke approaching her over the veld, or about Yiddish lullabies her father had sung by candlelight, there would have been a response – perhaps too much, for these days my mother is living largely in repeated memories of early childhood. Her shaky hand transcribes 'Klaver' from memory:

> *Across the River*
> *where the long hills lie*
> *side by side with the morning sky*
> *children's voices chipped out of silence,*
> *and as a child's undarkened breast*
> *is pure as the air she breathes*
> *so, free of dross a moment,*
> *the soul receives*
> *Thy Presence.*

Only those who know this primal scene are in a position to reach her; even then, to elicit a meaningful reply, it makes sense to supply a certain amount of information in asking a question, so that memory doesn't seize up in alarm. Since public discussion overrides this, she's at a loss in company. She's a different person – quite her old self – when we are alone.

The research is designed to elicit a preconceived diagnosis of dementia. I'm pressed to say that my mother is 'aggressive'.

'She's tense, anxious all right, as she's always been. Aggressive, no.'

This makes no impression, and I suspect that box gets ticked anyway. I fear an adverse Oxford report will influence my mother's doctors in Cape Town. It's obvious that the doctor in charge has not a clue about her calibre, nor does he recognise what's extraordinary about the memory she retains. Siamon tries to caution the doctor who, unbudged, sends a shuffling reply encased in medical lingo.

Fool I am to subject my mother to research that fails to take in the element of caprice in what we retain or let go. Her retention of her Klaver stories and her indifference to the Pope are not exactly aberrations; they point to a character inaccessible to questionnaires.

I'm resistant to diagnosis because I don't believe that my mother's condition can be defined, given how little we know about the brain. No one has asked if the barbiturate and Epanutin, which she's taken for decades, have finally had the effect she always feared. This is in part a story of a person who's had to struggle against the dulling that makes life livable, even as she finds a poetic subject in the 'abysms' and 'bolts' of illness.

Though my mother never read John Stuart Mill's *The Subjection of Women*, she came to the same conclusion that women's minds are even more vulnerable than their bodies to men who exercise unthinking authority. When I was her sister-child, she'd point out some man as 'a sadist'. Her chilling tone, and even more what she refrained from saying, drew me into the purview of Gothic horror. Her chief horror was the empowered medical man, who 'experiments on patients' or threatens a woman like herself with madness and incarceration.

In the background there was the spectre of Monica's mother –
put away when Monica was a baby – and many others (as Mary
Wollstonecraft testifies in *The Wrongs of Women*) who in one
way or another deviated from marital or maternal norms.

After my mother's post-partum crisis in 1944, she learnt to
conceal her oddity. As her sister, I knew from the age of four
that oddity was bound up with her rarity as an imaginative and
moral being. At the same time I was ashamed of her oddity, as
secretive as everyone else in our family, and often wished for an
ordinary mother. From the fifties to the eighties, the forty years
she was out in the world, she kept herself safe within women's
groups and, latterly, in the black and white women's friendship
club which brought out her freest verve.

In the later nineties Rhoda no longer left home.
With Olivia, then at Cambridge, Pip and Katie Erasmus

My brother does better by our mother. He takes her three times to consult Dr Frances Ames, Professor of Neurology at the University of Cape Town, who is alert to the individuality of memory loss. Dr Ames notes my mother's ploy to avert seizures by 'scrubbing' her palms. 'We should listen to patients,' she reminds her colleagues.

By the mid-nineties, journeys with my mother are fraught with difficulty. We drive for hours to Matjiesfontein to see a bare house, across the road from the railway station, where Olive Schreiner lived as a solitary, nursing her asthma in the dry Karoo air from 1890 to 1894. Here she wrote her *Dreams*, allegories of women to be. From this lone spot, one street ending in the veld, she spoke to the world. My mother is inattentive and finds the cutlery in the hotel unclean. Embarrassingly, she asks again and again for a fork to be replaced.

In December 1996 her brother Hubert dies, and we fly to Johannesburg for the funeral.

Next day we visit her middle brother, Sydney, at his home Inanda House. Sydney shows us around his indigenous garden, televised earlier in the day. It takes most of the morning to walk about the different gardens planted by his wife Victoria, a designer from New York with wonderful flair. Sydney is in his element, talking knowledgeably about trees and plants. He has imported some rare breed of grass, which remains green under a plantation of thick trees. I murmur 'a green thought in a green shade'. He recognises Marvell; he's a reader with his own formidable element of self-taught genius. He and Rhoda are too alike in their originality and self-absorption not to be strained when they are together, yet at a distance, he was attentive, sending her imaginative presents: a puffy chaise longue for reading; a light, warm-lined mac to wrap herself after swims.

That brilliant Highveld morning, where she has what is to be her last meeting with Sydney, she seems to accept his distance and keeps silent. I admire her restraint, for she'd like to reach through their reserve. But she judges correctly: their friction in the nursery and a lifetime's divide have held too long. He treats her with courtesy – 'mind that rock' or 'would you take some tea?' – yet his eyes turn away to his library, his trees, all that fulfilled the promise that had driven him. It was a long-ago vow to his shattered father after the Crash: 'I will save the family.' Whether these were his actual words, I don't know: by the time my mother passed them on, they were intoned as family myth.

Afterwards, my mother is fretful, and so disruptive on the plane coming back that it's impossible to contemplate her leaving home again.

By July–August 1999, my mother can sometimes no longer form a coherent sentence, though an urge to speak never leaves her.

I enter her room and find her wrestling with the phone; she wants to call Sydney, who died in 1997.

'Mommy.' I take the receiver from her, shaking my head. 'I have to tell you he died.'

Her face crumples. '*Don't* say.'

A moment later she's forgotten, and is phoning this brother again.

She's a prisoner in her own house, rattling the front door, locked in case she roams. To relieve this, I drive her to the mountainside gardens at Kirstenbosch, where she can roam freely. 'I'm feeling a little tired. Do you think we might go?' she says almost at once. I take a scenic route back via Hout Bay, but it's now, to her, alarmingly unfamiliar. 'If you don't mind, I think I'd like to go home,' she repeats uneasily all the way. By the time we turn into Avenue Normandie, in time for Friday night, she's so agitated that I'm afraid of her opening the car door and jumping out.

'Help me, help me,' she pleads, 'I'm ill ... ill ... ill.'

Misguidedly, I take her too suddenly off that addictive drug, Valium. She has a day or two of relief and natural happiness, followed by a seizure. 'It hurts,' she says, pointing to a bite at the side of her tongue. As I bend to look, we lock together. At night-time, we're alone in my flat overlooking the sea. I'm ironing, and she's seated near me with a cup of tea and a slice of cake. I open the sliding window and we lean out over a calm ocean beneath what she used to call 'a river of stars'. 'Beautiful,' she breathes. This scene holds in her memory whenever I bring it up, in the same way as she recalls peering into the lit houses on our evening walk in the climbing streets of Fresnaye. The old Rhoda is there when I read from *Poems on the Underground*, which I'd brought her a few years back. I read her favourites: 'Tyger Tyger, burning bright'; Milton's sonnet 'On his blindness'; Byron's 'So we'll go no more a-roving'; and 'O my Luve's like a red, red rose' by Robert Burns. Not twentieth-century poetry because she doesn't care for irony and mockery. Her affinities are still for the Romantics. the Wordsworth of the Immortality Ode with its memory of the child who trails clouds of glory from God, who is our home.

It was a mistake to take her off Valium while my brother, who monitored her pills, was away. She seems unsteady on her feet, and in September, after my return to England, she has three falls. Is her dose of her anticonvulsant drug, Epanutin, too low or too high? Doctors shift the dose this way or that, but she remains on the verge of seizures. The third fall breaks her arm. She can't understand why a cast is put on, and flails about

A last photo of Rhoda, taken by Pip, as they walk on the mountain

trying to rip it off. Instead of simply sedating her until she gets used to it, doctors decide on an operation to put a pin in. What they fail to consider is her state of mind: unfit for an unfamiliar place. After the operation she's wildly agitated in City Hospital, and the pin works loose. A second operation leaves her stupefied.

I fly overnight on Thursday, 30 September. Pip fetches me from the airport at six in the morning and fills me in as we drive through the bright air smelling of the sea.

'She doesn't want to live,' he says.

At home, I find her blank, eyes shut, refusing food.

It's obvious that the doctor, a locum GP, is overdosing her. He fancies a thyroid condition and won't listen when I say that it's not the case; nor does he want to hear about my mother's cramps from unnecessary purges.

'Can she be dying?' I ask. He concedes it could be.

'In that case, I'd like to have another opinion.'

The doctor stiffens unwillingly. My tactlessness does my mother no good. I've let him see how much I detest a know-all whose ego is fragile. The consultant doesn't return my call – she works through GPs, of course.

Something else does my mother no good, something I hide but she will sense. It's the trough a writer can fall into between books. No matter what has come before, it can be daunting to start again with an inchoate mass of material – what Yeats called, in creative terms, 'the dark of the moon'; it's easy to wonder if you can ever approach the full of the moon again. It's a year since I brought out a biography of two women and Henry James, and during this year I've done outlines for two very different subjects, one mysteriously private, Emily Dickinson, and the other a public figure, Mary Wollstonecraft. My New York agent likes the Dickinson proposal; my London agent would prefer to leave it for the time being. The outcome is still uncertain, and to keep the future at bay during the wakeful hours of the night, I tap out a diary on my laptop.

Saturday, 2 October 1999

It was a shock to see her sunk in what looks like a pre-death daze. Beyond speech, immobile, fed by syringe in the corner of a resistant mouth. In the afternoon, just before her onslaught of drugs, she opened her blue eyes – they stared at nothing, unseeing or not naming what she saw. She looked stripped, washed clean of life. At times, there is a hint of recognition – a faint smile in my direction when I said, 'I've been reading your writings on the plane,' and quoted 'Klaver'. A similar quiver back to life when I read aloud from passages she had marked in the psalms: how the Lord will restore thy soul. I speak in her own terms, reminding her that she is 'never alone'.

Mary, the night nurse, aged about fifty, has a round, smooth brown face with a merry smile. She said that she prays 'with your mother' through the night. 'I lay on hands,' she told me. She had wanted to be missionary, not a nursing aid, but there was no money for missionary school in a family of twelve children where the mother didn't work. We agreed that, in our generation, women working has caused problems in family life that didn't exist for our mothers.

This morning, when I came in to see my mother, Mary said she liked my brown Ghost dress. My mother smiled when I spoke to her, though she barely opened her lids. They say she's improved since I came, but it hardly seems so to me. Until now, when people have expected me to be shocked by my mother's condition, I'd felt that the real Rhoda was reachable – it was increasingly difficult, but alone with me, she would respond, even to humour when I read 'will you, won't you, will you, won't you, will you join the dance?'

Monday, 4 October 1999

Yesterday there was a breakthrough of sorts. It may not be due to my presence, alone; more likely to her own resilience and to the tender, skilled nursing of Evie (by day) and Mary (at night). 'Rhodie,' Evie coaxes her to swallow, stroking her arm. 'Do it for me.' Since I came last Thursday my mother had said only 'Sh . . . Sh . . . ' or 'mm . . . mm', which seemed, together with her closely shut, almost pointed lips, a negation of life. But yesterday it was as though she woke up and began to find a few words, though a lot is inarticulate babbling, oddly enough in Afrikaans – '... *hy is ... sy is ... altyd ... almal ... kom weer ... koer ... koer*'.

'Koer sounds like a bird's call,' I ventured, but this didn't tell – she wants to shape real words, and make them intelligible. She wants to communicate in Afrikaans, perhaps reverting to her early schooldays.

'*Almal, ja. Ons is almal hier,*' I said, face to face as she lay back on the bed. I was groping for words unused since I left the country in 1964. '*Evie is hier; Mary is hier; jou seun, Pip, kom weer môre, en ek is hier – ek is jou dogter, 'n dogter moet met her moeder wees.*'

She seemed to like this statement of duty, and took it as meant – not bare duty but a condition of being a daughter. '*Ons is familie,*' I repeated, feeling my way into this passage of forgotten words that rolled their own way, it seemed, from ages past.

Once again Rhoda nodded into my eyes, before lapsing into her daze. It's strange to be speaking to my mother in a language we've never used between us, but which appears to be the deepest residual language still in her.

Now and then, she's listening and even smiling when I repeat her name and her past, as though those facts gave her back herself.

'You are Rhoda,' I said, looking into her newly opened eyes. She nodded.

'Rhoda Stella Press from Klaver.' Another nod.

It's extraordinary how fast one's standards change: I was shocked at first; now am pleased to see the smallest improvement: open eyes, clear blue; words, in place of 'sh ... sh ...'; the odd smile; the flashes of recognition.

My mother still won't eat, and I've wondered if it is the

body's way of saying that this life should end. My impulse is NO. I want her to go on, to enter into the exchange of words, the taste of ice-cream, the ocean seething since Genesis – all she had before.

5 a.m. Tuesday, 5 October 1999

My mother took food willingly for the first time last night, opening her mouth for the chicken soup and then banana mashed with ice-cream. Yet I'm angry with doctors, who behave with extraordinary authoritarianism when they are in the dark: it was a wrong decision to operate even the first time on a woman in my mother's complex condition. An arm that might heal crooked is less important than a fragile mind.

My brother called in a psychiatrist. He came looking unprofessional, gross, as though he had rolled out of bed. He hardly stopped to speak to me, let alone the patient he'd come to see.

'Is she aggressive?' he asked abruptly. 'I believe she was aggressive.'

He made no attempt to know her; simply sat down at a desk and went into the prescribing routine.

Mary recalls instances where she made a correct diagnosis from experience, which the doctor would ignore. English-speaking doctors trained during apartheid will normally ignore Mary's intelligence, located as it is in a coloured woman who speaks the Afrikaans-English of the meaner streets.

She relishes language, and taught me the latest retort to a person, often older, who doesn't get the point: '*kom reg*', literally 'come right'. She likes my mother rambling in Afrikaans.

'Now you're speaking my language,' she says to her fondly. '*Lekker soppies,*' she smiled into Rhoda's wide eyes as she fed her mushroom soup.

They talk all night. When I can't sleep and pad up the passage towards my mother's room I hear '*asseblief tog . . . sê vir my . . .*' between her brief and urgent breaths.

Over Rhoda's restless body, I asked Mary how she bears the long hours of the night.

'I pray,' she said. 'I want to be something for others. If I'd been a proper nurse, I'd have been running things. This way I am close to people.'

I opened a chest of drawers in my mother's bedroom and found (as remembered) tapes of her classes and a typescript of a talk on Abraham, which opened with God's trials of this chosen man.

When I read this aloud to Rhoda, it roused her from her half-awake look to full attention.

'Like your own life with its trials,' I said, stroking the cast on her right arm. 'You are going through a trial now, and are learning, still, how to live.'

'*Ja,*' she nodded, putting up her hand to stroke my cheek with a tender look. It took me back to childhood, when I was entirely hers. The years of emotional estrangement recede into the wash of time. What's present is Rhoda's noble face – rather thinner, her high nose and white hair on the pillow of the hospital bed Pip hired. I see, sometimes, the girl she was with the dark skin and brown crinkly hair swept back, as that night when she lay on Lou's tweed arm in the dicky of the car and the stars were blown about the sky. There are flashes of her old intentness. These return me to the fullness of a daughter's tie to her mother as author of her being: awareness of others, words, nature and all that makes life quicken. I have the strongest sense of that mentor-mother still here, dimmed (as she's feared) by the pills, but rising again and yet again to the surface, which is why I don't want her to go.

Wednesday, 6 October 1999

The sawbones came yesterday to take out her stitches. When the cast was cut loose we saw a great cut up her arm, still looking raw. The doctor moved the arm rather roughly and my mother cried out 'Agony!'

'Please hold it,' I begged, but he went on with the job, smiling imperturbably.

'She's exaggerating,' he said, and the GP, who was there, backed him.

'But this is a brave woman,' I said tightly. To show fury wouldn't help. 'She never, ever complained of pain.' How easily the helpless are sealed off unknown, as Rhoda was largely unknown throughout her life.

The GP agreed to lessen the dosage, and she did pretty quickly gain animation; in fact, from the afternoon through the night, too much. It's a wall of words. If I say 'Rhoda!' her eyes turn, but almost at once return to their inward fixity. She's trying to say something, and her face at such times gains a meaningful look. There's a long way to go: she has to learn to walk again; and we have to get the medication right so that she doesn't talk all night. I've thought of Iris Murdoch refusing food, and John Bayley accepting this. Was it the humane thing to do, not to prolong so faded a life? Am I doing right by my mother who is unable to speak for herself? I look into her eyes and say, 'Tell me, I have to know as your daughter: are you unhappy?' Before, when I asked that question, she hugged me and indicated that she was happy enough. Now she listens but with some barrier between us. Her sound-language is often unhappy: a lot of 'mm ... mmm' from tight-pressed lips.

Pip took me to task for taking Rhoda off Valium in his absence last August.

'But she was saying "help, oh help me",' I protested. 'She was having panic attacks. The Valium seemed to be doing no good, and for two days it was bliss.'

'It was a DISASTER,' Pip shouted.

I walked out onto the stoep, paced a bit, then came back to say how much I've regretted this.

'It's my personality,' Pip said apologetically, when he calmed down.

'That's no excuse,' I retorted. I was compelled (though close to tears) to stand up to him.

Friday, 7 October 1999

Rhoda, even in her medicated state, charmed the new day nurse, Lulu (a Xhosa). She has an extraordinary attraction for anyone who serves her – what is it? She looks dignified, lean-ing back with eyes closed, her white hair swept away from her high nose and forehead. Then she will open clear blue eyes and smile gratefully into the face of a nurse, murmuring 'thank you', even though she can barely speak.

She was her 'real' self for about an hour yesterday afternoon: I read the closing lines of the Immortality Ode: 'To me the meanest flower that blows can give / Thoughts that do often lie too deep for tears.' She gave me that lovely smile of attention, so I read next the sonnet on Westminster Bridge. 'Beautiful' she breathed at 'all that mighty heart is lying still!'

Her well-worn anthology of English poems is inscribed 'Rhoda Stella Press, Good Hope Seminary, 1933'. It's full of notes and underlining, and includes a date, July 1938 [four months after Lou died], next to a heavy line under 'Dear as remembered kisses after death ... and wild with all regret; / O Death in Life, the days that are no more.'

As I read aloud to her, in the late afternoon when the effect of the pills wears off, I mull over the unlikely life of this housewife who 'felt through all this fleshly dress / Bright shoots of everlastingness'. Henry Vaughan speaks to her, and her eye meets Wordsworth's 'inward eye'. She too has seen 'gleams of past existence'. I choose poems that she has underlined – the only words to rouse her. For they speak to a part of her that lies deeper than memories: her intimations of eternity interfused with the face of creation, which for her are not daffodils on verdant English slopes around the Lakes but the harsh, unbroken horizons of Africa.

She completes certain lines, speaking in unison. Together she and the Psalmist walk 'with' their God.

When it comes to human ties, she joins Wordsworth on fraternal love, 'my dear, dear Sister . . . ', as Dorothy had been to him in their youth, when they trod their way above Tintern Abbey in Wales. Rhoda's sedated expression lights up; she looks into my eyes as I read. It's not me she sees, and the 'dear, dear Sister' is not Dorothy, but what she herself has been to Basil, dearest to her from the time he pulled a nail from her foot when he was six and she five years old in the dusty veld where they played.

I say to her GP, 'She remembers more than ninety-nine per cent of your patients ever knew.'

He is not impressed, and smiles kindly as he opens the gate to leave.

Sunday, 9 October 1999

Yesterday, after Evie managed to walk her to the lounge window, she sat on one of the dining-room chairs saying 'beautiful' as she looked out on the stoep, the vine just sprouting, the 'moon-flower' tree and what she called 'my mountain'. It was the pleasure of the patient who's been in bed for weeks, looking out on the world once more.

Pip dropped by this afternoon, on his way to a rugby match. 'Come and sit down,' I said, turning to the dining room.

'I have to make a call,' he said, bringing in the phone, but catching my look of surprise, didn't pick up the receiver. Just then, Evie produced our mother walking towards him.

'You're helping others to help you,' he approved. 'That's what I'm always telling you, Mom, you must help others to help you.' It's a more humorous tone than he sometimes takes with me, as one who's here to do his bidding.

'Speak English!' he pressed Rhoda, though her Afrikaans is idiomatic and rather amazing, as though the different being language brings out had been lurking there since early childhood.

'I'll try then,' she answered with the merest edge. We laughed.

'You're condescending to her, and she hears it,' I said.

He glanced at his watch. 'I'll be late for the match.' She'd been looking his way with delight, and was, I think, taken aback.

'You know that we love each other,' Pip said, kissing her goodbye.

'I don't know about that,' she retorted with a sudden return of spirit.

Later, when I sat on her bed and went over her life, she listened intently. Sometimes she put up her hand to stroke my face or hair. Once she held a strand of my hair, twisting it in a curl, round and round, as she used to make ringlets or curl her own hair while she was thinking. 'Blessings,' she said amidst the broken sentences. 'Goodbye.'

Wednesday, 12 October 1999

Reading my mother's poems and fragments, I'm struck by work a world apart from poems published in the lingering tail of the twentieth century. Their tiny ironies are post-post-Eliot, without the bolt of the 'unattended moments'. Rhoda's poems are visions, trials and prayers like the psalms.

Yesterday, the nurse who stood in for Eve put my mother to bed at four o'clock. She was tired, the nurse claimed. At six I had to stop her forcing pills on my mother's resistant lips. There has to be constant vigilance.

Thursday 13 October 1999

It is 5.45 a.m. and I've been awake since after one, reading Simon Brett's anthology of diarists – unexpected that I find more in Noel Coward and Barbara Pym than in esteemed diarists like Pepys, Evelyn or Fanny Burney (except one entry where she ran from the cries of a beaten dog). Of course I delighted in Virginia Woolf, Katherine Mansfield and Frances Partridge. Muggeridge, a loathsome man. Reading through the night was not a compulsive pleasure; it's become a way of holding off bad thoughts.

At 5.30 I took my coffee to the gate and looked my last on the outlines of Lion's Head and Signal Hill against the lightening sky.

Today, if my mother can walk (supported) to the car, I plan to take her to the sea for a drive. She seemed to like the idea. She's now calling me by name. Sometimes, I catch meaning in the jolting words. That catch at meaning comes from my knowledge of her and her past. No one else could do it, and this makes me uneasy about returning to England tomorrow. One moment she seems on course to modified recovery; another moment she looks dazed and disturbingly still.

I will regret leaving to my own dying day. Her two last words, when I phone from Oxford, are: 'Come home.' Hearing that she's eating well, dressing each morning and managing to walk, I put this off.

Sitting in her dining room with Maria, her companion, on 27 October, she states calmly, 'I think it's time for me to go.' She sinks outside her house four days later, a Sunday. On Monday morning Maria finds her transfigured with 'innocence'; the lines smoothed out, she looks 'like an eighty-year-old child'. She dies on Tuesday 2 November 1999.

16

Echoes of Kinship

'Souls live on in perpetual echoes,' George Eliot said. Is the end of a life the beginning of that life's reverberation in other lives? A biographer tunes in to echoes in the wake of a life and tests their authenticity. A daughter or son looks for the imprint of a life on the next and following generations. My mother's imprint is clearest on Anna, who at the age of four stood with her grandmother at the prayer door, alive to her 'awakened heart'.

'It was not about words,' she remembers. 'It was a meeting with a wordless self, entirely inward and silent.'

Anna is in India when she hears. She is carrying some of her grandmother's poems, and she sends 'The Priestess' with a fax for the rabbi to read aloud.

She looked after me as a baby when my mother was ill and she was a second mother to me. She gave me the greatest gift it is possible to give: she taught me, as a child, to be attentive the sound of the ocean, to see the mountain, to open my heart, to stand at the door of the sunroom and pray.

She told me stories for hours, late into the night. Under the pink duvet we ate peeled apples and argued about right and wrong through the ancient stories. I was titillated by the Canaanites and their orgies, while Gran was repelled. I could not understand why it was wrong to eat of the tree of knowledge and anyway, if it was God's will to create flawed people, what was he complaining about? I said it was wrong of Abraham to bind his son [for sacrifice], that a parent should put a child before duty, even to God. Gran always took God's side.

I'd thought my mother on course to recovery, and sent my passport for renewal to the South African office in London, with a view to seeing her in December. When she dies, the office won't speed up the process, so I'm not at the funeral.

At eleven in the morning, on Friday 5 November, Rhoda is buried beside Harry in the Jewish cemetery at Pinelands. Berjulie is the first to arrive, all the way from Canada. She does a quick round of family graves and favours Pip with her opinion that our father's shows the most spit and polish. Pip had the forethought to have the stone cleaned. He's helped, he says, by making arrangements. I'm helped by a stranger's meditation on death. My one time editor and friend, Marie Philip, passed on these words by Harry Scott Holland, a Canon of St Paul's Cathedral, which Marie read, she says, when her mother died:

I have only slipped away into the next room. I am I, and you are you. Whatever we were to each other, that we still are. Call me by my old familiar name, speak to me ... Put no difference in your tone, wear no forced air of solemnity or sorrow. Laugh as we always laughed at the little jokes we enjoyed together ... I am waiting for you, for an interval, somewhere very near ...

That afternoon I walk from the Tube at Marble Arch down Park Lane to Grosvenor House to see my cousin Barbara, eldest daughter to Uncle Hubert, who now lives in New York.

At a quarter to four, the November day is drawing in. Looking up at the bare trees of Hyde Park against the darkening sky, I see a world without my mother. Do I want to live in it? But of course, I do.

'Do you miss Uncle Hubert?' I ask Barbara.

'Terribly. I look for men who can teach me things. I've been going out with a man who is well-educated, who meets my train with bagels and cheese, who's even Jewish, but he spends his time raising money for Harvard. Why not raise money for the poor? I can't connect with him. I see men with this quality or that, but no one who has them all like my father.'

That evening, at a family Friday night, I see my mother's last remaining brother, Basil, who is eighty-four today. He has the long jawline of the Presses and likes to tell a story against himself. As a schoolboy, he relates, he asked my mother to help him with an English essay. She wrote the introduction and conclusion, and Basil filled in the sandwich. His master's comment was 'very good at the start and finish, but *poorish* in the middle.' When he and my mother were together, she'd be talking, she'd remember, while Basil would be thoughtfully munching leftovers from the fridge. He played up this Pooh Bear character, and played down his wisdom.

'Pooh was a bear of enormous brain,' he'd recite with relish when I was a child.

'Of enormous *what?*' I fill in, as he nods the cue.

'Well, he ate a lot.'

My mother adored 'my big brother Basil' for his stability, the opposite of her delicate frame and excitable imagination. Basil, immaculate in a blue tie and dark, well-cut suit, is not too well, and in London to consult a cardiologist. Yet he's serene, as my mother would say, admiring a temperament unlike her own.

'You still have an uncle,' he says as I bend to kiss him.

Next day, preparing lunch for friends, I switch on the radio this Saturday morning: it's Classic FM's hit parade.

'This was number one in 1916,' the announcer says, breaking the countdown with a curiosity. 'Caruso in *Santa Lucia*.'

Crackling through the old record, the great voice rises over the veld, rises and falls, and fountains higher, as Rhoda lifts her head in her candlelit room.

The day after the funeral, something strange happens to Anna in India. She's thinking of her gran, wishing she'd been with her, when an unknown Norwegian woman approaches with a box. It's a surprise, this woman says. Inside is a white and gold kitten, which a friend had sent to comfort Anna. The kitten, chosen from strays at an animal sanctuary, had been on a thirteen-hour bus journey.

'I took him home,' Anna relates over the phone, 'and tried to give him food and drink but he refused to take more than a sip or two. An hour later he had what looked like an epileptic fit or heart attack, and reminded of Gran, I held him on my heart, willing him to live. But fifteen minutes later it happened again and again and again. Four times he recovered and slept, and the fifth time died in my arms. I dug a hole between the sea and the river, and I felt the body freeze into an empty shell as I carried the kitten wrapped in a shawl to his grave.'

On the phone, Anna and I agree, as Anna puts it, that 'Gran formed us, she made us who we are, and I still feel her living inside me. I feel her now, a part of me.' Their closeness resounds in a startling comeback of her grandmother's voice almost two years later. On Anna's birthday, 9 August 2001, I'm away from home when she switches on the answering machine and to her amazement hears, she reports, 'a birthday message from my departed Gran. The machine went "... crackle, crackle ... I want to find Anna. I want to wish her a happy birthday."'

Anna concedes a logical explanation, that the answering machine was retrieving a message from the distant past. 'But even so, the timing was a coincidence.'

The message stirs Anna to say what she believes. 'I feel that we are always here, in one form or another, that our spirit is never born and never dies. So, if we miss someone who has passed, we can simply become still and feel the spirit of that person within the silence of the heart. We can learn to commune with the dead, as my dear grandmother reached out to me.'

I too have received a message of sorts. On Friday 19 November 1999, seventeen days after Rhoda's death, Maria phones to report a curious incident. When she moved my mother's desk, it collapsed, including the shelf of books at the back. One paperback, *The Bible and the Common Reader* by Mary Ellen Chase, a teacher at Smith College, fell open at the back flyleaf. And there, on that page, is an undated letter to me. My mother pencilled it on Rocklands beach, rocky, shelly, strewn with brown fronds of seaweed, where she used to swim, in the company of six diehards, throughout the winter. The icy water woke her from hated drugs. Towards the end her voice blends with an echo of the fourteenth-century visionary, Dame Julian of Norwich, who bore the scourge of the Black Death saying, 'All shall be well, and all manner of thing shall be well.'

Dearest Lyn —
    When it's so exquisite as it was at Rocklands this
morning I long to share it with someone & think of you —
the sea was so serene & crystal with one ship on the
horizon. I thought of Sirkka too & the spiritual joy that is

part of her lake-bathe. I thought of death & suddenly
heard across the sea & calm horizon all was well. The dark
background to life disappeared – this was Reality.

Have I a right to comfort? It would have been right to heal
our divide by yielding to what's wise in the scriptures. Would
it? I think back to one Day of Atonement when I'm fourteen,
standing beside her in Sea Point. I'm bored and privately at odds
with the dressy, sidelined girls, while the men sway (a gesture of
fervour traditionally reserved for males) and chant, 'Our Father,
our King, we have sinned before Thee.' The three Schiff sisters
make an entrance, flouncing down the aisle in new spring outfits with cinched waists and stiff petticoats. They apologise
profusely as they press their way into the front row, visible to
men. My mind flicks to iced cakes in the window of Maison
Mayfair on the Main Road; to youth leaders in the Movement,
where my mother has sent me to learn more about Our People;
and to one in particular with green eyes and a country accent
who dances in brown slippers because, people say, he's too poor
to afford shoes. They say he came first in matric. It's like the
start of a story to be so poor and brainy. The Movement urges
members to go to Israel, and my mother has promised to take
me when she visits someone very special at the end of the year.

'Our Father, our King, we have sinned before thee,' the
cantor laments in Hebrew with elaborate musical embellish-
ments. 'Hetanu lefanehah.' The closely packed congregation takes
up the lament. 'Selag lanu, kaper lanu.' Forgive us, let us atone.

She stands still in her plain dress and hat, absorbed in prayer
through all the hours of the fast. Her prayer book is open to the
list of sins: we have made false promises, we have been wanton,
we have corrupted, we have spread gossip, we have bad-
mouthed others. My mother fancies the prayer book's verbal
picture of 'running to do evil'. Not just evil, but running to do

it. Glancing my way, her finger points to the sin of the stiff-necked.

In 2003, my mother's friend Lilian Henry comes to England to stay with Vanessa, her adored granddaughter. At eighty-six, she travels alone by bus to Oxford. She brings the best gift ever: a typescript memoir of a youth shared with my mother, and filled with comic stories of the characters she lived amongst on Piketberg Mountain. She has a flair for stories, which I imagine comes from her Irish parents. At the dark end of a winter day we walk arm in arm through the rumbling bus station, and kiss goodbye as if for the last time.

'Another kiss for your mother,' she says.

Rhoda called Hubert's youngest daughter 'a story-book girl'. Linda was a child-reader of old-fashioned children's books. In 2006, as Linda Press Wulf, she writes a novel for children called *The Night of the Burning*. It's the story of Linda's mother-in-law Devorah Lehrman, who, aged twelve, is telling her story as a terrified survivor of a pogrom by Cossacks and neighbours on the Polish–Russian border. She becomes one of a number of orphans whom Isaac Ochberg ('Daddy Ochberg') transports from Poland to Oranjia. This was 1922, twenty years before my mother ran the library at Oranjia, but Linda imagines my mother into that scene under her second, preferred name. 'Once a week the library was opened by blue-eyed Miss Stella, who loved books as intensely as I did. As she walked down the orphanage corridor with her keys, calling to us like the Pied Piper, children rushed to choose the book they would borrow but especially to hear the stories she read aloud.'

As it happened, my mother never read stories aloud in the library – there was no time because so many orphans were lining up to check out books and receive their kiss. Her reading aloud is Linda's own memory of sitting beside her aunt in the sunroom as she introduced old-fashioned home girls, *Emily of New Moon* or *Little Women*, to a smiley blonde child, her little tongue curling excitedly around her lisp. The novel's dedication is in part 'For my Aunty Rhoda in the book-lined house on Avenue Normandie.'

Other echoes resonate from Rhoda's meeting with Sirkka Anttila, the Finnish sybil who in the summer of 1952 sent her on her way with awakened purpose. In late March 2002 Siamon attends an immunological conference in Oulu, in northern Finland, and on an impulse, he hunts up Sirkka's phone number in Helsinki.

The bold vigour of Sirkka's voice bursts out. 'All my inner life same with Rhoda. Not to be separated. All inner existence. Precious moments – all light Rhoda. Now, near to death, one only thankful and conscious. Brain is ischaemic, not to write or work, but still sense of humour and deeply conscious of life, death, eternity. Some way at home already.'

Sirkka, now eighty-four, lives on her own in Kallio, meaning hilltop, and (as I saw later) the flat is indeed on a hill overlooking the city. Sirkka's bedroom looks the other way, towards a church: a small, bare room with an iron bedstead. The flat is filled with Finnish folk art, including the three painted spindles Sirkka, aged twenty, rescued by night from behind the Russian lines during the Winter War. There's a portrait of her with her one-time husband Touko Markkanen, both in black and smouldering: two forceful characters. Touko had a hunchback, and Sirkka took to him the same year, 1953, as my mother sent her *The Little Locksmith*. Here are Sirkka's own publications: her '*mystikko*' poems, *Näkymättömän hymy*; a diary following her conversion to the Russian Orthodox church, when she entered, for a time, the Heinvesi Monastery of

Valamo; and a diary from the Winter War period, September 1939 to March 1940, published in 2000. Books lining the walls have the look of books that are looked at.

Still on the line to Siamon, Sirkka turns to these shelves. 'Books full of Jewish things sent by Rhoda.' She opens a copy of Buber's *I and Thou* sent from New York in 1966, and reads aloud the inscription: '"My sister Sirkka, Sirkka my dear and near one, I had a dark summer during which I have written to you, but none of these letters can be sent." Hey-hey.'

The final echoes are brief – a voice urging my mother to go alone into the arctic wilderness of Pallastunturi. 'Rhoda ... Rhoda ... Choice of life. Focus. Lapland. Boots.'

In the summer of 2004 I hear that Sirkka can no longer live unaided and has moved to a kind of sanatorium in the woods. That August I suggest coming to see her.

Dear Sirkka,

You may not remember me, the daughter of your 'sister'-friend, Rhoda. I found your letters to her, and would like to bring them to you, if I may. If you can put up with a visitor, I'd very much like to visit and read to you from these poetic letters (I understand that your eyesight is not good), and place them in your archive at the Finnish Literature Society.

I have lovely memories of staying with you in your lake place at Ukonvuori when your children were small, and your reading the *Kalevela* aloud in a rocking chair in front of the fire.

Hoping we may see each other,
Lyndall

On Sunday 29 August Sirkka's daughter, Saara Markkanen, who is my mother's goddaughter, takes me to her mother's flat.

It's about to be sold, and this is the last day or two, Saara says, that the flat is still intact. From there we drive to the sanatorium. On the way Saara warns me that Sirkka can no longer recognise visitors, not even her daughter.

The architecture, not drawing attention to itself, is extraordinary with light filtering through the leaves of the woods. Sirkka, whom I last saw in 1964, is seated at a table, grey of course, but her high cheekbones and slanting dark eyes are familiar. They look hard at me, and then at the photograph of my mother that I place in front of her. Suddenly her eyes light up and a smile of wonder breaks upon her face. I put down the letters on the table and as I read a few extracts aloud she beams, not speaking but strongly present. Then she tires and is led off to her room. Her mother's awakening is so unexpected to Saara that she's in tears.

Sirkka's papers are in the Finnish National Archives. I page through the Finnish of Sirkka's pocket diary until I come upon my mother's name on Wednesday 23 July 1952. The archivist, Anna Makkonen, translates Sirkka's first sight of Rhoda in the gallery: '*I met a woman writer at the Ateneum. Dark, wearing glasses, intelligent sensibility.*' There's our old address, 11 Avenue Normandie, Cape Town, and our old phone number, 46376 – I can hear her dialling Mrs Bass, the fishmonger, and her tired voice giving the order.

Amongst Sirkka's papers are my mother's letters. Weird to open a box in Helsinki and find her hand. '*I shall never forget that blessed time with you in Finland which shall live forever reincarnated perhaps as one of those gleams that grace a moment in future lives.*' That was at the end of 1958, when Sirkka gave birth to her twins, Antti and Anna.

Since Sirkka died, Saara and I keep in touch. 'You write vividly, as your mother did to mine,' I email her in 2008. 'My mother used to read aloud parts of Sirkka's letters. Her English, my mother said, was "vibrant", injecting something Finnish into English, which made us feel our language afresh ... I remember when you were born, and Sirkka sent a photo of you propped on her shoulder with her dark head turned tenderly towards you.'

As godmother, my mother kept Saara's drawings which, she told Sirkka, 'bring her close to me (leaning against my knees almost, with her hands in my lap in preparation for a story)', and she pored over the photos showing 'the shape of Saara's lovely head, her intense narrowed eyes' that came in fat envelopes with Finnish stamps. 'She sounds such a clever little girl whose way of being is so precious to me that I dare not speak of it,' she wrote to Sirkka in 1958 when Saara was three.

Mothering like this is universal, and yet it was rare for Saara and me to be daughters of women who lived for an infinity beyond human ties. In this sense our mothers were solitary and insistently obscure. Their triumph was to be the obverse of a celebrity who, like Emily Dickinson's frog, tells his name the livelong June to a surrounding Bog. A month after Sirkka and my mother part, Sirkka reveals herself as one who glides by in a silence where she's nothing. Life is 'moving nothingness'. So she puts it, on 7 September 1952, to Rhoda in London. Dickinson's sassy voice echoes behind them: 'I'm Nobody! Who are you? Are you – Nobody – too? Why then there's a pair of us.' Only when we accept nothingness, Sirkka adds, 'one is free to smile'.

A package from Japan arrives one day. In it are two landscapes. The artist, Yoshiko Aya, explains that the paintings are inspired by my mother's poems: 'Dawn' is based on the poem 'Klaver', and 'Morning Sky' on 'The Priestess'. Can this be another Meeting of my mother with a stranger, kin of her soul, from a far-off land?

It so happened that, twenty years ago, a graduate student from Tokyo came to St Hilda's College in Oxford. She was Atsuko Hayakawa from Tsuda College, founded by Madame Tsuda on the model of St Hilda's. As a very young woman, Tsuda had been one of the first students at St Hilda's after the college for women was founded in 1893. Atsuko brought me a miniature of a group of intrepid Japanese girls in search of education, standing in their kimonos at the prow of a vessel outward bound on its long way to the West. Tsuda is the smallest in the row of girls who lean ahead in their keenness to learn. Atsuko herself had been a pupil of Virginia Woolf's Japanese translator, and in Oxford she completed an insightful and delicately-worded thesis on Woolf's short fiction. Atsuko has since become a professor at Tsuda College, where she teaches a translation course.

During 2012 Atsuko returned to Oxford on sabbatical. When I talked of my mother, she asked if she might have copies of two poems. And this is how Yoshiko Aya came to read these poems, translated by Atsuko, her friend. Aya's vistas of dream-like light are Japanese landscapes with subtle colours, brush strokes and untouched space, cooler than Africa yet Aya's sky is tinged with the gold-smoke that crossed the veld to my mother as a child.

Ours is a dispersed generation. When we sailed to New York in 1965 we knew no one. By 2010, a number of younger cousins have settled there. Basil's daughter Jennifer, married to a New Yorker, has a party at Sotheby's, where she works. It's largely a family party for the publication of my new biography: a book on Emily Dickinson. Barbara comes, lovelier than ever. She has a weekly programme on local radio, discussing Jewish issues with a rabbi. Her brother Donald is accompanied by his partner John. Don is making a fold-out family tree, a work of intricate discovery. Uncle Sydney's daughter Caroline, a reader with tastes close to mine, manages a downtown newspaper. And Fran Miller, a teacher, comes, the daughter of my mother's long-lost cousin Ben, the only one from the Old Country to survive the Holocaust.

I stay with Jen in her apartment on East 79th Street. After the party, we look at a photo of my mother and Basil, who died in July 2003. They sit on his stoep looking out on False Bay. There's that glow in Rhoda's face whenever she's with him. 'Their love had no dross in it,' I murmur to Jen, 'no bad thought ever, though they were so different.'

Jen waits with me at the corner as we signal for a cab. I'm off to Penn Station to catch the train to Albany, and there, a limo from the summer writing course at Bennington College will take me into Vermont. Every June, for the last eleven years, I've travelled north along the Hudson River, recalling each time how Henry James made this journey by boat to visit his Albany grandmother. James, aged two, would hear, through the night, the hoots and churnings of the river traffic.

'Your father loved family tales,' I say to Jen as a cab pulls over to the sidewalk. I bung my case in the boot while the driver waits at the stop light for the midtown traffic roaring down Lexington Avenue.

'Those tales,' Jen says. 'Don has discovered that, in 1894, at the station when our grandfather left, his father, Benjamin, tried to wrest the ticket from his son. He thought he should go instead.'

The traffic light is changing. The cab revs.

Suddenly I remember something my mother said, her idea that her father, at the age of fifteen or sixteen, had a breakdown before he took off. If that happened, it would have added to the distress of the scene. Benjamin, she said, fainted at the station. It was not in his nature to leave home and he would never see his son again.

*

Tales make life, make us what we are. These days I tell tales to Olivia's son, the same as my mother told to me. Humphrey is in the neonatal ward at University College Hospital in London for his first five months. Then he goes to Great Ormond Street, where an Australian surgeon, Miss Cross, undertakes a long operation on a stomach that has yet to mature.

'When you're a big boy,' I tell him, 'you'll go to Cherry Tree Wood, and there will be ... ' and I picture the world he's not yet seen. 'Shall I tell you about the Bad Rabbit?' Humphrey's lips part, revealing his first tooth, as Peter Rabbit crunch-crunches on a carrot in Mr McGregor's garden. His serious eyes fix on mine as Mr McGregor comes on the scene, waving a rake and shouting, 'Stop, thief!' Then Humph smiles when I pant with Peter, 'huh, huh, huh', as he makes a dash for his mother's burrow. A new life quickens to the age-old tale of risk and home.

Glossary

bather bathing costume or swimsuit

coloured people of mixed race. In the apartheid hierarchy, the 'coloureds', as they were called, were second-class citizens who came between the whites and the third class, known as 'natives' – the black descendants of Bantu-speaking peoples, Xhosa, Zulu, Sotho etc

dennepits pine nuts

dicky a minute, unroofed back seat to a car, carved out of its boot. It held two windblown passengers, tightly pressed. Dickies were packed with partying boys and girls in Cape Town in the thirties and forties

dorp small village, sometimes used affectionately or pejoratively as a place of no importance

fynbos the indigenous flora of the Cape of Good Hope, with thousands of species unique to the region

gits a revision of 'gats' which is a euphemism for God in the context of surprise or disturbance. The closest English equivalent would be 'golly'. (Afrikaans, pronounced with a soft 'g'. With thanks to Anita Visser)

impi military platoon (Zulu)

joller a hedonist given to sprees

kiddush grace before meals, always recited by a male, on the Sabbath eve and on holy days

klaver clover. Because the dorp had this name, it's fair to surmise that clover grew easily in the region. It was one of our grandfather's crops. The correct (Afrikaans) spelling is

Klawer, but the place name was spelt Klaver by English speakers, including our family, in the first half of the twentieth century. Either way, the pronunciation is the same

kloof narrow passage between two mountain peaks

melktert milk tart, a Dutch South African delicacy

mielie corn on the cob

Nederlandskultuurgeskiedenis Dutch cultural history

Olifantsrivier Elephant river, so called in the eighteenth century by the first colonial explorers of the north-west Cape, who saw elephants bathing there. No elephants remained in my grandparents' time

ozeret literally, servant, but intending to convey a sense of domestic drudge

riempies leather thongs

sabra native-born Israeli

shaliah (plural *shlihot*) emissary (Hebrew)

shtetl Yiddish for a small Jewish village in Lithuania, the Ukraine and other areas of north-eastern Europe

skiet and donder shoot and rough-up, as in low-grade films and novels from overseas, marketed to the violent townships. The literal translation of *donder* is 'thunder', so that the meaning is somewhat stronger than 'rough up'

stoep veranda

tackies plimsolls or trainers

tickeys three-penny bits

Notes

1. 'Sister'

3 *'dwelt among the untrodden ways'*: 'She dwelt among the untrodden ways' is one of Wordsworth's Lucy poems (1799). Both this poem and 'Strange fits of passion' are about a dead woman who was true to her untrammelled nature, like the poet's beloved sister Dorothy.

4 *'Colossal substance of Immortality'*: Emily Dickinson, 'The Soul's Superior instants'.

5 *'Great Balls of Fire'*: A rock 'n' roll number performed by Jerry Lee Lewis.

2. Mothers

21 *Kausanai forest*: Simon Schama opens up the fate of his own Plunge family in *The Story of the Jews*, BBC 2, November 2013.

27 *the windy shore at Muizenberg*: It was on this beach that the British landed in 1795 and took the Cape colony from the Dutch.

28 *I know by heart*: Robert Louis Stevenson, 'The Swing', 'Where Go the Boats' and 'The Land of Counterpane', from *A Child's Garden of Verses* (1913).

3. 'Illness Was My Teacher'

29 *the Gardens*: The oldest part of Cape Town. Gardens were planted by the Dutch East India Company when it took over the Cape in the seventeenth century, to provide a refreshment station and citrus for sailors during long, scurvy-plagued voyages around Africa to the spice islands of Batavia and Java.

36 *Rhodes's thatched cottage*: Empire builder Cecil John Rhodes bought the cottage and died there, aged forty-four, in 1902.

4. Orphans and Stories

43 *Jock of the Bushveld*: A 1907 South African classic by Sir Percy FitzPatrick (1862–1931), about the adventures of his dog near Graskop in the Transvaal. These had been bedtime stories for his children; his friend Kipling urged him to turn them into what became an instant bestseller, never out of print.

54 *James James Morrison Morrison Weatherby George Dupree*: 'Disobedience', from *When We Were Very Young* (1924).

5. The Silent Past

60 *'clothes spread wide . . .'*: *Hamlet*, Act IV, scene vii. John Everett Millais painted *Ophelia* in 1851–2.

68 *. . . silent, bare*: Wordsworth's sonnet, 'Composed upon Westminster Bridge,

September 3, 1802'. At some later date, Rhoda pencilled 'epilepsy' in the margin.

68 *Wilfred Harris*: In his *Neuritis and Neuralgia* (OUP, 1926), he prescribes a strong drug, luminal, a derivative of veronal, for epilepsy in cases where bromide treatment fails. Virginia Woolf was given veronal during a mental breakdown in 1913.

6. 'Only a Housewife'

85 *Caledon*: Named after the Second Earl of Caledon, governor of the Cape Colony 1807–11.

87 *burly, shaggy bears*: 'Lines and Squares', from *When We Were Very Young* (1924).

87 *'crying with all ...'*: 'Rice Pudding', from *When We Were Very Young* (1924).

93 *'had humoured, or softened ...'*: The late Lady Elliott, mother of the three daughters in *Persuasion*.

7. School versus Home

114 *'worsted God'*: Emily Dickinson, 'A little East of Jordan' (*c.* early 1860).

8. 'Lapp Heights'

123 *Rainbow Valley*: By L. M. Montgomery (1919). One of the sequels to *Anne of Green Gables*.

9. Free in London

144 *'Finland'*: Published at the same time, October 1952, in *Finlandia* as 'Saalinen – Finland'. See p. 129.

145 *'Distrust the clouds ...'*: 'Voice and Vision', from a City Lit anthology.

10. Mother to Daughter

165 *Marie Bashkirtseff's diary*: Marie Bashkirtseff (1858–84) was a Ukrainian-born diarist, painter and sculptor who wrote about the struggles of women artists and contributed to a feminist newspaper in France. Her painting, *The Studio*, pictures herself in an all-women studio. She died of TB at the age of twenty-five.

167 *Ideal Marriage*: By the Dutch gynaecologist Theodoor Hendrik van de Velde (1873–1937). Despite the condescension, the manual was popular with women for dispelling ignorance.

11. At the Crossroad

179 *Muriel Spark's word*: *Loitering with Intent* (1981; reissued Virago 2007).

12. Dividing Dreams

194 *"The Hound of Heaven"*: By the English poet Francis Thompson (1893).

13. The Way Down

217 *Ben-Zion Goldberg*: His papers (including what I prepared on St Augustine, Rousseau and Nietzsche) are in the library of the Herbert D. Katz Center for

Judaic Studies at the University of Pennsylvania, www.library.upenn. edu/cajs/goldberg.html.

228 *made to have a fit*: Electro-convulsive therapy was first developed in Italy, in 1938, by Ugo Cerletti. According to Lisa Appignanesi in *Mad, Bad and Sad* (Virago, 2008), p. 367, he had seen pigs in a slaughterhouse become 'more manageable and less agitated when an electric prod was administered. Since the idea, later disproved, that epileptics didn't develop "schizophrenia", it was thought that if epileptic-like convulsions could be administered in patients, this would stop or ameliorate other forms of mental illness.' Some established figures in psychiatry claim that 'producing a fit and then unconsciousness' helps in some cases. This is a current opinion. Back in the mid-twentieth century, when Sylvia Plath had shock treatment following a suicide attempt, doctors believed more in its curative possibilities, and doctors believed that it helped in my case.

14. Lives for Women

245 *'I-Thou'*: *I and Thou* (1923), by the philosopher Martin Buber.

247 *Hannah, a friendly girl*: Recalled as a schoolmate by Jacob Bunka, the sole Plunge Jew to survive (because he was away in the Red Army). A wood-carver, Bunka (born 1923) was interviewed by Olivia Gordon for *Psychologies* magazine in 2006, and he appears in Simon Schama's BBC 2 documentary *The History of the Jews* (2013).

261 *'Nation shall not . . .'*: Isaiah 2:2–4.

262 *a challenge to this*: A speech reported in the *Jerusalem Post*, 8 August 1978.

266 *'men's bodies are . . .'*: Olive Schreiner, *Woman and Labour* (1913).

273 *reshuffles the order*: At first, she appears to have planned five sections: Childhood; Diary in Hell; Heaven is Here; Failure and Fall; Work in the World; with a coda Beyond Death: A Message. Then she decides on an unbroken sequence to cover her years from twenty-seven to her present age of seventy-two, shuffles the order and calls it variously 'Notes on a Journey', 'Records of a Journey' or 'Diary: Notes, Poems and Letters', or 'A Grandmother's Journey'. The epigraph is from Psalm 73, verse 28: 'That I may tell of all Thy Works', written in Hebrew – *l'saper col malhoteha*.

273 *"to tell of all Thy Works"*: Psalms 73:28.

15. Lost and Living Memory

298 *'will you, won't you, will you . . .'*: 'The Song of the Mock Turtle', from Lewis Carroll, *Alice in Wonderland* (1865).

303 *'Dear as remembered kisses . . .'*: Tennyson, 'Tears, Idle Tears' (1847).

Acknowledgements

This book is dedicated to my brother Philip (Pip) Getz, who provided an abundance of memories, points of view, photographs and translations of Hebrew letters.

Our mother was to be the focus, and I'd meant to be no more than a channel for scenes and experiences on which her poems draw. It was Lennie Goodings, publisher of Virago, who transformed this into a mother and daughter story. It was stimulating to have a reader respond with so sure a touch. I've been fortunate too to work once more with the editor Zoe Gullen.

Another thanks is for the imaginative empathy that fuels writing: this came from the literary agent Isobel Dixon, and in a different way from my daughter Anna Gordon, who read chapters at an early stage. Anna and my other daughter, Olivia Gordon, wrote passages that are included verbatim. Olivia, a journalist, provided details and photos from her visit to Plunge, Lithuania, in 2006, as well as her thoughts on motherhood. Her son Humphrey Clark, braving a traumatic start to life, has made his own special contribution to this book.

Atsuko Hayakawa translated two of my mother's poems into Japanese, and they inspired landscapes by the artist Yoshiko Aya. Their creative responses have been an unexpected gift.

Yet another unexpected pleasure was meeting Paula Deitz, editor of the *Hudson Review*. I was amazed by the alacrity with which she asked for an excerpt.

I am grateful to the Stellenbosch Institute for Advanced

Study (STIAS). The setting, privacy and good company offered ideal conditions for writing.

I should also like to thank the following for their help with memories, facts and material: Phillis Warshaw; Marie Philip of David Philip Publishers in South Africa; Naomi Press; Linda Press Wulf; Donald Press; Caroline Press; Suzanne Press; Victoria Press; Jennifer Roth; Annette Kessler; Garda Fig (for memories of the Black and White Friendship Club during many years of apartheid); Phillippa Cheifitz; Shirley Gelcer; Sylvia Magid; Tony Shapiro; Maria Bjat; Saara Markkanen; Anna Makkonen at the Finnish National Archives; Paula Alves (for kindly allowing me to see her flat in Maida Vale, where my mother lodged in 1952); Clare Bateman; Nicola Maye Goldberg; Milton Shain; the Gitlin Library in Cape Town (for an issue of the *South African Jewish Chronicle* of May 1955); and Professor Rachel Salmon of Bar-Ilan University, who explained about rabbinic reading. I took in Simon Schama's admirable stress on the Word in *The Story of the Jews*, shown on BBC 2 in 2013, as well as his record of what happened to the Jews of Plunge in July 1941. Above all, I'm grateful for a vivid memoir by my mother's life-long friend, Lilian Henry.

Georges Borchard, my New York agent, noted that 'Siamon disappeared' at a critical point. He was right, as always. There are no adequate words to thank Siamon for his tolerance of this challenge, and for his readiness to be amused and touched as each chapter unfolded. His character in this book and in an earlier memoir, *Shared Lives*, speaks for itself.

Cawnpore

Tom Williams

Published by Accent Press Ltd 2015

ISBN 9781783756032

Preface

The White Rajah, John Williamson's account of his life with James Brooke of Sarawak, was first published in 2010.Williamson had written the account as a personal record, not intending it for publication. It ended with him in Singapore, having left the man who had been his lover and mentor in Borneo.

Although much is known of James Brooke, I thought that Williamson had been lost to history after these adventures. About six months after *The White Rajah* was published, though, I received a package of papers from someone who has asked to remain anonymous. The papers had been in his possession for years and he had been uncertain what to do with them. He suggested that, following the success of the earlier book, I might like to see these published too.

The story follows on directly from the end of *The White Rajah*. Williamson apparently left Singapore and travelled to India. This book describes his experiences during the siege of Cawnpore in what was then called the Indian Mutiny. The siege of Cawnpore was one of the most comprehensive British military disasters of the 19th century and a source of fascination and horror to the Victorian public. One of the survivors, Captain Mowbray Thomson, published a book (*The Story of Cawnpore*) that was a best seller in its day. Williamson's manuscript suggests that he was thinking of publishing his own account. However, the work could never have been published at the time. Its open acknowledgement of his sexuality (when homosexuality was illegal), his ambivalent attitude to the rights and wrongs of the war, and his failure to play the part of the conventional Victorian hero, all made publication impossible. Perhaps he intended this as a first draft and then realised that editing it for the public would have meant removing all the details that make it such a unique and fascinating record.

The Indian War of 1857 was probably one of the best-documented conflicts in history, although many accounts differ as to the details of events. Williamson's record is typical in this respect. Overall, Williamson's account seems reliable, although I have added some Editor's Notes discussing some of the apparent discrepancies in his account and a short bibliography for anyone who wants to check the details of what happened.

Like most authors of his day, Williamson's spelling of some Indian words and the names he uses for Indian towns are not the same as they would be nowadays. I have retained Williamson's spellings, although where these have been inconsistent, I have edited them so that they are at least the same throughout the book.

Williamson used chapter headings written in the long narrative style of the day. They were more like tables of contents than chapter headings and I have removed them. Other than that, I have tried to let Williamson's words speak for themselves.

Tom Williams

Chapter One

It was in December of 1855 that I left Singapore. My time with James Brooke was generously rewarded and I found myself, if not a wealthy man, then certainly in a position to return to England and live out my days quietly and in comfort.

I was by now approaching my middle years, but I felt that I was still too young to retire to some country village. My time in the South China Seas had given me a taste for life in the Orient and James' stories of his experiences in India had left me curious about that country. So it was, when I took ship in the Swallow, I paid my passage just as far as Calcutta.

We celebrated Christmas at sea. The captain served a goose at his table and the crew entertained us with an impromptu concert that combined sea shanties and some carols, but otherwise there was little to mark Our Saviour's natal day. The sea looked much the same as the day before. There was a stiff breeze and, just before dark, there was a touch of rain.

We arrived at the red mud banks that mark the entrance to the Hooghly just as 1855 gave way to 1856. After three weeks at sea, I welcomed the proximity of land. Waking early, I joined the passengers clustered at the rails to watch the jungle passing in the pearly dawn light. For a moment, I felt myself back on the River Sarawak, seeing my first glimpse of Borneo. The Hooghly, though, was not the Sarawak. We were not feeling our way up an uncertain navigation. An East India Company pilot stood on the deck, alongside the captain, and we tacked our way confidently upstream.

When we arrived at last in Calcutta, no sooner had the ship docked than we were swarming with natives who hurtled up the gangplanks to inflict themselves on our poor vessel. Coolies, black and shining and naked but for a loincloth, came aboard, ostensibly for porterage. Most, though, seemed to squat idly or engage in animated but incomprehensible conversations with their fellows. Men claiming to be tailors, some armed with measuring tape and chalk as if to give proof of their profession, importuned any European who did not move rapidly out of their way, offering new suits at prices that would make a Singapore merchant blush. Other gentlemen, elegantly dressed in native drapery and turbans, glided toward me and, before I could effect an escape, they thrust into my face pieces of paper assuring me that the bearer had served this or that European as his khitmutghar, or major-domo, for so many months or years and that their services were in every respect satisfactory.

After I had assured several of my would-be servants that I intended to establish myself in a hotel before I made any decisions about my household, I decided to head for the shore and have my luggage sent on. Again, I found myself swamped with a crowd of natives. These were the boatmen, sinewy men, almost naked and so unlike the khitmutghars as to seem almost a different species. All offered their services at the top of their voices and all, on closer enquiry, demanded vast sums of money to paddle me the short distance to the shore.

When I had finally settled on a sum I suspect was scarcely more than twice that which old India hands would have paid, I descended the companion-ladder to an already over-laden boat and, after a few nervous minutes, I was deposited safe and more-or-less dry on the soil of India.

Now I had to fight my way through yet another crowd who jostled and pushed at passengers disembarking on the quay. Arms reached toward me, clutching begging bowls; voices shouted offers of services of every sort; while what seemed like thousands of other figures seemed to be joining the pushing throng simply from some social desire to do as everyone else was doing. In truth, I had little idea what any of them were saying as, although I had made some attempts to learn Hindustanee in Singapore, not one word in ten was intelligible. In the end, I turned to one fellow who was, in some approximation of English, offering the services of a palanquin. This, it turned out, was essentially the same thing as the sedan chairs of old England and, once I was safely aboard, four bearers carried me in curtained seclusion to my hotel.

The hotel I had chosen, on the recommendation of acquaintances I had made on my voyage, turned out to be a splendid place and I was soon safely ensconced with a good meal in my belly. Now, sat in my room digesting a leg of lamb that seemed all the more delicious after shipboard food, I felt it was time for some belated New Year resolutions. The first (and without it this might not have come to be written) was to make a diary of my impressions. When I had come to write of my early days in Borneo, I realised how many details of my experience had become blurred by time and I resolved that I would commit my new life to paper while it was still fresh in my mind. I had no inkling then that I would find myself at the centre of great events and that I would be writing an account such as the one that you are now reading, but rather I thought I would keep some jottings in a commonplace book that might stimulate fond memories in my later years.

My second goal was to find myself some employment such as would enable me to utilise the experience of administration that I had acquired in Borneo. I remembered all James Brooke's complaints about the power and the manifest failings of the East India

Company. Nonetheless, if I were to find employment in India, I would have to work for the Company which controlled the economy and government of the country with a grip no less firm for its being, to some degree, sclerotic.

I had feared that the Company would not be prepared to offer me any sort of position, as most of their recruits were the children or close relatives of existing employees, and those that were recruited in England were trained up in the Company's college at Haileybury. However, I was pleased to discover that, whatever his opinion of the East India Company, the Company held James Brooke in some esteem. Once it was known that I had been at his right hand in Borneo, doors I had expected to be closed to me were opened and I was soon being interviewed by a gentleman who declared that he was sure that a position could be found for me. His main concern seemed to be that I would find that employment with the Company failed properly to exercise my talents for administration. I assured him that this was unlikely to be the case. Even quite junior officials in the Company's employ would be responsible for a population that might be greater than in the whole of Sarawak and I was more than happy to seek a post that would be supervised by a more experienced officer. As it happened, there was a vacancy for a Deputy Collector in the city of Cawnpore in Agra, part of the North Western Provinces. Thus, it was agreed that I should make my way there, to work under the Collector, a Mr Charles George Hillersdon.

The journey to Cawnpore was to take the better part of two months and my new employers were anxious that I should make it as soon as possible, for the cool of January was held to be the ideal time to travel. So it was around the middle of that month (I look at my commonplace book and see that it was the 17th) that I set off from Calcutta. I had intended to travel light, but I was assured that no European could journey without servants. So, beside a man to drive my buggy, there was a separate groom to care for the horses and a personal attendant without whom, everyone told me, the natives would look on me hardly better than a vagabond.

Our caravan travelled fifty or sixty miles in a day, easing our way up the Grand Trunk Road. Each night we would stop at a Government post house, or dak bungalow as they are called, where I would be settled into a comfortable bedroom while the servants were herded away to sleep I knew not where. They seemed happy, though, such treatment being the custom of the country, and we progressed contentedly enough. At first, the journey was dull but, as the flat countryside around Calcutta changed gradually to hillier terrain, I gave myself over to the thrill of exploration, finding excitement in the constantly changing vistas. At times, the road grew so steep that I had to abandon the buggy and move to riding horses. This was no great inconvenience, though, as arrangements were easily made at the dak bungalows to hire another buggy when the terrain allowed. Any difficulties that were caused by changing conveyance were more than offset by the magnificent views from the summits we ascended.

I was told that we might be bothered by tigers but I saw no wild animals other than the monkeys I would glimpse from time to time among the branches wherever the road passed through trees. Once we did come upon a bear sleeping on the wayside, but it woke and lumbered lazily away without making any move toward us.

We had left hills and jungle behind us by the time we arrived at Cawnpore. The town lay stretched out on the plain alongside the Ganges, a fantastical confection of towers, minarets and domes that promised the real India – an India that had remained tantalisingly out of reach in Calcutta where the Governor's palace and the offices of the Company dominated the town. Here the buildings of the European Station clustered beside the river to the South, leaving native Cawnpore gazing down on the sacred Ganges as it has for centuries.

The company had arranged a bungalow for me and I arrived there around midday. It looked pleasant enough. The building, with high rooms and a shaded veranda against the summer heat, stood behind a mud wall that ran alongside the road, surrounding a fair-sized garden. Little grew there, though, save for some patches of grass, survivors from the rains, which pushed their way through the red soil.

I walked up the short pathway to the door to find it opened as I approached. A tall Indian in immaculate white robes and a turban stood within and greeted me, bowing with his palms pressed together.

'Welcome, sahib. Mr Hillersdon has asked me to serve you as khanasaman.'

A khanasaman, I knew, was almost like a butler. In Sarawak, James and I had been served by Freddy who had run our household with devotion and who had, on one famous occasion, saved our lives.[1] Freddy had been short and always somewhat rumpled in appearance, so about as different from the Indian before me as I could imagine, but I hoped that, despite his almost formidable appearance, he might become as valuable an ally as Freddy had been. I decided to try out my Hindustanee and greeted him in that tongue.

'*Namaste! Maiṁ tumasē milanē se khuśa hūṁ.*'

Far from showing any pleasure at my effort, it seemed to me the khanasaman recoiled a fraction before ignoring my proffered hand and salaaming even more deeply than before.

'Mr Hillersdon suggested that you might like me to arrange the hiring of your staff.'

---

[1] See *The White Rajah*

I persevered with my attempt at friendliness, favouring him with a broad smile.

'I'm sure there's no hurry. We can get to know each other first.'

The gentleman before me drew himself up and somehow looked even more formidable.

'It is essential that servants are hired without delay. I would have made the arrangements earlier, but Mr Hillersdon considered it appropriate to wait for your approval.' Then, scarcely pausing for breath, he started to enumerate the hirings he had planned for that afternoon. There was to be an abdar who would serve my wine, a khitmutghar to oversee my dining room, a second khitmutghar to assist the first, a cook, a second cook, a man to wash dishes, another man to wash clothes, and a third to iron them. In case these gentlemen should not ensure the eternal well-being of my wardrobe, I should hire my own tailor and then, as Indian servants come in pairs, a second tailor alongside the first. Beside these individuals, I was to employ various sweepers and gardeners and water carriers and, all in all, an establishment of some thirty or forty people. My attempts to explain that this was not necessary met, first, with incomprehension and then with dismay. 'Sahib,' he cried, 'I have been employed by the Company to ensure that your establishment is such as is suitable to a man in your position. You will disgrace me if you do not allow me to make the proper arrangements.'

It was pointless to argue. If I was to live and work as a Company official in India, I must maintain an appropriate style and that meant having servants – lots of servants. In order that I might give due honour to my position of Deputy Collector, I yielded as gracefully as I could and my khanasaman went off happily to engage this small army on my behalf. Only as he left did I realise that I did not even know his name. I think I realised at that moment that we were never going to become friends.

In the few hours of peace that I could expect before he returned, I explored my new home. The bungalow was a substantial building already furnished with such furniture as the Company considered suitable for a bachelor in its service – overstuffed armchairs and enough linen to make the most homesick of memsahibs feel that they were but a hop and a skip from London Town. I saw nothing that encouraged me to spend more time there than I had to so, after a quick wash and brush-up, I was ready to report for duty.

Finding the office where I was to spend my days was easy enough, for the Collectorate was an imposing building in the centre of the European quarter. It was built in a style halfway between the traditional Indian buildings and the offices of a British merchant bank. The stone facade with its fine doorway was separated from the street by a veranda that offered some shelter from the sun and the windows were high and unglazed, the lower half screened with the rush screens called tattis which would be soaked in water to provide some cooling of any breeze that might pass through.

I announced myself to the babu guarding a desk at the entrance. He was dressed as a European and spoke to me in perfect English. In fact, he seemed almost more English than most of the Englishmen I had met in India. He was the ideal gentleman, from his stiff wing collar to his perfectly polished shoes. Only the colour of his skin and the lustre of his hair gave away his Indian origins for, like most babus, he was the child of an Englishman and his Indian mistress and the more he tried to ape his European superiors, the more they would despise him. His efficiency, though, was in no doubt and, minutes later, I found myself in the office of the Collector.

Charles George Hillersdon, who also held the position of Magistrate for the district, was a few years my junior, being in his early thirties. He was slightly above the average in height, but a sedentary life had left him somewhat corpulent and he tended to stoop, making him appear older than his years. His office was a large room, but, despite its size, it seemed cramped, for the walls were covered in shelves where books and ledgers filled every available inch.

Mr Hillersdon pushed his chair back and rose to greet me. 'Welcome to my lair. See if you can find a seat somewhere and sit on it.'

There was a seat and, miraculously, it seemed to have hardly any papers resting on it. I moved a sheet or two and sat while the Collector outlined the work that I was to assist him in.

'We collect the taxes, oversee tribunals, inspect public dispensaries, check the schools are up to scratch, make sure the jails are sound, and the courts don't fall on the judges. A bit of everything really. As far as the natives here are concerned, I'm the Government. And you, too, now.'

It was much as my work had been in Borneo, only on a grander scale. I admit, it sounded daunting and I imagine that some of my concern must have shown on my face for Hillersdon hurried to reassure me. 'Don't worry. You won't be alone. There's a chap called Simkin who'll be as your right hand.' He smiled. 'I'll introduce you.'

We left the Collector's room and walked a short way down a corridor. On one side, a row of doors stood open, revealing offices that faced out onto the veranda. 'We never close the doors,' Hillersdon told me. 'It's hot enough with them open.'

Internal windows allowed air to cross the corridor to a single large room on the other side. There I saw twenty or thirty babus at rows of desks, industriously scratching away at the piles of papers in front of them, but Hillersdon ignored them and gestured for me to enter the next office. I did so, but the desk that stood in splendid isolation on a patch of carpet was unoccupied. Hillersdon, following me in the door, paused, a look of irritation on his face. 'Where the devil is Simkin?'

A note on the blotter, neatly centred on an otherwise empty desk, provided the answer. 'Gone to lunch,' it read.

Hillersdon sighed. 'The man's got to eat, I suppose.' He looked at me as if he had just that moment realised that the same was probably true of my constitution. 'You'll be hungry yourself.'

I assured him that I had breakfasted well – which was true for the food in the dak bungalows was generally excellent – but he insisted that he see me fed again.

We went to his Club, close by the Company's offices. 'We must fix you up membership. Everyone here's a member and they do a good lunch.'

I had never been inside a gentleman's club before. When I lived in England, my position meant that I would no more have dreamt of entering a club than of taking tea with the Queen. In Borneo there had been no need of such an institution, the gentlemen there all knowing one another and James Brooke and I keeping open house in any case. But I had heard of the London clubs and I had imagined what they might be like. The Club at Cawnpore was exactly as I had imagined gentlemen to repair to in London, though the height of the rooms and the slatted shutters over the windows were concessions made to the local climate.

Lunch in the club was obviously popular and the place was busy. Hillersdon introduced me to a dozen or more men in quick succession. All of them, like me, were respectably dressed in long jackets, high collars, and ties which, even in the cool of winter, were far from ideal clothing for this climate. Perhaps that is why my impression was of a parade of red-faced, perspiring English gentleman, most slightly overweight and, in the few moments of introduction each was allowed, all practically indistinguishable. Their names meant nothing to me nor mine to them, though several were anxious to try to place me.

'Are you one of the Surrey Williamsons?'

I had to confess I was not.

'Did I used to see you at Lady Forester's soirees?'

No, I had not had that pleasure.

'Did you know old John Marriot's lad?'

I feared not.

Hillersdon explained to each in turn that I had just arrived from Borneo and had worked there alongside James Brooke. At Brooke's name, one or two faces showed some sign of recognition, but for most, it seemed that my lack of any proper connections in English society was a grave disappointment.

Sensing my discomfort, Hillersdon steered me away to a quiet corner where we sat in stuffed leather armchairs in the reading room. Copies of *The Times*, shipped from London and filled with old news, were scattered around while the Indian papers lay pristine and neatly folded on the tables. We sipped gin until a native in a splendid white uniform came to whisper that luncheon was served. The food (roast lamb with mint sauce and potatoes followed by sticky toffee pudding), like the rest of the club, made no concessions to geography. Apart from the heat and the Indian servants, there was little to indicate that we were in India at all.

We lingered over coffee, but by three we were back in Simkin's office and Mr Hillersdon introduced me to a rotund young man with thinning fair hair, who at least had the grace to look embarrassed to learn that the Collector had been waiting on him. 'I'm so sorry, sir ... Most regrettable ... My wife ... new cook ...'

Hillersdon waved aside his explanations. 'Well, you're here now. Can you show Mr Williamson the ropes?'

The Collector retreated to his office and Simkin subsided into his chair. 'Oh dear. I think I may have blotted my copybook rather.'

I was not altogether impressed with Mr Simkin. 'I'm surprised you have time to get away at all. There seems a fearful amount of work needs doing.'

'Oh, yes. Fearful.'

'I hardly know how you can cope.'

'Ah hah!' Simkin tapped his nose with a wink. 'Organisation. There you have it. The secret is organisation.'

I sat, saying nothing. It seemed to me that young Simkin would expand on his point without encouragement.

'The natives are dishonest, feckless, and lazy but over centuries they have built up a system where each class exploits the one below it. We have a good relationship with one of the local bigwigs – chap called Nana Sahib. We flatter him and go to the parties he gives and he makes sure that all the local landowners hand on the taxes that they're supposed to pay. I have a couple of native clerks and they handle most of the day-to-day stuff.' He smiled with the confidence of one who had lunched well. 'Organisation, you see.'

I agreed that I did see and excused myself. I found my own way to my office and sat down with a weary sigh. Mr Hillersdon's intentions were good but I could see now why his office looked so busy. I had no doubt that mine would resemble it ere long.

Fortunately, Simkin was right about one thing. The babus were models of efficiency and, with their help, I was soon able to establish myself in my office and make a start on the tasks awaiting me. And if I could expect little help from below, I had Mr Hillersdon to aid me from above. For in an office where most of the Europeans seemed more concerned with following the fortunes of the runners in the famous Cawnpore races than in anything related to their employment, the Collector stood out as a model of conscientious behaviour. I soon came to admire him for his administrative skills and we seemed to rub along well enough together.

About a week after I arrived, he announced that now I had had a chance to settle down, I must dine with him at his home. 'You'll have to dine with everybody eventually but you might as well start with us.'

I think he realised that I was still not entirely comfortable in company. Dinner parties being one of the principal recreations of Cawnpore, I think he hoped to break me into the habit gently. In any case, I was the only guest of the Hillersdons that night, so just the three of us sat at table. Even with so small a party, though, we were waited on by no less than seven servants, one standing behind every chair, another to serve the wine, two to attend the table, and a khitmutghar who acted as a sort of major-domo. In addition, of course, there were the kitchen staff, who had prepared the food and Hillersdon's khanasaman who made an appearance at the beginning of the meal to ensure that all was in order.

With all the delicacies of the Orient at her disposal, Lydia Hillersdon had chosen to serve roast beef. I had tried, as tactfully as I could, to suggest that this might cause offense to the many members of her staff who were Hindoos, but she assured me that her cook was a Musalman and that he had no objection to our eating cattle.

Mrs Hillersdon was a pretty woman, barely more than a girl but already the mother of two children who were tucked away somewhere in the vast bungalow that reflected the Collector's status in Cawnpore. The meal, too, seemed designed more to astonish me with the profligacy of food available rather than to meet the needs of appetite. Besides the beef there was, as a concession to native cuisine, a chicken curry, and then eggs and mutton chops besides a concoction described as trifle but resembling nothing I had ever eaten before. Mrs Hillersdon was particularly proud of the mutton chops. They were so tough as to be practically inedible, but they had the virtue of being the product of her very own sheep for, as she was quick to explain, she kept a small menagerie of animals on the grounds at the rear of her bungalow.

'I have guinea fowl, turkeys, pigeons, chicken, and rabbits as well as the sheep. Alas! So many die in the summer heat, but I do enjoy looking after them and it is so rewarding to raise our own food for the table.'

Mrs Hillersdon, resplendent in her wide skirt trailing the floor and her immaculate white blouse seemed an unlikely stockwoman. Then again, when she looked at me, dressed as a gentleman with my stiff collar and my cravat under a jacket of the latest pattern, she probably did not imagine that I had started life as a farm labourer in Devon. Relieved to find a common interest, I ventured to question her on matters of animal husbandry.

'Do you keep your own ram, madam?'

'A ram, Mr Williamson? Whatever for?'

'So you hire a ram to tup your ewes?'

'Tup, Mr Williamson? Pray what does that term mean?'

Mr Hillersdon saved me from further embarrassment remarking on the charm of the lambs. 'Our boy has made quite a pet of one of them. I hardly dare mention where his chops come from.'

Lydia Hillersdon could not let mention of her son pass without telling me all about his attachment to their flock and the shepherd's smock that her tailor had run up for him. The conversation moved on and the danger was passed. Fortunately, Mr Hillersdon was more amused than annoyed by my *faux pas*, explaining the next day that his wife's involvement with her miniature farm was limited to occasional inspections while her servants did the actual work. She employed a shepherd for the sheep and a murgh-i-wallah for the fowl and the rabbits. This seemed to me an extraordinary amount of care to lavish on a few animals for the table but Mr Hillersdon assured me that her efforts were, by the standards of many of the Europeans in the Station, quite modest.

James Brooke had frowned on British women joining our community in Borneo, so dinners there were more relaxed, bachelor affairs. I had felt somewhat constrained before my misunderstanding with Mrs Hillersdon, and after that I fear I left Mr Hillersdon carrying most of the burden of conversation himself. He was a good host, though, with a store of entertaining stories that kept the table amused until more servants arrived to clear the meal. We withdrew into a parlour cluttered with furniture, much of which appeared to have been shipped from England, having no sign of native design or manufacture. In pride of place was a fine upright piano where Mrs Hillersdon sat to entertain us. The instrument was not entirely in tune, as the climate of India means that pianos have to be tuned almost monthly, but it was clear that she was a good player and I appreciated her attempts to entertain a stranger in her home.

I left at around ten, having found the evening trying after so many years of living in a bachelor establishment. The weeks that followed, though, made me realise just how pleasant a hostess Mrs Hillersdon was and how enlightened her husband.

I was invited to dinner party after dinner party. I would set off at around seven, leading a train of servants, for to arrive without them would be considered a grave discourtesy. I would take a vile sherry with the master of the household while my servants and the host's servants and the servants of the other guests all navigated themselves around the over-stuffed furniture and the occasional tables covered in sculpture chipped from the walls of the local temples. Our host's khitmutghar would announce dinner and we would traipse through to a dining room where we would be seated at a table that would not be out of place in a grand dining hall. An array of cutlery would be displayed, guaranteed to confuse me for all that I was now generally able to pass myself off as a gentleman, and dish after dish would be set before me in the confusion of over-spiced lamb and under-boiled beef that passed for Anglo-Indian cuisine. As a bachelor, I was invariably placed between two young women who would simper at me in the hope that I would relieve their parents of the embarrassment of unmarried daughters. We would struggle to make polite conversation, which, in these circles, meant empty chatter about English fashion and London Society. Sometimes the ladies would ask for advice on a horse they were considering purchasing. Here I thought I might impress, horses being, so to speak, in my blood from childhood. Unfortunately, I would barely have started on my enquiries on the finer points of their proposed purchases than I would see the light die in their eyes and I realised that they were no more truly interested in my views on horseflesh than my attitude to the latest colour for an evening gown.

I would stagger home from these evenings, my head aching from the heat and the interminable chatter and my bowels already complaining as they tried to digest the execrable food. I wondered what these people were doing here in India when they so clearly wanted to pretend to be in Surrey and to ride to hounds after the fox. (They did, indeed, ride to hounds in Cawnpore, but had to be content with chasing jackals.)

The contrast between these dinners and the quiet evenings spent at the Hillersdons (for there were to be many more after that first night) made me appreciate the virtues of the Collector's household. They kept a small establishment by local standards (though, even so, they must have had around forty servants) and they treated them kindly. They might eat beef at their table but they respected the religious sensibilities of their staff in their direct dealings with them and were generous with gifts on the many and various holy days that the Hindoos and the Musalmans celebrated. Indeed, in his role as magistrate, Mr Hillersdon was often distressed to hear of cases where Europeans had beaten their servants because a chop had been over-cooked or the leather on their horse's bridle had not gleamed from recent polishing when they chose to ride out unexpectedly. Although it was impossible, given the relationship between the races, for the Collector to side openly with the natives against their rulers, he would often take the delinquent master aside and speak so severely to him in private that his behaviour would be moderated for weeks or months to come.

In part, Hillersdon's attitudes seem to have been tempered by his relationship with Nana Sahib. 'Old Nana,' as Mr Hillersdon called him, was apparently a particular friend of the Collector as well as having the more general reputation of being well disposed to all the Company officials in Cawnpore.

'He's a jolly fine chap,' Hillersdon assured me. 'He heard that Lydia was a bit peaky last summer and said that if she ever needed a change of air, she was welcome to stay out at his guest house.'

Nana Sahib lived something over ten miles outside Cawnpore and a visit to his guesthouse was viewed by the European community as a pleasant change from the dust and heat of the town.

'He's an excellent host and extraordinarily well disposed to Britain – surprisingly so, given the treatment he has received.'

'We've treated him badly?'

Hillersdon had been explaining land ownership in the

area, but now he pushed aside the books on property rights in Agra and reached for a bundle of papers tied in a green ribbon.

'These are copies of Nana Sahib's petitions to be recognised as Peshwa. That was his father's title, but dear old dad was a naughty boy. He raised an army down near Bombay and decided to drive the British out of India. We smashed his army and exiled him here with a pension to keep him quiet. When he died, Nana naturally assumed he'd get the title and the pension. The Governor-General doesn't agree. Poor old Nana is stuck here with hundreds of courtiers and retainers, all demanding pay and pensions and regular gifts. He even has his own little army to escort him around the place and let him play at being a great lord still. It's all very splendid but it doesn't come cheap. The old Peshwa left a fortune, but the well must run dry soon. Nana Sahib writes petition after petition and quite a few of us have put in a word for him but Dalhousie won't be moved. You can see why Nana Sahib might have it in for the British but far from it. I couldn't get things done half as easily if he weren't around to smooth things over with the natives when difficulties arise.'

I picked up the petitions, almost without thinking, and spent the rest of the afternoon making notes on exactly who was responsible for the tax on the hundreds of farms in the countryside around Cawnpore. As I did so, I noticed how many were ultimately owned by Nana Sahib and, where they weren't, how often his name was mentioned as having adjudicated disputes on field boundaries or inheritance.

That night, after a dinner eaten alone but watched by four different servants, I settled to read through Nana Sahib's petitions. I wasn't surprised that the East India Company was no longer prepared to pay the eight hundred thousand rupees a year that they had used to buy off his father but some of the other measures – notably their refusal to recognise any of his hereditary titles – seemed cruel. Did the East India Company not understand how important titles and honours were in the East? And if they did, why were they antagonising someone who had shown nothing but good will toward their country and their Company?

By now, my understanding of Hindustanee was considerably improved. I would talk to my household servants in their own language (much to my khanasaman's disgust) and I would listen to the conversations I heard in the bazaar to try to understand the politics of the place. The Collector's offices were full of reports from European officials and native spies, but I felt that these looked only at the surface of things. I sensed deeper currents that would take events I knew not where – but I was sure that without understanding the Nana Sahib I could never really understand native politics in Agra.

Mr Hillersdon noted my interest and sought to gratify it by suggesting that we pay the man a visit.

'You'll have to meet him sooner or later. Everybody does – and, of course, he'll be interested to meet you as you're the new Deputy Collector. Why don't we ride out to Bithur tomorrow?'

We set off early. We had twelve miles to ride and we intended to take it gently. In the summer, we would have taken a carriage, but the winter chill was still on the mornings, so we preferred the possibility of some gentle exercise to sitting swaddled in blankets for the journey. We did not breakfast before we left as Hillersdon assured me that we would be more than adequately fed when we got there.

Our journey took us North, past the old town, nestling against the Ganges to our right. In less than a quarter of an hour, we had put Cawnpore behind us and were riding across a wide plain with only occasional hamlets and the odd grove of trees to break the monotony of miles of open ground. Even here, though, were constant reminders of the sheer number of people living in India. We passed holy men who raised begging bowls, farmers carrying food to the Cawnpore markets in great baskets strapped to their backs, and finely dressed men who Mr Hillersdon identified as the Nana's land agents, off to collect rents or adjudicate disputes with his tenants. Every mile or so we would pass fields scratched from the thin soil, a few straggling plants all that stood between the farmer and starvation.

Despite the plentiful evidence of hardship, the early light lent softness to the scene. It filled the landscape with a promise of romance so that the journey was as pleasant as I had hoped. It ended unexpectedly in a tree-lined boulevard that led to the Nana's palace. This was not as exciting an outlook as I had expected, for everyone who had visited it had told me what a splendid place it was. The whole compound was enclosed in a high wall which presented a dreary prospect to the arriving guest. At the gate, a magnificently uniformed sentry leaned against the wall. As we approached, he recognised the Collector and hurriedly pulled himself to attention, giving an adequate salute as we passed through.

Once inside, we found ourselves in a pleasure garden with orchards and fountains as picturesque as anything I might have imagined. I relaxed after the ride and sat easily on my horse, admiring the monkeys that chattered in the trees alongside the path, when I heard a lion roaring nearby. I shortened rein, ready to gallop for my life, but Hillersdon, seeing my alarm, reached out a hand to calm me.

'Relax! Nana has his own menagerie. The lion is far from the most remarkable beast there. We'll take a look later.'

He rode on toward the house and, minutes later,

servants were leading our horses to the stables while we entered the home of Nana Sahib.

Outside, the palace had little to recommend it architecturally. The long frontage was crudely coated with some sort of plaster. There was no decoration to speak of and, had I seen it in an English park, I would not have recognised it as the home of a great man. Once we had climbed the steps to the main doorway, though, the interior was another matter. We passed down a marbled corridor, lined with woven tapestries, the sound of fountains in dozens of tiny courtyards echoing on the stone. We were led to a dining room where, beneath a fine chandelier that had nothing of native manufacture about it, I saw, as Hillersdon had promised me, a full English breakfast. There was kedgeree, sausages, some fried eggs congealing in a chafing dish, devilled kidneys, mutton chops that looked scarcely more appealing than those produced by poor Lydia Hillersdon, ham on the bone, and slices of greasy bacon on a silver salver.

I was hungry after our ride and if the food had clearly been cooked by someone who was a stranger to British cuisine and if it was served on mismatched (but expensive) china, it was still welcome. We set to with a will, while I admired the life-sized portraits of Nana Sahib's ancestors and tried to ignore the apparently arbitrary selection of paintings of European beauties that were mixed among them.

We had finished our meal and were relaxing with a cup of tea and a cheroot apiece when a young man in native robes entered the room and asked us to accompany him. His name, he said, was Mungo Buksh and he was a cousin of Nana Sahib, come to lead us to greet our host.

We followed young Mr Buksh along the marbled corridors, through more and more splendid rooms, some furnished like the dining room in European style, some with just cushions or daybeds on the floor. At last we came to a pair of ornate brass doors with guards, smartly uniformed in the style of Indians in the Company's army – that is generally like our own troops, only with turbans on their heads and the long curved scimitars that they call tulwars held at rest. As we drew up to them they came to the salute with their swords and unseen hands within opened the doors.

Our guide gestured toward our riding boots and I followed Hillersdon's lead in removing them before entering the room where Nana Sahib sat on a carpet waiting for us.

My first thought was that he seemed very young to be such a prominent personage. He was, I judged, not thirty years old, but already beginning to run to fat. He did not make a particularly imposing figure. To my surprise, he wore glasses perched on an aquiline nose, decorated underneath by a neatly waxed moustache. A small turban balanced lopsidedly on the top of his head – he was almost bald – and looked, frankly, ridiculous. Add to that the gold embroidered waistcoat he was wearing together with a pearl necklace, and the effect was as if a rather tubby child had been let loose on a dressing-up box. Still, he greeted us with a smile and a pretty speech of welcome which Mr Buksh translated for us (the Nana having not a word of English).

Hillersdon smiled in return and introduced me as one friend to another. Nana Sahib nodded and gestured to the carpet in front of him. 'Do please be seated, Mr Williamson.'

I sat cross-legged like him and he smiled again, this time with more warmth. 'You have been some time in India, Mr Williamson? You sit comfortably while poor Mr Hillersdon is still at a loss when deprived of his chair.'

I looked across to where the Collector was, indeed, visibly struggling to settle himself on the floor. 'Not in India, sir, but in Borneo.'

'Borneo!' Nana Sahib's brown eyes sparkled with enthusiasm. 'A land of mystery! You must tell me all about it.'

So Mr Buksh was kept busy interpreting as we talked about Borneo and my time there and the work that James Brooke and I had done in Sarawak. Nana Sahib interrupted from time to time with intelligent questioning while poor Hillersdon fidgeted uncomfortably beside me. Nana Sahib was particularly interested in the basis of our rule in Sarawak.

'So the East India Company has no rule in Borneo?'

'No. Sarawak is independent of the Company and of Britain.'

'And the titles of the native lords are recognised?'

'Of course.'

Nana Sahib turned to Hillersdon, whose agitation was by now not entirely due to the cramp setting in in his legs.

'It seems to me,' and his eyes glinted as he spoke, 'that we could all learn much from the administration in Borneo.'

Hillersdon stretched his lips into a smile. 'Indeed. I am sure we will all benefit from Mr Williamson's experience.'

At that, Nana Sahib appeared satisfied and our audience was over.

Mungo Buksh accompanied us as we left, expertly navigating the maze of corridors and hallways. He smiled comfortably when he caught my eye on him and, as Hillersdon's expression was much less encouraging, I concentrated my attention on our guide. He was, I guessed, in his early twenties; a good-looking young man with an open, friendly face. Although he had said he was a cousin of Nana Sahib, I could see no family resemblance and I asked him if he and his cousin were close.

'Close?' He looked puzzled for a moment. 'Oh! Because I am his cousin.' He smiled. 'Nana Sahib has a hundred cousins. I see him only some days. I am useful to him because my English is good. He asks me sometimes to look after his English guests.' He paused, looking between me and Mr Hillersdon. 'I know the Collector has been here many times, but would you like me to show you around?'

For a moment, I thought Hillersdon's irritation at my apparently impolitic comments during our audience might make him object but it was not in his nature to be petty. He had matters to attend to in Cawnpore, he said, but he was happy to leave me in Mr Buksh's care.

We saw the Collector to the door and then my guide took me back into the building. 'Saturday House was built by the Peshwa Baji Rao when he established himself in Bithur in 1819.' He had obviously made this speech a thousand times before and he uttered it mechanically.

'Why Saturday House?' I asked. I had hoped to interrupt his rehearsed tour and elicit some more spontaneous response, but he had obviously been asked that question a thousand times too.

'It's named for the Peshwa's residence at Poona, which was also Saturday House.'

'And why was that given such an unusual name?'

'Because the building was started on a Saturday.'

I laughed. It seemed so ridiculous. Young Buksh, though, appeared quite indignant at my response.

'It is true. The building of the palace at Poona began on January 10th in your year 1730. It was a Saturday. It was a very auspicious day.'

He made me feel as if I were mocking him and his beliefs in auspicious days and, as this had been far from my intention, I apologised. He smiled. 'Most English people find the name amusing but they don't apologise when I explain it.' He turned abruptly down a marbled corridor that we had passed earlier. 'Come. We'll be just in time.'

The corridor was something over twenty-five yards long and every yard along it there was a niche in the wall and each niche held a clock. Some were carriage clocks that sat on top of pillars; others were grandfather clocks, standing proudly on the floor. All were ticking noisily, the sound echoing on the bare marble. And all showed the time as two minutes before noon.

We walked to the middle of the corridor, my companion grinning broadly, while my ears seemed to quiver in anticipation of what I feared was coming next.

One of the clocks must have been badly adjusted, for it started to strike the hour while the others were still silent. A few seconds later, though, the rest joined the mechanical chorus.

There were twenty-five clocks in that corridor and every one of them was striking noon. Carriage clocks tinkled, grandfather clocks tolled sonorously, one sounded the chimes of Big Ben, another trilled as if in imitation of a caged bird. All rang out at once in the marbled corridor, combining into an unspeakable din. For several seconds I stood dumbfounded and then, careless of the proper way to behave in such circumstances (for surely someone, somewhere must have decided what is the proper way to behave when faced with a potentate's clock collection) I put my fingers to my ears and waited for the assault on my hearing to end.

I looked toward young Mungo and caught him laughing heartily – though I couldn't hear him over the racket of the clocks.

One by one, Nana Sahib's horological tormentors fell silent and my guide, still laughing, led me onward.

'You didn't appreciate the chimes?' His face puckered into a mischievous smile. 'Nana Sahib is very proud of his collection. Every one of them has been shipped here from Europe and then adjusted until they tell the time perfectly. He has three jewellers who have learned the skills of watchmakers and whose sole duty is to care for the clocks.'

'I am sure the clocks are wonderful. But I can't help feeling that twenty-five clocks are not twenty-five times as impressive as one. Especially at noon.'

'Ah, yes.' He laughed again, a sound of shccr dclight escaping his throat. 'We were lucky to arrive in time. Imagine how disappointing it would have been had you arrived only an hour later.'

I grinned back. My young companion was no longer the solemn guide and he led me through mirrored halls pausing to admire shrines with images of various Hindoo deities, many of which were garlanded with fresh flowers.

'This is my favourite.' We were standing in front of a statue of a man-like figure with a monkey's face and tail. 'This is Hanuman. He was always full of tricks and frequently naughty but in the end he was a brave warrior and he gained wisdom from the gods.'

I looked at the brass face of the idol. There was, indeed, something in his eyes suggesting an impishness that I could see would appeal to the young man at my side.

'There are real monkeys outside,' he said, and we were off to explore Nana Sahib's menagerie like a couple of schoolboys on a holiday.

There were indeed monkeys – and the lion I had heard when we arrived, and snakes. 'A man plays a pipe to them and they dance,' said Mungo Buksh, 'but he isn't here now. Do you want me to have him come?' I assured him I was happy to see the snakes left peacefully asleep while I admired the birds in Nana Sahib's aviaries, the deer, the tigers pacing their cage and, in pride of place, a rhinoceros that stood like a statue on a patch of bare earth surrounded by solid iron bars.

'The elephants and the camels are kept separately because they are working animals. Would you like to see their stables?'

Of course I said, 'Yes.' The afternoon flew by as we explored Saturday House and its grounds but, all too soon, as children are summoned by their mothers' cries, so our afternoon ended as we remembered our duties. Mungo vanished into the palace and I set off back along the dusty road to Cawnpore.

Chapter Two

The days that followed allowed little time to think about my visit to Saturday House or the friend I had made there in Mungo Buksh, for it was that February that the East India Company, having fenced around the issue for years, finally annexed the Kingdom of Oudh.

Cawnpore was not itself in Oudh, but one of the main reasons the Company had such a large presence in the town was to guard the gateway to that kingdom. The Ganges at Cawnpore marked the Western border of Oudh. Inevitably, the excitement occasioned by the imposition of direct British rule in Oudh led to tremors in the usual calm of life on our side of the river.

Alongside the administrators, merchants, engineers, and men of business who made up the Civil Station of Cawnpore was an even more substantial military population who lived in cantonments on the outskirts of the town. My bungalow – like those of most of the Company's servants – was situated between the military settlement and old Cawnpore, so the sight of soldiers swaggering to and from the markets of the town was a common one. That February, though, there was more to-ing and fro-ing than usual. The native troops would gather in groups in the old town, while their European officers strode purposefully here and there or pushed their horses through the crowds blocking the roads to the bazaars.

I had no idea what the point of this martial enthusiasm might be. My own experience of the military mind in Borneo had left me unwilling to become closer acquainted with it. The view of most of the civilians working for the

Company was not that different from mine. The Civil staff generally avoided the military as the military avoided the civilians, each considering themselves superior to the other.

Whatever led to the flurry of military activity, things soon quieted down on that front, for the annexation was achieved with not a shot fired. It created a deal of work for we civilians, though, as much of Cawnpore's business involved Oudh and contracts that referred to the government of the kingdom now all had to be re-written to take account of the new administration. There was also a positive storm of new regulations as we sought to harmonise the laws of Oudh with those of the rest of British India. The storm engulfed all of the Company but it beat hardest against those nearest to the kingdom.

The pressure of work was increased by the unfortunate coincidence that Dalhousie had no sooner put his plans for Oudh into effect than he was replaced as Governor-General by the Viscount Canning. Mr Hillersdon was anxious that we have everything in good order for, as he said, Viscount Canning was a new broom, and every new broom feels the need to prove itself by sweeping cleaner than its predecessor. 'And I fear,' he added, 'that Charles Canning may feel he has a lot to prove, for they say he was appointed on the reputation of his father, rather than his own abilities.'

It was rare for Mr Hillersdon to express a view so clearly political as this, but I had no time to consider the merits or otherwise of the new Governor-General or the reasons for his attaining such an exalted position. Instead, for almost a month, I immersed myself in the mechanics of government. It was an invigorating opportunity to master the rules and regulations that governed every aspect of life in India and to understand how these were implemented in practice. I found myself arriving at my office early in the morning and often not leaving until the night watchman knocked worriedly at my door to enquire if all was well with the sahib. Mr Hillersdon did not need to spend as long in the office as I did, for his years of experience in India meant that he was able to digest the astonishing volume of memoranda, notes, policies, regulations, and official advice with an ease I did not expect to be able to emulate for years. But he was thorough and conscientious, with an unerring ability to go directly to the crux of any matter put before him. Although his grasp of the native tongue was limited, he had a real affection for the country and its people and he was quick to understand the implications of Company actions for the local people.

'Mark my words, John,' he would say (for we were on familiar terms by now), 'no good will come of this Oudh business. It's getting the natives agitated.'

If Hillersdon had any intimation of the storm that was to break on us, he was almost alone. For most of the Europeans in Cawnpore, the annexation was of importance only insofar as it interfered with the comfortable indolence of their regular lives. I was almost sorry for Simkin, forced to appear punctually at the office and work harder than he had in years. As the weeks passed and we moved into March, the weather grew steadily warmer and, by the end of the month, it was regularly over ninety degrees at midday. Most Europeans rose with the dawn, when it was still cool. While I welcomed the chance to make an early start in the office, I discovered that Simkin (like most of his colleagues) would start the day with a ride, claiming that the exercise was essential to his health. He would then breakfast ('I can hardly work on an empty stomach, can I?'), arriving at his desk – if all went well – by 10.00 a.m. or thereabouts. He would make a vague attempt at dealing with his correspondence before announcing that the heat was insufferable and returning to his home to spend the afternoon lying on his bed being fanned by a native employed specifically for that purpose. When I raised the question of his behaviour with Mr Hillersdon I was assured that, unsatisfactory as it was, it was the custom of the Station and there was little that could be done about it. The Company's servants, thousands of miles from home, could hardly be discharged from their employment. The climate did not encourage enthusiasm and a certain level of indolence had become accepted as a perquisite of the job.

Irritating as the behaviour of my fellows might appear, by April I had some sympathy with them. The mercury would often hover around one hundred degrees and I, too, would take to my bed in the midday heat. The pankha fan (an enormous construction some fifteen feet long) no longer seemed a ridiculous affectation. My khanasaman with his usual enthusiasm for increasing the size of my establishment, had already hired not one but three boys to act as pankha wallahs. They took turns day and night to sit in the corridor outside my bedroom pulling at the ropes that, by an ingenious system of pulleys, kept the fan turning and thus agitated the languid air within the room.

So life settled into the routine of the hot dry season. The flurry of activity that had marked our annexation of Oudh died away and was forgotten. The soldiers that we saw about the place, both native and European, no longer strutted with self-importance but idled through the heat like mere mortals. The Company's servants and their families spent most of the daylight hours hidden in shaded rooms, while any natives who could not emulate them would sit in the shade of the trees that grew on street corners or in the empty plots of dust that separated the houses of the Civil Station.

Only in the evening did the temperature drop to a point where I could work. The papers that passed across my desk were now, for the most part, routine but, however many I dealt with, the pile brought to me every morning by my babu never seemed to shrink. There were requests for medicines to be supplied when outbreaks of this or that fever struck nearby villages, appeals from landlords saying that their tax had been wrongly assessed, requests that the Company involve itself with this or that dispute with a tenant, leave requests, accommodation requests, requisition slips for horses and camels and elephants and bills for feeding of aforementioned horses, camels, and elephants. Matters serious and matters trivial – but all matters, apparently, that the Company must rule on.

Others had wives and families to distract them, but I had no one. I had left the only one I cared about over two thousand miles away in Borneo. I was invited to the evening picnics that the womenfolk organised and introduced to young ladies who had travelled to India from England apparently for the sole purpose of improving their matrimonial chances. These entertainments made me uncomfortable and I would excuse myself as often as I could, preferring to stay in the office about my business.

Hillersdon noticed the hours I was putting in and admitted himself concerned. 'Take it easy, old boy,' he said one afternoon as he set off to join his wife at a concert given by one of the military bands. 'People are taking advantage of you. You're doing the work of half a dozen others while they rag about you in their clubs and laugh because it's known you do their work for them.'

'The work needs to be done.'

'It does indeed. And if you weren't here at all hours doing it, I could make some of the idlers on our staff pull their weight.' He looked up from the papers he was tidying away and, seeing that I was making no reply, said, 'Take a couple of days' leave, John. Take yourself out to Nana's place. He'll put you up and the change of air will do you good.'

Nana Sahib's guesthouse was a regular talking point in Cawnpore. Although the Nana never visited Europeans in their homes, he was a generous host. In the grounds of Saturday House he kept a separate building for his visitors and there was no one of any significance in our community who had not stayed there at least once. Mr Hillersdon had often visited the Nana with his wife and he insisted that a few days there would be good for my health.

'You've been overdoing it, old boy. You take a break from your toiling here and when you return you'll be able to work all the better.'

So, with Mr Hillersdon's assistance, all the necessary arrangements were made, and on the last Monday in April I rose early so that I might make the journey to Bithur before the heat of the day became oppressive.

This time I travelled in a carriage. This was in part because the weather made riding, even in the early morning, quite exhausting, but also because Mr Hillersdon was emphatic that if I were to arrive as a guest I should travel in a style that would reflect my status. 'Not to do so,' he assured me, 'will not only diminish you in native eyes but will be taken as an insult by Nana Sahib.'

For the same reason, I was to travel with a valet to take care of my personal needs, a groom to take care of the horses, and a coachman to drive me. I was perfectly capable of dressing myself and driving my own carriage and the horses would be stabled in Nana Sahib's own stables where his grooms would attend them as a matter of course but none of this was of any account. I was to travel in state because that was the way that things were done. So I bumped my way to Bithur (for Indian carriages are woefully inadequately sprung) and arrived hot and tired and very glad indeed that my journey was over.

As the gates of the compound opened, a servant, who appeared to have been waiting there for my arrival, ran forward to guide the coachman to the guesthouse in the palace grounds.

Rounding a bend in the carriage drive, we came

suddenly upon the guesthouse, secluded in a rhododendron grove. I had not seen it on my previous tour of the grounds, so its incongruity struck me with a force that nearly made me laugh aloud. For here, in the Oriental splendour of the Nana's grounds, was a bungalow: a perfect replica of the houses that the Company had built for its servants in Cawnpore.

My valet, who had been riding alongside the coachman, carried my cases inside while I stretched myself after the ride and looked about me. To my delight, I saw, hastening along the gravel, the lithe figure of Mungo Buksh.

'Greetings, John,' he called as he hurried toward me. 'I am sorry I was not at the gate to welcome you, but I had matters to attend to.'

My young friend was dressed today in loose trousers such as many of the better kind of Indian wear and an open jacket. Both were of red cotton, much embroidered with gold. Around his waist was a golden sash. He looked as if he had just stepped from a picture book.

'I'm so glad to see you.' I stepped forward and embraced him.

He returned my embrace and asked, 'Have you been inside yet?'

'No, I just arrived.'

'Let me show you round.'

He led the way through the door and introduced me to my home for the next few days. It was about the size of my house in Cawnpore but, rather than being crammed with furniture that aped European fashions, it was elegantly equipped with everything of the finest native manufacture. Beds and tables had been made high off the floor, rather than low to the ground in the native style (for Indians do not generally use chairs and prefer everything to be accessible to a man seated on the ground) but they were carved from teak and mahogany, decorated and gilded in the ways I had observed in the furnishings of

Nana Sahib's own quarters.

'Your lord does me too much honour.'

I spoke formally. Mungo Buksh should have replied with a similarly flowery phrase indicating that the guesthouse was not nearly fine enough for the use of one so exalted as myself but instead he just laughed. 'It's a house, John, not a mansion.'

I relaxed, taking my cue from him. 'It's still remarkable. I'm impressed that Nana Sahib should have gone to such trouble for his guests. He must have a hundred rooms in Saturday House, yet he has had this built specially.'

Mungo Buksh laughed again. 'Do you really not know why it was built?'

I shook my head. My companion obviously thought my ignorance a huge joke but I truly had no idea why he was so amused.

'It's so that you don't pollute the palace.'

My expression must have reflected my confusion so he explained the situation. Nana Sahib, being of the highest caste, would be polluted by intimate contact with those of no caste like ourselves. A bed we had slept in could not be used by any of his religion. Plates we had eaten from would have to be ritually cleansed before they could be used again. If even my shadow fell across a bowl of food prepared for the men of his household, the food would be unclean, fit only to be fed to animals.

The preparation of the guesthouse, which I had taken as an honour, in fact reflected the contempt in which Nana Sahib's religion held us.

I fear that the distress that this realisation caused me must have shown on my face for Mungo Buksh clasped me by the hand and, his young face suddenly very serious, said, 'You must not be concerned, John. It is the rule of our Brahmins. It is like when your Brahmins say that they eat human flesh and drink human blood. It is a thing that you do in your religion. But I do not worry that you are going to eat me.' He smiled reassuringly.

I was not reassured but I let him think that I was. It was not that I felt insulted, but that I was suddenly aware of my ignorance. I had come to live in India but, for all that I was learning Hindustanee and would speak a few words with the natives in the bazaar, I had no real understanding of the lives of the Indians around me. My khanasaman jealously guarded his domain over the servants, growing visibly agitated if I had any more dealings with them than were necessary to see my meals placed on the table and my linen cleaned and pressed. My babus insisted on maintaining the fiction that they were European and would refuse to converse in anything but English and so, though I was surrounded by natives, I was positively discouraged from coming to any proper comprehension of their lives.

I realised, with a start, that my hand still clasped that of Mungo Buksh and, in the same instant, came the realisation that I did have one friend who could help me understand the people who filled this vast country.

That afternoon, Mungo Buksh took me around the palace again. This time we didn't look at the animals or the clocks but concentrated our attention on the idols in their flower-bedecked shrines. We started by revisiting Hanuman and my guide tried to explain how Hanuman had led an army of monkeys to free another god who was imprisoned on the island of Ceylon and how they had been opposed by demons with necklaces of skulls. He spoke as if it was a story that everyone should know but, in truth, it seemed so long, confusing, and foolish that I gave up trying to understand it.

Mungo took mercy on me and we moved on, finding idols everywhere we walked. Some dominated small courtyards, some were in niches carved into the stone walls of rooms or corridors, some sat on shelves high on the walls. All were, to my eye, alien and grotesque. There were human heads on animal bodies and animal heads on the bodies of humans. Some had four arms, some six, some eight. One had five heads. An elephant was depicted carried by a mouse.

While I struggled to remember their names, Mungo explained which each of these gods were and what they represented. At first, I tried to recall simple things about them. Lakshmi seemed easy because she had four arms.

'Lakshmi is the goddess of wealth.' Mungo pointed to the coins in one of her hands. 'She pours gold out, bringing blessings to the world.'

We moved to another courtyard, where a statue showed a beautiful young girl, decorated with jewels.

'Who is this one?'

Mungo looked at me as if I were a particularly stupid child. 'This is Lakshmi.'

'But she has only two arms.'

'That is because this image shows her as the goddess of beauty. Lakshmi brings so many good things.' He bowed reverently to the statue, his hands pressed together. 'She is the goddess of beauty and of wealth and fortune. When she brings wealth, she has four arms that she can distribute good things more generously.'

'But in this statue she has only two.'

'Of course. Would you think a girl beautiful if she had four arms?'

I hesitated, trying to imagine such a thing. 'Probably not,' I agreed.

'Then of course she cannot have four arms.'

He bowed to the statue again and moved on. Clearly, there was no more to be said on the matter.

So the afternoon went on. By evening, my head was aching with the effort of keeping track. I was hopelessly confused, but intrigued. For the first time, I was looking at these idols not as exotic decoration but as the visible expression of the beliefs that penetrated every aspect of Hindoo society, from their objections to the killing of cattle to the eighteen holy days on which they fasted; from the direction their houses should face to the way they styled their hair.

It had been agreed that I should spend four days at Saturday House, arriving on the first and leaving on the fourth. After my introduction to the Hindoo deities on that first day, I decided to devote the rest of my stay to trying to understand the religion. To this end, I prevailed on Mungo Buksh to spend most of the second day in repeating the stories of the deities while I made careful notes in my commonplace book.

'These stories have been written down,' he said, as I asked him, yet again, to list all eight of the avatars of Ganesh. 'Would it help if you were able to read about them?'

It would indeed, I replied. Like many who have come to reading late in life, I had an almost superstitious conviction that books contained the knowledge of all the world and that if I could only find a book describing these gods, then all would become immediately clear to me. So Mungo took me by the hand again and led me through corridors and up stairs and around courtyards and thus, eventually, to Nana Sahib's library, a gracious room with wide, high windows and reading desks arranged to best catch the light. He ran lightly to the shelves and returned with a book that he opened to a page illustrating ten avatars of Vishnu.

'Look,' he said, pointing happily, 'it's all explained here.'

And it was. But it was written in Devanagari, the Hindoo script, and though I could by now speak the language passably well, the script was no more to me than a meaningless scribble across the page.

Again, I was forced to realise the depths of my

ignorance. I knew that the Indians had a written language (or languages, for the Musalman script was based on the Arabic and looked entirely different). I had seen their writing on signs by their businesses but I had not thought of their having a literature and libraries to store it. It was not that I considered them ignorant – for I did not – but that I had not considered the matter of their literature at all.

It seemed that to understand their religion, it would be as well that I learn to read their script.

Mungo Buksh watched me sigh and turn defeated from the volume he had placed before me and he quickly divined the reason for my sudden gloom. He laid his hand reassuringly on my arm.

'Do not despair. I will show you how to read this.'

And so my lessons started.

I could not help remembering the days I spent with James in Borneo when he taught me to read. Now I found myself struggling again with marks on paper that at first meant nothing to me. I would peer at them, trying to draw meaning from the scribbles and then I would look up to see the brown eyes of Mungo Buksh watching me and I would remember those other brown eyes that had watched over my earlier struggles.

Despite Mungo's best efforts, I could learn little in the time I remained in Saturday House, but I at least started to probe the depths of my ignorance and to overcome them with diligent study.

When I returned to Cawnpore I could hardly describe myself as rested, for my last two days at Saturday House had been spent hard at work with pen and paper, copying and pronouncing the letters of the Hindoo alphabet and my brain fairly ached with the effort. Yet far from feeling fatigued, I came back to work reinvigorated, to the delight of Mr Hillersdon who insisted that the break had so improved my health that I must make another visit to Nana Sahib as soon as my duties allowed me.

I was happy to fall in with this suggestion, for my attempts to master the ancient script were unavailing without Mungo Buksh to help me. So I got into the habit of spending every day that I could be spared from my duties out in Bithur and, slowly but surely, I began to progress in my studies.

I was helped by the relative calm of life in Cawnpore. The most exciting thing to happen was the arrival of a new commander for the garrison. General Wheeler arrived to take over the Cawnpore Division soon after the rains began around the middle of July. I recall meeting him at a formal dinner to welcome him to the town. It was given in the Assembly Rooms – a grand building but, I always thought, rather comical in those surroundings. The fine front with its Corinthian columns and the elegant interior with its ballrooms, the fine panelling, and the chandeliers – all would excite enthusiasm in an English provincial town, but here it was as ridiculous as if an Indian lord had set down a minareted mosque in Regent's Park.

Wheeler had arrived in a closed carriage but he insisted on standing in the rain while attendants hurried up with umbrellas to shelter his wife. I was waiting in the hallway with those who were to be the first to greet him and I was touched by the way this small, elderly man stood to attention, water soaking into his red jacket and pouring from the gold braid on his shoulders, while his wife slowly descended the steps that had been pushed against the carriage for her convenience.

I had heard about Lady Frances Wheeler, of course. The scandal was the talk of every Station in India. It had happened over forty years ago, but it was almost certainly the reason why Wheeler was here in Cawnpore. Nearly seventy years old, and the most senior and experienced of the Company's generals, Hugh Wheeler was to see out his service as a Divisional Commander, passed over for further promotion. I don't know if people were more shocked by the fact that Lady Frances had been married to another man when she bore Wheeler the first of their nine children or that she was, with her dusky skin and graceful beauty, clearly the result of a union between a European officer and an Indian woman. Simkin had made it all too clear what was the prevailing view of such Anglo-Indians, as people generally referred to them. In one of his earlier (and more than usually misguided) attempts to ingratiate himself with me, he had suggested that we might call on some 'ladies' he knew who might entertain us for an evening. When I asked what sort of unchaperoned ladies would entertain two men he explained, with a leering wink, that these 'called themselves European but had more than a touch of the tar brush to them,' and hence they were automatically viewed as little better than harlots.

Stories of the snubs that had been delivered to Lady Frances from the self-styled protectors of European morality in India were rife. Even as the wife of a man knighted by the Queen herself, Lady Frances was not received in many a Calcutta drawing room. The posting to Cawnpore, where the hospitality of Nana Sahib was typical of the easy relationship between the races, must have been a great relief to her, if a disappointment to her husband.

Although the General seemed at ease at the dinner and his wife appeared a lady of refinement, I did not expect to come across him in the daily life of the station, for civilians and military tended not to socialise together. The occasional officer might be invited if his family were known to the host but generally the swagger of the military men did not sit well with the administrators of the Company, though we all served the same masters. The distinction was maintained not only socially but geographically. All but the most senior officers were housed in military bungalows along the perimeter of the huge camp to the South and East of the town and I found only a couple of occasions a year to visit that quarter. I was, therefore, not a little surprised when Charles Hillersdon suggested, early in August, that I join him at an informal dinner they were hosting for the General the following evening.

'Just a few of us at home,' he said. 'Nothing special.'

I was always delighted to receive an invitation to dine with the Hillersdons. I think Charles had some inkling of my nature. At least he did not seat me beside young ladies fresh from England and desperate to make a suitable match. Such girls, all coquettish charm and sly smiles, were the bane of my life and I suspected that suspicions about my immunity to their wiles underlaid Simkin's proposal that we visit his Anglo-Indian 'ladies.' So it was that I hummed cheerfully to myself the next evening as I dressed in a dinner suit made by the tailor my khanasaman had insisted on hiring. I had decided to ignore the suggestion that the dinner was 'nothing special' and to torture myself with stiff collar and bow tie. When I arrived at the Hillersdons it was clear that I had made the right decision. The place was rapidly filling with guests and Lydia Hillersdon, usually the calmest of women, was visibly flustered.

'John, thank goodness you're here. I asked the servants to borrow an extra two chairs from our neighbours because Charles has just explained that the General is bringing all three of his children.' (The remaining six children, fortunately for Mrs Hillersdon's catering arrangements, had not joined the general in Cawnpore.) 'Charles swears that he told me that a week ago but I'm sure he did not. And I fear he may have invited Simkin and now they're pretending not to understand and I know you can speak to them.'

She was waving her hand in her agitation and I caught it up and kissed it.

'Don't worry, Lydia. I know Simkin isn't coming

because I saw him just an hour ago sulking because he was not asked. And my Hindustanee may not be up to much but the servants know better than to pretend they can't understand me. So you shall have your extra chairs.'

She smiled prettily. She did everything prettily. She was a sweet child and made her husband very happy.

I was a few minutes rousting out a servant and sending him off for the chairs. When I returned to the dining room, the General had just arrived. I almost could not see him: he really was quite a short man and he had chosen a dinner jacket rather than his red uniform, so he was nearly submerged in the throng of the Hillersdons' guests and the servants who accompanied them. I noticed Lady Frances before her husband. She was not much shorter than him and she held herself with the casual grace of the native women, which somehow made her seem taller than the General, for all that the he stood erect with the habits of a lifetime of military service. She was wearing a russet dress in the latest style yet, despite the conventional European clothes, she retained an air of the exotic which was visibly disturbing some of the other ladies present. Her daughters had inherited much of her beauty: the older girl seemed to take more after her father but the younger, Margaret, was almost as dark as her mother with a glint in her eye that suggested she was well aware of the effect her looks might have on the young men of the station.

The son, Godfrey Wheeler, was by contrast, quite severe in his appearance and his bearing was every inch that of a soldier. There was something in the half protective, half subordinate way he hovered just behind the General that would have made me guess that the young man was on his father's staff even had I not known he was his aide de camp.

Beside the Wheelers, the most important guests were Thomas Greenway and his wife. The Greenways were part of a family whose commercial activities, from banking to indigo planting to running the general store, penetrated every part of European Cawnpore. The formidable Mrs Greenway oversaw the business but she was, she claimed, too old to enjoy dining out and so the company paid its respects by entertaining her son.

Some Company officials, wives, and daughters made up the numbers. (Wheeler was the only man there to have his son at the Station with him.) With such a crowd sat at table, there was a constant bustle of servants. The Wheelers had, of course, brought their own people with them and the chaos caused by so many strangers getting in each other's way with every course made it difficult for me to follow all the conversation. Despite the interruptions, though, I was able to enjoy most of the General's anecdotes. He had built up his store of dining-out stories over a lifetime's campaigning and if some were so polished as to suggest they had been told a hundred times before, still they were fresh for me.

It was late by the time I came to make my way home and as I bade Hillersdon farewell, I congratulated him on the success of the evening. 'You did well to bag the Wheelers so early on. I doubt they'll have a free evening the rest of the year.'

Charles smiled at that but his eyes were wary. 'I hope so, John. I really do.'

I was puzzled by his response but I imagined it to be that he was tired at the end of the evening and I thought no more of it. But the weeks passed and I found myself joining Charles and his wife as he entertained the General almost weekly. It seemed that while Hillersdon enjoyed the Wheelers' company, there was, even in Cawnpore, a strange reluctance to entertain an Anglo-Indian in the home.

The prejudice was all the more incomprehensible to me as I would often meet my colleagues when I was staying at Saturday House. It seemed that, just as Nana Sahib was happy to have European visitors so long as they did not stay in his own house, so the Europeans were happy to meet with the better class of native so long as it was not under their own roofs.

In my case, I fear Nana Sahib's taboo was broken, though he was, I trust, unaware of it. The demands on the guesthouse were such that on several occasions Mungo Buksh was unable to procure accommodation for me. After two or three of our meetings had been prevented in this way, he suggested that I stay in his quarters. 'There's plenty of room,' he said. 'No one need know.'

I told myself that this was simply a sensible way to make sure that my studies were not disrupted but, in my heart, I knew better. Since I had loved James Brooke, I knew my true nature. Just as I saw no attraction in the vapid prettiness of the women who were so regularly pushed forward for my inspection, so I could not pretend that I was not moved by the beauty of Mungo Buksh. I have heard people talk of the Indians as black but Mungo's skin was the colour of a cup of rich chocolate. He was, like most natives, short in stature and delicately built. His cheekbones gave his face the shape of an angel and his eyes were huge and deep and brown. He moved with an easy grace, sometimes – when excited – fast, at other times lazily stretching into motion as if enjoying the pleasure of feeling the life in his own limbs.

I could not pretend that he could be my soul mate. James would be forever the man that I had truly loved. But Mungo had youth and charm and a laugh that lifted my spirits whenever I heard it.

Mungo's apartments were small, but more than adequate for a minor courtier whose needs would all be met by the palace servants. He had one room where he could read or entertain or eat, if he chose to eat in his own quarters, and one for sleeping. Generally, he would bathe in the grand baths that were available to all in the royal household, but there was an alcove off his bedroom where a tub and a ewer allowed him to perform his ablutions in private, should he wish to.

Latticed windows high in the walls gave light and air but allowed Mungo his privacy. The floor was of marble and the walls were tiled. The place was beautiful, but as I looked around, admiring the elegant furniture and the statue of Hanuman in a niche on the wall, I could not help but notice that there was no provision for guests.

We spent the afternoon in the library. My studies were going well and Mungo was even more than usually cheerful, constantly praising my efforts. We returned to his room to find fish and rice laid out for us by one of the ubiquitous palace servants. (When Mungo had said that no one need know I was in his apartments, I fear he had simply ignored the servants as being not worthy of consideration.)

We ate slowly and then talked about the gods I had studied during the day. As the light faded and we grew sleepy, I became increasingly conscious of how close we were sitting, the smell of his body, and the warmth of his breath on my cheek.

The feelings that had been creeping up on me as long as I had known Mungo were now too strong for me to ignore, but I resolved that I would not give way to my baser desires. I told Mungo that I would sleep on the ground. The night was very warm and I would need no bedding. But my young friend would have none of it. 'Don't be foolish,' he said. 'My manjaa is big enough for two.' He patted the string framework of the low day bed he was sitting on.

'Your charpoy?'

He laughed. He laughed so easily. 'You call it a charpoy but truly it is a manjaa. The word is a Punjabi word and it is a Punjabi manjaa.'

I shrugged. What he called it was scarcely the point. It

was a bed, albeit a primitive bed, lacking mattress or sheets. And he was suggesting we share it.

I hesitated, but I knew what it was that I wanted. I nodded. I hope it looked like a simple manly nod of affirmation but inside I felt like I imagined a schoolgirl must feel before her first kiss. I confess my hands trembled as I shed my day clothes and donned the silk shirt and linen drawers that are the universal nightdress of the East. My nervousness was increased by the look of bemused amusement on my young companion's face. I fear I blushed for I was sure that to a youth the body of a man my age was bound to be a source of mirth. But it seemed his amusement was at the idea that I should dress for bed as, once I considered my toilette complete, he simply stripped off his trousers and tunic and settled down beside me.

Even now, I feel a stirring at the memory of that perfect body, the brown skin smooth and supple. He was almost hairless about his person and looked more like a living statue – one of those gods I had spent so long studying – rather than a mere mortal.

As he pressed his body against mine, and I felt the warmth of his flesh against my flesh, my desire almost overcame me. But he was so young and so beautiful that I felt that any touch of mine would be a defilement. And, in any case, surely he could not be offering himself to me – old, pale-skinned, graceless with the ungainly ways of my race. So I smiled at him and turned away, lying with my back to him and hoping that sleep would come upon me quickly before I should yield to temptation and foolishness.

A moment later, I felt his arms around me. He pressed himself against my back and the warmth of his body passed through my silk shirt as if I were naked too. His hands reached around my chest, brushing my nipples and he moved lazily against my buttocks.

I turned then and seized his face in my hands and kissed him. It was not like the gentle kisses that James and I had shared, but a hungry kiss, trying to consume him, as I was suddenly consumed with desire. It was the crudest form of lust that overcame me. I tore off the drawers I had just put on and thrust at him with an urgency that shocked me, but he seemed unsurprised. Indeed, when I tried to regain control of my impulses and pull away from him, he reached for my organ and drew me back.

Later – how much later, I had no way of knowing – we drew apart. I was drenched in sweat but his body was just lightly sheened with perspiration, which seemed rather to add to his unworldly beauty than to diminish it. My mind was in turmoil. Everything that I had done with James Brooke had been sanctioned by love but I felt that I had no such excuse to offer now. I thought I should explain myself or grovel for understanding or at least say something of my behaviour but, though I opened my mouth to speak, I could think of no words to say. And then, while I sat in great confusion of mind, Mungo placed his finger on my lips, as you might hush a fractious child, and he drew me to him and I slept.

I woke late, to find Mungo sitting cross-legged beside the bed with a breakfast of fruit that he had cut up and prepared for me. As soon as I was stirring, he insisted that I eat and I was glad to do so for my eating avoided the necessity of conversation and I was still far from sure what I should say.

I think Mungo recognised my confusion for, while I was eating and in no position to discuss the events of the previous night, he started talking about Hindoo gods. At first, I scarcely paid any attention to what he was saying. I was usually more than happy to learn from him but, at that moment, the details of the Hindoo pantheon seemed of little importance. Then, as if I were waking from a dream,

I heard a few phrases of his soliloquy.

'... many of our gods have both male and female aspects ... any activity that brings joy is blessed ... temple carvings showing two men engaged in carnal ...'

I set down my fruit and concentrated on his words. Now that he could see he had my attention he began to speak faster and to concentrate on particular tales. He described the birth of Sabarimalai Sastha whose parents were both male deities. Vishnu had disguised himself as a woman and another god, Shiva, intoxicated by her beauty had had sex with her. The result had been the god Sabarimalai Sastha, born from Vishnu's thigh.

'You must remember, my friend, that our gods can take many forms, sometimes that of a man and sometimes that of a woman. Shiva often takes the form of Ardhanarisvara, neither man nor woman. Hindoos accept that all that is made by the gods is good. There are men and there are women and there are those of the third sex. In the South the third sex even worship their own god, Aravan.'

His hand shot toward the tray of fruit and he snapped up two grapes. He threw one into his mouth and, as I opened my own to reply, he flicked the other into mine. 'Let's not waste more time in talk. The library is waiting for us.'

Chapter Three

So summer passed into the cool of winter. Life in Cawnpore continued much as usual. Lydia Hillersdon was with child again, to her husband's evident delight, but they continued to entertain. Every week they would invite the Wheelers to dinner until Charles' example began to have its effect. One by one, the ladies of the European community overcame their distaste for their mixed race sister and allowed Lady Frances into their dining rooms. General Wheeler approved plans to extend the military cantonment with a series of new barracks to the West of the main camp. More civilian engineers arrived from Bombay to survey the approach of the railway that was planned to link Cawnpore with Allahabad. A tiger took to raiding some of the villages to the North and a hunt was organised: soldiers and civilians set off together, mounted on elephants, and returned bearing not one but two tiger skins as evidence of their success.

At Bithur, my command of the language improved to the point where Mungo swore that I could pass for a native. 'I think perhaps in a previous life you were an Indian, for you speak the language so well.'

'Good enough for you,' I said. 'But I think you are not a fair judge.'

'Very well,' he said and his eyes sparkled with mischief. 'I'll put you to the test.'

Commanding me to wait in his apartment, he whisked out of the room. I had seen that sudden enthusiasm before and it usually meant that Mungo was up to no good and so it was to prove on this occasion.

He returned almost an hour later bearing a bundle of red clothes wrapped around a sword.

'What in the name of all the gods do you have there?'

Proudly he unrolled the bundle, revealing a curved tulwar in its scabbard. The clothes he laid out carefully on the floor: a long red tunic, white britches, a black belt and a wide cross-belt to wear across the breast.

'I couldn't carry the boots as well. I'll have to go back for them.'

'But what on earth is this?' I knew the answer, of course. I had seen enough of the Nana's sowars, his proud cavalrymen, to recognise their uniform when I saw it. 'And where did you get it?'

Mungo tapped his nose, knowingly. 'What do you English say, John? Ask me no questions and you'll be told no lies. Put these on while I'm away.'

And, quick as a flash, he was out of the door again.

I looked at the garments spread before me. This was all too ridiculous. But then again, they were there: I might as well try them on.

I was dressed in this finery and trying to admire my turnout in the hand mirror that Mungo used for his toilette when he burst into the room again, carrying a pair of black riding boots, complete with clanking spurs.

'You look splendid,' he said. 'Turn around. Let me see it properly.'

I did as he asked and he admired the fit of the uniform, insisting that it was perfect on me.

'But now,' he said, turning his mouth down with a comically exaggerated expression of dismay, 'you will have to take it all off.'

'But why?'

He gave no reply. Indeed, he was already unbuckling the belt. Laughing, I let him strip me. When I stood naked, he started to kiss me, but as soon as he saw I was aroused he pulled away, putting his hand to his mouth in mock horror.

'I've forgotten myself. There was a reason I had to have you naked and it had naught to do with my desire for your body. Stand still!'

From the pile of his own clothing (somehow that seemed to have been removed as well), he retrieved a bottle of dark liquid and a sponge. While I stood still, he carefully covered my hands with it, carrying on up my arm until well above where my sleeves would have ended, had I been wearing the tunic. Then he repeated the procedure with my face, working down my neck to the top of my chest.

'It's walnut juice,' he said, anticipating my question. 'Your skin is dark from the sun but I think that to look truly like a native of my country, you need a little assistance.' He worked on, patiently.

'And to apply this to my face and hands, it was absolutely necessary to remove my trousers?'

'Oh, absolutely necessary.' He grinned and slapped toward my buttocks. I tried to retaliate but he ordered me to stand still, lest I disturb his handicraft. 'Though, truly, you need to take care not to get this stain on those lovely white britches. You'd best stay naked until it dries. And stand very still.'

He took his time finishing the staining, all the while making me stand there while he took advantage of his insistence on my immobility to tease my body in a dozen ways that left me desperate to move, yet hoping that the stain might never dry.

'You can move now.'

At once I made to seize him but he twisted from my grip. 'Not until you've proved yourself.'

'How?'

'Get dressed first.'

Reluctantly, I pulled back on the clothes I had so recently taken off.

'One more thing.'

Mungo produced a length of black cloth that he wrapped back and forth around my head, topping off the uniform with a fine turban. 'I must teach you how to do that for yourself but I want to play this game out.'

Taking me by the hand, he pulled me after him into the corridors of the palace.

Before long, we passed one of the tall mirrors that Nana Sahib had dotted around the place in what he imagined to be the latest European style. Had I not seen the strange figure reflected back at me still holding Mungo's hand, I don't believe I would have recognised myself. I must admit that I preened a little, much to Mungo's amusement.

'Wait here, my brave soldier!' We had reached the end of one corridor and Mungo vanished around a corner, leaving me wondering how I would explain myself if anyone were to come upon me standing there. I need not have worried, though. In less than a minute, he was back – but his face wore the grin I had come to dread.

'There's a guard in the next hallway. Walk past him and then turn back and criticise his turnout. There'll be something wrong. There always is. If you can't think of anything else, tell him his boots need shining. Tell him he's a disgrace and he should report himself to his havildar. Get his name and the name of his havildar and then we'll see tomorrow if he believed you to be what you seem or if he could tell you to be a white man.'

'We won't have to wait until tomorrow. We'll know I've failed as soon as he draws his sword and skewers me with it.'

'Be brave, John Williamson! And, in any case, if he does detect you, I will explain it was a trick of mine and I will bear you safe away.'

I was not entirely reassured but Mungo was implacable and, a few minutes later, I found myself walking down the hallway with a swagger that perhaps over-compensated for my nervousness.

In the end, it was almost too easy. The sentry was apparently transfixed by the splendour of my equipage and, looking at the stains on his tunic, the missing buttons and (for Mungo had been right, of course) the unpolished boots, it was easy to see why. I found I had a real sense of grievance on behalf of Nana Sahib and I castigated the man at length before stalking off and leaving him quivering at attention in my wake.

After that, Mungo would often dress me in a variety of native dresses and he would set me challenges that tested my linguistic skills and my understanding of the world he was leading me farther and farther into. One day he decided I should beg as a mendicant in the streets of Bithur. I protested that it was a foolish jape, for were the mob to penetrate my disguise I did not see how he could have protected me and I was sure that it would take more than walnut juice to change me from a European to an Indian. But Mungo insisted.

'Do you not keep telling me that you would learn more about the ordinary people? And how better to learn than to go among them?'

I was far from confident, but there was no arguing with Mungo once he had an idea firmly in his pretty head. I was stripped of all my clothing and then Mungo shaved off my body hair. Fortunately, I am not a hairy man, but Mungo considered that I was, nonetheless, still too hirsute to pass as a native. After my barbering, Mungo covered me from head to foot with walnut stain before allowing me to wrap a loincloth about my nakedness. Then he thrust a staff into one hand and a begging bowl into the other and sent me off to fend for myself.

'You are a little too well fed to be utterly convincing,' he said. 'So you will have to take care to stoop and shuffle and generally try to look less the European gentleman and more the Indian mendicant.'

I duly stooped and shuffled my way around the streets and alleys of old Bithur.

It was not a very prepossessing place. Before Nana Sahib had built his palace there, it had been just a fisherman's village on the shores of the Ganges. The fisherman's houses – little more than mud huts – were still there, facing the muddy foreshore of the river, which was running quite high, it being not that long since the rainy season. The fisherman's village was quiet, most of the men being in their boats on the river, hauling their nets, casting their lines, or dozing under canvas awnings while they waited for the fish to bite. On shore, there were just children running in the streets and women, most of whom kept modestly indoors.

Behind the old fishing village, further from the muddy stench of the foreshore, a new Bithur had grown up, full of shops to serve Saturday House and those who lived there and houses for the families and hangers-on of the fortunate inhabitants of the palace.

Here was the bustle and noise that I had come to associate with all but the smallest Indian villages. Shopkeepers displayed their wares on mats in front of the shabby buildings where they lived and traded. Even fine silks were spread out for inspection where every footfall raised more dust to dull their vibrant colours. Samosas and chupattis were piled on plates ready to eat, while butchers hung carcasses from hooks on the front of their shop-houses. Hawkers wandered by, selling their own goods from bags slung over their shoulders or trays hung round their necks. Their cries competed with the shouts of the shop owners to raise a cacophony in which my plaintive cries for alms at first went unheeded.

The streets were thronged with the Nana's men, who were all-too-eager to demonstrate their wealth and status by purchasing luxury goods with an aristocrat's disdain for the price. Once these people had caught a glimpse of my begging bowl they were quick to buy food that they could give me. In the villages of India, at least, it seemed that no one gave money, preferring to honour the tradition that beggars should be fed. I was careful to mix the offerings together, honouring the equally ancient tradition that all the food I was given should be treated equally and I could not pick out the dainties to separate them from the poorer man's gift of plain boiled rice.

In all the bustle, no one seemed to notice that I was, perhaps, a little well fed for a beggar. Or perhaps Mungo had exaggerated the hardship of a beggar's life, for I found that my bowl was soon filled with a more than ample meal, which I took to the river's edge to eat with my fingers, as I now ate all my food when I was not dining with Europeans.

As I ate, I thought how differently the Indians viewed indigents such as myself from the way that they were viewed in Europe. Here, it was not unusual for a man of my age to retire from the world and spend his life contemplating the mysteries of philosophy while trusting to the kindness of strangers for his basic needs, while at home the parish beadle was always on the lookout to ensure that Christian charity was never extended beyond the minimum set down by law.

After my meal, I found shelter under a banyan tree and spent the hottest hours of the day in the shade, half-sleeping. With one lazy eye, I watched the passage of a sacred bullock making his privileged way to the river to drink. At this time of year, the days were still cool enough for a rest in the open to be pleasant. I realised why so many Indians spent the noon hours in this way, which the Europeans saw as 'idle', considering that a man should rest in the privacy of his home or spend his time in honest toil.

Refreshed, I returned to the market where, after the midday pause, people were already beginning to buy and sell again. My stomach well satisfied, I did not hold my bowl out for alms, but leaned on my staff and watched the ebb and flow of business. There was no school in Bithur and children ran amongst the adults, adding to the noise with their laughter. Occasionally I would hear a father call to a child to stop his play and come to help, holding this, counting that or just watching his father and learning from what he saw.

A knife sharpener appeared with his grindstone and suddenly the street was filled with women, flitting from their homes like a flock of birds in brilliant saris, chattering to each other in gentle voices.

I moved from the main street to a smaller alley that cut through to the high road back to Saturday House, ducking aside from time to time as people made their way to the market, sometimes bowed down by the weight of goods they were carrying. One man, presumably aware of the Nana's penchant for European furnishings, was somehow managing to carry an entire French bureau roped to his back so that he resembled a donkey more than a man. The alley was scarcely wide enough for some of the more heavily laden porters to pass but we all made our way well enough and, however burdened down they were, all found breath to exchange greetings with me as they squeezed their way by. Suddenly, ahead of me I heard a raised European voice.

'Out of the way, you fools! Make way there!'

Ahead, I saw, to my astonishment, a large man on an even larger horse. He was presumably one of the Nana's guests and had, for some reason, decided to take this path to the market, rather than follow the high road. Still, with everyone pressing themselves to any gaps they could find, he was able to push his way down. I was so astonished at watching his progress that I forgot myself a moment and failed to move aside as quickly as I should. He leaned forward, striking out with his whip and opening a cut across my shoulder. A man sheltering in a doorway behind me reached to pull me from his path and he was gone.

One or two of those who had seen what occurred looked at the cut on my shoulder and shook their heads in sympathy, but, within minutes, the interruption to the normal rhythm of life was forgotten.

I made my way back to Saturday House and slipped in past the kitchens, where beggars often came and went. A few minutes later, I was safely back in our apartments and Mungo was inspecting my wound and cursing himself for putting me in such a situation.

We had regularly dined in Mungo's apartment. As I was usually at Saturday House for only a few days at a time, a bowl of fruit, a few chupattis or some nan bread and a samosa or two were quite enough to feed us. If we wanted to eat more, a servant would appear at the door and bowls of fragrant rice and spiced meat would be placed on the low table.

Mungo even gave me an Indian name to go with my character: Anjoor Tewaree. Never was I the subject of the least suspicion in Bithur, although, some of the Europeans in Cawnpore must have wondered at the change in my complexion. However much I scrubbed, some of the stain always seemed to remain, and I saw the odd peculiar glance at the Club. No one was so vulgar as to comment on it, and I imagine that most decided I had simply been spending too long in the sun. Hillersdon noticed, of course, but then he had always encouraged my visits to Bithur. I think he realised the reason for the change in my appearance and recognised, even before I did, that my ability to pass as a native might one day be of value to the Company.

As the weeks passed, what had started as a game came to have a more practical use. Although all seemed normal in Cawnpore, European visitors to the Nana became reluctant to leave the palace to explore the streets of Bithur. It was not that there were any positive reports of difficulties with the natives – just a general surliness that made the venture unpleasant. I went out one evening without first disguising myself and I found my horse's path blocked from time to time by groups of natives who ignored my shouts, responding only with angry looks and muttered curses. It was not until I struck out with my whip that I was able to proceed. When I told Mungo of what had occurred, his face took on an expression of unwonted seriousness. 'I think, John, that it would be best if you wear native dress when you visit me. I think the days are coming when your pale skin will attract attention we could well do without.'

I thought Mungo too cautious, but it cost me nothing to humour him. Indeed, I enjoyed the charade. I would insist on leaving my carriage in Cawnpore and ride out on the Bithur road in European clothes, stopping in a grove of trees to change into native dress for my arrival in Saturday House. The element of subterfuge added to the frisson of danger that made our illicit friendship even more exciting. A few weeks later, though, I was riding toward the palace in my disguise when a fakir threw himself in front of my horse and seized the bridle. I resisted the impulse to strike him, for though the fakirs are often frauds and beggars of the worst sort, it is as well to remember that they are viewed as holy men. I reached instead for my purse to throw him a few annas and be on my way but he showed no interest in my money, instead calling on the gods to bless me and repeating over and again, '*Sub lal hoga.*' 'Everything is to become red.' I shook my mount free of his grip and rode on and when I turned to look back, he was still standing in the middle of the road, his arms raised to heaven and chanting, '*Sub lal hoga. Sub lal hoga.*'

The incident, though trivial, worried me for some reason and I told Mungo about it. He did admit to having heard the phrase here and there before but insisted that it was simply a warning about the growth in power of the British and meant only that with the annexation of Oudh, it was but a matter of time before our scarlet uniforms was seen throughout the sub-continent.

I was unconvinced. The tone of the fakir had not been that of a man discussing the latest trends in Company policy and I wondered if the reference was to something thicker than water and of a deeper crimson than a British uniform.

My fears were reinforced as the days again turned cool and 1856 drew towards its close. I was studying alone in the library (this time dressed as a scribe) when Mungo came in great excitement to urge me to join the throng gathering in the Nana's audience hall – a great pillared court, half open to the sky, where Nana Sahib would sit in state.

That afternoon, Mungo said, the Nana's personal astrologer was to make a great prediction for the year 1857. I was intrigued, for there seemed no obvious reason why a Hindoo astrologer should see anything of import in our Christian calendar, so I squatted in the crowd, inconspicuous in sandals and loincloth, while the astrologer – a tall fellow in a red robe – came before the Nana.

With a great palaver, he produced a chart of the heavens which he pointed to and scowled over. The Nana's barely concealed boredom suggested he already knew what was to come, but the courtiers around me seemed very impressed and excited by the whole performance. Finally, the astrologer wallah came out and told us that 1857 would see the hundredth anniversary of the Battle of Plassey, which had marked the start of British rule in India. 'And on that anniversary,' he declaimed (for he had worked himself into a state of considerable excitement by now) 'the Europeans will be driven from our land and the rule of the British will end.'

There was a deal of excitement at this, as you can imagine, and I could swear that I heard more than one of those around me mutter, '*Sub lal hoga.*'

I tried to convince myself that this was nothing, but by January I could not ignore the rumblings of discontent which, by then, had spread to Cawnpore. British rule in India depended on the army, but the army in India, though officered by Europeans, relied on local recruits. These sepoys, as they were called, were uniformed, equipped, and drilled just as our British soldiers and, for almost a century, we had taken their loyalty for granted. The dark looks in the lines of the Native Infantry and the stories of seditious meetings in the hours of darkness were therefore a source of real concern. The immediate cause appeared to be rumours that the new cartridges to be issued to our Indian troops had been made using the fat of pigs and cattle and were hence offensive to both Musalmans and Hindoos. Yet something deeper was threatening our peace – something that affected civilians and soldiers alike. It was something that hung in the air like the wretched red dust that choked the city whenever the wind blew but, like the dusty air, it was intangible. I took to walking the streets of the Old Cawnpore, usually dressed as a beggar. With my wooden bowl held out for gifts of food, I could linger for hours without exciting suspicion and more and more often I would hear that ominous phrase: '*Sub lal hoga.*' Yet still there was nothing specific I could report to Hillersdon.

In the European Station, life went on as usual. The Collector was peevish because he had applied for funds to improve the embankment North of the town, where the Ganges would often flood some of the older houses where the poorer people lived, but the revenue board would have none of it. General Wheeler, by contrast, was kept in funds to build new barracks. I shared Hillersdon's irritation that money could always be found for the army while the civil authorities had to make do and mend but it had been ever thus and I could hardly hold it against Wheeler that he, at least, could expand his empire.

The 53rd Native Infantry arrived from Cuttack to reinforce our garrison in February, but the new barracks were nowhere near ready and they were billeted in the existing lines. I was concerned that this might lead to them being infected with the alienation we suspected already abroad amongst our troops. I did say something of the sort to Hillersdon, but he replied that in the absence of other accommodation it was not to be helped and there was an end to it. We could only hope that we might soon be sent a British regiment to dilute the predominance of surly brown faces in the cantonment.

February gave way to March and, with the coming of warmer weather, came yet more signs and portents.

On one particularly warm morning, I arrived at my office at the usual time to find a note from Simkin on my desk, asking me to look in on him at my earliest convenience. I was somewhat taken aback by the idea of his being at his desk before the appointed hour – or indeed within thirty minutes of it. But, on putting my head into his office, I saw him sitting there in a state of some agitation.

It transpired that Simkin (who had some small responsibility for the chowkedars, or local policemen), had been told by one of these men that he had been approached by a comrade who had run up and given him two chupattis before running off, apparently in a state of high excitement.

I calmed Simkin down, telling him that there was nothing in it and that making a gift of these unleavened loaves was a regular custom but, I admit, I lied. I had heard talk in the bazaar of waiting for the coming of the chupattis. No one seemed to know exactly what they signified but there was no doubt that, like the coming of a fiery cross, they indicated that some great mischief was planned. They seemed to be sent as a warning that men should prepare themselves for a day that was nigh upon them. I saw no advantage to having Simkin more agitated than he already was but, whilst affecting an air of nonchalance, I made my way directly to Hillersdon's office to see what experience he could bring to bear on the issue.

Charles greeted me in his usual cheery way but his face grew grave as I passed on the news and when I had finished he sighed, wearily.

'So it's among the townsfolk, too.'

My expression must have made him realise that his response puzzled me.

'I'm sorry, Williamson, I should have told you. General Wheeler has informed me that his officers have reports of lotus leaves being distributed in the same way.' I tried to remember what Mungo had told me about the symbolism of the lotus but, while I was still racking my brain, Hillersdon explained. 'The leaves are a symbol of war. The chupattis could, I suppose, have some innocent explanation, but taken together there is no doubt that they presage some sort of trouble. I just don't know what.'

So things continued as each day brought a rise in mercury in the thermometers and, less clearly visible yet all too real, a rise in the tension that pervaded Cawnpore. Servants were surly, mistresses more than usually ready to find fault, and masters quick to lash out with fist or riding crop at any native they thought insolent.

Wheeler, though, was determined that the routine of life in the station should carry on as ever. The military band took its place on the bandstand to entertain any who braved the heat to listen to them. The sound of marching feet could be heard in the quiet of the mornings, reassuring us that the Native Infantry still drilled obedient to their officers.

While insolence and petty pilfering might be rife, the courts were strangely quiet. Indeed, Hillersdon suggested that we close the local court on Wednesdays as, he claimed, the judges' dockets were almost empty and they presided over nothing but heat and dust.

In my own establishment, there was always a degree of petty theft. It was a regular part of any life where fifty servants swarmed around with little to do save plot mischief. Like every European, I pretended outrage but, in fact, tolerated the losses as part of the cost of maintaining staff. Now, though, silver spoons began to disappear at an alarming rate and the number of plates broken in a week necessitated new deliveries of china. I visited the servants' quarters, cursed fluently in Hindustanee, and dismissed on the spot the men I suspected of causing the most trouble. I blessed Mungo Buksh for the lessons he had taught me, for my confidence in dealing with natives in their own tongue was all thanks to him and my performance awed them into good behaviour.

Other households, though, were not so lucky. Noxious herbs appeared in the feed in Simkin's stable and his Arab, a rarity in those parts, died, foaming at the mouth. Poor Mrs Hillersdon hardly dared entertain, so often did she find the meat her butcher delivered was corrupted. Yet no one could prove these were not simply accidents or the result of the seasonal heat.

Europeans began to avoid the bazaar, promenading only on the Course, that stretch of road that ran up from the military cantonments and which, being straight and smooth and lined with trees, was favoured by those who would exercise their horses in safety and comfort. Now, to its other manifest advantages was added the fact that it was seldom frequented by native civilians and that the soldiers using it, being close to their camp, were generally well disciplined and polite. As the Deputy Collector, I shared their caution, riding up and down the Course and otherwise straying as little as possible from the concentration of European houses sandwiched between the military cantonments and the native town. But in my other life – the life I shared with Mungo Buksh – I spent increasing hours in exploring the lanes and alleys of both Cawnpore and Bithur and everywhere there were dark mutterings about a Red Year and old resentments of the British were being aired. Yet still all remained rumour and whispers on the wind.

Mungo swore that everything would yet turn out well. 'The rains will come in June and all the evil will be washed away.' But, for all his soothing words, he would warn me to be careful in riding along the road to Bithur and, though he begged me to spend every day I could at Saturday House, he insisted that I never show myself there in my European clothes.

'But I scarcely ever do.'

We were eating in his quarters. A palace servant had brought dishes of fowl and mutton served in sauces so different from what my own servants produced under the generic title of 'Curry' that I scarce recognised them as being even nominally the same dish. Mungo took some rice, rolled it into a ball with his nimble fingers, soaking it in the sauce and transferring the whole lot to his mouth with no mess, no spills and the merest trace of sauce on his fingertips.

'I wish I could eat as tidily as you do.'

He smiled. 'It's practice, John. It will come. But you're changing the subject.' There was an edge of tension in his voice that did not sit easily with his naturally relaxed approach to almost all life's problems. 'I know you seldom appear here in your European guise. But I think it best that from now on you never do.'

'What's worrying you, Mungo? You can't believe that I would be in any danger in Nana Sahib's home.'

'No, no.' He took my hands between his, pressing them

as he sought to reassure me. 'Nana Sahib has always been a friend to the British.'

'Then why your concern?'

'It is …' His eyes darted about the room, as if seeking an answer hidden among the cushions or behind the tapestry that covered one wall. 'It is difficult. The Nana is loyal but there are those in his court who do not wish the British well.'

'Don't be ridiculous, Mungo. The Nana is an absolute ruler within his court. If he is loyal, then I am as safe here as anywhere on Earth.'

Mungo did not reply but his discomfort was obvious. I could not understand why he should have any fears. 'The Nana is loyal, isn't he?'

My friend gave me a tired smile. 'You speak our language so well and you understand so much of our lives, I sometimes forget that you are, in the end, an Englishman.'

'Mungo, what do you mean?'

'You remember our gods. The ones that may have six arms or two? That may be a man or a woman? With skin of blue or of white?'

I said nothing.

'These are our gods, John. They are important. Their quality tells you something of our quality.'

'That you can have six arms or two? That your skin may be blue or white?'

Mungo had been fidgeting, picking at the string of his day bed, but now he raised his face to mine. 'Or that a man may be loyal and disloyal.'

I stared at him in horror. As people had become nervous of taking the air in Cawnpore, so even more women and children had been sent to enjoy the hospitality of Nana Sahib. Only two days before we had this conversation, Hillersdon had confided in me that he was thinking of sending Lydia to Saturday House. 'She'll be safe out there with Nana Sahib,' he had said.

'I do not mean he is untrue.' Mungo was, by now, wringing his hands in his agitation. 'I mean just that nothing is certain. There are those who urge him to act against the British who have denied him his birthright and insulted his name. Yet he is a friend to many of the British officers and the men of the Company. He offers them his hospitality and it is honestly meant. He cannot hurt those with whom he has broken bread.'

I forbore to point out that Nana Sahib did not, in fact break bread with his European guests. Mungo's distress was painful to watch. Nana Sahib was his cousin and he owed him fealty: it was simply cruel to make him question his lord's integrity. But I took his advice to pass myself as a native whenever I was at Bithur. And I decided to keep a closer eye on the behaviour of Nana Sahib. The Nana's behaviour, though, was beyond reproach. Over the time I had spent in Cawnpore, I had seen him ride into town, parading himself on his elephant, surrounded by his own troops, half a dozen times and his visits were always well received by the native population. In March he made three such excursions, explaining to Hillersdon (whom he was careful to acknowledge with due ceremony on each visit) that his presence had a calming effect. There seemed to be some truth in this. As the Company's native troops became more sullen and disaffected, the sight of Nana Sahib's well turned out guard seemed to promise a security that I feared our own soldiers no longer offered.

The next time that the possibility of open revolution was raised at dinner, the circumstances were very different. Early in May, I was again invited to join Wheeler at the Hillersdons. The General was accompanied only by his son and he looked tired and old. Our meal was eaten quietly, the sombre atmosphere having its effect even on the usually lively Lydia. Her pregnancy was advanced by now and she tired easily. She was happy to withdraw as soon as the meal was over, leaving just the four of us (there were no other guests) to sip our port and chew nervously at our cigars.

Hillersdon waited until we were settled before broaching the topic that had obviously been on his mind for some time. 'There's rumours all over the country that the native troops are on the edge of mutiny. As one gentleman to another, I'm asking you, Sir Hugh, if there's any truth in it.'

'I'll not dissemble with you, Hillersdon.' The General paused and turned his cigar, making sure it was burning evenly. 'Things could turn very nasty. There's rumours flying about the new cartridges being greased with pig and beef fat and the natives don't like it. I think my chaps are reliable, but we could be in for a nasty couple of months.'

I remembered Mungo's words. 'Some of the natives are saying that the crisis will pass when the rains come.'

Hillersdon pursed his lips. 'That's all well and good and I trust you're right, but meanwhile I have the Treasury for the whole province here in Cawnpore and it's guarded by troops we can't be sure of. If there's even a chance they might be mutinous, surely leaving the Treasury in their hands is just putting temptation in their way?'

Wheeler nodded. 'There's something in what you say, but I don't have a lot of choice. The only British regiment I have is the 84th Foot. There's only a hundred of them, and it sometimes seems that most of them are in the hospital with one thing or another. As far as the Treasury guard is concerned, it's Native Infantry or nothing.'

'Not necessarily.' Hillersdon picked up his port glass and swirled it round, watching the ruby liquid swill up the sides. 'We could always call on Nana Sahib's men.'

'You can't!' I spoke without thinking and the three other men stared at me in surprise. I blushed and started to mumble some sort of explanation. 'I mean … If we're going to trust native troops, surely we should trust our own men.'

Hillersdon was usually the most easygoing of superiors but my sudden outburst, in front of the General and his son, had clearly irritated him. 'General Wheeler has intimated that our own troops are not entirely trustworthy. Are you suggesting that we cannot trust Nana Sahib either?'

That was, indeed, my belief, but I was reluctant to say so at Hillersdon's table.

Charles considered the Nana a friend and would take it amiss if I were to say that I thought him unreliable. In any case, what evidence did I have? Merely the remarks of Mungo Buksh, which I was hardly in a position to discuss. In any case, however much Mungo's comments had ignited my suspicions, he was himself convinced that in the end the Nana would be loyal. So I stuttered out some prevaricating nonsense about how I thought it a poor show when we stood down our own troops and put local soldiery in their place and generally played the part of a pukha-sahib, while the others stared at me and wondered if the heat had softened my brain.

'Well,' said Hillersdon, when I finally stammered to a halt, 'if there is no specific objection,' (he laid an ironic emphasis on the word 'specific') 'then would you have any problem with my approaching Nana Sahib, General?'

'In principle, I'd have no objection. But things are at a delicate stage now and I don't want to make any move that might precipitate disaffection amongst the men. Let us wait until the situation becomes clearer before we apply for local assistance.'

Hillersdon did not press his point. The General had been generous in accepting the idea of having such an important task as guarding the Treasury transferred from soldiers under his direct command to those of a native ruler, however loyal. He had achieved all he could hope for at this stage and was quick to move the conversation to a broader discussion of the unrest now being reported all over the Northern provinces. Not that this topic was without its dangers. Wheeler had been an Indian Army officer for over fifty years and was reluctant to allow that his troops might rise up against the British.

'The sepoys can be foolish, I admit. Like children, sometimes. But they're loyal. I'd stake my life on it.'

He did admit that rumours about the fat on the new cartridges and other, even more implausible, stories had led to a degree of discontent in the ranks. 'I have never seen the men as nervous as some of them are now. But I don't blame them. The trouble is caused by the missionary societies interfering in matters they do not properly understand. These chaps come out from England and start telling the natives that their religions are all wrong and they should all convert to Christianity. You can see why they get suspicious. There's stories going about that the Company intends the forcible Christianising of the whole nation. One of my lieutenants swears he heard a sepoy explain that we were shipping our own army widows out to India where the native troops would be forcibly married to them so that they would be dragged to baptism by way of matrimony. It's madness and I rather agree with our friend,' – he nodded toward me – 'that once the rains start, the wilder stories will be washed away in the flood and life will get back onto some sort of even keel.'

So the port circulated and we exchanged stories of mutinies in the past (for here and there a regiment misbehaved every few years) and how all had blown over. As we puffed our cigars and allowed ourselves to relax after a good meal and sip our fine liquor, we convinced ourselves that this, too, would pass.

The week that followed that dinner saw the temperature in the town edge its way past 110 degrees. As the mercury rose in the thermometer, so the tension in the town grew more palpable, but still the soldiers paraded and the band played, our sepoys smartly turned out, the European officers going about their business as usual. All seemed quiet in the province and life in the Company's offices moved even more languidly than usual.

Then, on Thursday 14th May, everything changed.

I had ridden out early when the temperature was barely 80 degrees, which we accounted cool in May. I wanted to judge the mood of the population so, instead of having my cook prepare breakfast, I ate at the club. Simkin was there and he asked if he could join me. Generally, I ate alone, finding I had little in common with the other members. They, I think, sensed that I was not of their class and so I was left to my solitary meals, and arrangement which suited us all. Now that Simkin chose to break with this convention and impose himself on me, I could think of no reason to refuse his company. I was forced to listen to him droning on while I ate my devilled kidneys and bacon. He was full of rumours of the insurrection that was anticipated any day but he had no actual news. The bodies of Europeans, he said, had been seen floating in the Ganges, and for a moment I thought this might be real intelligence and I enquired as to where I might see these portents for myself. At this, Simkin admitted that the bodies, if they existed, were not at Cawnpore but at a village some distance away, the name of which he had forgotten, or had never known.

By the time I had finished my breakfast I was sure that the situation was just as it had been the day before and the week before that and the month before that. Wheeler was right; Mungo was right: we were starting at shadows. If we could but keep our nerves until the rains came, all would be well.

I made my way to my office, determined to make inroads into the returns required in Calcutta. How much tax had we collected? How many staff had we paid? How many hours had they worked? How many dependents did they have? Calcutta's demand for numbers, its appetite for neatly completed questionnaires was insatiable. I thought of Hillersdon's embankment and the peremptory refusal of funds for its construction and wondered, not for the first time, if joining the Company had been a mistake.

I was reaching for a ledger kept on a high shelf by the window when I heard Hillersdon call for me from the corridor. He was usually a carefully courteous man and calling for me in that way was unlike him. And I heard something in his voice that frightened me.

I remember pushing the ledger back into place and turning toward the door as Hillersdon entered.

'Williamson,' he said, 'we must see the General at once. I have terrible news.'

The same four of us that had drunk port and smoked cigars together at that dinner party, now sat in Wheeler's house.

'It's best we talk here,' he'd said. 'It's more discreet.'

His son grimaced. 'Discreet or not, this will be all over the Station by evening.'

The old man nodded. 'That's as may be, but at least we can discuss the news calmly before we have to deal with the panic.' He turned to Hillersdon. 'You're absolutely sure of this?'

'It's an official telegraph. I imagine the delay has been to give them time to confirm the truth of the story.'

'Meerut.' Wheeler shook his head, unbelievingly. 'There's more European soldiers stationed there than anywhere else in the country. How the devil could they have let it happen at Meerut?'

He had rolled out a map on the table and we all looked at the point where a cross marked the garrison town of Meerut.

It is hard to credit now, when every schoolboy in the Empire knows its name, but until that day, I was scarcely aware that the place existed. Almost two hundred and fifty miles North-West of Cawnpore, Meerut was a base from which to protect the border with the Afghan tribes we had only recently defeated. Over four thousand troops were based there, around half of them British and half natives. On Sunday 10th May, the native troops had mutinied, shot their officers, burned and looted in the town, and marched on Delhi.

'You say this happened on Sunday.' I turned to Hillersdon. 'How could we not know of this 'til now?'

'They cut the telegraph.' His tone was grim. 'Law and order seems to have broken down entirely. The roads are unsafe. Messages are undelivered. What news we have is unreliable. But there is no doubt that Meerut has mutinied and that Delhi is now in the hands of what is, in effect, a rebel army claiming to be re-establishing the Mogul Empire.'

We looked back at the map. Delhi was just forty miles from Meerut, still over two hundred miles from us.

'I think we still need to remain calm.' Wheeler was on his feet, peering at the map and it struck me again how short a man he was, and how old. 'The men here should yet prove loyal.'

His son nodded in agreement. 'We should take no precipitous action, to be sure, but I think that it would be wise to make plans for defending ourselves should we need to.'

Wheeler nodded. 'We don't have the men to defend ourselves against a full-fledged attack but, judging from what happened at Meerut, if there is a mutiny, we can expect a day of riot and then the rebels will march to join their brethren in Delhi. We should have a place of security prepared where the European community can gather with such protection as we can provide, to wait in safety while the storm blows itself out.'

His son unrolled a plan of the military cantonment. 'We

could dig a protective trench around these two barracks here.' He gestured at two buildings that stood between the main lines of the cantonment and the European part of the town. 'One of them is in use as a hospital, which is a convenient type of building to have to hand if there might be casualties. The other is currently unused. There is a well, and a kitchen, some warehousing, and the usual offices. If we dig a rampart around it, it will be as good a rally point as any 'til the natives have had their fun looting the town and make off to Delhi.'

His father placed his finger at the point Godfrey had indicated, tapping at the paper with a preoccupied air. 'It can do no harm to make ready, I suppose. Explain to the engineers what we have in mind and we can get coolies out digging. But I want no fuss. Nothing must be done that might alarm the troops and increase their concerns.'

And that was that.

Hillersdon and I walked back to our office, neither of us anxious to discuss the meeting we had just attended. Godfrey Wheeler, I suppose, went off to instruct the engineers. The General had seen us to the door but his wife had come out of her sitting room to forbid him from walking out with us. It was too hot, she had said. 'You must think of your health, dear.' And so he had bade us farewell and returned to his study.

The rest of that Thursday had an air of unreality. Hillersdon and I carried on as if we had heard no news, ignoring the rumours that, as Major Wheeler had predicted, were everywhere by nightfall. It was said that all of the country was ablaze, the Mogul Emperor restored in Delhi and his army, a hundred thousand strong, was setting out to sweep the British from Indian soil forever.

By Friday, an awful confirmation of the story Simkin had told me of Europeans in the Ganges floated downstream. A body was caught in the current on the Oudh bank and it was decided not to attempt to recover it.

On Saturday, I was in my office, trying – and utterly failing – to concentrate on some correspondence about Hillersdon's plans for that wretched embankment, when Charles said that we had been summoned by the general.

'I fear it is unlikely to be good news,' he said. 'I am thinking that it might be best to get Lydia away.'

'I know some people are trying to send their families to Allahabad but there are rumours that rebels control the river.'

'No, travelling through the country in the present situation is unthinkable for Lydia, especially in her condition. But Nana Sahib has let me know that she would be welcome to stay with him until things calm down. She could take the children, too.'

I had hardly seen the children, for Hillersdon was firmly of the opinion that they should be seen as little as possible and best heard never – at least when there were visitors in the house. Still, he was, I believe, a conscientious and caring father and the idea of his family being caught up in any untoward events in Cawnpore was a constant concern. The idea of sending them to Bithur seemed sensible. Lydia had been a frequent guest of the Nana and even if my suspicions of his loyalty proved true, I could not imagine that he would harm the family if they were left under his protection.

'It's worrying, of course. I don't like the idea of her being miles from a European doctor if she were to …'

'Absolutely.' I nodded again.

So Hillersdon passed our walk to Wheeler's house worrying about his domestic arrangements and I spent it sympathising for, though I could not imagine ever finding myself in his position, it was clear that he was in an agony of doubt what to do for the best.

When we arrived and a servant had ushered us into the presence of the general, he wasted no time with conventional civilities. 'I have new intelligence,' Wheeler announced, almost as soon as we were seated. 'I have it reported that yesterday one of the sepoys' sons was heard boasting to another child that he was in the secret of what his father's regiment was to do to strike a blow for his people.'

I stared at him, astonished. 'Is this our intelligence? Idle chatter in the school yard?'

'Mr Williamson!' Wheeler tried to sound magisterial but ended up simply querulous. 'There has been seditious talk also from the sepoys. One of the Musalmans in the 56th has been spreading stories that we intend to gather the native regiments together at their next pay muster and blow them to Kingdom come with mines we have been secretly constructing under the parade ground. The problem is that some of his comrades appear to have believed him. He's in irons now.'

The General wiped his face with his hands, as if trying to wipe away his doubts and anxieties. The Indian Army had been his life and I realised now how desperate he was to believe that his men would not betray him. On the plain on the edge of town, a ditch and an earthen rampart was being painstakingly scratched from the baked earth. I had seen it that morning: a bank just three feet high, it would not serve to stop a child. Wheeler had to believe he would not be attacked, yet everywhere from the schoolyard to his own sepoys' quarters rumour spread – and rumour begat fear and fear was already giving rise to panic.

'Perhaps …' Hillersdon was speaking. 'Perhaps now is the time to move the Nana's troops in to guard the Treasury.'

Wheeler nodded. 'I'll send for European troops from Lucknow. That may calm things. But if it gets any worse, we might have to use Nana Sahib's men. It will reassure the townspeople that there is still order in the place and it will show the sepoys that there are other troops to do our bidding if they are recalcitrant.'

I was about to demur, but I knew Hillersdon was determined on the wisdom of this move and, after my earlier outburst, Wheeler was unlikely to respond favourably to any interjection by me, so I kept my peace.

My concerns remained, though, so as I walked back to the office with Hillersdon, I suggested that I should take some time away from my desk to take the mood of the people. Hillersdon was no fool and he knew that I used my facility with the native language to judge mood in the streets, although I took care for him not to learn how completely I was passing myself off as an Indian. I think, too, that while he would hear nothing said against the Nana, he welcomed the idea that I should satisfy myself that all was well.

That afternoon, I slipped away from Cawnpore and hurried to Saturday House.

If Hillersdon had hoped that I would be reassured by what I saw, he would have been disappointed by my reception at the Nana's palace. At the gate, instead of passing sentries slouched in their usual casual indolence, I was challenged by guards who had the air of soldiers already sensing battle on the horizon. Fortunately, Mungo's repeated urgings of caution had had their effect on me and I was immaculately turned out in the uniform of one of Nana's own men, so a sharp salute and a word or two of greeting was enough for me to gain admittance.

Mungo was not in his apartments when I arrived. I fidgeted, uncertain what to do with myself. I had, as usual, brought my commonplace book with me to Saturday House and I recorded the meeting with Wheeler. Reading my words again left me even more troubled. I picked up one of the books I had been studying with Mungo and turned the pages, reading the Devanagari script with practised ease. But I found that I could not concentrate on the text. I needed Mungo to reassure me that all would be well and that Nana Sahib's troops would truly keep the peace in Cawnpore.

I replaced the book on the table and opened the chest where Mungo stored his clothes. I found myself pressing my face into them, inhaling the lingering traces of his scent. It was not just his news about Nana Sahib I needed; I needed him. His presence, his youth, his vitality. With the ordered world of British India no longer secure, it was to Mungo that I turned as the one safe and certain point I knew.

He came in so quietly that he found me still sitting there with my face buried in his clothing. I should have been embarrassed, but he reached for me without a word and pulled me to him and the faint remembrance of his scent gave way to the heady reality of his presence.

He slipped off his tunic and unbuttoned my shirt and I clung to his body, kissing the soft, warm flesh while he stroked my hair, murmuring reassurance.

We made love slowly, as if both if us wanted to extend the moment and delay all talk of politics, mutiny, and murder. But, at last, as we lay together, sated in each other's arms, we could prevaricate no longer. I explained that Wheeler was requesting the Nana for help and I asked Mungo to tell me if he was to be trusted or not.

'I would not ask so bluntly, but I have to know. At Meerut they killed women and children and burned the town.'

Mungo lay quietly, looking up at the ceiling, where a gecko sat motionless above his head.

'Nana Sahib has been insulted by the British and they have refused him his pension. There are those who say that he should avenge the insults and seize the money that is his right. But when the British defeated his father, they did not kill him. They allowed him to live here. They paid him a pension. So Nana Sahib has always been a friend to the British. He entertains them here at Saturday House. He is polite to their wives and kind to their children. And he has shown respect to your Mr Hillersdon and to all the officers of the Company. This he does because the British treated his father honourably – and because he knows your army is strong and that when his father rose against your army, he was defeated.'

I lay alongside him, thinking of what he said.

'Our army is still strong.'

He turned from the gecko and propped his head on his hand, looking at me as he spoke. 'We are the people of this land. We do not need the telegraph to know what happened in Meerut.'

'Meerut was one town. Britain has soldiers in countries all across the globe. Once her wrath is roused, she will crush the rebels entirely.'

'Yes.' His eyes gazed into mine. 'I think you are right. And so do many in the court. And they tell Nana Sahib that he should stay loyal to the British.'

'So he will send troops to assist us?'

'He will send troops.'

'And they will be loyal?'

Now Mungo's gaze turned back to the gecko. 'Why do you dig a ditch around the old barracks?'

'It's a precaution only. General Wheeler has a military mind, so he is preparing a defence in case one should be needed.'

'A child could climb it.'

'We hope it will never be needed.'

'It should not have been done.'

Something in his tone alarmed me. 'Why not, Mungo?' I asked.

'Because it is weak. And Nana Sahib is loyal because he thinks you are strong.'

I made no reply. The two of us lay beside each other on the bed, watching the gecko until, as if conscious of our gaze, it moved away.

Chapter Four

I returned to Cawnpore the next day. Although it was the Sabbath, I decided that I should call upon Hillersdon and let him know how things stood.

Charles received me cordially enough, but Lydia was only a few weeks from her confinement and it was obvious that he did not want her agitated. So we sat and talked of the price of fish and whether they should buy a quieter horse so that Lydia might be able to ride out as soon as she was recovered from the birth and what the fashions might be for the ladies when the dancing season should come again with the rains.

Our increasingly desperate attempts to avoid any discussion of those events that were all that anyone in Cawnpore truly cared about created the very atmosphere of tension that we were trying to avoid. Fortunately, Lydia, who was as intelligent as she was pretty, had the good sense to tell us that her condition made it imperative that she take to her bed for a while and she withdrew, leaving Charles and me alone.

Hillersdon spoke immediately his wife was out of the room. 'I take it you have news and that is why you have called.'

'I do.' I paused, for now that it came to it, what positive news did I have? 'Do you trust my judgement, Charles?'

'You know I do.'

'Then you should be careful of Nana Sahib. He is loyal for now but there are factions in his court who sympathise with the rebels. He will stand by us while he thinks the British will be triumphant but if he sees us weak, he can't be relied upon.'

'Are you sure?'

'You said you trust my judgement, Charles.'

He pursed his lips, his brow furrowed with concern. 'Frankly, John, I'm not sure that anyone can be totally relied upon. The question is: is he safer than the troops guarding the Treasury at present? I have reports that natives who call there with all the proper papers are harassed and threatened and may be sent away with nothing unless they find favour with the guard. The sepoys there are becoming a law unto themselves.' He rose from his chair and strode back and forth across the room, hardly recognisable as the affable administrator I had come to know. 'The Treasury is my responsibility. There's upwards of a hundred thousand pounds in there. I have to know it's safe.'

'Nothing is safe, Charles. Not now. You know that.'

He stopped his pacing. 'Very well. We have the sepoys, who are already semi-mutinous, and the Nana's men who may rebel in the future. As you say, nothing is safe. But the danger with the sepoys is already present, while the risk with the Nana is a problem for the morrow. I shall ask Wheeler to call on the Nana's troops as soon as practicable.'

'And Lydia?'

'Do you think there is any possibility he would harm her?'

'I would doubt it.'

'Yet if he were to declare for the rebels, she would be trapped in the enemy's camp. A white woman a prisoner of the niggers.'

Although I had heard some men – Simkin came most readily to mind – speak of the natives in these terms, I had never before heard Hillersdon use that word and it was a measure of his distress that he did so then.

'No,' he said. 'I cannot do it.'

We spoke a while longer but all that mattered had been decided. The Nana was to be invited to post his troops to Cawnpore but Lydia was not to go to Saturday House. I could see that Hillersdon was in great distress of mind about both these things and it seemed best to leave him.

I shared some of his agitation and felt I would not be able to settle if I went straight home, so I rode instead to see what progress had been made on the Entrenchment Wheeler had ordered. What I saw did not reassure me. The coolies had struggled to make any progress digging in the sun-baked soil and neither the ditch nor the mud rampart provided a convincing defence. The whole thing was a rough rectangle with bulges here and there to accommodate artillery, although, as yet, no guns were mounted in position. I feared Mungo was right: it looked like an act of desperation, rather than the military preparedness of a great army. I just hoped that things would remain calm until reinforcements arrived from Lucknow.

The days that followed seemed never-ending. Each morning we woke in the hope that we might receive news that the rebellion was quashed or that we might see the promised reinforcements march into town. And then, as the day wore on and the heat became unsupportable, all pretence of work stopped. Men sat idly at their desks, or walked toward the cantonments to see what progress was being made on the fortifications. In their bungalows, the memsahibs took to their beds or berated their cooks with near-hysterical outbursts over the failings of the last day's dinner or this day's luncheon. Even among the natives, a greater than usual lassitude descended. Then night would fall and shadowy brown figures would move among the native lines or through the streets of the old town and any European abroad would be greeted with suspicion and disrespect.

On Thursday, Wheeler ordered all the women and children in the Station to report to the Entrenchment. They were to sleep there, he said, simply as a precaution. Hillersdon chose to accompany his family.

The next morning, he was rather later into the office than usual. He explained to me that his wife, his two children and himself had been sharing a small room with two other families. There were only two barrack blocks into which all the women and children of the Civil Station were crammed willy-nilly.

'Wheeler was most insistent that the women and children shelter there for the night but there was no question of their staying in that awful place all day. So I had to arrange for us all to get home and then I had to settle the children, who were tired and fractious, and then I needed to perform my ablutions for there are no proper facilities in the barracks and, anyway, it's all made me a little behind.'

I smiled, in what I hope was an understanding way. 'It almost makes me glad that I have no family and was therefore able to spend the night in my own bed.'

'Humph.'

Hillersdon's expression left me thinking that perhaps my smile hadn't been as understanding as I had hoped.

Although his day had scarcely started well, Hillersdon was in the best of tempers, for that Friday the Nana's troops were finally to arrive in Cawnpore and, he felt, he would again see the Treasury safely under the guard of men he trusted. He was in and out of my room all morning, fidgeting while he waited for news. It was a considerable relief when, at about half past ten, a brilliantly turned out cavalryman presented himself at our offices and announced that the Nana's guard was about to arrive in the town. Did Mr Hillersdon want to meet them at the Treasury?

Mr Hillersdon could hardly wait. Mr Hillersdon had

had a groom standing by at the door all morning so that he could ride to inspect what I am sure he thought of as 'his' troops.

'Aren't you coming, John?' he asked. 'It will be a fine sight.'

Unlike the Collector, I did not have my groom standing by so I had to organise myself a horse. The Treasury was about three miles away and I had, in any case, no intention of being the only pedestrian surrounded by mounted officers both civil and military. Hillersdon was fairly bursting with impatience, so he rode off and I followed.

When I finally arrived at the imposing stone building that was, effectively, the European bank, I saw that Hillersdon had been joined by Wheeler and his son. Nana Sahib's state elephant was kneeling nearby and the Nana himself had dismounted and was conferring earnestly with the Collector and the General. The Nana had brought about three hundred men, both infantry and cavalry and they even towed two guns with them. They were lined up in neat rows, as well turned out as our own troops had ever been and much better than the sullen sepoys of the 53rd Native Infantry, whose normally smart appearance was just a memory from happier days.

Hillersdon was smiling and looked more relaxed than I had seen him for weeks. If my warning had given him any temporary doubts about the Nana's loyalty, he had clearly put this behind him. The only one of the party of officers who looked unhappy was the colonel of the 53rd. I could see him gesticulating angrily and shaking his head as I approached. By the time I was in earshot, Wheeler was trying to placate him.

'The 53rd are not being relieved. Of course we trust them. It's just that the Nana's guard can share their duties, allowing some of the men to move onto garrison duty in the cantonment.'

Colonel Gibbs was clearly still unhappy. 'Look here,

General, it's difficult for me to present this to the men as anything other than an insult. Even if a few of the 53rd remain here, most are being replaced by local troops who are not even under my command.'

Wheeler had obviously had enough. 'Mr Hillersdon has suggested to me that the men of the 53rd appear to be under your command only in the most limited sense. The troops of the Nana Sahib are well turned out, well disciplined, and command the respect of the local populace and of me. The troops of the 53rd, sir, do not.'

Wheeler beckoned for his horse and his son assisted him in mounting while the unfortunate Colonel Gibbs looked fit to burst with apoplexy. Indeed, given that the sun was approaching its zenith, I had some real concern for his safety in the heat.

I congratulated Hillersdon for having secured the Treasury, joined him in accompanying the Nana in a sort of informal inspection of the troops and then, the heat being intense, made my apologies and returned to the office. The place was almost deserted, most people having decided to retreat to the cool of their homes. I decided I would remain at my desk and await Hillersdon's return, for I was sure that he would want to record details of the new guard in his official paperwork.

I had almost decided that I was mistaken in my belief when, an hour or more later, I heard the thud of hooves on the dried earth followed by Charles' arrival in my office, mopping perspiration from his brow and complaining of the heat.

I agreed. 'You shouldn't be riding out at midday. It's a recipe for heatstroke.'

He shrugged. 'I didn't really have a lot of choice. I had to stay and chat to the Nana and he said that he intended to remain in Cawnpore and camp beside his men. Showing the flag and all that sort of stuff. Can you get Simkin to make sure that it's all sorted out? I don't want complaints that he pitched his tent on Company property without a permit or any such nonsense. I did offer to pay for forage and provisions for his men but he wouldn't hear of it. Good man!'

And, with a smile on his face and a spring in his step, despite the heat, Hillersdon passed on to his own office and left me to my thoughts. The first of which was that it I was more likely to see a phoenix sat on my desk than to find Simkin in his office and as far the Nana's camping arrangements were concerned, I had best ensure that the proper formalities were observed myself.

It is remarkable how much paperwork a tent can generate – at least when it is accompanied by an elephant and three hundred troops. The job took me most of the day and involved another expedition to the Treasury, though I took care to wait until the worst of the heat had passed before I undertook that.

The Treasury was firmly situated in the Civil Station, though it was quite close to the army's magazine which, for reasons lost in time, was situated four miles or so from the military cantonment. The Nana had drawn up his army a mile or so back from the river, where there was open space in which his soldiers were bivouacked. The men were obviously expected to sleep on the ground under the stars but Nana Sahib himself had an elaborate pavilion erected in the centre of his force, with guards on piquet duty and his elephant resting nearby under the supervision of its mahout.

The whole arrangement, with muskets neatly stacked by each group of sepoys, the horses of the cavalry tethered in rows, and the guns ready on their limbers all gave the impression of an army that meant business. But whether they were ready to protect us from our own forces or to aid in an Indian rebellion against European rule, I could not guess. I suspected that at that point, the Nana was not sure himself. I decided, though, that it would be best to ride out to Saturday House the next day and see what intelligence I could gather.

The excitement and bustle that had permeated Saturday House when I was last there had vanished with the Nana and his troops. As had always been the case until the last few weeks, I was able to enter with only the most cursory of glances from a sentry slumped into a shady corner. Inside the palace, I made my way to Mungo's rooms, passing servants idly pushing brooms along passages that would usually be swept clean early in the morning.

When I arrived at his apartment, I found Mungo no stranger to the general air of idleness. As I entered (doors were never locked in Saturday House) Mungo was pulling on a tunic, his hair rumpled and his eyes still swollen from sleep. When he saw it was me, he simply pulled off the tunic and lay back on the bed, motioning me to join him.

'Lazy bones!' I chided, though I was taking off my own shirt as I spoke. 'Do you have no duties to be about?'

He reached for me and pulled me to him. 'Nana Sahib is away and we can play all day,' he said. And then his mouth was busy with other things than words and we spoke no more.

Much later, as I held him in my arms and stroked his hair, I reminded myself that I was there to gather such intelligence as I could as to the Nana's intentions. I asked how long the Nana was expected to be away.

Mungo did not want to speak of it, which I felt ominous in itself, so I persisted and he grumpily told me that the Nana intended to stay with the army in Cawnpore.

'But what does he intend to do there?'

'It's his army.' Mungo rolled away from me and started to pull on his tunic. 'You understand so much about India that sometimes I forget that you do not belong here.'

He was standing by now, pulling on trousers under the tunic, busying himself with tying knots and searching for his shoes – anything to avoid meeting my eye.

'Mungo, what have I said wrong?'

Now he turned to me and I saw the beginning of tears. 'You ask why he is in Cawnpore. His father was a great man who ruled over an area of hundreds of miles, tens of thousands marched under his banner and millions acknowledged him as their lord. Nana Sahib has lost all this. You will not accord him his titles. You do not fire your guns in salute. His army is a few hundred men and his rule extends only over this palace. And now you need him, he is here for you and his army marches to Cawnpore, where your army is failing. And he rides with it upon his elephant for now he is as his father once was, leading an army in his own country. It is his country, you see, John. And you ask, "What does he intend to do there?" Is it not fairer to ask what the British intend to do, thousands of miles from their homes, their soldiers no longer true, hiding in their bungalows. It is not truly your country, John. It belongs to people like Nana Sahib.'

I was still sat on the bed and I felt my head fall into my hands. 'Then Nana Sahib will turn on the British and take the country.'

'No.' Mungo shook his head urgently, trying, I think, to convince himself as much as me. 'The Nana will stand by the British and you will see that he is a good friend and when the rains come and all is quiet again, you will reward him for his loyalty.'

I said nothing. Perhaps, when Dalhousie had been Governor-General, this might have happened. But under Canning? The man who so adamantly refused to recognise the Nana's titles that letters that were signed with them were returned unread? The man who, if he had not annexed Oudh, had presided over the imposition of British administration there? All things, of course, were possible – but if I were Nana Sahib, I would not pin my hopes on Canning.

I think Mungo saw my doubts about Canning, just as I saw his about the Nana, but we chose to pretend that all was well. And, indeed, for all we knew, the crisis might pass. The Nana could still preserve the European community in Cawnpore. He had the respect of the local people and troops at his command to keep order if there were to be unrest. Wheeler was an old India hand and could be counted on to do everything he could to calm the talk of mutiny and, meanwhile, European troops were promised from Lucknow. The rains could start in a month. Things only had to stay quiet until then.

That afternoon we explored the palace as we had the day that I had met him. We walked along the corridor of clocks and stood hand-in-hand to watch the lion pacing in his cage. We cooled ourselves in the waters of the fountains and our eyes were soothed by the green of the lawns.

That night we made love again, slowly, savouring each moment. It was as if we knew that something evil was coming but that we wanted to cherish what we had while we still could. We woke the next dawn to another day of calm. Mungo took me to the audience chamber where I had first met Nana Sahib. The door was open and there was no guard. He sat on the Nana's mat and told me he was ruler now and I bowed and called him 'Your Highness' and 'Great Majesty' and he laughed and then was suddenly pensive. 'If only the British would do him honour and call him "Your Highness". It's all he wants.'

I said I would ride back to Cawnpore and talk to Hillersdon and see if anything could be done that might ease relations. Mungo, sitting in the Nana's place seemed to weigh my words as if he really was a ruler, considering matters of high state and diplomacy and then, in a more than usually thoughtful tone, he said, 'You should stay here. You can do nothing at Cawnpore now. Mr Hillersdon is a good man but he does not have the power to change things. I don't know that any of us can change things now.' Then, with a flash of his old mischief, he was on his feet and almost running to the door.

I followed as fast as I could, hampered by the sword on the sowar's uniform I now wore more or less as a matter of course around the palace. ('It's safer,' Mungo had said. 'People will not challenge an officer.') Mungo, in his tunic and loose trousers, had almost vanished down the corridor before I was out of the door and he led me an undignified chase through the palace for most of the afternoon.

I thought I knew the place by now but it was vast, with separate quarters for different families related to the Nana by ties of blood or state and for the garrison and the servants. There were cellars storing food and cellars filled with bottles of wine (for the Nana's tastes had grown cosmopolitan over the years he had entertained the English). There were cellars with forage for the beasts of the place and one cellar Mungo hurried me through, muttering angrily that he had not intended to bring me there and where I saw pikes and muskets stacked neatly in racks against the walls. There were no attics but stairs led directly to the roof, marked off with walls protecting the ladies of the harem who might seek to take the air up there, while we wandered safely out of sight of them, looking across the parapets at the dusty countryside between Bithur and Cawnpore.

Mungo let me catch up with him there and we held each other as we looked out along the road.

'I have to go back,' I said.

'I know.' He slipped his hands beneath my clothing and held me to him. 'Stay tonight,' he said, 'and then go if you must. But,' – and here he turned his face to mine and I saw real distress in his eyes – 'if all you fear comes to pass, then come back here to Saturday House and I will protect you.'

I returned his embrace. How could he protect me? He

was little more than a boy. But I looked across the parapet and saw an alien country. Somewhere below the horizon was Cawnpore where the European community relied for their protection on one hundred white troops and tried to convince themselves that this made them safe. As I looked down at Mungo's face, he gave me a smile of reassurance.

This was his country. He would protect me.

I returned to Cawnpore on the Monday, still no wiser as to what the Nana's plans really were. At the Collectorate, Hillersdon was in the best of humours. Nana Sahib's men had firmly established themselves at the Treasury and their presence did seem to be calming the locals.

I took myself to my office and settled to work as best I could. There was plenty to do. The end of the week would be Good Friday and work in the office would stop while the Europeans took themselves to church for a day of prayer and fasting.

That evening I did not return directly to my bungalow but, instead, called in on the Club. I was not a regular visitor for I never felt truly comfortable with the gentlemen there. Still I took care to call in often enough that neither my presence nor absence caused comment. This evening I wanted to judge for myself the atmosphere in the European community.

All seemed much as it had been on my last visit a couple of weeks earlier. The waiters moved quietly from table to table pouring more brandies than might have been expected in quieter times and the newspapers were tattered from the number of people reading them but there was no sign of panic. Indeed, the promise of Easter seemed to be calming nerves. The stately rhythm of the ecclesiastical year seems to promise that the present crisis would pass. The story of the Resurrection and Christ's triumph over death reassured believers (and none would admit to doubting) that the Lord would see them safely through their present travails.

So the days to Easter passed with no further excitement and, on Good Friday, I joined the faithful in St John's Church to repent my sins. I listened to the murmured prayers of the men and women around me and wished that I could share their faith and their belief, but I could not, and I left the service still weighed down by the guilt of all that had happened in Borneo. Every Good Friday since I had stood by and watched my friend destroy his enemies, I had repented my sin, that I had not stopped him. Yet I did not believe that God had forgiven me.[1]

My spirits were lifted the next day when I dined again with Hillersdon. It was a quiet evening with Charles treating me almost as one of the family. Lydia suffered with the heat, given her condition, but was as bright and cheerful as could be expected and we parted with best wishes for Easter Day.

The service on Sunday went well. The bright red of the officers' uniforms enlivened the place and their voices covered for any weakness on the part of the choir. All the European families had turned out to celebrate and decorated eggs were handed to the children as they left the church. Listening to their laughter and seeing their mothers in their Easter bonnets, it was easy, for a moment, to imagine ourselves back in England and the air of menace that had filled every waking moment for so long seemed temporarily lifted.

The promise of redemption was short-lived, however. I woke on Easter Monday to find breakfast late and my khanasaman berating the boys in the kitchen. When the shouts began to be interspersed with the sound of breaking

---

[1] Williamson had accompanied James Brooke at the massacre of Beting Marau. His account of this can be read in *The White Rajah.*

crockery, I abandoned protocol and went into the kitchen myself to find out the cause of the trouble.

One of the boys was on his knees gathering up pieces of a broken plate while the khanasaman was standing over another with his hand raised to strike him.

'What the devil is going on?' I looked about for the cook. 'And where is Cook?'

The boys scurried to hide themselves in corners while the khanasaman explained to me that the cook was nowhere to be found. 'He is a stupid man and is frightened by stories.'

'What stories?'

No stories in particular, the khanasaman assured me. Just idle chitchat. He himself had heard nothing.

By now, I was becoming alarmed. Whatever had happened had been serious enough for my cook to flee. The khanasaman clearly knew what was going on and equally clearly had no intention of telling me. I decided to get directly to the office to find out the news and to breakfast later at the Club.

Instead of the normal morning calm of the office, I found almost every desk occupied but there was no sign of any work being done. I was accosted on all sides by staff – both Europeans and babus – who demanded to know the latest news. Unable to tell them anything, I made for Hillersdon's office, trying to look like a man who knew what was going on.

I was not surprised to find the babus so agitated, for they were prone to temperamental behaviour, but the excitability of the Europeans was a shock. Even men like Simkin would usually maintain some impression of *sang froid*, especially in front of the natives. The full extent of the panic only became obvious, though, when I entered Charles's office to find him rigid at his desk, pale as death under his tan, staring at the desk in front of him. When he heard me enter, he raised his eyes and gestured for me to sit.

'I fear the worst, John,' he said.

'What on earth has happened?'

'Last night some damn fool subaltern was going home drunk. He was challenged by a patrol of native infantry. They were right to challenge him, there's no doubt about that. Instead of identifying himself, the damn fool took out his pistol and shot one of them.' He passed a hand over his face. 'You know, while you were away, Wheeler ordered that the guns should not be fired on the Queen's birthday, in case the sound of the salute should alarm the native troops and make them think we were attacking them. And now some drunken lieutenant shoots a sepoy who is simply doing his job. It defies belief.'

I sat silent, as horrified by his news as he was. We were sitting in a powder magazine and some young fool had dropped a lighted match.

'I'm taking Lydia and the children to the Entrenchment. I'm leaving you in charge here. I suggest that you tell all the men with families to go to their homes and get their women and children safe. Anyone else who has revolvers should bring them to the office. But tell everyone to be discreet. I don't want the natives to see us running around with guns.'

He left and most of the men in the office left with him. A few of us bachelors remained behind with a handful of handguns to defend our files if insurrection were to break out. But the day passed in an awful stillness and in the evening I found myself, somewhat to my surprise, still alive.

I had heard no firing. The streets, when I ventured out, were quiet. Even so, I resolved to spend that night in the Entrenchment. I made a quick visit to my house to take a bath and eat an early supper, and then set off to Wheeler's earthworks. I decided not to ride, for I reasoned that there would be far too many horses there already and no provision for stabling. Instead, I walked the mile or so to where, on the edge of the great parade ground just to the East of the military lines, a crumbling embankment marked out the boundaries of our refuge.

I entered through a gap in the earthworks where a storeroom had been adapted to make some sort of gatehouse. Some men of the 84th Foot were standing around, almost lost in the mass of civilians who thronged around the entrance. It took me several minutes to get through. When, at last, I did, the place seemed scarcely less crowded than the gateway. The earthworks had been thrown up to enclose two long barrack blocks but these were almost entirely obscured from view by the tents and shelters erected haphazardly in the open ground around them. These were not the neat rows of army-issue tents that one might expect in a military establishment, but a shanty-town of canvas with which the civilian families sheltering under the army's protection sought to ensure themselves a modicum of privacy and shelter from the cruelty of the sun.

It was immediately apparent that the Europeans gathered in these shelters were those who lacked position or patronage and I made my way as best I could through their gypsy encampment until I reached the more Northerly of the two barrack blocks which, unlike the other, had a roof of tile rather than of thatch. Covered verandas ran along both sides of the building and the interior was broken up into a number of rooms which, between them, would probably have housed a company of a hundred men when they were in regular military use. Now at least twice that number were packed inside while as many again clustered onto the verandas which at least offered shelter from the sun and, being arcaded, some sort of privacy.

I found the Hillersdons sharing a room with the Greenways and two other couples whom I knew only vaguely. One of them had two children around the age of the Hillersdons' children and they were playing together rather lacklustrely in the heat. I stooped to pat their heads and congratulate Lydia on their good behaviour, for all around I could hear other children crying and whining and hers were really making the best they could of their situation.

Lydia rewarded me with a tired smile but Charles beamed his approval and, having established that I intended to spend the night in their encampment, he insisted that I find a space in the room with them. There was a certain amount of muttering from one of the other couples but the Greenways supported the Hillersdons and soon I was settling down on the floor.

I cannot say I slept well. There were no punkahs to stir the air and the windows were open with no wetted screens to cool it. All around were the sounds of men and women in uneasy sleep and the cries of children. After my years in Borneo, I did not suffer from lying on the packed earth floor, but very few people had even camp beds and, for civilians used to the luxury of mattresses and feather pillows, the unwelcome novelty of their situation made repose difficult.

When Charles and I woke the next morning, we were in no fit state to go directly to the office. Fortunately, Hillersdon had arranged for his family to move temporarily into a new bungalow quite close to the barracks and he shepherded me with them to make myself presentable in his new home.

I must confess I felt guilty as I followed Charles to where I knew I would find a clean bath and all the other necessities of modern life. All around us less fortunate families were beginning to form queues for the two privies that served the barrack block and mothers were squatting on the ground trying to clean their children with cloths dampened from jugs of water.

Charles caught the direction of my gaze and misunderstood the look of concern on my face.

'Don't worry, John. There's plenty of water. We have a well over there.' He gestured toward the space between the barracks but I couldn't see a well for the crowd and the tents that seemed even more closely packed now than when I arrived.

'Is there just the one well?'

'It's enough. It's never failed us yet.'

I looked again at the mass of people who apparently relied for all their water on one well that stood in the open. I was no soldier but even I could see the danger inherent in this situation. If there were to be a mutiny, the Entrenchment would provide shelter from the first blast of the storm but, with no proper fortification and only that one exposed source of water, it could not sustain us against any prolonged attack.

I said nothing to Hillersdon of my fears. What good, I reasoned, could it possibly do? And by noon I was beginning to think myself a fool to have been so concerned for, at last, we received our promised reinforcements.

One hundred men of the 84th Foot and fifteen of the Madras Fusiliers arrived in a convoy of bullock carts. Tired and dusty as they were from the road, they dismounted on the edge of the town and marched into camp. Hillersdon closed the office for an hour to allow everyone to join the crowds cheering as they marched by. The babus made way for me so that I might stand near the front and I must admit to drawing comfort from the sight of those homely English faces under their uniform hats. They marched with a swagger that promised a restoration of the rightful order and we all convinced ourselves we had been saved. Small as the contingent was, the look on the faces of the native troops as they, too, watched the Europeans march into camp showed how much they felt the situation had shifted to their disadvantage.

Imagine, then, our shock as news came that General Wheeler had ordered that fifty of these men should be sent on immediately to Lucknow, where there were rumours that the European community faced dangers similar to our own. Simkin, on hearing that the fifty were already on the road referred to General Wheeler as 'a bloody idiot' in tones that were clearly distinguishable in the general office, where some of the babus started to actually wail. Hillersdon called me into his office and asked me to do what I could to calm their fears.

'After all,' he said, 'it is surely the strongest possible evidence of General Wheeler's confidence in the situation that he should sacrifice our defensive forces here to ease the concerns of our colleagues in Oudh.'

I tried to persuade myself that he was right and I perhaps half convinced at least some of the babus. That evening, though, Hillersdon and his family again sought the shelter of the Entrenchment and I was not ashamed to join them. The crowding was, if anything, greater than that of the previous evening and there was a pervasive stench of unwashed bodies and, I fear, worse, as the privies were inadequate and the number of children in the encampment meant that small bowels were forced on occasion to empty themselves wherever was convenient. Yet things had come to such a pass that the squalor and discomfort seemed preferable to a night isolated in my own home.

I returned to my office the next day feeling fatigued and – despite again enjoying the hospitality of the Hillersdons in order to bathe – dirty.

The place was quiet. The European staff were all at their desks, though most looked tired and strained and I doubted that many were in any fit state to do anything useful. In any case, our paperwork relied on the efforts of the clerks and more than half of the babus had stayed away.

Like the others, I found it impossible to settle to any

real work and sat in my office irritably moving papers around my desk. When one of the few babus there knocked at my door to tell me that there was a native soldier who claimed to have an urgent and personal message for me, I nearly told him to go to hell. Native soldiers seemed to me to be at the root of all our present troubles and I could think of none who had any proper business with me. Just in time, though, I calmed myself. I would not allow myself to be caught up in the hysteria that saw every native trooper as a threat. I would be as civil to this visitor as to any other.

My clerk returned a few minutes later and ushered in, not one of the Company's native troops, but an impeccably turned-out sowar of the Nana's force.

He bowed, his hands together in respect, and then held out a letter, heavily sealed with wax.

'I am instructed, sahib, to bring you this letter and to place it in your hand only.'

I took it and he immediately bowed again and made to leave.

'Are you not to wait for a reply?'

'No, sahib. I am to give you this letter and then leave.'

'Well,' I reached into my pocket for some coins and pulled out a rupee, 'you should at least be rewarded for your effort.'

The soldier shook his head. 'I seek no reward, sahib. I have brought this message to pay an obligation to the sender. My obligation is discharged by its safe receipt and I require no other reward.'

And with a smart salute he was gone.

Intrigued, I broke the seal. Inside was a short letter written in Devanagari script and, as I translated it, the soldier's behaviour was explained.

My beloved friend

I send this message by the hand of one I trust. He has ties of blood and obligation. Even so, it is dangerous to write. But I have to send this message to you.

It is dangerous for you to stay any longer in Cawnpore. I beg you, as you love me, come directly to Bithur. I beg of you that you do not tell your friends where you are going or why. You cannot save them and you will only put yourself and me in danger.

I trust you, my beloved. And I wait for you here.

M

It was not yet noon but the day was too hot to contemplate riding to Bithur until closer to the evening and then there was every chance that night would find me still on the road. With the country simmering on the edge of anarchy, I was unwilling to travel after dark. Yet the message suggested an immediate danger.

What danger could Mungo know of? Was the Nana planning treachery? There was no evidence of this. His troops, I knew, remained camped out at the Treasury and, though there had been stories from some of the richer locals that the Nana's men had threatened them or demanded money, there was no evidence that this went beyond the misbehaviour of some individual soldiers. I could not even be sure that the stories were true.

Should I take the letter to Hillersdon? But what could he do if I did? It would simply be one more rumour in a town full of rumours. Anyway, Hillersdon and his family would sleep in the encampment again that night and that would be as safe as anywhere.

Perhaps Mungo's fears, like so many peoples', were simply based on rumour and there was no imminent danger? Yet, in writing to me, he had taken a real risk. No one of note knew of our relationship and Mungo was anxious to keep it a secret. Yet he had taken the risk of sending a message to me. Could I ignore his warning? And, if I did, would he trust me again?

There was nothing for it. I would have to ride out to Bithur.

I left the Collectorate soon after four. The afternoon was still blisteringly hot, but I did not want to risk delaying further. I had told Hillersdon that I had heard rumours that the European community might be attacked but that I needed to investigate further before I could give him any details and I intended to do so immediately. He took me at my word. He did not ask me where I had heard the rumours for he understood that I would not be specific. He shook my hand as I left and I think he suspected that I would not return.

I called in at my bungalow to collect the bundle in which I stored my sowar's uniform, hidden with some souvenirs of my time in Borneo and my commonplace book. I sensed that I would want to have a record of the days ahead of me. I warned the khanasaman that I might be away for a while and that he was to take whatever measures he deemed necessary to protect the premises in my absence.

I had two horses by then, in the small stables behind my bungalow. One was an Indian pony, quite large enough to carry me and tough and wiry. The other, a bay hunter. I had named him Kuching in remembrance of my time with James and, though he was less suited to hard riding in the Indian climate, he was a thing of beauty and admired by both Europeans and natives alike. In the end, I chose to ride Kuching, arguing that he was faster and stronger.

Then I was off, heading North. I paused in the shelter of some neem trees to pull off my European clothes. I stood naked, staining my face and hands with walnut juice, working with the aid of a hand mirror bundled in with the clothes. Then I pulled on my uniform and stepped from the trees a soldier in the Nana's army.

I wasted no more time, proceeding alternately at canter and trot until my poor horse, eyes wild with the heat, finally came in sight of Saturday House. Only then did I feel safe to rein in, covering the last half mile at an easy walk that gave Kuching a chance to recover.

At the gate the guard stopped me. I worried for a moment that my hunter might be leading him to suspect that I was not the native I was pretending to be, though I knew that many of the sowars would ride a European horse if they could get one, as the animals made a brave show. To my relief, the sentry had stopped me, not to challenge my entry, but to ask what news there was from Cawnpore.

'Has the mutiny started yet?'

This was the first I knew that a mutiny was planned and that the plans were apparently common knowledge at Bithur, but I did my best not to let this shock show.

'There was no mutiny when I left,' I said, 'but it cannot be long now.'

The sentry grinned broadly. 'It must be soon,' he agreed and waved me past him.

I left Kuching at the stables, where the Nana's grooms cared for all the animals of the household, and made my way directly to Mungo's quarters. The place was almost as deserted as it had been before, yet where my last visit had revealed ill-disciplined idleness, now the few servants I saw in the corridors moved sharply about their business. The Nana's apartments were guarded by sentries who stood smartly to attention and saluted as I passed. Even Mungo seemed infected by this new alertness, though in his case the tension visible in his lithe body as soon as I entered his room was more about his concern for me than the general situation.

'Thank the gods you are safe,' he said, pulling me to

him and hugging me until I thought I would not be able to breathe. 'I think you escaped just in time.'

'So a mutiny is planned and the Nana is involved?'

Mungo turned away from me, as if ashamed. 'There will be a mutiny. It should start today. The Nana knows of it. Everyone knows of it. That does not mean that he has planned it or that it is of his doing.'

'I should warn them.'

Mungo shrugged. 'And tell them what? That their army is on the verge of mutiny? I think, John, that they probably know that already.'

'But people here know more than that.'

'They know that the mutiny will start today. It has probably already started. There is nothing you can do about it now.'

I sat on the bed with my head in my hands. If Mungo was telling the truth, what could I do? He sat beside me, holding me to him.

'I need to know what is happening.'

'If there's news, it will arrive at the garrison first. We can go there and wait.'

Mungo started off through the maze of passages. Fast as he moved, I found myself passing him and striding ahead, for so many hours had we spent exploring the place together that I was now almost as familiar with it as he was and I was desperate to learn the latest intelligence.

Although from the outside Saturday House appeared one single building, inside the warren of passageways and courtyards created separate areas for the different elements of the Nana's enormous household. So it was that the garrison was quartered in dormitories that led onto the same open space where a statue with six heads held a positive arsenal of weapons – a spear, a bow, a sword and half a dozen more – in an improbable number of arms. I knew by now that this was Murugan. Mungo had pointed him out to me all those months ago when he had first been teaching me about the different deities – or (as I had come to learn) the different aspects of deity. Then the statue had been unadorned but now it was hung about with garlands of flowers and, alarmingly, lotus leaves like those that had been distributed among the native troops in Cawnpore. If I had had any doubts as to the seriousness of the situation before, the sight of all these offerings to the god of war made it all too clear that the Nana's soldiers were convinced they were about to go into battle.

The courtyard was arcaded but the centre was open to the air and, even at evening, the place was light and pleasant. We were obviously not the only people waiting there for news. When we arrived there were already knots of men gathering, talking, and gesticulating excitedly together. As we waited, more people entered from the corridors that led from the rest of the palace. A few off-duty soldiers strutted about, enjoying the admiring glances of the civilians. One came over to me and asked for the latest news. For a moment I nearly panicked, convinced he would recognise me for an imposter. I would be torn apart and Mungo, who was standing beside me, would be compromised. But I kept my composure and told him that all had been quiet when I left, but that we expected to hear more shortly and he went his way satisfied.

We had been there for an hour and torches had been lit to illuminate the courtyard when there was the sound of shouting in the distance and word spread through the crowd that Nana Sahib was returning to Saturday House.

Now everyone was thrusting their way back through the halls and passageways, pressing toward the main entrance of the palace. I started to try to push through the crowd, but Mungo plucked at my sleeve.

'Don't waste your time. You'll never get through that way. Follow me!'

He darted off and I realised that there were secrets of the palace's geography that I had yet to learn. We darted down corridors of bare stone, up narrow staircases, across a roof, down a flight of wooden steps, and finally emerged through a postern gate just in time to see the Nana's entourage arrive.

Indian elephants are quite small and not nearly such splendid beasts as they are usually depicted in pictures. Even so, the Nana, seated atop his State Elephant, was a commanding presence. The elephant towered over the crimson uniformed figures of his escort. From the howdah, the Nana waved regally at the few privileged courtiers who had been allowed to greet him at the door and then dismounted to be escorted by half a dozen of his men who marched beside him, swords drawn and held smartly at attention.

He vanished into the Palace without a word.

'Is there then to be no news at all?' I asked Mungo.

He shook his head, in disappointment, I think, rather than negation, and turned to go back into Saturday House. At that moment though, a havildar of the guard came to the entrance and, raising his voice, addressed the courtiers who had made up the welcoming party.

'Nana Sahib, the Peshwa Seereek Dhoondoo Punth, desires that his loyal subjects should know and take cogniscence of the rebellion of soldiers of the 3rd Oudh Native Artillery, who have left the employ of the British.'

That was all, though the cheers of the courtiers suggested that they, at least, thought this an announcement of great moment. For Mungo and me, though, analysing every word of that brief statement back in his apartment, we were little wiser than before. I noted that Nana Sahib had said nothing himself and that he was here in Bithur, far from any mutiny. Mungo, too, was in no doubt what this meant. 'Nana Sahib has not yet committed himself to the rebel cause. If the British stand firm, he may yet support them.' On the other hand, the use of the title of Peshwa and his formal names, although not threatening in itself, was sufficiently unusual to suggest that the Nana was at least aware of the possibilities that a mutiny might offer for him to consolidate his own position.

I slept restlessly that night and by the next morning I had almost persuaded myself to return to Cawnpore, but Mungo insisted that I wait until he had more news. 'Stay here and eat. I will see what I can discover and then I will return and we can plan what you should do.'

He kissed me and vanished out of the door. I lay on the bed, my mind running through all the possibilities over and over again. Yet however much I worried at them, every alternative seemed fraught with peril. In any case, whatever I did or did not do, it seemed it was now too late to avert mutiny.

I was still lying there when Mungo returned. His smile suggested he had good news but his first concern was that I had not eaten and he refused to tell me anything until I had at least nibbled at some of the fruit that he offered me.

'There has been no bloodshed. The men of the Artillery ran away from their officers. People say they crossed the Ganges into Oudh. That is all that has happened. Nana Sahib is returning to Cawnpore today. I think that which you feared may yet be averted.'

Perhaps it would be all right. Perhaps the mutineers would drift away in the night and the one hundred and fifty British troops would be left guarding an empty cantonment until this whole ghastly mess was over and some kind of normality was restored.

I looked up at Mungo who stood, his face unwontedly serious. Beyond the door, I could hear a sweeper cleaning the passage. A smell of incense wafted in the high window. This, I realised, was normality in India. European rule was a one-hundred-year-old experiment that seemed now to be coming to an end. Could one hundred and fifty troops really make any difference when we faced an entire nation who saw us as alien and who now might simply wish us gone?

'What should I do, Mungo?'

'Stay here. Rest.' He paused a moment, and then added, 'Pray to your God.'

I took his advice as to staying and resting. I even tried prayer, but the words wouldn't come.

In the afternoon, I wandered the palace until I found a shrine to Ganesh. The elephant-headed god was my favourite. He was a popular choice, bringing luck, and his shrine was heaped with offerings. I had begged a fistful of incense sticks from Mungo and now I lit them all, the acrid smoke rising from the courtyard to the heavens above. Somehow I felt that Ganesh might favour me with good fortune even while the God of my childhood turned his face from me.

Thursday passed and on Friday I woke to the prospect of another long, hot day. Mungo was nervous of my wandering alone about Saturday House. The tension that had pervaded life in Cawnpore for so many months was beginning to make itself felt in Bithur too, though here there was more a sense of anticipatory excitement, rather than dread. Still, Mungo felt that it would be safer for me to stay in his room while he found out the latest news.

Mungo had left me with a book about the history of the Peshwas and I found myself caught up in reading the story of the power that Nana Sahib's adoptive family had held before they were overthrown by the British. Immersed in the tale, I was able to forget my troubles for a while.

Then Mungo returned and my troubles with him.

Chapter Five

The mutiny had started in the night, while we slept. The 2nd Native Cavalry had risen, firing their barracks and riding to the Native Infantry lines to call on their comrades to join them in revolt. In the confusion, with the weeks of fear and suspicion working on their minds, the British had fired indiscriminately on the native troops, driving any who had remained loyal to join their fellows in mutiny.

'The Nana opened the Treasury to them.'

I looked up at him from where I sat cross-legged in native fashion. 'Then he has made his choice.'

'Your friends are in their fort.' He meant the Entrenchment. I knew the Indians called it a fort. It was mockery: the Entrenchment was no fort and would never survive attack.

'There has been some looting. A few – very few, I think – have been killed. But the rebels say they will march to Delhi to join the Emperor.'

I noticed he said 'Emperor'. So the King of Delhi was already seen once again as the Mogul Emperor his ancestors had been. This did not bode well for the Company.

Mungo was still talking, trying to reassure me. 'If they march to Delhi, your friends will be left safe. I do not think you need to worry.'

The native troops had mutinied, the Nana had thrown his lot in with them, and the people were clearly ready to join a general uprising but, according to Mungo, I had no need to worry.

I tried to smile, but I felt my lips twisted with

bitterness.

Mungo reached down to embrace me and I felt his tears falling in my cheeks.

'I am sorry, my love.' His hold on me tightened. 'Just stay here and I will look after you.'

Now I found it easier to smile. Here was my Mungo – little more than a boy – promising me his protection. How could I not smile?

The wonder of our situation was that Mungo was, indeed, well placed to preserve me from the fate of those Europeans who had been caught out of the Entrenchment when the soldiers mutinied. There had already been murders. As the day went by and word came back to Bithur of events in Cawnpore, Mungo brought news of not only Europeans but the half-caste babus being killed wherever they were found.

Businesses which had supplied the European community were looted and the houses of rich Indians who had become too close to the British were broken into and robbed. But most people had slept for safety in the Entrenchment or fled there as soon as the mutiny broke out and there, it seemed, they remained unmolested.

I thought of the heat and the stench that I had experienced in my nights there and tried not to dwell on how things must be under the blazing noon sun. Poor Lydia, so close to her confinement and forced to rest on the hard packed ground, with no relief from the heat. And the children! Charles must be distraught.

I stayed in Mungo's apartments all day and I could not help but compare my situation with that of Charles and his family. I was sheltered from the sun, the marble floor cool to my naked feet, even at midday. Ewers of clear water were there for the asking and Mungo insisted on bringing constant delicacies for me to enjoy.

Still, I told myself, soon the rebels would be on their way to Delhi. The Europeans would return to their homes.

All would be well. All had to be well.

By nightfall, I had convinced myself of the truth of this. At least, I had convinced myself enough to be able to sleep. I'm not sure that I ever really believed it.

The morning brought confirmation of all my worst fears. I woke from an uneasy sleep to find Mungo already dressed. As soon as he saw me stir, he was on his feet, his face grim.

'Nana Sahib is returning to Cawnpore.'

At first, I did not understand. The rebels were marching to Delhi. If the Nana was returning to Cawnpore, had he decided at last to abandon them and throw in his lot with the British?

I don't remember what I said. I must have asked some sort of question that made Mungo realise my mistake. He spoke gently, trying to ease the blow.

'He is leading the rebels back. He intends to use them as his own army, to take back the power of the Peshwas.'

Gentle as he was, there could not really have been any doubting the meaning of his words, yet I lay there in his bed puzzling over them.

'Back to here?'

'Back to Cawnpore.'

'But what can Nana Sahib have to do in Cawnpore?'

The anguish on Mungo's face should have told me all. I should have faced the truth on my own but I had to make him complicit. I had to make him spell out the detail of his master's treachery.

'They intend to drive the British from Cawnpore.'

Still I pretended to myself that we were not utterly betrayed. 'The British will be happy enough to leave. Men have been trying to get their families out for months but the countryside has been too dangerous. With the Nana Sahib giving safe passage, they'll be off like a shot and glad to see the last of the place.'

'John ...' There were tears welling in his eyes. 'There will be no safe passage. They will attack the fort. They intend to destroy the British.'

At the sight of his tears, for the first time I allowed myself to try to comprehend the horror that awaited the people I knew.

'Damn it, Mungo. There's women and children in there.'

He said nothing, and his silence, more than his words, forced me to accept that this was really happening. Nana Sahib, at the head of his own troops and our disaffected regiments, was to lay siege to the miserable earthworks that demarcated the refuge of every European man, woman, and child left living in Cawnpore.

'I should go to them.'

Mungo shook his head gently, like a mother comforting a fractious child. 'It would serve no purpose.'

'But I should go there. These are my friends.'

Still Mungo shook his head. 'Are they truly your friends? Mr Hillersdon – yes, I think he is a friend to you. But the others? If they are truly your friends, then why, now, are you here with me? Here you eat with me, enjoying the food of our people.' He managed a wan smile. 'You even manage to eat your rice with hardly any lost on the floor. Why are you not eating with the Europeans, if they are your friends?'

I thought of the dinner parties I had suffered through. The frightful women I would be sat between; the endless, pointless prattling about London fashion, London Society, and London theatres. I had never lived in London and I would sit almost silent, wondering what I was doing there. Mungo had scored a fair point.

'And you speak of Mr Hillersdon often and with affection. But of whom else do you speak?'

I closed my eyes and saw Simkin leering at me with his suggestion that we spend an evening with the Anglo-

Indian women he had offered me. I saw the sun-reddened faces of the men at the Club, peering out from behind their London papers, complaining that their servants had been slow to come at their call, or had not checked the girth strap on their mount (God forbid that they should check it themselves), or had had the temerity to fall ill. Not everyone was like that, of course. General Wheeler was a decent man, but he was of a different generation and a different class and, though I admired him, he was not a friend. And the engineers up to plan the new railway were good sorts, but they tended to keep to themselves, there being enough of them to form their own society.

'You speak our language, you know our gods. I know you prayed to Ganesh the other day. I saw the bundle of joss sticks and recognised the knot.'

I shook my head but the gesture lacked conviction. Mungo smiled; a sad smile that made him look suddenly older. He pulled me toward him. 'Here is where you belong, John. Here with me.'

He held me. I felt his heart beating in his chest and I felt not aroused, but safe. He was right. I was where I belonged.

For the next day or two, I was able to convince myself that I should stay in Bithur with Mungo. However, by Sunday news was filtering back to Bithur of what the Europeans in Cawnpore were undergoing. Nana Sahib had decided not to sit and starve them out of their refuge but, rather, to destroy the Entrenchment and all within it. The mutineers had taken with them some of their artillery and, added to the Nana's own small field guns, he now had the firepower to bombard Wheeler's position day and night.

I thought of Hillersdon. I remembered Lydia, always trying to keep cheerful in the terrible heat of the barrack block, and the children, and their efforts to behave as their parents would wish them. How were they coping, sharing that one small room with four or five other families, with no respite from the noise and the dust? How were Charles and Lydia explaining the cannonade to the children? Did the barracks offer any shelter from the artillery or were they exposed to the enemy's fire?

I fretted all afternoon, desperate for information. By nightfall I could not sleep.

'I shouldn't be here, Mungo.'

'We've talked of this. In any case, Wheeler's fort is surrounded. You could not enter even if you wished, and if you entered you would surely not leave alive.'

'I need to know. I have to know if they are alive or dead. I have to see if there is anything that I can do to help them.'

'There is nothing.'

He spoke so calmly. I couldn't contain my own emotion any longer.

'I have to know! I have to go there. I have to know!'

I did not realise that I was shouting in English until I saw Mungo's calm expression give way to alarm. He wrapped his arms tightly round me. 'Hush! People will hear. Calm yourself.'

He tried to kiss me, but I pushed him away. I was quieter now, for the foolishness of my outburst was apparent even in my excited state. Even as I tried to calm myself, though, I was still determined on leaving.

'John! Don't be a fool. You can achieve nothing now but tomorrow I will see if there is anything I can do.'

As suddenly as it had started, my outburst finished. I found myself weeping, clinging to Mungo for comfort.

'Can you really help me?'

He stroked my hair. 'Yes,' he said. 'Yes, I think I can.'

Mungo's plan, when he revealed it the next morning, was as simple as it was audacious. I was to dress in my sowar's uniform and simply ride out to the Entrenchment and see it

115

for myself.

'You must be careful. If anyone challenges you, tell them that you have a message for Rao Sahib. He is not there; he is still here in Bithur. If anyone tells you this, say that you were told he was at Cawnpore but that if he is not, then you must ride immediately to Bithur. I do not think anyone will be sure where Rao Sahib is, though. So you may ride wherever you wish, to deliver this message.' He handed me a parchment, folded, addressed and sealed with an impressive amount of red wax. 'See. You even have the message.'

I smiled, despite myself. 'What does it say?'

'It asks him to dine with me tomorrow night. In the unlikely event that it is ever delivered, I will have to order in something exceptional.' He laughed. It was a feeble jest but I joined his laughter. It was the first time I had laughed in too long.

Within the hour I was swaggering to the stables in my uniform. Kuching seemed pleased to see me, for I had not ridden out on him since the crisis had been upon us. The grooms had looked after him splendidly, but he was fretting from his days of inactivity. As soon as I mounted, he was as anxious as I to be off on the road.

We started at an easy trot for I wanted to get as far as I could before the heat of the day made the journey intolerable. I soon realised, though, that the journey would take longer than in the past. Instead of just the odd farmer taking food to sell at market or a party of priests making their way to the Ganges, I passed people every few hundred yards and I was constantly forced to slow as I pushed my way through the traffic. There were cavalrymen like myself, carrying messages out or bringing word back, some with despatch cases strapped to their saddles. Some wore the same uniform as me, others sported the insignia of the Company's troops. There were soldiers, most in ones and twos, but every mile or so I would pass a group of ten or twenty marching in step, as smart as any I had seen drilling in Cawnpore. There were civilians too, rudely armed with whatever they had to hand – here a sword, there a scythe, and a few with old muskets that I would not trust not to explode in my face like the pipe muskets of Borneo. I saw the look on their faces and recognised it from my time with Brooke, for it was the look I saw on the faces of the Dyaks who had joined with us to destroy the pirates. These were the faces of men who were taking up whatever weapons they could find to drive an enemy from their land.

I had never realised before how much the British were hated.

I did not reach town until late in the morning. There were fewer travellers now, for the heat was driving people to seek shelter. As I rode down the road that separated the European quarter from the buildings of the native city I found myself alone. On my left were the offices and bungalows which, but a week before, had been the beating heart of a thriving community. Now, what a melancholy aspect these buildings presented. They stood silent in the noontide heat, an almost palpable air of desolation the more pronounced because here and there a swinging door or a broken shutter evidenced their rapid abandonment or the first signs of looting.

Moving South, there were more obvious signs that a mob had ravaged through these properties. Papers lay scattered outside opened doorways, the shutters on a dry goods store had been wrenched off and the interior, naked to the street, was in terrible disarray. From one or two windows, wisps of smoke betrayed the damage caused by carelessness or arson.

Now the eerie silence of the Quarter was broken by the distant crash of cannon fire. I had slowed to a walk but now I kicked Kuching on and, defying the heat, we trotted down to the military cantonment.

The stillness and emptiness of the European Quarter had been disturbing enough, but the sight that now met my eyes was one of horror. Smoke billowed from every side of the Entrenchment where cannon blasted in ragged volleys. I had to slow my horse to push through the throng of armed men who filled the road toward the cantonment. The bungalows of the officers were but ruins from which smoke still rose but the new barracks – still not yet completed – stood as they had been when I last saw them, forming a line of buildings to the South of the Entrenchment. They were the closest structures to Wheeler's position and the sight of rebel troops moving in and out of them suggested that they were being used as cover from which to fire into the British camp.

I headed my horse in that direction. Mungo had been right to suspect that I would not be challenged, for the scene was full of men walking here and there with no apparent order or direction. At first I thought this presaged well for the British force, as their opponents clearly lacked discipline, but then I saw a rifleman rise to stand on the half-finished roof of one of the barrack blocks. He stood completely exposed, fired down into the Entrenchment, shooting over its pathetic little wall of mud and then, still exposed, calmly reloaded his weapon. I realised then that the lack of order was not a sign of weakness but came from the rebels' perception of their strength. They were treating the siege as a high holiday with the option of firing into Wheeler's position much as we might shoot at fowl on a hunting party – except that it would be considered unsporting to shoot fowl that could make no attempt to fly and escape the guns.

As I rode nearer, a sepoy reached for my bridle and urged me to dismount. 'The British will not spend their shot on a man on foot,' he warned me, 'but they might fire at your horse.' I offered him a few annas if he would hold my mount while I went forward and he was happy to do so. 'Though you will not be able to kill them with your sabre,' he grinned. 'You will have to wait your turn. Now is the time for the infantry.'

I forced a smile, promising myself that if I should ever see the man alone in Bithur, I would kill him.

I made my way across the open ground toward the unfinished barracks. For the first minute or two I had to steel myself to walk normally, as the multitude of other troops in the area seemed to be doing. I could not believe that at any minute there would not come the crack of a bullet to bear me away from this world. Yet the sepoy had been right. The only real danger seemed to be from the rebels' own artillery passing over our heads toward the enclosure beyond.

I decided not to walk to the furthest barrack but to move away from the line taken by the other troops and cut straight to the nearest building. As I tried to do so, urgent voices shouted to me in warning. 'Away from there!' There was mocking laughter from the sepoys who liked nothing better than to see a cavalryman shown up on the field. 'The British are in there.'

Improbable as it seemed, I thought it best to take them at their word and to stay a safe distance from the barracks in the centre of the line and to make my way to the most Southerly of the structures which, coincidentally, were the furthest from completion. Arriving there I was greeted by a crowd of sepoys who, it seemed, were waiting their turn to climb onto the roof for the honour of putting a ball or two into the enemy position before giving way to the next man. There was much laughter and good-natured joshing, much of it aimed at me and the fact that I carried no musket. It was difficult to believe that these men were at war and engaged in the distinctly unamusing business of shooting into a crowd consisting in large part of women and children.

One man offered to lend me his gun so that I could join

119

in the fun. Disguising my feelings of revulsion, I accepted his offer with a hearty smile. Not only was I anxious to do nothing to cause suspicion, but accepting the gun gave me reason to mount the roof and look down on the Entrenchment to see the state of things within – and though I would fire the wretched thing, I could take care not to hit anyone. So, after waiting a while for my turn and entertaining my fellows with tales of the British I had ridden down and killed on the road, I clambered up a rickety ladder and emerged on the roof beams.

The half-finished building had offered shade at this, the hottest time of day. Now I emerged into the blazing sunlight and the heat struck me as if I had stepped into an oven. Coming from the shadows of the interior and suddenly emerging into the full light of day, I was dazzled for a moment and had to screw my eyes up against the sun before I could see anything.

The roof itself had hardly been started when the coolies had been ordered to abandon it to dig the defences that I now looked down on. From my precarious perch I had an excellent view of Wheeler's arrangements. The first thing I noticed was that a line of upturned carts and barrels now stretched from the fort to the barrack building I had been warned away from. In daylight, this would provide entirely inadequate cover, but I could see that at night a picket could move into or out of the Entrenchment, enabling Wheeler to maintain a sort of forward post. It was bad enough that I could sit on the perch where I now found myself but if the whole row were to be controlled by the rebels, it would bring their lines to within two hundred yards of the Entrenchment. Yet the defence of that barrack block must depend on just a handful of men, isolated from the main force. I could well see why they saved their ammunition to guard against a frontal attack and must perforce put up with rebel sniping.

The thought of sniping recalled to me the purpose for

which, in the eyes of all those waiting below, I was up here. I raised my gun and made pretence of taking careful aim. This gave me every opportunity to look into the Entrenchment and what a miserable sight it was. The open space was littered with the wreckage of the shelters that people had made for themselves when they first arrived. Now no one ventured into this open ground. Here and there lay a body that showed what would happen to anyone foolish enough to try. Men, some in uniform, some civilians, but all armed, lay pressed to the earth, trying to shelter behind the rampart. But the miserable height of the defences meant that they were pathetically exposed and some already lay so still that I was sure they would never move again.

Driven from the open ground by musket fire, the women and children had sought shelter in the two barrack blocks but, as I had seen when I spent my nights there, these were not nearly large enough to hold the mass of people trying to force their way into them. People crowded into the verandas, which offered some shelter from the sun but no protection from musket fire.

There was a constant jostling among the pathetic crowd as they sought to move away from the sides of the barracks which were exposed to my position, which was the only high point within musket range. But the women could not protect themselves from the artillery that boomed from every side of the compound. As I watched, the sound of a cannon came from the East and gunpowder smoke rose from the direction of St John's church. There was a crash as the ball struck home and a panicked rush of children from the cover afforded by the nearer barrack block showed where the round must have landed. A young woman braved the open ground to call the children back. I could not make out her features. Perhaps I had dined with her a few weeks ago. I may have seen her at the bandstand, calling her little ones not to stray too far from their picnic.

What a desperate contrast was the scene before me! The woman, arms waving frantically, her mouth open in a scream I fancied I could hear above the gunfire. The children paused and turned and then scurried back toward the shelter of the building.

I fired my musket, taking care that my shot should fall well short but as I did so I heard another cannon sound. This time the shot came from behind me and the round struck the earth parapet, taking a chunk from the top of its already inadequate height. Slowing, it bounced across the open ground, falling just short of the barracks. To my amazement, I saw two troopers run into the open to seize the ball and carry it back toward the rampart.

I remembered that the Nana's forces at the Treasury had been based next to the Magazine so the rebels had been ideally placed to seize all the ammunition they could desire while Wheeler's men had only that which they had carried with them to the Entrenchment. And now they were reduced to salvaging the rounds that were fired at them to return against the enemy.

There were shouts now from below me that I had had my turn and others were waiting. Reluctantly, I started back down the ladder, pausing as another crash from the rear presaged a cloud of dust and plaster from the nearer barrack block as it was struck.

The sepoy grinned as I returned his gun. 'Were you successful?'

'Truly I was. A woman ran from cover to save her child and I shot her.' Remembering just in time that he would be able to see the bodies lying there, I added, 'She dragged herself back behind the barracks but I think her wound is mortal.'

The fellow clapped me on the shoulders. 'A fair attempt for a sowar.'

So it was that I was congratulated for the heroic business of killing a defenceless woman! And I had to smile and conceal my contempt.

I made my way back to where I had left my horse, careful to maintain the easy swagger that sowars affected though I wanted to stop and weep at what I had seen.

I found the sepoy and gave him a few more annas. He didn't expect to be paid twice but I had handed him the money without thought. Indeed, I seemed incapable of doing anything that involved mental effort. I did not even mount, just took Kuching by the reins and followed the milling throng.

The drift of the crowd carried me vaguely Southward to where I had heard the cannon behind me. Now it sounded again. I saw the smoke rise and heard the whoosh of the ball in flight. I imagined it crashing into the feeble buildings that were all that offered shelter to the wretches trapped behind those mud walls.

Ahead of me, something over a mile away, a small hill rose from the plain. I remembered it as an empty spot. There was a rather grand house built there, but it had fallen into disrepair and the place was now just used by the military to store unwanted equipment. Looking up at the hill now, though, it seemed a centre of activity. From where I was, I could not see the house, but I could make out some tents of gold and red fabric. These were by far the most distinctive structures on this side of the Entrenchment so, in the absence of any better plan, I made my way toward them.

The nearer I got to this encampment, the more splendid it appeared and, remembering that Nana Sahib had had a tent erected for his stay at the Treasury, I guessed that this must be his headquarters for the siege. I hesitated as to whether to approach it more closely, fearing that my disguise might be more carefully examined as I drew nearer the seat of power. Then I reminded myself that I had never been questioned, even as I roamed his palace. I was simply allowing the horrors of the battlefield to rattle my nerves. I would not skulk home to hide with Mungo.

I turned to pet my horse, stroking him, ostensibly to calm him but, in fact, as much to calm myself. Then, drawing myself up and trying to radiate the confident arrogance of a cavalryman, I carried on toward the tents.

The Peshwa (as he was now calling himself) had chosen the site well. It was far enough away for there to be no danger at all of being hit by a stray shot, yet its height above the Entrenchment allowed the Nana and his generals an excellent view of the action. Judging from the number of soldiers gathered around, he was keeping a substantial personal guard near at hand, though I imagine they may also have served as reserves, ready to throw into the battle if needed. Given the one-sided nature of the conflict, though, the reserves were unlikely to be called for. With nothing to occupy them, groups of armed men lounged around or squatted beside cooking fires. I noticed, though, that for all the apparent lack of order, piquets had been mounted and the soldiers on guard seemed attentive and alert.

I decided not to try to pass the piquets. I could see enough from where I was and there seemed no point in risking a challenge from the sentries. I mounted my horse, for a man seated on a horse looks as if he has a purpose in life while the same man standing beside the horse looks like a loiterer. From the saddle I looked down over the field. Cannon boomed at irregular intervals from all sides. Inside the Entrenchment there would be puffs of dust from the ground or from the walls of the barracks as the balls landed. From time to time a man would leave cover to make off with a cannon ball that could be recovered for the garrison's use or a child would dash from shelter pursued by a desperate mother. Once I saw a woman fall and her child turn to her as if willing her to rise again. There was another distant crack as a musket fired from the roof of the abandoned barracks where I had lately stood and the child dropped beside its mother.

I could watch no more and turned my attention to the tents. There was no sign of the Nana, though a regular coming and going of officers in smart uniforms of red or French grey, adorned with sashes and braid, confirmed that the tents were the centre of the Nana's command.

As the day grew hotter, I bypassed the guards on the tents and made my way around to the old Savada House (for such had the mansion been called in the days of its glory). In the strip of shade on the North of the building an elephant stood tethered by the leg, its presence confirming that Nana Sahib was still presiding over his troops.

At a safe distance from the royal transport, soldiers were also seeking shelter from the sun. It being time for tiffin, most were cooking. Only half an hour earlier I had felt sick to my stomach at the sights I was seeing, but suddenly the smell of spiced meats reminded me that I was hungry. The body knows its needs and will soon assert them. And would my going hungry achieve anything for those poor souls on the plain below?

I dismounted by one group of sepoys and sniffed appreciatively. Once I might have thought of their meal simply as 'curry' but my time with Mungo had taught me better and I was able to distinguish the scents of chilli and paprika, coriander and bay leaves, all mingling with the aroma of the lamb that simmered in their pot. There was even a sprinkling of saffron, suggesting that they had been busy looting in the town, as saffron was hardly a regular ingredient in a soldier's dish.

I had chosen to greet a group of mutineers, as I felt more secure from questioning than if I had approached men who, like me, wore the uniform of the Nana. I did wonder if there might be some awkwardness on account of our different loyalties but I was welcomed immediately as a comrade.

'You like the smell of our tiffin, eh?'

The speaker was a big man, with a thick moustache that curled down the sides of his mouth. He had abandoned his uniform trousers for the loose folds of a dhoti, leaving his legs bare below the knee.

I grinned at him without thinking, the simple response of anyone offered food and companionship by a fellow. And when I stopped to remember that it was a rebel who spoke to me, still the gesture seemed right. However much I hated the mass of Nana's soldiery as mutineers and rebels, I could not reconcile this hatred with my feelings toward the individuals making up that army. I had eaten alongside the Nana's soldiers in Saturday House. The man offering to share his meal now was probably a distant cousin of someone who had paused to salaam me when I was dressed as a scribe in Bithur. Perhaps he had tossed alms into my dish when I was disguised as a beggar. Besides, if I were to hate the Nana's soldiers, should I not hate his courtiers more? And was not Mungo kin to Nana Sahib and served him at Saturday House?

He pushed a tin dish toward me. 'You'll have to share my bowl.'

I smiled and bowed my thanks. Last week, serving the British, he was an ally. Tomorrow, I might have the chance to stop him from shooting a woman or a child and I would kill him as my enemy. But for now, he was a man offering to break bread with me and I would treat him as a friend.

One of the sepoys was crouched over a cauldron that bubbled gently above a small fire. He was apparently the cook for the group and now he ladled the stew into bowls and slapped unleavened bread onto a plate. My host tore a piece off and scooped food from the bowl between us. I followed his example and, for a few minutes, we concentrated on eating.

'Ahhh!' He gave a contented belch. 'So what brings one of the Peshwa's sowars to mess with the common soldiery?'

'I'm just a messenger,' I said. 'I have a letter for Rao Sahib but no one can direct me to him.'

'Don't they know over there?' He gestured in the direction of the tents.

'He's not there. I think he may be back at Bithur.'

'It's possible.' He paused and turned his attention to the food for a while. 'There's people coming and going all the time.'

'But the Nana remains here.'

'Oh, yes!' He grinned. 'Old Nana Sahib stays here. He's changed sides often enough. We want to know he's on our side now.'

So Mungo had been right all along. Nana Sahib had been playing a waiting game, holding back until he was confident he knew which side of this conflict was going to come out on top. Looking down on the Entrenchment and the mass of men and artillery that surrounded it, I had to admit that he seemed to have chosen well.

The sepoy followed the direction of my gaze. 'I'll say this for the British. They're stubborn and they're brave. We should have overrun that place in an hour but they're still there.'

'Why don't you just rush them? That wall won't hold you back.'

He grinned. 'And you sowars can lead the charge, eh? Get all the glory while we have to do the dirty fighting in their camp?' Now the grin faded. 'A charge will not be so easy. They have artillery and they lay their fire well. You do not see them fire because they are conserving their ammunition. But if a body of men were to rush at the fort,' (and I noticed he used the word quite seriously) 'then you would see them cut down with ball and canister. And the men you see lying waiting behind the walls – they took all the muskets they could find. Each man has two or three or four beside him, so they can fire again and again. Their women come from shelter and reload for them. I had never thought to see a memsahib do such a thing but they do and it means the men can fire repeatedly while we are in the open and can fire only once.' He shook his head. 'No, a charge will not be easy.'

We returned to our food. Between scoops of spiced lamb, we looked out over the battle.

One-sided as it was, it was true that the rebel forces were not moving forward. Though the artillery kept up its bombardment and the snipers took their toll, it seemed to me that destroying Wheeler's position by attrition was likely to be a drawn-out affair.

'Are you planning to starve them out?'

He shrugged. 'I think they have enough food. And there is water.' He pointed to the one exposed well I had noticed when I was with Hillersdon in the barracks. 'They have to show themselves to draw it, though. Then we can shoot them. But they generally use the well only at night now. Still, we can hear the windlass creak, so we can fire at them even in the darkness.'

I thought again of the conditions inside the barracks. Out at Saturday House there was not the same obsession with the exact temperature that pervaded European life and I had not seen a thermometer for days, but I judged that it must be well over a hundred degrees. Here, on raised ground, the whisper of a breeze made the day just about bearable. But in the barracks below us, crammed together with the windows shuttered against the detritus thrown up by the shelling and the constant risk from musket fire, there the heat must be excruciating. The women and children now sheltered there were used to spending their days in elegant rooms cooled by pankah fans with freshly watered tattis to protect them from hot air through the windows. How terrible must they be finding their new habitation. And with every drop of water bought at immediate risk of death at the exposed well, there would be none for the luxury of bathing – even if the conditions allowed for the possibility of a bath. There would be hardly enough to satisfy the basic requirement for life. They must be continually thirsty, especially the children.

'Do you feel no pity for them?'

The sepoy shrugged. 'I am sad that they must suffer so. But I never asked them to come to my land. I never asked that they should seize Oudh from its rightful ruler. My family have lived in Oudh for more generations than I can count. And now the British come and say it is theirs. It was never theirs. We are just taking back what was always ours.'

'And the women? And the children?'

He shrugged again. 'It is a war. These things cannot be helped.'

We were both silent for a while after that. At one point, between the noise of the cannon, I thought I had the cry of a child carried on the breeze, but we must have been a mile from the barracks and it was probably my imagination.

When I spoke again, it was to ask about his family and his home in Oudh. He had a wife there, he said, and five children. 'Three sons. One day they will be warriors like their father.'

'And whom will they serve?'

He paused then, picking at some meat that was stuck in his teeth.

'The Peshwa now leads a mighty army. He is a Hindoo but the Musalmans follow him. The old King in Delhi may call himself Emperor but he is weak. The Peshwa is young and strong and full of cunning. I think the Peshwa will be a great lord in India and I will serve in his army.'

Our bowls were empty and I felt it was time to be moving on. I smiled my thanks. 'Perhaps one day we will be comrades in the Peshwa's army and I will be able to return your hospitality.'

'Perhaps.' As I prepared to mount, he rose to his feet

and clasped me to him as one comrade to another. I clasped him in return and then, with repeated assurances of mutual respect and affection, I was in the saddle and walking Kuching back the way I had come.

The sun had passed its zenith and the hottest part of the day was coming to its end. I passed slowly through the crowds of soldiers. There seemed no proper cordon round the Entrenchment but such was the number of those assembled to attack it that I could see little prospect of anyone smuggling themselves out. I supposed that I might make my way in by working my way along the abandoned barracks until I came to the pickets who kept vigil in the building that was linked to the Entrenchment by the line of carts. But once within, what could I do? I would be one more mouth to feed, one more person for whom water would have to be drawn from the well under the pitiless rebel fire.

Everything I had seen suggested that the situation was very different by night than by day. During the day, the rebels were unwilling to show themselves on open ground because they feared the fire of the enemy. But after dark, the Europeans' advantage of accuracy in fire would be negated. On the other hand, at night the Europeans would have freedom to manoeuvre around the Entrenchment in a way that was impossible when they were under targeted fire during the day.

I considered the possibility of waiting until nightfall to observe how things turned out under these very different conditions but I decided against it. By nightfall, I would be exhausted and I had promised to return to Mungo who, I knew, would not rest until I was safe home.

So I made my way slowly back to the town. It was still infernally hot and I walked Kuching easily to spare both the horse and myself. We ambled up the Course and I remembered the mornings I had ridden here for exercise in the cool of the early hours. I had been in Cawnpore less than eighteen months, but my memories of those early days seemed like a dream now. Was it only a year ago that Company men had walked this land like the emissaries of the gods, the servants of the greatest power India had ever seen? And now they and their army cowered behind a mud wall and their homes and offices were abandoned to the mob.

As I approached the neat bungalows of the Civil Station, I decided that I should make my way through them to the river. It might be some time before my horse had another chance to drink and I felt I would benefit from the opportunity to cool myself in the water, even if I did not trust it for human consumption.

Here, walking past the tidy gardens and listening to the screeching of the swifts darting under their eaves, I was more than ever struck by the changes that so short a time had wrought. There was Mr Hart's place where I had dined just a few weeks ago; there was that couple with the sweet little girl with the big black dog. I wondered what had happened to the dog now. Somehow, it was easier to worry about the dog than the girl.

We arrived on at the edge of the river. At this time of year, toward the end of the dry season, the Ganges here was very low and I had to lead the horse carefully down a flight of steps (which the Indians call a ghat) to get to the level of the water. Even then, there was an expanse of muddy shallows between us and the river proper, but at least there was enough for Kuching and, taking care not to get mud on my white britches, I was at least able to cool my face in water scooped from the ground.

The height of the banks here gave some shelter from the sun and the water passing by seemed to have some cooling effect, so I rested there awhile before carefully walking my horse back up the steps, his hooves slipping once or twice on the worn stone.

Back among the bungalows of the deserted colony, I

mounted and, kicking Kuching to a trot, I set off along the road to Bithur. In the distance, I still heard the sound of cannon fire but I did not look back.

I will not dwell on my dispute with Mungo the next morning. I had told him that I intended to return to Cawnpore in the evening so that I could see how matters fared in the hours of darkness. He called me a fool and said that I loved those in the Entrenchment more than I loved him and that I would die and that I deserved death and a hundred other things I know he did not truly mean. He was cruel but, I think, in the end I was the crueller, for I would not be shaken from my purpose. Late in the afternoon, having rested as well as I could in the face of Mungo's fury, I prepared to set out again.

I was still in the guise of a sowar for this had served me well so far but I knew that if I were to approach closer to the Entrenchment it would have to be on foot. My tulwar with its long, curved blade was an ideal weapon for fighting on horseback but not well suited to combat on foot. When Mungo saw that I was determined to go, he vanished from our quarters. I waited almost an hour for him to return and was about to depart, leaving just a note to assure him that I would come back safely, when he rushed in through the door carrying a pistol and a bayonet in its scabbard.

'Tuck them in your belt. If you must risk your life, at least these will give you a chance in a fight.'

There were tears in his eyes as he spoke. I put them in my belt, as he suggested and, saying nothing, I held him and kissed him. He kissed me back and then pushed me from him.

'Go, if you must,' he said.

I went.

With all the movement between Bithur and Cawnpore, the stables were a constant bustle of activity, but the men there knew their jobs and my horse was ready for me.

The road was even busier than the day before. More people were moving in the cool of the evening, either returning to their homes in Bithur or, like me, hurrying to join the army at Cawnpore. At one point, I was greeted by a group of sowars, who were heading to their barracks for the night, and who urged me to turn back with them. 'There'll be no cavalry attacks tonight.'

'I've despatches for the Peshwa,' I told them and they waved as I passed.

The native town of Cawnpore was alive with movement and excitement, while the European quarter was even more desolate by night than during the day. No lights showed. All was silence.

I hurried past both, made my way down the Course, and then swung off the road toward the abandoned barracks. If I were to have any communication with the Entrenchment's defenders, the piquet they maintained in the middle barrack had to be the safest course. This outpost, well beyond the defences of the Entrenchment, was their most forward position. The British maintained their outpost in the centre of the row of unfinished barracks while the rebels controlled the buildings at either end.

It was full dark by now. The only light came from the fires of countless groups of soldiers spread across the plain around Wheeler's position, cooking evening meals or just keeping a fire against the fears that even brave men might feel in the darkness. The figures I passed now were no more than grey shapes and it took me a while before I found one who would tend my horse. I had no fear that he might steal it, for a poor Indian with a horse would be detected immediately and dragged before the Nana in the hope of reward – but I was concerned that I might be unable to find him again in the dark. I left him near one of the fires and, taking my bearings on two of the rebel artillery positions, which still kept up a desultory fire, I trusted that I would be able to retrace my steps to this point.

I moved forward, as near as I could tell along the path I had taken the previous day.

'Hush, you fool!'

The voice came out of the darkness on my left and hands pulled me off the path and down toward the ground. There, huddling in the darkness, were twenty or so sepoys.

'What are you doing here?' I could barely see the fellow's face but the voice was urgent.

'I'm sick of you infantry having all the fun. I came to lend a hand.'

Light caught on his teeth, grinning whitely in the shadows. 'Do you have a musket?'

'I have a pistol.'

'Then you are welcome to join us. Now you will see some real soldiering. Move quietly!'

There was a stirring in the darkness and the men around me rose and moved, crouching to the shelter of the nearest of the barracks.

'Have a care. We don't know exactly where they are.'

The building we had arrived at, though roofed, lacked doors and windows and we were able to climb inside with only the odd scuffling to reveal our presence.

The barracks were laid out with rooms leading off from either side of a central corridor. In the darkness, we slipped from one doorway to another, moving forward a room at a time, uncertain whether the enemy had sent out patrols which might be moving along the building from the other end. Our caution, though, was unnecessary. The British had not pushed out so far from the building they controlled and this barrack block was empty.

We gathered in the room at the far end and waited in silence.

In the distance, I heard the creaking of a windlass and

suddenly cannon fire opened up from all the rebel positions and the crack of musketry came from the barracks ahead of us. I remembered what I had been told about the attempts of those trapped in the hell of the Entrenchment to draw water by night and how the creak of the windlass would betray them. I thought of a man crouched at the well while shot and shell ripped through the darkness around him.

There was a moment's pause in the firing and then I heard it still: the steady creaking as he stayed at his post, drawing up the water that was life itself to all in that dreadful place.

'Move when the firing starts again.'

The bombardment resumed and we were out of the barracks and running to enter the next, some by the door, some by the windows.

There was a confusion of sound against the gunfire from outside. Someone shouted a challenge.

'Just fire, you fool!'

The voice was in English and a moment later came a shot, echoing off the bare walls of the unfinished building.

'Corridor's clear.'

The central corridor was, indeed, empty. At the first sound of voices, we had dived for the rooms that led from it on either side. Around me, I felt, rather than saw, half a dozen black bodies tense.

Booted feet moved cautiously toward us. In the room across the corridor, I heard the slap of a sandaled tread on the ground. In the dark, I was suddenly aware of how different was the sound of European footsteps to that of the natives. My own boots would sound as heavy as any of the Entrenchment's defenders, but would be all too easily distinguished by the jingling of my spurs. I cursed myself for not removing them but I could not do so now without making more noise than if I just stood still.

'No one in here.'

Then they were in the next room. Some of our party were waiting silently and as soon as the searchers entered, they were on them. There was the sound of shots and then the clash of swords. Around me, men made for the door in the darkness, desperately pushing at one another as they ran toward the sound of combat.

I followed.

As soon as I passed into the corridor, all was confusion. There was even less light there than in the room we had taken shelter in, for the corridor had no windows. Though my eyes were already grown used to the gloom, I saw nothing but shadows. In the darkness, men had abandoned their swords for there was as much danger of cutting a friend as an enemy. Instead, they came in close, using all their senses to identify their foes.

I found myself struggling with one man whose lithe body suggested he was Indian. I kicked toward his legs and, as he sought to regain his footing, I heard the slap of his sandal. I knew then he was one of those with whom I had entered the building and who would have thought me a comrade. But now, fighting with Wheeler's men, the men I had come to help, I must see him as my enemy. My bayonet was already drawn and in the darkness I stabbed toward his gut, twisting as I withdrew it.

In the chaos, no one saw me.

Again, I heard the sound of sandals and another figure brushed past me. I seized his arm. 'Wait!' I whispered the word in Hindustanee. He alone heard me; he paused. My bayonet swept across his neck.

An English voice shouted, 'Ready!'

An instant before the light flared, I had realised what was to happen and I was already diving for the patch of grey that was a doorway. As I did, light burst forth from a shaded lantern, now uncovered. Three men, two kneeling and one standing between them, blocked the corridor, muskets levelled toward the Indians. As soon as the light allowed them to distinguish their targets, all three fired and two black bodies fell to the ground. The rebels now raised their muskets in their turn but already the lantern was shaded. Two or three shots sounded but there were no cries from where the British had been standing so I presumed that, in the darkness, they had missed.

I strained to hear any sounds in the room where I now found myself. The noise of deadly combat continued to dominate outside but in here all seemed quiet. I moved, as silently as my spurs would allow me, back toward the door.

Before I could reach it, I heard boots run down the corridor and into the room. I heard him stop and I imagined him listening, as I listened, peering intently into the darkness to see if he could make me out.

I concentrated on his breathing and, guided by the sound, I could just see his pale face in the shadows. I was still, taking care to breathe softly, and my face was stained, so I had the advantage of him. I could have killed him easily but I had come to help, not to destroy. My problem was how to convey this to him before he struck me down.

Slowly, taking care to make no sound, I crouched down on the ground. Only then did I say, as quietly as I could while taking care my every word was heard, 'I am a friend. Stay calm.'

His first response, as I had expected, was to strike blindly in the direction my voice indicated I was standing. The blow struck the wall above where I was crouching. I leapt up and grabbed his arm. 'I'm a friend!'

This time the words reached him through the fear and the desire to kill.

'You're British!'

'Yes – but keep quiet. I came in with them and they must not know.'

Even as I spoke, there were more shots, screams and the sound of running feet.

'I don't think you have to worry about them.' The languid voice reminded me of a world that, in little more than a week, had come to seem impossibly remote. 'I think you'd better meet Captain Moore.'

Outside the room, lanterns now provided a steady light and I had my first sight of the men who had cleared the rebels from the building.

Their appearance was a terrible contrast to their voices. While their accents remained those of English gentlemen, the wretched figures I saw before me were scarcely recognisable as those of my compatriots. Their uniforms were filthy and torn. All showed signs of some injury or other, blood staining their tunics and filthy scraps of bandages showing through rents in trouser legs and sleeves. Their faces showed the strain of days and nights spent under constant bombardment. Above all, they stank; as men without access to water for washing and inadequate facilities for the necessities of the toilette will stink after days baking in the Indian sun.

The tallest of the group, his badges of rank barely visible through the filth and blood, glanced over at me and spoke to the man at my side. 'Don't waste time, Kirkby. Just kill the bugger.'

'Beg pardon, sir. He's not a prisoner. He's one of us.'

The captain turned and stared at me. 'Don't be a fool, Kirkby. The man's a nigger.' He held the lantern toward my face to make the point and I took the opportunity to speak.

'Captain Moore, I take it.'

Moore's eyes, incongruously light blue in the filth of his face, widened in surprise.

'I have that honour, sir. And who the hell are you?'

'I'm the Deputy Collector.'

For a moment, he looked nonplussed and then, without questioning me further he simply grinned, put out his hand to me and said, 'Well, Mr Deputy Collector, you must have a tale to tell.'

'And one I am to tell quickly.' I sketched out the circumstances that had allowed me to escape the Entrenchment and hide among the rebels, skipping over the details and explaining simply that I had disguised myself and penetrated the enemy camp.

'I can enter these buildings at night and bring anything that I can conceal about my person. What do you have most need of?'

'Food is always welcome. Most of our diet now is gram.' He wrinkled his nose in distaste – gram, or ground chickpea flour, was the basic food of the poor but featured only sparingly on European menus. 'I fear you can't carry enough food in your pockets to make any difference. Bandages might make more sense.' He gestured at the fabric visible through a bloodied hole on his sleeve. 'We've been reduced to tearing up petticoats, as you can see. I fear the ladies are in rags.' There was a rattle of musket fire against the wall and the lights were doused. 'Look here.' In the darkness, the Irish lilt in his voice was somehow more obvious. 'What we really need is intelligence. News in and news out. Try to get word to Lucknow that we're in a jam. We can't hold out much longer. I've lost count of the dead and there's precious little we can do for the wounded. We've basic rations but nothing to cook with and that damn well is so exposed that we never dare draw as much water as we should. And we need to know what the rebels have planned.'

'That last is easy enough,' I said. 'They will just stay round and about until they've killed you all. There's no organisation to speak of but they outnumber you by hundreds to one and they are in no hurry.'

'They're not worried that we'll be relieved?'

'From where? The countryside has risen. Nana Sahib is calling himself the Peshwa. The King of Delhi is calling himself the Emperor. Every princeling in India will be

Lord of this or that by now and they all want the British out.'

Mr Kirkby was looking cautiously round the edge of the window and now urged that they pull back to the central block. 'I'm not sure but that I can't see movement out there, sir.'

'Two minutes, Kirkby, if you please. You may fire from the window if you are concerned.'

I felt, rather than saw, Captain Moore turn his attention back to me as Kirkby fired out into the darkness. 'Look, Williamson, things seem pretty dark. First thing is to get word to Lucknow. Second is to see if there's any way we can get safe passage out for the women and children. The men can hold out for as long as it takes, but this is no place for families. Find out what the rebels plan and let us know. Write it down and leave it in the room we are in now. If you can, bring in bandages and any medicines – iodine would be especially welcomed. Food if you can bring it safely.'

Kirkby fired again and was joined by two of the others.

'Time to go, I think,' said Moore. 'Good luck!'

There was the sound of running in the darkness and they were gone. I waited a few minutes and then made my way back the way I had come, slipping quietly through the doorway and, bending low, across the open ground back to what passed for the rebel lines.

I had worried that my solitary return might lead to awkward questions but I need not have been concerned. In the darkness and the excitement, I had not been aware of my own appearance but, back in the company of the mutineers, I saw myself by the light of their torches. My uniform was covered in blood, which I was quick to assure them was that of our British foes and I was treated as a hero for my endeavours.

I had an unpleasant quarter of an hour while I struggled to find my horse, for all the care I had taken in marking the spot but, once I had done so, I was safe away back to Bithur.

As I rode, the horror of the night's events returned to me and I swayed uneasily in my saddle. Fortunately my horse was steady and, by then, knew the route to take so I arrived back at Saturday House without mishap. The sentries, bleary eyed as they were, still noticed the blood upon my clothing and saluted sharply but otherwise my return excited no attention.

Two hours before dawn, I was back in Mungo's rooms to find him trying to read by the light of an oil lamp.

'I couldn't sleep.'

'Am I forgiven, then?'

He said nothing but opened his arms and held me, bloody clothes and all.

I had thought that the hardest part of the tasks that Captain Moore had set me would be to get a message through to Lucknow. Surely, I thought, the roads would be sealed and, in any case, with the populace hunting down and killing any Europeans that they found, who would be foolish enough to attempt to carry a message on behalf of the hated foreigners. To my astonishment, when I explained my problem to Mungo, he said that he would be able to arrange this with no difficulty at all.

'There are messages being sent to Lucknow all the time,' he assured me. 'Every foreigner who has gone to ground anywhere within a hundred miles is desperate to get word to Lucknow. And every Indian who ever served them and who sees no possibility of employment in the future is desperate to take their money to see these messages delivered.'

'I'm sure they take money but do they really see the messages delivered?'

Mungo shrugged. 'There are thieves everywhere. I'm sure you have some in England too. But remember that though people say they hate the British that does not mean that they hate each and every person from that country. I'm not too fond of the British myself but I would do anything to save you.'

All that remained was for Mungo to find a messenger, which was but the work of an hour or two. Following his instructions, I spent the time that he was away in writing a concise account of the situation of Cawnpore and transcribing this in letters a small as I could manage onto a thin sheet of paper which was rolled into a tiny cylinder to be secreted in the clothing of our courier.

That afternoon the message was on its way and Moore's first commission was completed.

Finding out what Nana Sahib's plans were proved more difficult. The chaos in the rebel ranks meant that all Mungo's attempts to discover their intentions were producing nothing. When my frustration led me to complain that he was not exerting himself enough, he pointed out that I had actually fought in the rebel army and I still had no idea what their strategy was.

The confusion was in part, I think, because the Nana lacked good generals, but was also an inevitable consequence of the nature of the rebel force. Although all the troops besieging Cawnpore owed nominal allegiance to Nana Sahib, it was less a single army than a ragtag coalition. There were mutineers, the Nana's own troops, local Musalman troops, and local Hindoo troops – the last two being almost as likely to attack each other as the British. Added to this confusion of loyalties were thugs with no loyalty at all. One of the first acts of the rebels had been to open the jails and the rogues that were released saw the opportunity for good pickings in the confusion of war. There were few rich merchants who did not have some connection to the British and many was the household broken into and looted for no better reason than that they were rich and had once done business with an

Englishman.

The one thing that was completely clear was that the rebels intended to show no mercy to any foreigner who fell into their hands. In the days immediately following the mutiny there was regular news of Europeans who had been away from Cawnpore when the trouble broke out being rounded up here and there throughout the area. These were not soldiers but businessmen, engineers, or, like myself, Company servants. The storm took the lowest and the highest. Even the Eurasian clerks were liable to be dragged from their homes and killed while the matriarch of the Greenways survived as a prisoner with her immediate family. 'They have promised a ransom of 10,000 lacs,' Mungo told me, awed at the vast sum that was to buy their lives. 'But I am not sure it will save the men.'

For those without the wealth of the Greenway family bank behind them, the end was at least quick. They were taken to Savada House and led before Nana Sahib. In almost every case, the women were imprisoned but the men were executed on the spot.

I seized on the fact that most of the women had not been killed. 'If he spares the women, then perhaps he might let them leave the Entrenchment.'

'I don't think so, John His father's widows still live here at Saturday House and they are a power in our land.' He gave a wry grin. 'I think that Nana Sahib would as soon that they were not. He was adopted, remember. His father's widows have no reason to love him. And it is the widows who have insisted that he spare the women he has captured. He gives them their way on this because there are few women prisoners and it is easier not to cross the widows. But I do not think he will want to have scores of these women. What will he do with them?'

'He could offer them safe passage.'

'To where? All India is aflame.'

'When last I heard, Lucknow was safe.'

'After Cawnpore, Lucknow will be next.'

Mungo saw the look of horror on my face. 'John, it is known. It is decided. I cannot pretend to you that this will not happen. The Peshwa has cast the dice and now he is committed to fight. War will continue until all the British are forced out of India. Already there is an Emperor at Delhi. Here, the Peshwa will extend his power and Oudh will acknowledge him as their liberator. The old kingdoms will rise again and all will be as it was.'

'So my people have to die so that Nana Sahib can show that blood can be spilled as easily in Cawnpore as in Delhi?'

For the first time, I saw Mungo angry, his chocolate skin darkening with emotion.

'Your people? Are these truly your people? And, if they are, can you dare to complain that they are driven from this land by force of arms? Did the Peshwa choose to live in Bithur or was he dispossessed by British armies? Did the Emperor resign his power voluntarily to live half-mad in Delhi under your guard? Or did you seize his lands from him?'

With a visible effort, he calmed himself. 'I know you, John. I know you are better than that. In Borneo, you ruled with the love of the people and they accepted you because they knew you cared for them. And here you have tried to understand our ways and to see our people fairly treated. It is not by chance that you are here and not trapped with the men of General Wheeler.'

'And the women? And the children?'

Mungo shrugged. 'It is sad. Truly, it is sad. And I will help you pack food and medicine to relieve their suffering as much as I can, though I know it is very little. But this is India. There are countless women and children trying to scratch a living in this country. And every day, thousands of them die. When you confiscate lands, do you make sure that all the pensioners of those you have dispossessed are provided for? When you build your roads and your barracks and your grand buildings, do you worry that the land you are taking may have supported a household? When the Europeans of Cawnpore dismissed a servant who had not pleased them, did they concern themselves with how the man's family was to live? For a hundred years, the British have ruled in India and Indian lives have been held cheap. Now, we take back what is ours. Should we hesitate because the innocent may suffer alongside the guilty?'

Now it was my turn to shrug, for what words could I say?

Chapter Six

The next afternoon, I was again on the road to Cawnpore. Mungo and I had spent the morning thinking what were the most useful things I could carry with me. I would not be able to take any sort of bag into the barracks for a sowar carried his kit upon his horse and any pack would excite curiosity. Nor did my uniform have any pockets. There was a small leather pouch on the belt and iodine went in that. Otherwise, all that I carried had to be concealed beneath my tunic.

We slung two bags, such as sepoys might carry, across my shoulders, sewing the straps short so that they lay across my chest. Not much could be placed in them without my chest taking on a swell that might remind a literary observer too much of Falstaff. So chapattis and slices of dried meat that could lie flat against my body made up the bulk of my supplies. Bandages, such as a medical orderly would have about him, were not easily come by in Bithur but we cut cotton into strips and wrapped it around my waist.

I spent an hour trying to compose a letter to Captain Moore. Telling him that I had sent news to Lucknow was the easy part, though even there I felt I had to caution him that other messages had probably got through and had no effect. Then, though, I had to admit that I could offer no intelligence as to the rebels' plans beyond their intention to maintain the siege until all were destroyed and that the women and children could expect no mercy.

I drafted and redrafted my note until, at last, I told the simple truth and, with a heavy heart, I placed it in one of the canvas bags, alongside the pitiful provisions we had assembled there.

The cotton and the canvas against my skin meant that the journey to Cawnpore was even more unpleasant than usual and I was covered in sweat when I arrived back at the siege. Little had changed, though the number of vultures that glided in lazy circles over the field of battle had increased. From time to time one would brave the firing to drop to earth and feed on the remains that lay around the Entrenchment's defences. I recognised some of these pathetic remnants as horses but other shapes were smaller and I took care not to look too carefully at what they might be.

The Nana's cannon had been joined by two new pairs of mortars and the weight of artillery now being brought to bear was such that the crash of firing echoed across the plain every few seconds. Even the brief interludes of quiet were interrupted by the crack of muskets as snipers kept up their fire into the compound. Most of the Indian troops, though, just lounged in such shade as they could find, waiting for the defenders to die without the necessity to engage them in open fight.

I joined the loungers, grateful for a chance to rest and allow my body to cool. We talked idly of our homes or the women who waited there or the possibility of a good supper. I noticed that people did not talk of the siege or of the Entrenchment, as if these things had already become simply part of the background to their lives. As the darkness drew in, though, these men drifted away and a few others gathered – quieter fellows with a grim look about their faces. One or two looked at the bayonet which I again wore tucked into my belt and they nodded quietly, recognising that there could be one reason only why I should carry such a weapon.

The oldest man there, wearing the uniform of a havildar in the Company's army, was recognised by the sepoys around him as their natural leader and he set out our objectives for the night for all as if he was still fighting for the Company and briefing his men there.

'Tonight we shall move forward together until we make contact with the enemy and then defend our position. We do not try to drive them out. We will hold our position until daylight. If we are still in the barracks when the light comes, then we will be able to overrun them. They are few and in the daylight we can defeat them.'

His thinking was sound. Captain Moore and his men had succeeded by being better organised in the dark. They shot a disciplined volley when the lantern was uncovered and moved to new positions while the native force was divided and confused. The havildar might well lead his men to success. The implications of this could be disastrous, for if the British were driven from their outpost in theses barracks, the rebels would command a line of buildings where they could muster men for an attack less than a hundred yards from Wheeler's defences.

The havildar's strategy was also a direct threat to my own plans for the night. I was relying on separation and confusion to allow me to take off my jacket and leave the supplies I was carrying safely in some dark corner to be found once the attackers had withdrawn.

Fortunately, I had an excuse to separate myself from their plan.

'I fear, comrade, that I cannot remain all the night in the barracks, for I have not stabled my horse but have him in the charge of some ragamuffin I am paying two annas to guard him until my return. But I am happy to scout ahead of you. When I encounter the enemy, you will know that you must prepare to defend your position. Then I shall withdraw, leaving you the glory of the field.'

There were mutterings of appreciation at this, for the idea of one of the Nana Sahib's own cavalrymen leading an action on foot was seen as most gallant. My desire to withdraw after the fighting was done for the night was thought of as just another aspect of my heroic nature. The only problem with the plan, from my point of view, was that it involved my being in the forefront of the attack when I had good cause to know the deadly efficacy of the British fire.

I had little time to dwell on my predicament, for the dusk is short in India, and with full dark we started across the open space toward the barracks.

Our adventure at first followed the pattern of the previous night, though this time I had the forethought to remove my spurs. We crawled through the darkness, slipped into the first building, and made our cautious way along its length. The havildar's strategy meant that the force moved as one group, slipping silently from doorway to doorway, invisible in the dark but their breath warm upon my neck as I kept my promise to take my position at the front.

Again, we waited for the noise of firing before we slipped from the first barracks to the second. The group moved forward as a single unit, silently slipping into the first two rooms, either side of the central corridor.

We paused for a moment and then I felt a gentle push from the havildar. I stepped cautiously through the door and started up the corridor. After I had gone a few paces without challenge, I felt the stirring of the air and heard the barely perceptible sound of footsteps following me.

I moved forward in the darkness, step by careful step. My fingers felt along the wall for the next doorway. Surely we must have reached it by now? I seemed to have been walking forever.

Now I felt the door and slipped inside. Half of the rebels followed, half entered the doorway opposite.

Again, a brief pause and then I was out and moving again. This time, the rebels were slower to follow and I was almost at the next doorway before I sensed them behind me. Obviously they, like me, feared that we were moving ever closer to the British and that at any moment we would come under fire. Not yet, though – we had gained the third doorway.

Now we paused a little longer, but, all too soon, I was once more in the corridor.

Something ahead of me moved. I felt a whisper of a breeze and threw myself to the floor at the very instant that the corridor filled with the thunderous crash of musket fire. Behind me, I heard a single cry. Had the rebels all been following me, I would have heard more. Almost all, I guessed, were still in the rooms, leaving me exposed alone in the corridor.

Already I was scrambling to my feet, throwing myself forward to the shelter of the next doorway. I could not see it but I knew it must be there.

There was a sudden light as, just as they had done before, the British opened their dark lantern and those who had not fired in that first volley took their aim. But the light showed me the doorway and I threw myself through it as the musket balls flew past.

The lantern was closed and it was dark once again. I heard the booted feet in the corridor.

'There was one ran in there.'

I flattened myself against the wall but stayed as far as I could from the door, which I could just make out as a fractionally blacker rectangle in the darkness. There was the sound of boots and there was the slightest deepening of the shadow of the doorway.

My ears told me that two men had entered the room and now stood in the centre. My guess was that if I remained silent the next step would be for someone to enter with the lantern. I decided not to wait for that.

I spoke as softly as I could. 'I'm British. Get Captain Moore. And clash your swords together so it sounds as if you're fighting me.' As I spoke, I was already pulling off my jacket and pulling the canvas bags over my head.

Fortunately, my two unseen compatriots were quick on the uptake. They clashed swords most convincingly while shouting for their captain and a light. The rebels hiding in the next room in the corridor would have every reason to think that I was putting up a desperate struggle.

Moore came in at a run, accompanied by a man in civilian clothes who carried a musket in one hand and the lantern in the other.

By now the bags, my letter and the iodine were on the floor and I was unwrapping the bandage as fast as I could.

'Captain, don't speak. You can scream if you want.'

Moore looked at his men, still striking each other's swords with vigour and immediately understood the situation. He gave a bloodcurdling yell.

'They're all in the next room and the one across from there. Pull a couple of your men back with a lot of noise and the rest wait here. I'll lead them to you.'

Moore gestured the two men who were still enthusiastically clashing sword on sword. One broke off and ran into the corridor followed by the other.

Their screams and yells moved into the distance while the rest of Moore's men assembled around their captain. The lantern was closed and they remained in darkness while I made my way back into the corridor, yelling imprecations in Hindoo.

'Cowardly dogs! Come back and fight, you scum!'

For a moment, I thought that the rebels were not to be fooled but then I heard them leaving the rooms behind me to start down the corridor. They moved without caution, confident that I had cleared the way ahead and that the British had fled.

As they passed the room where Captain Moore and his men waited, the British fired into their flank and followed this up with a furious charge. Shocked and confused in the darkness, the rebels never had a chance. In a few minutes, it was all over and Captain Moore's outpost was safe for another night.

I had sheltered in another room, anxious not to be caught up in a battle where I could easily have ended up killed by either side, but now the lantern was lit again and I presented myself to Moore. My pathetic gifts were enthusiastically accepted, though my summary of the contents of the letter was received sombrely. I asked how things lay in the Entrenchment and their grim looks told me more than they were prepared to say in words.

'We pray for relief from Lucknow, but your intelligence suggests our prayers will not be answered.'

'I fear not, but the situation changes daily. Lucknow may yet come to your aid.'

'Then we will stand and fight until all hope is gone. But you must stay safe. Don't come here again unless you have intelligence we can use. Every time you come is fraught with danger and you may yet have something to tell us that could make a difference. Stay safe, John Williamson, and watch for news that may aid us in our plight.'

'And if I ever do, how will I get it to you?'

'I'm sure you'll find a way.' He grinned. 'You're very resourceful.'

I took his hand and shook it. 'Then I must be off.'

'Not just yet '

I was puzzled. The longer I stayed with them, the more chance of being discovered as a spy.

'All the others are dead and you are unmarked.'

He was right of course, and his solution to the problem was right as well, but I could wish that his men had not been so damnably enthusiastic about it. Still, I was convincingly bloody as I recovered my horse and started yet again on the road to Bithur.

I had planned to spend the next day – the 12th – resting, but word came to Saturday House that there was to be an

153

assault on the Entrenchment that evening. I could think of no way to warn the defenders in time but I reasoned that they would be able to see the preparations for the full-scale assault that was planned. I decided, though, that I should once again journey to Cawnpore to see how the Nana's ramshackle army behaved when ordered into action.

In the event, I had to admit they acquitted themselves rather well. They dug a trench from a drainage ditch that passed by the opposite side of the Entrenchment from the empty barracks and used this to enable themselves to advance under cover. At the same time, other rebels moved forward on the blind side of the unfinished barracks. Every ruined wall was used for shelter as some five thousand rebels closed from all directions on Wheeler's two hundred men.

The Nana's artillery now set up a concerted firing, such as I had not seen them do before and which I would have thought beyond their organisation. Alas, it was all too clear that it was not. For almost two hours the bombardment continued. It was as if some infernal thunderstorm was rolling across the plain with musket bullets sounding like hail between the claps of the artillery.

Artillery and infantry were both being thrown against Wheeler's defences, such as they were. The cavalry, though, was being held back so I rode to the promontory where I could observe the efforts of the defenders.

Looking down into Wheeler's position, I was struck again by how inadequate these defences appeared. Men lay in depressions scratched into the ground, offering no real protection against the mass of shot that fell into the compound so thickly that it was visible even from where I now stood.

For the first time I saw Wheeler's artillery in action. There were no proper breastworks to protect the gun crews and the pathetic wall of dried earth that the soldiers sheltered behind offered no protection at all when they stood to fire their field pieces. There were fewer than a dozen guns in the compound and every time a crew rose to their feet to load and aim, the intensity of musket fire increased. Again and again I saw men fall at their posts to be pushed roughly aside as others crawled to take their places, the air above them thick with lead.

The defenders' cannon did not fire that often, but, when they did, the skill and training of their European crews showed in the accuracy of their shots. While most of the Indian fire was wasted, often falling short and sometimes overshooting the compound altogether, the Europeans were deadly accurate. When a group of rebels found a strong position from which to fire, it was only a matter of minutes before canister shot would drop around them. I saw black bodies shredded as the canisters burst, spraying metal in all directions. Sometimes the screams could even be heard over the racket of the firing.

The musketry of the defenders was also impressive. There were few rifled weapons in the garrison and the secret of success with musketry is not accuracy but rate of fire. Each of the figures lying behind the earth bank had several muskets beside him and fired each in turn. From where I sat I saw women, their dresses torn and filthy, crawl across the open ground to take the empty muskets and bring reloaded ones. Some loaded lying beside their men: a difficult exercise when it was impossible to kneel to drop in the ball or wad down the charge for the rebels were quick to fire at any exposed person of either sex.

I thought of the silly chattering wives I had known, and could hardly believe that these same women now lay in the dust alongside their men, doing what they could to hold off the enemy's advance.

Every minute I expected to see the Nana's forces rise from cover and charge forward, overwhelming the Entrenchment by sheer weight of numbers. Yet they never did. Now and then one rebel, braver than the rest, would rise to his feet, gesticulating to his comrades to follow him, but every time he would be cut down by musket or artillery and his fellows would once more sink to cover to consider the danger of exposing themselves to European fire.

As darkness fell, I was sure that the natives would use the cover of night to accomplish by stealth what they had so signally failed to achieve by open assault. Yet this was not to be the case. The coming of night seemed to quell their spirits and the firing fell away. Wheeler's tiny force had survived an organised attack by the full might of Nana Sahib's infantry. I left that night wondering, for the first time, if the garrison could, against all the odds, survive the siege.

What can I say of the days that followed? I spent much of my time with Mungo, who listened assiduously for every scrap of gossip he could gather. His efforts yielded rumours aplenty. Nana Sahib was to march to Delhi to take the throne of the Emperor; the British had sent an army from London but the fleet it was travelling in had been intercepted by the Turks and utterly destroyed; a group of Musalmans had killed a cow and roasted it in the rebel lines. There was, it turned out, some truth in this last story. For a few hours, it seemed possible that the Hindoos might turn on the followers of the Prophet and the Nana's army might have disintegrated in an orgy of fratricide, but the Nana restrained his co-religionists and passions were calmed.

The welter of confusion and lies, contradictory report after contradictory report, moved us no further forward. I did my best to add to the confusion. When I was seized by the arm by some inhabitant of Saturday House anxious for news from the battle, I would purse my lips and say that the troops feared to approach too close to the enemy because they believed the area to have been mined. Or I would say that I had smelt the odour of roasting flesh from the defenders and I feared that they had more provisions than we had believed.

In such petty ways I did what little I could to undermine the morale of the rebels, but when I rode to Cawnpore, day after day I saw the same sad spectacle with only minor alterations. The barracks where Captain Moore maintained his piquet sprouted a strange construction on the roof – a sort of crow's nest where a man could sit concealed from hostile fire but himself shoot out at anyone approaching the building. These efforts made an assault across the open ground that much harder and reduced the amount of sniping from the other buildings but the rebels continued to fire sporadically into the compound. The rebel artillery, too, kept up a steady bombardment, despite desperate sallies by night that had seen some of the nearer guns spiked. It seemed now that every time that I climbed that accursed promontory, there were more corpses lying exposed in the Entrenchment and the vultures had taken to landing at the centre of the camp, pecking at the flesh of the dead until a weary hand heaved a stone in their direction and they flapped ungainly away.

I did wonder why the open ground was not piled with the European dead but a rebel sepoy explained to me that at night the bodies were dragged to a well outside the Entrenchment and deposited there.

'We hear them doing it,' he said, 'and sometimes we fire toward the sound but ...' He shrugged. It seemed that even in this ugly battle, there were limits to what most of the sepoys were prepared to do.

For all the casualties inflicted by the rebels' fire, the most deadly enemy of the Europeans was the heat. It was the hottest time of the year. Every day we waited for the weather to break but the monsoon rains held off. Even the natives began to feel the effect of the heat. After my years in the tropics, I was as inured to its effects as anyone, but by midday, the least exertion was intolereable. Even a short walk involved an enormous effort and the idea of undertaking any strenuous activity was impossible. I would sit sweating in the shade, remembering stories I had heard of men struck down by heatstroke; fit and healthy at breakfast and dead by noon. The natives were as helpless as I in the hottest hours of the day. Even to load and fire a gun taxed their strength and there was always an easing of the amount of fire at noon, which must have offered some relief to Wheeler's men. It might have gone some way to make that time of day just bearable, for the tortured souls in the Entrenchment had no relief from the sun beating down on the hideously over-crowded barracks that were the only shelter remaining.

Wheeler's promise that the well would provide enough water to sustain life seemed to be being kept. By now, the brickwork at the top of the well had been completely destroyed by the artillery that rained upon it whenever a creaking in the night betrayed the unfortunate at the windlass. The sepoys told me, though, that they would still hear the rattling of a bucket against the bricks of the shaft as the garrison was supplied with the liquid it needed to stay alive. With every drop drawn at terrible risk to the men at the wellhead, there would be none to spare for bathing or to splash on hot children. No dampened towels might cool the fevered brows of ladies used to sitting in the airy shade of their drawing rooms while a pankah wallah worked to keep a cooling breeze. Here the air was disturbed only as cannon shot tore through the walls of the buildings, bringing terror and death to all those huddled within. I saw those shots smash into the old barracks and, remembering the families packed in there when I had shared their shelter less than three weeks before, I saw in my mind's eye the trail of blood and entrails that would follow the ball as it carved its way through the interior.

The kitchen block still stood but by now there could be

little left to cook in it. The desperate state of the garrison's supplies was reflected in the way they opened fire at any sowar within range, even if he posed no threat to the Entrenchment. Short as they were of ammunition, they would always try to hit a horse. The sepoys warned me of the danger. 'If they can kill it, then when it is dark, they will sneak out to cut off the flesh for food.'

'I can't just stay here and do nothing.'

Mungo sat cross-legged on the floor while I paced around the room. He didn't speak.

'Say something, for God's sake.'

He shrugged. He had a very eloquent shrug.

'They're dying there.'

'We're all dying, John.'

'I should do something.'

'You cannot help them.'

'If I could save just one person … If I saved just one, I would feel that I had not been entirely useless.'

Mungo rose to his feet in a single graceful movement.

'Not everyone made it into the fort.'

He was right, of course. Europeans had been rounded up here and there and either killed on the spot or hauled off to the Nana and killed there, except for a few of the women who had been spared to appease the old Peshwa's widows and one or two men it was rumoured were being held for ransom.

Mungo stood in front of me and held me by the arms, stopping my pacing. 'John, you can do nothing for those trapped with General Wheeler. But you might, perhaps, save some of your compatriots who are hiding in the country.'

Mungo's suggestion showed how well he had come to know me. Riding the countryside searching for fugitives would give me an outlet for the nervous energy that was eating me up. And he was right – I had more chance of saving lives out in the open country than in Cawnpore, surrounded by Nana Sahib's army.

I started that very afternoon, making a wide circuit North and West of Bithur. The country was, by and large, open fields, but there were occasional stands of woods and ditches where a man might hide. I was handicapped by my appearance. I had to wear the Nana's uniform to guarantee myself free passage but I knew that any Europeans who saw me approach would take care to conceal themselves. So I had to search as thoroughly as if I were truly an enemy come to destroy them.

That day, and for days to come, I pushed my horse through the woody groves, branches scratching at my face and tearing my clothes. I dismounted to clamber into dusty ditches that proved empty as far as the eye could see. I demanded peremptorily of villagers if they had seen any ome, as the foreign devils were called. Each day, though, I returned to Bithur hot, tired, and covered with the grime of a long ride but without having found any Europeans. I did come across evidence that there were refugees surviving somehow in that hostile country. A villager, anxious to please, denounced a fellow as having sheltered a family a few days previously but further enquiry revealed that they had left the district and no one knew where they might be now.

A ruffian walking along the road was carrying a pocket watch, clearly stolen. At first, he denied it but I drew my sword and made to strike him with it and he admitted he had found a man hiding in a ditch and he had robbed him.

'But he wept and pleaded that I should spare his life, saying he was a merchant and had never cheated the Indians he had traded with, so I left him.' He paused to spit. 'It was no matter. He had no food and no water. He will be dead by now.'

I had him tell me where he had found the man and I rode there and searched but I saw no sign of him.

Once, beside a shrine, I saw the ground disturbed with a new grave. Dogs had scratched at the turned earth and part of a red coat showed through. No native would have been buried thus, so I knew I had found one of those I was searching for but too late, too late.

About a week after I had started my quest, I was riding in the later part of the morning across open land where ditches separated the poor fields. The heat was near insufferable. I had just turned toward a cluster of huts some mile away, where I planned to rest in the shade, when a movement drew my eye to the ditch ahead of me.

Heaped in the red dust was what I first took to be a pile of clothing but, as I drew near, I saw it to be the huddled body of a man. He had scraped a hollow at the bottom of the ditch and sought to shelter from the sun with his jacket draped over the shallow declivity.

When I first saw him, he was lying motionless, as if hoping to avoid detection but, as I approached, he must have realised that he would be seen and he started to scrabble desperately along the ditch. I called to him in English and, at last, he stopped and turned to me. From his look of terror, I think he stopped only because he recognised the futility of his attempts to escape, rather than because he was reassured by my words.

The ragged remains of his clothes showed that he had once been a man of substance but now, it seemed to me, he was scarcely a man at all. His shirt and trousers were torn and filthy. His features were burnt by the sun and his hair a wild tangle. I dismounted and walked slowly toward him, holding out my water bottle. Judging from his cracked lips, he must have been desperate for drink and I think that is all that made him face me.

While he drank, I explained that I was English and was there to help him. I had chapattis and dried figs in my saddlebag and he seized these ravenously.

'You are safe now,' I said. 'I will protect you.'

He made no reply, as if unwilling to draw breath for explanations until he had eaten and drunk all that I could offer him. Even then, he said little and much of what he did say made no sense. As far as I could tell, he had been a week on the run with scarce anything to eat and drinking foul water in any place that he could find it.

'They spill it from the wells when they water the cattle in the evenings and it may lie puddled until dark,' he said. 'And once I stayed two nights beside a river but there were people and it was not safe.'

I learned his name was Mr Ashley and he had been a telegraph engineer. He spoke of a woman but whether this was his wife, lost in India, or some English sweetheart, I could not ascertain. It seemed that the heat, the hunger, the thirst, and the constant fear had addled his brain.

I was so thrilled that I had at last found a survivor of these outrages that it was some time before I started to worry about the practicalities of helping him. It was possible, I knew, that a combination of threats and bribery might buy him shelter in the village to which I had been heading. However, this was far from certain and I was reluctant to reveal myself by riding in with him under my protection until I had sounded out the disposition of the inhabitants. If they seemed to me unreliable, I could move the man to shelter in the woods nearer to Bithur until such a time as Mungo and I could between us make some more secure arrangement for his safety.

Looking back at it now, it seems obvious that I should have made some proper plans for how I was to deal with such a situation before starting my search. At the time, though, finding some survivors seemed so urgent a goal that I had concentrated all my thoughts on that, confident that once I had found somebody I would be able to develop a plan to succour them. Even faced with the immediate problem of providing shelter for Mr Ashley, I was confident that I could secure his safety. Convincing

Mr Ashley of this proved, though, immensely difficult. His troubled mind had seized on the notion that I was his saviour and he clung piteously to my legs begging me not to go and leave him. In vain did I assure him again and again that I left only to secure a safe place in which to shelter him and that I would return to bear him away.

At last, he seemed to understand the situation but he said that he feared to be left alone and defenceless. Could I leave the pistol he had seen holstered on my saddlebag? Armed, he thought he would be able to wait for me with some confidence.

I was reluctant to part with the weapon, especially to one whose mental state seemed so uncertain, but it did seem the easiest resolution of the situation. So I handed the pistol to Mr Ashley and, mounting, turned my horse again toward the village.

I had ridden no more than a hundred paces when, behind me, I heard the sound of a single shot. I did not hurry my return, for I already knew what I would see. There in the ditch lay the mortal remains of Mr Ashley, my pistol gripped in his fist and his brains a mess of blood and grey matter, already drying into the parched soil.

I returned to Saturday House in the blackest of desperate moods. Mungo sat cross-legged and silent while I poured out the story of my failure.

'I thought it would be all right if I saved one person. One person, Mungo. Is that so much to ask?'

At last, after I had raged and wept, he rose to his feet and kissed me. 'You are a good man, John. We will see you save one soul yet.'

As so often, he took quiet charge. 'I have a cousin who lives some ten miles North of Bithur. His name is Dara. He has high walls around his compound and no neighbours. The servants are loyal. I was going to wait until it was needed before I made any arrangements, for, though the risk is small, there is always some risk. And servants, though loyal, are more reliable when bribed. But I will put all in train now and then, when you find another lost soul, paradise shall be ready to receive him.'

He smiled with a confidence that went some way to restoring my faded spirits and, though Mr Ashley's death still weighed heavy on me, after some hours I fell into a fitful sleep. From time to time, I woke to find Mungo bent over me, soothing me with his hands and his kisses and each time the dreams that had wakened me would fade and by morning I was almost recovered.

Mungo insisted that I not ride out the next day but rest at Saturday House while he made arrangements with his cousin. I promised faithfully that I would ride nowhere and I kept the letter of my promise. Once Mungo was safely out about his business, though, I decided to use my enforced rest to resume what I fancifully thought of as my intelligence activities, though I could think of nothing I was likely to discover that might help my compatriots.

I decided that a sowar conspicuously absent from the field might be the subject of contemptuous remarks and would learn nothing of value. So, instead, I dressed myself in a beggar's rags and slipped quietly through a side entrance and into Bithur.

The village was quieter than the first time I had visited it in this disguise. The fishermen's boats were still there, bobbing on the river while the men busied themselves with lines and nets. The market, though, was almost deserted. Many of the Nana's courtiers had decamped to Cawnpore to fawn on him at his new headquarters. Merchants who could transport their produce to Cawnpore had followed, leaving the street I remembered as being so busy with a faintly desolate air.

I walked about, occasionally knocking my staff against the bowl. After an hour, though, it was still almost empty. The mob might feast on the plunder of Europeans and

Anglo-Indians in Cawnpore, but little of that wealth found its way to the villagers of Bithur. Even the porters and idlers who used to swagger the streets or lean against the walls of alleyways in a vaguely menacing way – even they had gone. The owners of the shop-houses, trapped in Bithur by their properties, and the fishermen, whose families had lived beside the Ganges for generations – these were the only people left in the village.

A merchant beckoned me to the shady interior of his shop and cast a handful of rice into my bowl.

'I'd give you more, but times are hard.'

'I thank you for any gift and I grieve that you are finding the times troubling. But are these not good times for our people, that the white men are being driven from us?'

The merchant hesitated, stroking his chin before responding. 'It is good that the *feringees* go. But their going brings turbulence and when the river is troubled, a boat may be broken.'

'So do you feel it were better that these present troubles had not started?'

'Oh, no!' His eyebrows – bushy for an Indian – climbed his forehead as he expressed his indignation at the idea. 'I only wish the Europeans had been driven out years ago. Once they are gone, life will be good again.'

'Then it is good that they are being driven from Cawnpore.'

'Ha! I doubt they are being driven out. Rather I hear that they will stay for eternity in the town.' Then he grinned. '*Sub lal hoga.*'

Everything is to become red.

I smiled as best I could, thanked him for his gift, and turned away.

The next day, Mungo having made the necessary arrangements with his cousin, I once again started my search for survivors. It seemed, though, that the luck that I had thought changed with my discovery of Mr Ashley had once again turned and I found no one.

By now it was the middle of June and rumours began to spread that there would be an assault on the Entrenchment on the anniversary of the Battle of Plassey, fulfilling the prophecy that (at least as far as Cawnpore was concerned), the British would be driven out on the hundredth anniversary of their first great victory in India.

Any news of a new attack was, of course, important, but this assault was to be especially significant for me as the story was that the cavalry was to be deployed in force for the first time. I had tried to avoid over-much contact with other sowars, as I feared that any true cavalryman would soon spot me for the impostor that I was. However, I had used the disguise so regularly that by now I was a familiar face about Saturday House and I feared it would be noticed if I was absent from such a significant event.

Although I had always been a reasonable horseman, I rode in a style that reflected the rough riding of my childhood on an English farm. I was not sure that I could hold my own with the cavalry-drilled sowars of Nana Sahib's guard. And even if my basic horsemanship passed muster, I had no experience of riding to war. The notion of finding myself in a cavalry charge was utterly terrifying.

Much of the time that I would have liked to have been out looking for refugees was spent in earnest debate with Mungo. His first response to the news was that I should discard my sowar disguise and stay safe at home in his apartment. I turned this idea down flat. I had adopted the uniform because it was the safest way to allow free passage in Bithur, Cawnpore, and all the countryside around. Without it, I could do nothing but skulk behind Mungo's protection until, somehow, the horror of the mutiny was ended or, as I sometimes feared might be the case, I grew old in hiding.

The only alternative to ignominious retreat seemed to be to learn enough of the cavalryman's art to pass myself off not only to the uninitiated, but to the Nana's sowars themselves. It took a full day of argument before Mungo accepted that I could not live with myself were I to give up now. As ever, though, once he had been convinced that I was in earnest, he did everything in his power to aid me. It turned out that another of his invaluable cousins had himself ridden as a cavalryman in the service of a local lord whose little kingdom had long ago been swallowed by the British.

'The skills he learned will be similar enough to the Nana's men.' If Mungo was convinced that my idea was insanely dangerous, he had at least decided not to let me see how terrified he was on my behalf. 'And you are going to have to tell people you have transferred here from elsewhere. You can hardly turn up claiming to be an old servant of the Nana when none of the sowars here will ever have seen you in their lives before.'

'I think that there may be difficulties in my just "turning up", whatever my story.'

Mungo grinned. 'Sometimes I forget how English you are, John. This is India, and an India at war. There are no regimental rolls and movement orders. The word goes out and soldiers come. As it happens ...' (by now Mungo's grin threatened to split his chin from his face) 'one Mahmet Mazullah fell from his horse last week and there is some doubt as to whether or not he will recover. If you study hard with my cousin, you should be ready to replace him when his service ends.'

'"Mahmet Mazullah". A Musalman?'

'Why not?'

'Serving Nana Sahib?'

'Serving the Peshwa. Fighting in India for freedom from foreign conquerors.'

By now, it should have come as no surprise. The

horrors of Cawnpore, the bloated bodies floating in the Ganges, the remains that jackals dug from shallow graves – all these things confirmed the hatred that the populace felt for the foreigners in their midst. Yet it still shocked me that Musalman and Hindoo would put aside their traditional enmity and fight alongside each other to destroy the Christians.

'I had best start studying with your cousin as soon as may be.'

The anniversary of Plassey was now less than a week away and I feared that I could not hope to gain the skills I needed in the few days available to me. I need not have worried. Soon after dawn the next day, Mungo introduced me to his cousin on an empty plain a few miles West of Bithur, remote from any road and away from prying eyes. Amjad (for that was his name) was a wiry man but, though I still found it difficult to judge the age of Indians, I thought him too senescent to be in any shape to teach me. As soon as he mounted the skinny little pony he had brought to our meeting, I realised my mistake. The man was a magnificent rider, relaxed yet secure in the saddle as he galloped his mount in what seemed impossibly tight circles.

After a few minutes, he reined back and cantered toward a lance he had left upright in the red earth. Without pausing, he plucked it from the ground and wheeled again. As the pony turned, the lance was already couched under his arm. He kicked once and galloped straight toward us. My horse shied as Amjad raced just inches past my face and lowered the lance to the ground. A moment later, he raised it. There on the point, was a tent peg he had hammered into the ground before our arrival.

Twice more he turned at the gallop and the lance dipped to the earth and each time he raised it with another peg speared on the tip.

He trotted over to me and passed over the lance.

'You try.'

Thinking this a joke, I laughed, but Amjad's scowl showed that he was serious. I looked to where he had speared up the pegs and saw another three forming a neat line alongside them.

I tucked the lance under my arm. It was surprisingly light. I turned my horse but, before I could start toward the pegs, Amjad was shouting at me with a string of criticisms. I didn't hold the lance properly; I had failed to adjust my weight to take account of the new balance point I would need as it dipped; my left hand was loose on the reins. There seemed a hundred other things but these were all I could remember.

I sat on Kuching, feeling more and more ridiculous as he poked and prodded me into what he thought was a satisfactory position. Finally, I was allowed to kick in my heels and start toward the tent pegs.

I had taken barely half a dozen paces before I was subjected to another torrent of complaints. I had shifted my weight again as soon as I had moved, my kick was wrong, the horse didn't understand me, I had allowed my body to slump, I had pulled too sharply on the reins, I had taken my eyes off the pegs …

On my third attempt, I got as far as a canter before the abuse started; on my fourth I almost reached the pegs. By now, Mungo was struggling to keep a straight face. I, blushing furiously under the tan which was now almost as effective a disguise as my walnut stain, tried to hold onto my temper. I was, after all, no mean horseman. I had grown up with the beasts and, if I had not ridden during my sea-faring years, I had more than made up for my lack of practice during my time in India. Yet I had to admit that I did not have the smallest part of the skill of the old man now offering a devastating critique of every aspect of my riding. Even so, I doubted that his comments would be truly useful. Surely his skill was that of a native, born to his way of life. How could a morning spent subjecting myself to being treated like a child at a riding school make any difference to my own abilities? As the day grew hotter, I found, to my astonishment, that I could catch the tent pegs on my lance, if not at a gallop, then at a respectable canter. And my newfound ability to turn my horse back on itself without slowing impressed Mungo to the point where he caught himself clapping, despite Amjad's scowls.

Before noon, we had to stop. The heat had reached the point where neither man nor horse should be in the full sun, and we walked our beasts slowly toward a grove some half mile away, where we sheltered under the trees and Mungo made us a picnic of cold rice with curried fowl, and mangoes and figs for a fine dessert.

Amjad enjoyed his food though, like many older men, he ate sparingly. I took advantage of the break to question him about drills. He was undoubtedly improving my horsemanship but I was still no clearer as to how the Nana's cavalry drilled. Having watched the Company's cavalry on parade, moving seamlessly from 'advance by column' to 'advance in line', responding, as if by magic, to the sounds of the bugle, I was all too aware that I had no knowledge of how to perform these manoeuvres. I was sure that as soon as anything more complicated than following the man in front was required, I would be exposed as an imposter.

Once I had got Amjad to understand my question, he laughed so much that he nearly choked on the last of his figs. Yet again, I had forgotten that the way that Indians organised their armies was totally alien to the British approach to matters military.

'Ride along with your fellows until they order a charge, then draw your sword and charge with everyone else. Your horse will know what to do if you don't.' He laughed again.

'What about the lance?'

'If they charge, you won't need the lance. It's for showing off and sticking pigs. The first man you strike with it, it will snap off. And if it doesn't, you can hardly ride around with a body dangling from your lance, can you?'

Mungo passed him water, because we both feared that he would choke if he laughed much more.

'So why have I spent the morning learning to use the lance?'

Amjad spluttered and water splashed onto the baked earth.

'Because showing off is nine-tenths of what makes a sowar. But don't worry – once the day cools, I'll show you how to use that fancy sword of yours.'

We lazed under the trees, digesting our meal until the worst of the heat was over. Then Amjad was as good as his word. We did not leave the grove but Amjad stuffed a bag with leaves and soil and hung it from a branch. Then, swinging his heavy tulwar, he rode through the trees toward the bag, which was slashed open in an instant.

'Now you try.'

My first attempt ended with my nearly falling from the horse as the weight of the sword unbalanced me. Having mastered the whole business of staying in the saddle while whirling my blade around, I twice buried it in tree trunks before I reached the sack. A few more passes rocked the bag to and fro but failed to cut it. Only as the shadows of the trees were stretching long in the afternoon did I finally manage to despatch my enemy well enough to satisfy Amjad. Even at the end, though, he had his doubts.

'Mungo tells me you don't really want to kill anyone,' he said. 'That's probably just as well.'

Chapter Seven

Mahmet Mazullah died that night and, in accordance with the custom of the Musalmans, he was buried the next day.

I had intended to introduce myself into the company of the Nana's cavalry that same day but my efforts with Amjad had left me so stiff and tired Mungo said it was better that I rest in his apartment, while he massaged the aches and pains from my body. 'Tomorrow will be soon enough,' he assured me. I was not certain that his advice was truly impartial, for he was never slow to enjoy the opportunities offered when he massaged me but, in truth, I was too tired to argue and happy enough to allow him the freedom of my body for a day. The next morning, though, I was up early to force myself into the uniform and, trying to look dashing and military, rather than just stiff and uncomfortable, I made my way to the quarters usually occupied by the cavalry.

I was nervous of introducing myself, but Mungo had been right: I just told people that I was there to replace Mahmet Mazullah and no one questioned my presence. Perhaps this was at least in part because everyone had a more pressing matter on their minds. Word had spread that, after weeks of standing by while the infantry failed to take the Entrenchment, the cavalry was now to be given their chance. On 23rd June, the hundredth anniversary of the Battle of Plassey, Nana Sahib had ordered that his sowars should ride against the British and finally drive them from Cawnpore. So it was that only four days after my lesson in the basic skills of an Indian cavalryman, I was to see action against my own people.

My first thought, on finally hearing confirmation of these plans, was that I should warn the garrison, but how could I achieve this in the days that remained? With the cavalry about to be deployed, I could hardly join a raiding party such as I had before and I could think of no other way of getting information to the British, trapped in their Entrenchment.

As ever, it was Mungo's common sense that reassured me.

'The British have calendars,' he said. He was straddling me as I lay on the floor and he rubbed oil into my calves, easing the stiffness that remained even three days from my lessons with Amjad. 'I think they'll know to be prepared on the anniversary of Plassey.'

He was right, of course. The Indians had always been predictable in attacking on anniversaries, or lucky days, a custom that the British had long understood. The 23rd June would see Wheeler's force as ready as, given their situation, they could ever be.

On the Monday morning, the Nana's cavalry was assembled together at Bithur and we rode at dawn to avoid the worst of the heat. We took the road to Cawnpore that, by now, I knew so well. I had thought that the ride would be a sombre affair, with people's minds on the battle that they would face on the morrow, but none showed any sign of fear or concern. Instead, they rode easily, talking and joking amongst each other. Several edged their horses alongside mine to greet me and welcome me to their company. They would ask where I was from and what experience I had. I answered with details of the history I had rehearsed with Mungo. I had come from Dharampur, far enough from Bithur for there to be little chance of anyone who might claim to know the place. It was in Oudh and, though I had left military life to settle with my wife on a small farm, my anger at the annexation had driven me to join the Peshwa. The story had the advantage that any mistakes in my riding could be excused as carelessness after so long away. The idea that I was an old cavalryman returned to the fray also explained why a man of my comparatively advanced years would still be riding into action.

As we rode, we came across other forces of cavalry. Some were mutineers or deserters from other places where troops had turned on their officers, others were attached to local rulers who, while less significant than Nana Sahib, still had small honour guards they had contributed to the Peshwa's campaign.

We passed through Old Cawnpore and, once in the European quarter, we made our way to the Assembly Rooms where I had met General Wheeler. Could that have been less than a year before? So much had changed. The streets here were wide thoroughfares where parasoled ladies had walked with their beaus away from the native rabble. Now, though, the street had been turned into a makeshift camp for some of the thousands who had flocked to join the Nana. Tents blocked the highway. Indians, in all sorts of uniforms and none, filled every available space. Nana Sahib was to address his men in the Assembly Rooms and everyone wanted to be there to hear their Peshwa urge them to victory on the morrow.

Over four thousand men gathered. Most could not enter the Rooms themselves but stood outside in the street, scorning the shelter of their tents and craning their necks for a glimpse of their leader. They cheered the Nana's arrival and they cheered again and again when they heard shouting from those lucky enough to have found space within the Rooms.

I sat on my horse with the rest of the cavalry, for we thought ourselves above pressing our way through the sepoys and, besides, we did not want to leave our mounts.

We stood there, in the baking sun, for the better part of an hour. At last, with a final exultant cheer, men began spilling from the Assembly Rooms. Many were still in their Native Infantry uniforms (though most had discarded the trousers for loincloths, which were more suitable to the heat.) These joined men from their regiments who had waited outside and from all directions came voices of command as troops formed up. Even my fellows sat to attention and we nudged our horses with our heels until they formed smart lines.

Now Nana Sahib emerged onto the steps of the Assembly Rooms. It was the first time that I had seen him since he established his headquarters at Savada House and I was struck by the change in his appearance. He looked much older and his face, which had been relaxed and easy to smile, was now etched with worry lines that betrayed the cares that had come with his new responsibilities. The glasses were gone and, as his glance darted from side to side to take in the thousands mustered for his inspection, I found myself wondering how much he could see or if the men in front of him were just an anonymous blur. Still, he looked quite grand with a golden sash tied around his waist and a torque of gold at his throat. The pistol and sword tucked into the sash added a martial touch, suited to his new role as army commander and when he raised his hand to acknowledge the salutes (somewhat ragged in many cases but salutes nonetheless) the cheer from his troops was loud enough to unsettle the horses.

Eventually the Nana withdrew back into the Assembly Rooms and gradually the mass of men dispersed, some marching off in tidy columns (a few still carrying the colours of their old regiments), others drifting away in small groups or ones and twos. The Bithur cavalry headed to the European villas where some servants, undecided as to the eventual outcome of the revolt, were keeping faith with their old masters to the extent of watering the patches of lawn around the houses and thus providing some basic grazing for our horses. By now it was late so, after setting small fires on the ground and cooking companionable meals, we made ourselves as comfortable as we could for what might well be our last night on this earth. Some of us settled to sleep on the ground; some commandeered the bedrooms in the bungalows. For a mad moment, I wondered about returning to my own old home to sleep there, but the danger of recognition was too great so, still somehow uncomfortable with the notion of invading my neighbours' homes, I wrapped a blanket around myself and settled for a night under the stars.

We were not to sleep for long, however. Though the cavalry was to attack in the morning on the anniversary of Plassey, the rebel infantry kept up scattered firing throughout the night to deny the enemy their rest. Of course, it denied us rest as well. I lay awake listening to the fitful musket fire – somehow more disturbing than the constant noise of artillery, which I was by now used to. I wondered whether Charles Hillersdon was listening to the same shots and whether he could sleep as he waited for the dawn. Was he even still alive? And poor, pretty Lydia – had she survived childbirth lying on the earth floor?

When I did sleep, I dreamt of them – Lydia, Charles, and the children. They came to me, emaciated and bleeding, and asked me why I had abandoned them. I told them I would see them in the morning and, in my dream, I mounted my horse and rode into the Encampment. I had my lance and I galloped at the Hillersdons and the children were on the ground next to a newborn baby and I gathered each on my lance. Amjad was standing alongside Charles Hillersdon and he turned to him and asked if he did not think I had held my seat well.

I woke before dawn, shivering, though it was warm even at that hour. My attempts at sleep had left me more tired than if I had spent the night in useful activity. I cursed myself for not having tried to make contact with the garrison – though with the attack already under way, I could think of no useful intelligence I could have added.

We roused ourselves as soon as there was light to see. The Musalmans amongst us stretched themselves out on the ground to make their morning prayers, while the Hindoos, with me among them, performed our ablutions as best we could with the water available, for the Hindoo values cleanliness of the person.

We took chapattis and dried meat from our saddlebags and ate them as we mounted. Today was not a day for a leisurely breakfast.

The cavalry was to rendezvous at the army riding school, a quarter of a mile North of the Entrenchment. It had been burned down in the early days of the Mutiny and was now little more than rubble, but it remained the last cover available before the plain where Wheeler had made his stand. I wondered if some Indian with an ironic sense of humour had chosen the building where the British had trained their riders to be the gathering place for their nemesis.

We reined our mounts. Now that the moment was come, we sat silently in our saddles. There is an abundance of life in India, which breeds, in its turn, a philosophical acceptance of death. But, faced with the immediate imminence of destruction, even the most stoic of men is liable to pause and reflect on the fate that may await him.

The Nana's batteries had fallen silent as we assembled but now they opened up all at once and the air was so thick with artillery that it seemed for a moment that the Entrenchment lay under the shadow of an unnatural cloud.

Now the bombardment stopped and, for a moment, all was silent. Then came the unsteady notes of a bugle at the lips of a man who clearly lacked experience with his instrument. Cracked as the sound was, though, even I recognised the order to charge. We rode from the ruins of the riding school, forming a ragged line as we emerged onto the plain. For a few moments we were trotting. I drew my sword, already finding it difficult to control the heavy blade against the movements of the horse. I worried that if we lurched I could end up pricking my own mount with the point and I wondered how I would cope at the gallop. Already some of the horses were stretching themselves to their full speed. Instinctively, others joined them. My own horse pushed forward and I could hardly have held him back, even had I wished to.

There was still half a mile to the British defences and we were hurtling forward. Dust rose all around, mingling with the smoke which still hung in the air from the artillery barrage. My ears were filled with the thunder of hoofbeats and the cries of my companions.

'Deen! Deen!' 'For the faith! For the faith!'

We rode on. Now, from the saddle, I could see across the pitiful defences to where my fellow Europeans lay with their muskets ready at their shoulders. Beside them, I saw crouching figures dressed in rags. I did not at first recognise them as the white women of Cawnpore, their finery destroyed, their beauty tarnished. Yet, seeing them steadfast beside their men, ready to reload and pass new weapons to the warriors, I had never thought them finer.

Now we were two hundred yards from the parapet. Now one hundred. Still we rode, with no fire from our enemy. Already, the horses were tiring and the impetus of our charge had been lost but we were almost upon them. Then, when we were just fifty yards from their defences, Wheeler's tattered army opened fire. Three nine-pounders belched flame and smoke. One round of grapeshot found our range. All around me, men and horses were thrown to the ground. Had we not galloped the whole way from the riding school, the speed and exhilaration of our charge might well have carried us to the parapet despite our losses, but the horses were already slowing. As riders tugged desperately at their reigns to avoid the welter of bodies beneath our horses' hooves, the animals swung about, causing even further chaos in the line. Within seconds, the charge had turned into a mass of wheeling, panicked horseflesh, riders yelling in impotent rage, scarcely more rational than the beasts they rode.

Ahead of me a horse fell. Its forelegs scrabbled to raise it from the ground but then it collapsed, whinnying its pain and terror. Instinctively, I kicked Kuching on and we jumped the doomed creature, but now all around was chaos. I swerved to avoid another fallen horse, reining back until Kuching stood, flanks heaving, eyes rolling in terror. Again and again, the British muskets fired. All around, it seemed, men were falling to the ground. Exposed to the rebels' fire by the inadequacy of the mud wall that offered their only protection, the British gunners nonetheless stood at their posts and I knew that it would be only seconds before the cannon were ready to fire again.

The charge was broken, the sowars turning and riding hard back the way they had come. I pulled at the reins, turning Kuching toward safety and joined the flight. Before the nine-pounders could fire another round, it was over.

That was the end of the cavalry's attempts to take Wheeler's position. I think we all knew then that the day was lost but, to be fair to the infantry, they made a better showing than us. For now they tried where we had failed.

The Nana's generals had come up with a new plan. They had raided the storehouses along the river and seized the giant bales of cotton that had been left there ready for shipping. Now the infantry advanced pushing the bales ahead of them as mobile parapets. Behind these, the sepoys were able to move in safety, showing themselves only to fire at the Entrenchment before ducking back into cover.

The British were pouring fire toward the infantry but without effect. The cotton bales moved steadily onward and I began to believe that the prophecy of victory on the anniversary of Plassey could yet come true. Those of us who had survived the abortive cavalry charge began to see a possibility of redeeming ourselves. As soon as the infantry reached the parapet, we could follow, moving up behind their cover and then passing through them to bring death and destruction to the enemy camp. Officers ordered us back into our lines and we began to edge forward.

At that point, as we thought that the battle was turning in our favour, we saw smoke rising from the foremost of the bales. As they moved closer to the British guns, so the hot shot was firing the cotton. Minutes later, most of the bales were alight and, suddenly robbed of their cover, the soldiers were at the mercy of the defenders' fire. Like the cavalry before them, the infantry now broke, turning and running back toward us.

So the anniversary of Plassey passed and the British were still there.

No one ever ordered us to disperse. One by one or in small groups, we slipped away. There was no point in pretending that we might charge again. The sun was by now high in the sky and the day too hot for another open assault. The artillery barrage continued unabated but the Nana's troops rested in the shade. There was one small consolation for the rebels. About midday, there was a great explosion within the Entrenchment and it seemed that a lucky shot had struck a store of the defenders' ammunition but the blow came too late and would not, in any case, have been decisive.

Some of those who had assembled for the assault now left the rebel lines but most settled back to the comfortable monotony of the siege. I decided that I, too, would stay in Cawnpore. The events of the day and the valiant defence put up by General Wheeler made me wonder if the defeat of the British was truly inevitable. If they were not doomed, but had, perhaps, even the remotest chance of seeing things to a successful conclusion, did I not have an obligation to fight with them? The men of the garrison were by now physically exhausted after weeks of constant bombardment but I was rested and healthy. Could I not make a useful contribution, especially if I were able to carry in food and medicine?

In the time since my last foray to Captain Moore's position, the eyrie that had been built on top of the unfinished barrack had discouraged such raids. I had seen, during the attack earlier in the day, how one or two men in that vantage point could pick off so many attackers that few were prepared to take the risk of moving into range of Moore's sharpshooters. Reaching the Entrenchment by way of the empty barracks no longer seemed a realistic option. But perhaps, I thought, there might be other possibilities.

I set off to ride along the roads nearest to the Entrenchment to see if there was any sensible path that might allow a determined individual to reach the British position.

By now, the sun was setting and the brief Indian dusk was upon us. To my right I saw some British move out to retrieve any of the abandoned cotton bales that had not been destroyed by fire. With piquets around them to guard against attack, the defenders rolled the cotton back toward their base where the bales made a useful addition to the mud parapet that was their only defence. Despite the guards, the British took a big risk by exposing themselves in the open like this. With hundreds of Indians still lurking under cover following the day's reverses, a massed attack must have killed many of the men in the open – a loss that their tiny garrison could not sustain while any casualties would be negligible to the Nana. It seemed to me that the fight had gone out of the rebels. They no longer believed that they were going to win this battle.

On my left were the remains of St John's, the soldiers' church. This symbol of an alien God had been set ablaze early in the revolt and now the ruined walls were a sad reminder of what it had once been. As I came up with the remains, I saw a group of sepoys, still wearing the uniform of the 1st Native Infantry. They were silently looking toward a storm drain that ran between the Entrenchment and the road. I reined in and, following the direction of their gaze, tried to see what it was that exercised their attention.

Barely visible in the failing light, I could just make out the figure of a native crawling along the drain. Although I could not be sure, he did not appear to be carrying a weapon and, certainly, those who were watching him did not seem prepared for action. Indeed, several had stacked their muskets against the rubble of a wall.

Urgent voices called from the shadows, urging me not to linger in view of the sentries but to ride on.

There was something about the group that made me hesitate. They shuffled like naughty children caught out in a trick. They were nervous but their nervousness did not look like that of men preparing for battle. Besides, with the casualties the 1st Native Infantry had taken that morning, no one would expect them to fight again today.

Rather than ride on, I dismounted and led my horse among the shadows.

Now the sepoys huddled together, casting only occasional suspicious glances in my direction. Although infantry soldiers could be unfriendly to the cavalry, I had not encountered such open hostility at Cawnpore before. I tethered my horse to one of the less unstable columns of rubble and approached the sepoys with as friendly an expression as I could muster. I stopped and placed my hands together in greeting. 'Namaste.'

My greeting seemed to calm them and there were mutterings of 'Namaste' quiet in the darkness. There were no Salaams and it seemed that all the sepoys here were Hindoos and my appearance as a Hindoo was in some measure reassuring to them.

'Who do you watch, my brothers?' I asked.

One of the men moved forward. I noticed that the others deferred to him and I guessed him to have been their naik, or corporal when they served under the British flag. He seemed to have the habit of command though, as the naik wore no rank badges, I could not be sure.

'A brother seeks to enter the fort.'

While we spoke, the dark shape of the figure in the drain seemed to move fractionally further forward. The sepoy's answer told me nothing that my eyes could not see for themselves.

'Why does he seek to enter the fort, my brother?'

'He would know the disposition of the British.'

The sepoy had chosen his words with care. The man who still moved inch by inch toward the European camp was to report how he found the enemy. To a loyal sowar, this should mean that the man was gathering intelligence that would aid us in our next assault. Try as I might, though, I could think of no information that was needed beyond the number of defenders and the strength of their artillery and we had gathered more than enough intelligence as to those during the debacle of the day. I looked again at my companions. They were Hindoos, who mostly harboured less intensity of rage toward the British than did the Musalmans. And they were mutineers, rather than rebels who had travelled to Cawnpore out of a commitment to the destruction of the Europeans. These men had served with the British for years. They would have known many of the officers now trapped with Wheeler, they would have greeted their wives and, often enough, played with their children – for soldiers as a species are sentimental about children and the Indian sepoy no less so than his European brother. The fact that they still wore their uniforms showed them to possess some residual feelings for their regiment and the life they had abandoned with the mutiny.

I decided to make a neutral response but one which might encourage the mutineers to speak more freely of their intentions.

'The British fought well today.'

The naik fixed his gaze on my face, as if trying to discern my expression in the gloom. Still choosing his words carefully, he said, 'They fought like tigers. They may yet escape the fury of Nana Sahib.'

He had given me my cue. 'Nana Sahib', not 'the Peshwa', It was my turn to give some indication of my loyalties.

'I have known many sowars who have fought with the British. They are mighty warriors and, moreover, they know how to use cavalry. If the British had commanded the attack this morning, it would not have failed.'

Now the other sepoys began to join in. The British had paid them regularly but the Nana, though generous when pay was issued, could go for weeks without paying them at all. The Company's army had been disciplined and proud, but here they fought alongside the scum of the bazaars and discipline was forgotten. Many of them admired their officers, but here they were ordered into battle by Nana Sahib's advisers who were completely unknown to them.

The complaints were little more than the grumbles that you heard from soldiers everywhere. Listening to the anger in their voices, though, I felt I was listening to men who had deserted the British and were no longer convinced that they had picked the winning side.

'And your friend in the ditch?'

There was a pause in the flow of complaints from the sepoys. The naik spoke in the silence.

'He is to find our officers and ask if we can return to our duty.'

'You would join the British in there?'

'You saw what happened today. The Nana's army is

weak. The British are strong. They fight bravely and, it is rumoured, they have mined their fort and they will blow it up if the Nana's army enters it. They will die but we will die alongside them.'

I smiled to myself in the darkness. It seemed as if the rumours I had started had become common currency amongst soldiery.

The naik went on and I felt he was trying to convince himself as much as me with what he said next. 'If a few of us were to join with the British and attack the hill where the Nana hides from danger, then I think the Nana would run. And once he runs, the revolt is over. There are many of the Company's soldiers who feel as we do. There are many who were led into revolt by a few bad men. If they see the British forgive us and allow us to fight for them again, they will join with us. The revolt will be defeated and we will be forgiven and rewarded.'

I made no reply but joined them as they watched their comrade moving inch by inch toward the British position. Could there be any hope in their wild plan? Crouched beside them in the darkness, I began to wonder if it could be so. There was no doubt that, just as the British had had every cause to doubt the loyalty of their troops during the months preceding the mutiny, now Nana Sahib could not rely on them. Most of the sepoys were the sons of soldiers who were themselves the sons of soldiers. Their greatest desire was to serve as soldiers but, like all soldiers, they wanted to be on the winning side. If the mutinous sepoys thought that the British could yet prevail, then perhaps they might desert the Nana just as they had deserted us. And any disaffection amongst the Nana's forces would be exacerbated by the tensions already visible between Hindoos and Musalmans in his ranks.

But even if the sepoys – or many of them – were to rejoin the Company's ranks, could they fight their way out of Cawnpore and across rebel-held country until they reached some place where the British still held out in strength?

For a few minutes, I allowed myself to believe it was possible. The sepoys' envoy would be received by a grateful Wheeler; the native troops would march once more under the British flag; the Nana would be defeated and this nightmare would be over.

From the darkness, I heard a British voice shouting and the crack of a rifle from the Entrenchment. From somewhere between us and the British breastworks, there came a scream, then a desperate sobbing and then silence.

The sepoys looked at each other and then me. Not a word was said and they slipped silently away into the darkness.

I sat alone for the better part of an hour, staring across to where I knew my countrymen would be trying to rest and eking out such rations as they had left. From time to time, there would be the boom of a cannon somewhere in the rebel lines and a crash as shot or shell smashed into the Entrenchment ahead of me.

There, alone in the dark, I doubted that the sepoys' plan had had any real chance of success, but it had been the only hope the garrison had. They were surrounded, outnumbered, and outgunned. They had little food and scarcely any shelter. Their defences were no more than mud walls and any day now the monsoon rains would start and they would be washed away. If I joined them, I, too, was as doomed as they. Yet was I not British? Was it not my duty to stand by the men and women of my race even if it was a pointless gesture that could end only in my death alongside theirs? I thought of Mungo's rooms in Saturday House, of his arms around me, his mouth seeking mine. But still some small part of me wanted to cross the open ground to the Entrenchment, to join my fellows there and to die like an Englishman.

It made no difference what I thought. The sepoy's

death had shown what fate would befall me were I to attempt to enter the Entrenchment. I had made my decision and abandoned my colleagues to their fate. I could not change things now.

I had no intention of attempting to journey back to Bithur in the dark. Even in normal times, the road was not so good that I would care to risk the health of my horse by riding it at night and the war had brought its own perils. The rebels had opened the jails, releasing all manner of villains. That, combined with the destruction of the usual institutions of police and magistracy, meant that the road could be a dangerous place after sunset.

At this time of year, the night air was no threat to my health. In fact, even at midnight I was more likely to feel too hot rather than chilled and I settled to sleep in the ruins where I had watched the unfortunate sepoy crawl to his death.

I woke at around six. The air was somewhat cooler in the early dawn than it had been when I lay down to sleep the night before, but the sun was already bright in the sky.

I decided that I would stay at Cawnpore until the afternoon, to get some idea of how the previous day's reverses had affected the rebels. Were the sepoys of the previous night an isolated group or were many of the Nana's men ready to give up the siege?

My horse had long since eaten the sparse foliage sprouting amongst the rubble and was now pawing at the dirt in the hope of finding anything edible hidden in the dust. The beast obviously needed food and I was sure that there would be fodder available at Savada House, where Nana Sahib still had his headquarters. A visit there might also give me a clearer view of how things were progressing with the rebels.

I carried on with the circuit I had started the evening before, moving away from the town and turning South with the Entrenchment on my right. I passed the great empty expanse of the parade ground where the vultures were already flapping about the remains of yesterday's dead and then I walked my horse up the little knoll toward Savada House.

The place had a more permanent feel than when I had last been there. Nana Sahib's personal standard flew over his tent, still some way ahead of me. It reassured the people that he was still living among them. Around that pavilion had grown up a little village of tents and shacks. The place was bright with banners – the green of the Musalmans, orange flags of some of the Hindoos, regimental colours from mutinous troops, and the heraldry of a dozen minor lords who had pledged allegiance to the Peshwa. Looking at them, I realised for the first time how the reforms that the British had introduced to land ownership had alienated the landowners who were the ancient aristocracy of India and now these petty princelings had found a common cause. And, of course, the poor of the land, who we had thought our reforms had benefited, now flocked to their lords' banners. As my horse pushed its way through the mass of servants and beggars, I was conscious that they were fighting for their right to be robbed by the men whose families had robbed them for generations rather than pay their dues to a European interloper.

Approaching Savada House, I could not help but think of those Europeans who had been taken before the Nana and hacked down beside this building, or of those who even now repined within its walls. This was where the Nana kept the women he had spared and, it was said, here was old Mrs Greenway and her family, who were being held for ransom. It seemed, though, that the Nana now had more prisoners than he could accommodate in the old house. I had seen the looting and destruction that war had brought to Cawnpore. Here was evidence of the new rulers' attempts to maintain some sort of order. A few yards from the house was a crude bamboo stockade, thrown up around a grove of mango trees. Within it, a couple of dozen natives, men and women, squatted disconsolately in the dust, watched over by four men standing with swords drawn. The rebels may have started their revolt by emptying the town jail but they had already produced an alternative.

The mass of humanity became thicker the nearer I came to the Nana's headquarters. This was now the centre of the Peshwa's court. This was the honey pot that attracted everyone who held hopes of advancement in the new India that was to arise after the British left. The men of rank had pitched their own tents round and about but they, in turn, had their own servants and followers. So many people, quite without any proper sanitary arrangements, made for a stink noticeable even to my nostrils, which, after a year and a half in India, had generally become inured to the odour of unwashed humanity.

Such was the stench arising from the human population, that I could not immediately distinguish the ammoniac smell that led me to the horses of the cavalry. Once I did, it was easy enough to find some of my fellow sowars. Many of those who had ridden to defeat the previous morning had slipped quietly away but the best of them had decamped here, to be at hand should their Peshwa call on them.

I greeted those I recognised and was welcomed into their ranks. As I had foreseen, they were well supplied with fodder. The Nana employed grass cutters to bring fresh grass for the horses at Bithur every morning and some had obviously been sent to join the other servants at Savada House, for generous piles of grass were scattered about for the cavalry mounts. Nor had the riders neglected their own welfare. A square of canvas had been erected to shelter them from the sun and some carpets and pillows, scavenged from who knew where, provided a modicum of comfort. I tied my horse to one of the posts that had been erected for the purpose and settled down with my comrades to drink tea and, perhaps, chew the odd betel nut.

As the morning wore on, men came and went moving between periods of duty and idleness with the casual lack of discipline that characterised the rebel forces. Usually there were at least four or five of us resting there and the talk was naturally on the events of the previous day. There was reluctant agreement that the cavalry had, as a body, not distinguished itself in the engagement. People could not agree, though, on who was to blame for the debacle. Chimnaji, one of the older men and as near as our little group had to a leader, blamed the failure on men from Oudh, whose martial qualities, he claimed, were much over-rated. Others said it was the fault of some Parthans who had travelled from the North West to join the revolt. The only thing we could all agree with confidence was that Nana Sahib's own sowars had fought valiantly and well.

There was some particular criticism of whoever had caused the bugle to sound the charge so far from the defences. One or two of the younger men suggested that this must have been the result of incompetence by the army's commanders but this led to nervous glances in the direction of Nana Sahib's tent and a shift of the conversation into safer areas.

If the sowars were unhappy with the way that the revolt was going, at least they were not on the verge of deserting like the men I had seen the previous night. But, as with every other army, the cavalrymen had a status denied to the infantry and they would be the most loyal of the Nana's men. Indeed, they were aware of discontent amongst the infantry and they spoke dismissively of many of the men who had flocked to the rebel cause.

'Company soldiers who have half a mind to run back to

their old masters; old men who serve their lords loyally but who have never before seen a battle; farmers who bring sickles for want of swords; and every badmash who has a reputation with his fists. They all called themselves the Peshwa's soldiers when they thought the British would be overrun in a day or two. But now they find that they have to fight … Well, it's a different story.'

There was much nodding of heads and then Chimnaji started on some yarn about a battle he was in years back. 'Now that was real fighting.' And then Appa, one of the younger men, tried to top his tale with another and soon everybody had a story to tell and so the morning passed away until it grew hot and time for tiffin and we interrupted our boasting to eat.

Once we had finished our meal, our talk became more desultory until it finally dwindled into silence. The hubbub of the rebel camp was quieted as those around us, from the Nana Sahib himself to the poorest of the beggars beside the road, all gave themselves over to the stupor that Indian and European alike fall into in the hottest part of a June day.

I had just composed myself comfortably in the shade when I was disturbed by the passage of several men hurrying past our little camp in the direction of Savada House. Any movement in the heat of the day was unusual enough but as more and more people passed, I roused myself to see what could be so extraordinary as to rouse people from their idleness so soon after tiffin.

As I approached the building, it was clear that the centre of attention was the makeshift bamboo prison. A crowd, already a hundred or so strong, had gathered but I could not see what had drawn them there. I pushed through, ordering people aside with the arrogance that a genuine sowar would show and in a few seconds I was standing close against the bamboo palisade.

The source of the excitement was apparently a new

prisoner. He seemed exceptionally tall for an Indian, though the appearance of his height was accentuated by the emaciation of his body. Indeed, he looked almost like a scarecrow, wearing a turban, a loincloth and a cook's coat smeared with grease. He seemed an unprepossessing fellow and I asked around to see why he was the cause of so much interest.

Most of the people I enquired of had, like me, been attracted by the noise and the gathering crowd and knew no more of the man than I did. However, eventually I asked one young fellow who said that he had followed him as he was escorted into the place and that his guards said he was a refugee from the Entrenchment.

I looked at him with renewed interest. His thinness was now explained but, other than that, he seemed in reasonable health. I was surprised that somebody could have lived in the conditions that must have existed inside that camp and not being more visibly marked by their suffering. This man, although looking understandably nervous, had something about him that suggested an inner strength but I could not put my finger on what it was that gave me this impression.

The crowd was still growing and there was a sense that something must be about to happen. We waited a full fifteen minutes, though, before two of the Nana's guards arrived and, with much shouting and waving of their swords escorted him through the crowd toward a mango tree that stood a few paces away from the grove, outside the stockade.

In the shade of the tree was a dirty carpet and on it sat an elderly man whose nondescript appearance was belied by the guard standing to attention beside him. I did not recognise him but I knew enough of the protocol of the Nana's court to realise that he must have been a senior official.

The guards gestured the prisoner to stand before him

and the old man, after fussing with his spectacles and arranging his writing materials, started by asking him his name and where he came from. He replied that his name was Budloo and that he was from Allahabad.

These preliminaries had excited little interest. None of the audience (still growing by the minute) seemed to know anyone named Budloo and nobody claimed to remember him from Allahabad – a city just far enough away that not many at Cawnpore would have known it. Now, though, the old man moved on to more important matters.

'What do you know of the British fort?'

'Nothing,' he said. 'Nothing.'

'You lie! We know you were in there. Tell us what you know of the condition of the British.'

'I was there but I worked as a cook. I was kept in the kitchen and the soldiers watched me in case I ran away. I know nothing outside the kitchen.'

Again, the old man called him a liar and the soldiers guarding him swore at him and raised their swords to strike.

A voice from the crowd shouted, 'If he was so carefully watched, how then did he escape?'

The old man nodded. 'How, indeed?'

The prisoner looked nervously about him as the shouts and threats from the mob grew steadily. It seemed to me obvious that he was lying and desperately trying to think of a credible story. Just as it seemed certain that he would be beaten, he spoke again.

'After yesterday's attack, there were so many bodies that they could not all be buried during the night and the soldiers slipped out of the fort in the morning to throw the last corpses into the well. I bore a helping hand, but while they were busy with the bodies, I slipped away from the well and hid amongst the piles of bricks until I got the opportunity to escape.'

Implausible as this story seemed to me, it satisfied the

old man who changed his line of questioning. 'If you were in the kitchens, you must know how much provision is left and the number of fighting men still alive.'

'Well, I will tell you as far as I know. I have often heard the soldiers say, while in the cookhouse, that they can pull on with the provisions for another whole month.'

Now, once again, the crowd exploded into anger, with one voice after another denouncing him as a liar. The old man leaned forward pointing angrily with his finger. 'We know full well the *feringees* are starving.'

Now the prisoner roused himself to anger. 'If you know the situation, why question me? I have nothing more to say to you.' At which he hunched his shoulders, and, staring at the ground lapsed into silence. The guards abused him, calling him a dog and the son of a whore and one made to strike him, but the old man raised his hand to stop them and, adopting a conciliatory tone, asked if he had any other intelligence of the enemy's position.

At this he told his inquisitor, with apparent reluctance, that some two dozen soldiers had died from sunstroke and a very few from shot and shell but that there were sufficient fighting men still left to defend the place and all were determined to fight to the last.

As I heard this, my spirits rose but the news that was so pleasing to me was as displeasing to his captors who again violently abused him. However often they taxed him with being a liar, though, he simply shook his head and repeated his claims.

The insults offered by the guards were joined by those of the natives who had gathered to watch the sport. For several minutes, it was impossible to hear anything that the prisoner might say. On his carpet, the old man shouted for silence and, little by little, the noise subsided and he was able to recommence the questioning.

'Is it true that the European dogs have mined the perimeter of the encampment and will destroy all who enter it?'

It was all that I could do to stop myself from laughing at this further evidence that the rumours I started had grown to the point where so many believed them. Fortunately, this question started the spectators again in their chorus of jeers and abuse and, if my expression betrayed my inner elation, no one gave it any attention.

The prisoner looked puzzled at this question but eventually replied that he was not sure what was meant by 'mining' but that he could most positively assert that powder was buried in several places within the camp.

You can imagine my surprise at this. I wondered if my invention might, indeed, be no more than the truth. Yet it seemed unlikely. Had any such plan been intended, I would surely have heard of it in the days when the Entrenchment was being prepared. If that were the case, then the prisoner must be lying to his captors with the same intention of causing fear and confusion that had led me to start the rumour in the first place.

Knowing this, I looked at him with renewed interest. There was something about him that did not look quite right. As I had already noticed, he was taller than the average native and, though he continually lowered his head and often put his hands before him in entreaty, there was that about his manner which suggested a latent pride unlikely to have been found in the breast of a low caste cook.

Although my suspicions were by now fully aroused, the old man and the guards seemed to be accepting their prisoner as what he claimed to be. His inventions about the mining of the fort generated such excitement that within minutes his inquisitor was heading toward the Nana's tent as fast as his aged legs would carry him.

The prisoner was escorted back into his compound and gradually the crowd dispersed. Some settled back to sleep through the heat under the shade of the mango where the prisoner had been questioned. Intrigued as I was by this Budloo, I decided to join them.

The carpet had been rolled up and removed. Dirty though it had been, I would have welcomed something to rest on other than the bare earth but I saw no alternative. I settled cross-legged on the ground where sat or lay the other natives who had chosen this patch of shade.

The prisoner had also decided to rest in the shade and had laid himself out under one of the trees on his side of the bamboo fence. Within a few minutes, it seemed, he was asleep.

I continued sitting in the dust. Despite the shade of the tree, it was hot, even for the summer. There were, of course, no proper facilities for the throng now inhabiting this place and the stench was offensive. I began to wonder if I should return to my cavalry companions who were a little removed from the hoi polloi. The smell from the horses was vastly preferable to that from the mass of humankind and the memory of the cushions the sowars had acquired grew steadily more attractive the longer I sat on the hard ground.

I had just decided that my vigil was pointless when the guards were joined by another rebel sepoy who bustled over from the direction of the Nana's headquarters and immediately started a series of whispered conversations with his fellows.

I moved myself by inches to the very edge of the shade and strained my ears to hear the news that he had brought. Fortunately, as the sepoys grew steadily more excited, so their voices grew louder. One said, 'So it will end,' and the others hushed him and looked about them.

What might end? Could they conceivably be talking of an end to the siege? My discomfort was forgotten in an instant and I scarcely noticed the heat. My whole being seemed concentrated in my ears as I struggled to catch odd words and phrases.

'… cannot succeed by assault …'

'… mines …'

'… powder magazines set to explode …'

'… hundreds could die …'

'… they cannot be defeated …'

Finally, I was sure.

'The Nana will offer terms …'

I wanted to run, shouting, toward the Entrenchment, 'The Nana is to offer terms! The siege is to be ended! You are saved!' Instead, I had to sit squirming in the heat, trying not to betray my excitement.

I had been so taken with eavesdropping on the sepoys that I had neglected to watch the prisoner. Now I noticed that the cook, though still lying stretched out beneath a tree, was exhibiting the same twitches of excitement as I was. As I stared toward him, trying to make some sense of what I saw, he opened his eyes and caught my gaze. When he realised he was watched, he grew visibly alarmed, and, tugging his turban down over his forehead and hunching his shoulders into his cook's jacket, he seemed to be trying to conceal his features.

It was this very effort to hide his face that made me realise that I had seen it before. But where? I was sure that it was not the face of a cook.

I was still searching my memory when there was yet more movement from the direction of the Nana's tent. A short fat man, perspiring in the heat, approached with clearly unaccustomed briskness. His importance was signified by the smartness of his dress and an escort of not one but two guards. The sepoys at the enclosure promptly ceased their conversation and stood to attention as he wobbled his way to the stockade shouting for 'the prisoner Budloo' to be brought before him.

Budloo was already on his feet and, seeing the guards making toward him with expressions suggesting they would not be gentle in carrying out the order, he hastened to stand before the visitor.

This time there were no secret whispers. In a voice clearly audible to all in the vicinity, the official demanded to know whether the Europeans were anxious to leave the Station, and, in the event of an offer being made to that effect, if it would be accepted.

I could swear I saw a flicker of triumph pass across Budloo's features but, as fast as it appeared, it was gone and, with downcast eyes and hesitant tone, he replied that he could not exactly tell. 'The women are certainly anxious to get away by any means and to take their children with them,' he mumbled. 'I think that the soldiers would accept an offer if it allowed their women to escape.'

The official nodded vigorously at this reply and turned to scuttle back toward his master.

Intrigued as I was by my growing certainty that Budloo was no cook, I decided to follow the fat official back to the Nana's tent. It seemed that things were moving to some sort of conclusion and the Nana's headquarters was the place to be if I wanted the latest news.

I settled to outside the tent, though to call it a 'tent' does it scant justice. As the Nana had established himself, so the tent had grown into an elaborate pavilion of coloured silks. The glimpses I had of the interior suggested that it was divided into separate rooms. I could, obviously, see only the entrance chamber but even that was carpeted with low tables dotted about and (a reminder, no doubt, of Saturday House) mirrors hanging on the walls.

My presence at the entrance attracted no attention, for there was a continual passage of people entering and leaving as well as a crowd always loitering around in the hope of gathering some crumbs from the rich man's table or just, like me, anxious to hear the latest news and gossip.

Word that something of importance was to pass had clearly spread through the camp, for the crowd of idlers was growing by the minute. Nor was this audience to be deprived of the spectacle they sought. Various officials, gorgeously robed, came and went with earnest faces, pretending to ignore the crowd but, in fact, strutting before them like actors in a second-rate play. Now came a Brahmin, now a mullah; orange robes, white robes, green fringes, red cloth – a veritable rainbow of rank. Even the guards who pushed their way past the onlookers were immaculately turned out in white tunics and turbans of blue or red.

The scent of incense drifted from the tent, going some way to disguise the reek from the unwashed bodies massed around me. From time to time more incense and the smell of rosewater marked the movement of such of the neighbouring rulers who had sworn fealty to Nana Sahib as they hurried from their own tents to their Peshwa's pavilion. I searched their faces for any indication of their mood. It seemed to me that they expected good news but most kept their features masks of disdain for the common folk and it was difficult to discern their feelings.

Now the guards who had set out were returning, beating a path through the onlookers with the flats of their swords. They formed a tight group and, at first, I could not see whom they escorted. Then I caught a glimpse of a white arm, a grey head, the bedraggled remains of a dress. It was Mrs Greenway! It is almost impossible to imagine the shock I felt on seeing this dowager, the respected matriarch of Cawnpore's most influential family, hustled by her guards like some common criminal. Though I had seen the European quarter looted and burned and watched the sepoys firing on their European masters day after day, it was, I think, the pathetic sight of this old woman hurried before the Nana that truly brought home to me the totality of the destruction of European power and all that I had known of British rule in India.

By now, the afternoon was well advanced. There was no more urgent coming and going but I was content to wait on events. The mass of natives around me seemed to share this view for scarcely any moved away while, even now, others drifted over to join us.

For a time, nothing happened. Then there was a sudden eruption of sepoys who ran off in all directions, shouting for horses. I thought for an instant that I might volunteer my own mount and thus maybe find myself privy to any messages the Nana was despatching. My horse, though, was with the other sowars and the messengers were already scattering away from the tent. Besides, if the Nana were sending out new general orders, I would know them soon enough, while any more specific news would best be gleaned by staying where I was.

Again, the crowd settled to wait and I waited with them. A quarter of an hour passed and there was no sign of anything happening. Then came a stirring, an uneasiness, amongst the mass of men around me. I shared their unease, a feeling that some great change had taken place. The heat and the stench were the same as ever but something was different.

I heard a dog barking in the town below and I realised what it was. After days and nights of cacophony, one by one the Nana's batteries were falling silent. By late afternoon, all the rebel firing ceased and only the lazy flapping of vultures' wings broke the eeric silence that lay across the plain around Wheeler's position.

An hour passed. Then two. Still the silence was not broken. Finally, toward evening, the Nana's guards emerged again with Mrs Greenway.

This time she was not hustled along like a criminal but, rather, escorted as if to do her honour. She stood erect, guards on either side, and though her gown was dirty and, in places, torn, she stood up proudly, as if she were robed as a queen.

At some stage during her captivity, her shoes had been taken from her and she walked now on bare feet. Yet, still she stepped forward bravely. The guards walked with her down the little hill. I followed, as did most of those who had been waiting all afternoon for some excitement and who now felt it was only right that they should be able to see whatever show these new events might offer.

Arriving at the edge of the great parade ground, the guards stepped aside and Mrs Greenway started out toward the Entrenchment on her own. With the rest of the crowd, I stopped on the edge of the plain. It was not fear of the British guns that stopped us, I think, but the sense that this plain, where so much Indian blood had been spilt, was somehow alien. As Mrs Greenway walked on, she walked alone, a frail figure in all those acres of empty land.

We watched as she neared those feeble defences that had stood so defiantly for the weeks of the siege. In her right hand, she held what I at first thought to be a walking stick painted white. As she approached the Entrenchment, though, she flourished it in the air and I recognised it as a symbol of envoy, as Europeans might wave a white flag.

Now she was almost at the breastworks. She began to sway slightly, her strength clearly exhausted. Faint on the evening air came cries of command from the besieged garrison and then an officer was clambering over the debris of the defences and catching the old lady as she finally succumbed to faintness and collapsed into his arms. Together the two made their way into the Entrenchment.

'We shall see no more tonight.'

Others around me took up the same refrain. Some said we would see no more of Mrs Greenway even if we waited until the next day.

'The Peshwa was holding her for ransom. Surely she is ransomed and now she has gone back to her people. She will not return.'

Hearing this, the guards – who stood now with the rest of the crowd – joined in with the enthusiasm of gossips who are privileged to know more than their companions.

'She'll be back. The Peshwa still holds her family hostage against her safe return.'

One fellow, bolder than the rest, demanded of the guards why the old woman had been sent to the British in the first place.

'The Peshwa has decided that the British can do no more harm. She carries his message to them. They are to be offered safe passage if they lay down their arms and leave this place for ever.'

A murmur of excitement ran through the crowd at this apparent confirmation of the rumours that had been flying around the Nana's camp all afternoon. Even now, I can scarce describe my own feelings. It seemed that there was indeed a God who was merciful to his creation and who was leading his children out of the fire to which I had feared he had consigned them. As night fell, with the suddenness of the darkness in these latitudes, so my fears were carried away by a night breeze and, for the first time since the Entrenchment had been surrounded, I felt sure of their escape.

Most of the men around me shared my mood of relief, though their reasons may have been different from mine. Few will have cared for the Europeans in the Entrenchment but they were tired of the deaths and, I believed, tired of the killing. Now they would have their victory without the need for further bloodshed. Men relaxed, laughing and joking with each other. Sweetmeats appeared from the folds of robes, confections of sugar and fruit that were passed around and shared.

The sun had long set and we watched across the plain by moonlight until a moving shadow resolved itself as the limping figure of an old woman. Mrs Greenway's guards fell in beside her and escorted her back to the Nana's tent and the crowd, deprived of the possibility of further entertainment, finally dispersed.

I made my way back to Chimnaji and the others. My

elation was somewhat tempered by the number of trips and stumbles that I suffered in the darkness, but my spirits were lifted by the enthusiasm with which my fellow sowars greeted me on my return. They had heard the rumours, but considered their pride prohibited them from mingling with the common throng to learn more. They were, however, more than happy to benefit from my willingness to humble myself in that way and we sat up around a small fire while I rehearsed the events of the day.

It must have been close to midnight when I finally lay down to sleep. The fire was scarcely necessary, for the night was still warm, but it provided a little light and comfort and I found my mind slipping back to the days before the Mutiny. And suddenly I knew where I had seen the prisoner before. His name was not Budloo and he was no cook. He was Jonah Shepherd, one of the babus in our offices. Now his answers made sense, for his insistence that the defenders were well supplied and the Entrenchment was mined had served to convince Nana Sahib that it would be wise to offer terms.

I resolved that as soon as it was light I should return to the stockade to see what aid I could offer him and, with this thought in my mind, I was soon in the arms of Morpheus.

I roused myself at dawn the next morning. Though I had rested for only a few hours, still I was well refreshed, for the change in the fortune of the Europeans had revived my spirits and I had slept more soundly than for many a night past. I made my toilette as quickly as I could and, telling my comrades that I would scout for more news, I hurried to the stockade to find it empty.

Determined that this time I would not fail a European who had so far survived the tragedy, I enquired of the guards on Savada House as to what had happened to the prisoners.

'The Europeans are here,' they told me. 'The old

woman was returned in the middle of the night and they are safely behind these walls.'

'And the others?'

'Oh, them.' It seemed that, even in captivity, the old caste lines were maintained. The Europeans may be hated now but the guard's tone betrayed the fact that he considered the native prisoners to be of no significance compared to his charges. 'They've been taken to the old cavalry hospital, where they can be more safely held.'

The hospital was some half a mile away and I decided to collect my horse and ride over there, not only to spare myself the walk, but in the hope that my presence might carry more authority if I were on my hunter. So it was, by the merest chance, that I was mounted and passing near the Nana's tent when an officer appeared in the entrance and, seeing me, raised his voice to command that I immediately attend upon him.

My first thought was that my disguise had been penetrated and I considered fleeing but I saw the mass of men round about and considered that I would have little hope of escape. In any case, the officer's tone was peremptory rather than angry so I rode to him and dismounted.

'Another envoy is to be sent to the British. It is to be an old woman again but we don't want her wandering around half dead like the other one. She is to be transported in a palanquin. She should not be fired on, for the British themselves have asked that we send her, but it is best that there be an escort and if she is to be carried, the escort should be mounted. You'll do.'

I had heard the sepoys complain that the rebel officers behaved less well toward them than had the British, but this was the first time that I had personal experience of the way that the army was treated under the new regime. The British might consider themselves a superior race but they had the utmost respect for the soldierly qualities of the

Native regiments. By contrast, the men appointed by the Nana to positions of command were, mostly, courtiers and they allowed the contempt they felt for the common soldiers to colour all their dealings with them. I found myself resenting him still more because I was no mere sepoy but a sowar. I still hated the man, even as I recognised how ridiculous I was to allow this to concern me.

Taking care to keep my expression respectful, I mounted again and waited until four men came trotting along the path from Savada House, carrying a litter bearing the figure of a half-caste woman. Her dress, though less dirty and ragged than that of Mrs Greenway, suggested a person of a lower social rank, but she seemed to have fared better in her captivity, being somewhat plump. She may have been the wife of a soldier and, though she was a mature lady, she was far from Mrs Greenway's age. Unlike that matriarch, though, she made no attempt to maintain a show of dignity but half-sat, half-lay in the palanquin as we set off across the open ground.

As we approached, I saw the men of the garrison strolling around, taking the air as they had done in the mornings before the Mutiny. As they walked to and fro behind their breastwork, I was reminded of how inadequate that defence had been and how they had been unable even to stand erect without exposing themselves to the rebels' fire.

Now the women came out from the ruin of the barracks that had sheltered them, joining their husbands to watch our approach.

The defences were by now so reduced that the bearers were able to carry the litter over the rubble and directly into the Entrenchment, where the passenger was immediately mobbed by the European ladies, content for once to associate with one whose skin was several shades darker than their own. Not that the women of the garrison still had the peaches and cream complexions that they had protected so carefully from the Indian sun. Few now had any bonnets and none sported parasols. As their shelter was destroyed and as they took their places beside the men, loading their guns and salving their wounds, so their skin had been burned almost as brown as that of the babus they had previously despised.

Once our passenger was safely within his camp, General Wheeler himself emerged from what was left of the barracks, accompanied by Captain Moore and some other officers I did not recognise. Moore's attention, naturally enough, was concentrated on the Nana's envoy, but he cast a swift glance over the scene and I saw his eyes swivel back to my face. I gave him the slightest of nods and, as the General and his aides hustled the woman toward the guard post at the gate – one of the most substantial buildings still more or less intact – Moore drifted over to where I was now standing beside my horse. There was no reason why, under these circumstances, a British officer could not speak to one of the Nana's cavalrymen and Moore felt safe to ask my news.

'I'm safe enough, though I've been of little use to you or anyone else. I saw Shepherd yesterday. He has convinced Nana Sahib to offer you safe passage, though now he's been moved to another jail and I'm off there later to see what assistance I can give him.'

'The stout chap! We all feared that he had been lost when he did not return from his scouting expedition.'

'He was taken but has persuaded Nana Sahib that you are so strong and well-supplied that you can hold out for weeks yet.'

Moore gave a short bark of laughter.

'We'll struggle to hold out another couple of days. The men don't mind dying. Most of them are soldiers and it's our trade. But it hurts to see the women suffer like this and to know that they are doomed too. Is he serious about safe passage?'

I thought of the disaster of our cavalry charge, the soldiers I had seen trying to make their own peace with the British, the conviction so many rebels held that Wheeler had mined his own position.

'He's not sure that he can keep his men together for the time it will take to win. No one can believe you've held out so long. I think he's sincere. He will do almost anything to bring this to an end.'

'I'll make sure Wheeler knows that.'

He turned to join the other officers with the General. Suddenly, I felt desperately alone. It seemed so long since I had seen Mungo. I spent my days and my nights keeping company with men who would kill me if they had any notion who I was. Stepping quickly after him, I reached my hand to Moore's sleeve. 'Perhaps I should just stay here?'

Moore did not hesitate. 'No. This meeting has to go smoothly and the Nana's envoy must be returned without any fuss. It's our best hope.' I think he must have seen the dejection on my face. 'Beside, you still have to try to do something for Shepherd.'

He strode into the guardhouse. I was left alone with the bearers and a small crowd of English women who looked at me in my native uniform with eyes that held nothing but contempt.

Chapter Eight

I do not know what happened at the conference Wheeler held with his staff that morning. I have heard some say that it was Captain Moore who spoke most strongly in favour of accepting Nana Sahib's offer. If this were so, I pray my words were not the reason for it. I only know that some two hours after I had arrived at the Entrenchment, I was escorting the woman back to the Nana's pavilion and that the truce, which had started the previous afternoon, still held.

I took advantage of the ceasefire to ride directly across to the old cavalry hospital where I had been told that Shepherd now lay imprisoned. I might have achieved little for those in the Entrenchment but I hoped that I could at least do something to help the prisoner.

When I arrived, I found the door to the jail was open, to allow more air to those incarcerated therein. A guard squatted nearby, chatting to a friend. When I asked to see the man in charge, he vanished inside, returning a few minutes later with an elderly Hindoo who introduced himself as the subadar. I asked after the prisoners and was assured that all were safe. I told him that I was especially interested in the welfare of Budloo and asked if there were any chance he might be released into my custody, but the old subadar was emphatic that this was impossible. 'And even if I could,' he added, 'I don't know that I will be doing him any favour if I let him go. It's all right for you and me – we are armed and have the authority of our uniforms to protect us but for the likes of him, they are less likely to come to harm in here than if they were roaming free on the streets.'

There being no obvious way to procure Shepherd's release, I slipped some coins into his palm with the promise of more if the prisoner Budloo came to no harm. The subadar assured me that he would do all in his power to protect him. 'For he's a pleasant enough fellow and gives no trouble.'

I felt I had done little for him, but I believed the subadar would be true to his word.

My business at the jail concluded, there were no immediate duties calling for my attention. It being now the hottest part of the day, I settled myself under the shade of a tree to rest until the sun was lower in the sky.

Usually I had no trouble in sleeping through the midday heat, even when I was disturbed by the occasional sound of firing. Now, though, I found I could not settle. I tried to tell myself that this was because the day was exceptionally hot (which it was) or that the silence, after the weeks of shelling, was by now more disturbing than the thunder of cannon fire.

In my heart, though, I knew the true reason for my unrest. With the ending of the siege, there was no reason why I should remain a stranger to my own people. I should stay here at Cawnpore and, at the first opportunity, insinuate myself back into the Entrenchment, to leave under the promise of safe passage that the Nana had made to the garrison. Yet, were I to do so, I would never see Mungo again.

I thought of his impish smile, his young, taut body and the pleasure it gave me, his kindness and his caresses. Was I just to walk away from this with no word of farewell?

Nor were Mungo's physical charms the only thing that I would miss if I were to leave Saturday House behind me forever. In my time there, I had come to understand something of what life in India had to offer – its religion, its literature, its art. I thought of the meals I had eaten with

Mungo and compared them in my memory with the spicy mess of food that Europeans called 'curry'. Having lived so long in the East, the life that Mungo had shared with me at Bithur was no more alien than the world of the European Station in Cawnpore.

I thought of the pleasure that Mungo and I had shared, enjoying our love not only in its sweaty, sticky, physical manifestation but in the quiet hours spent alone, walking through the gardens of Saturday House or in his room where he struggled to teach me to play the sarod. It is true that we were careful not to be overly demonstrative in public, but there must have been those at Saturday House who guessed our relationship. Servants came and went all the time and the laundryman, if no one else, must have been aware that Mungo was no celibate. Yet, at Bithur, this did not seem to be the criminal scandal that it would have been at Cawnpore. A return to my old life would be a return to a world in which I could never be open about the sort of man I was. It would be a world in which I might never truly love or be loved again.

As I tossed on the ground, the shade of the tree providing only the smallest relief from the heat, I knew the only decision I could come to. I had left Britain when I was barely a man but I could not pretend to be other than I was. India was turning against the British and, if they discovered who I was, they would turn against me. It mattered not that I loved Mungo or that I cared for their customs or that I could pick out the unfamiliar melodies on the sarod. I was a European. The Indians, no less than the British, would have me know my place.

After an hour or so of wakefulness, I gave up trying to sleep and braved the heat to make my way back toward the Nana's tent. It seemed to me that with communications now opened between the rebels and the Entrenchment, there would likely be opportunities to pass from one to the other carrying messages for the Nana. In this way, I might escape the rebels and rejoin my countrymen.

As I neared the Nana's headquarters, I was surprised to see almost as many people round about as there had been that morning. I had expected that the heat would have driven them to shelter in the shade and that most would still be dozing but instead the crowd was quite lively.

At first, I worried that something untoward might have occurred and that the truce was to be broken, but the smiles on the faces all around reassured me. When I asked what had passed, I was told that at one o'clock the Nana's chief minister – a scoundrel called Azimullah, who many considered responsible for corrupting his lord – had met with Wheeler's senior officers on the open ground before the British camp and that the arrangements for the surrender of the garrison had been successfully completed.

My delight on hearing this news was tarnished only by my realisation that had I been there as the delegations met, it would have been easy to insinuate myself into Azimullah's escort and so carry out my plan to slip away into the British ranks. Having missed this opportunity, though, I made careful enquiries as to what exactly the plans for the British departure were, so that I could choose the best time and place to escape the rebels.

The first few people I asked all told me that the British were to depart that very afternoon. I was alarmed that they might go without my finding an opportunity to join them, though I reasoned that if the worst came to the worst I could simply ride up to their column as they left and announce myself to Captain Moore. However, without knowing any details of how things were to be managed, I worried that this might not be possible, so I was reassured when others told me that the British had refused to leave immediately but had insisted that transport be arranged before they quit their camp.

'They are to travel down the river to Allahabad.' The man who told me this wore the remnants of the uniform of the 56th and his tone suggested that he was not entirely sure that he would not like to be travelling to Allahabad with them. 'They are to board at the ghat by Sati Chowra, where the Peshwa is providing boats to carry them away in safety.'

I knew the place. Sati Chowra was a fisherman's village, scarcely more than a few huts. It was on the edge of the European Station, near to the spot where I had watered my horse on my first visit to the siege. The ghat, little more than a flight of steps to a small stone platform on the riverbank, was a favourite spot amongst the Europeans, cool and tree-shaded, except in the very height of summer. I had often ridden there myself, early in the morning or at the end of the day. There was a little temple overlooking it and young ladies would often tell me how romantic they thought it was. I think part of its romantic appeal was that the river's banks there were very steep and anyone walking at the water's edge would have a degree of privacy not readily found elsewhere in Cawnpore, but perhaps I misjudged them. It was certainly very pretty.

As an embarkation point, it was conveniently situated, being about as close to the camp as the Ganges ran, but my recollection of the river, even when I had taken my horse to drink over two weeks earlier, was that the water was very low. I did wonder how the women were to get across the muddy shallows to a point far enough out for the boats to float off. And even if the women felt that after their weeks in the filth of the Entrenchment they could cope with some mud, there was the more serious question of how to carry aboard the many injured soldiers who would have to be evacuated with them.

The boats would be ready the next day, I was assured, and by the night, the British would be gone.

The atmosphere in the Nana's camp was relaxed, even celebratory. Late in the afternoon, an Englishman appeared on foot, carrying a letter which, I heard, was the formal acceptance of the Nana's terms. There was some cheering as this news spread through the crowd. When he re-emerged from the Nana's pavilion several men went to put their arms about his shoulders at which he quailed as if he were to be attacked and we all laughed at his discomfiture.

I lay down to sleep that night with an easier mind than I had in the afternoon. The British were safe and my decision was made. The next day, I would join them in time to leave Cawnpore with them.

That night I dreamt that the garrison arrived at the river to find it empty of water. Wheeler was mounted on an elephant.

'There's nothing for it, lads,' he says. 'We'll have to float them off on our blood.' At which the men march to the riverbed and slash their arms open with their bayonets. The blood gushes out and the boats are floating but now the women refuse to board. Lydia Hillersdon turns to me (for I was there, mounted on my horse and still wearing the Nana's uniform) and says, 'How can we cross that blood? It will make my dress dirty.'

Then the Nana appears, standing on the temple that overlooks the ghat. 'If the women won't enter the boats,' he cries, 'then they must come with me to Saturday House. They'll be quite safe there.' He turns to go and where he had been standing, the corpse of Mrs Greenway balances for a moment before falling with a great splash into the river. Her fall disturbs the blood which swells like a great wave, carrying away all the women and wrecking the boats. It runs around my horse, which rears, throwing me into the blood …

I woke, sweating, my heart beating against my ribs so that I thought I might fall down in a moment and die, like those struck by the heat. But it was not yet dawn and the air was as cool as it ever was in June.

I lay back on the ground and composed myself again to sleep. But I resolved that in the morning I would visit the

Sati Chowra ghat and see the condition of the boats for myself.

I awoke refreshed but with memories of my dream still disturbing me despite the promise of the new day. I joined Chimnaji and the other sowars for breakfast. We shared a meal, supplied by one of our number who had requisitioned it from a respectable citizen's kitchen the night before. 'Though,' he grumbled, 'there was little enough there. And the rogue demanded payment. I told him that he'd get paid when we did.'

The problem of our pay – or the lack of it – was increasingly difficult to ignore. The token military force that Nana Sahib had been allowed under the British had been joined by thousands of others who had flocked to his cause on the promise of better pay than the British gave their troops. The money looted from Treasury in the first days of the revolt had meant that, initially, these promises had been kept. By now, though, the money from the Treasury was gone. All that was left was that which Wheeler had been able to spirit away before the Nana's guard barred the doors. That money was in the Entrenchment and forfeit under the terms of the surrender. Nana Sahib needed the money and needed it immediately. Allowing Wheeler to depart with the honours of war was a small price to pay.

Why, then, was I still uneasy? Between mouthfuls of chapatti washed down with weak tea, I tried asking my fellow diners their views of the likelihood of the Europeans being able to get safely into the boats and off down river.

'Why ask me?' The man who had scavenged our breakfast tore off part of his chapatti and threw it onto the fire where we boiled water. 'I'm no fisherman.' He spoke the word with all the contempt that a high caste soldier would feel for a lowly river dweller.

The man beside me reached across to pour more hot water onto his tea. 'So long as the British leave, I don't care what happens to them.'

I didn't pursue the subject, but, once we had eaten, I excused myself to exercise my horse and soon I was making my way toward the river.

I decided to take the route that the British would follow, along the metalled road that led from the Entrenchment toward the ruins of St John's church and on to the Ganges. This meant starting at the farthest side of the Entrenchment from where the Nana's camp was situated. The quickest way would have been to cross the plain, a safe enough undertaking now that the guns were silent but, though it seemed a foolish superstition, I could not bring myself to do so. This patch of ground, that had been so long fought across and where so many men had lost their lives (for almost a thousand of the rebels were reckoned to have perished), seemed unclean and I could not bring myself to ride across it. The path I took instead carried me not far from the cavalry hospital where Mr Shepherd was imprisoned and I decided to stop by there in the hope that I might be able to offer him some more assistance or, at the least, to ensure that the money that I had paid to his jailer was having its effect.

Arriving at the jail, I soon found the subadar and enquired after his charge.

He smiled at me, reassuringly. 'He is well. He is safe here.'

'I hope that soon he will be safe anywhere. His crime was that he was in the Entrenchment with the British,' I said. 'But the British are to be allowed to leave. Is it possible that he might be allowed to leave with them?'

I had thought my question innocent enough, yet the subadar's smile vanished. He was an old man who looked as if he had been given the job for years of service to the Nana and he seemed an honest enough fellow. Yet now his eyes darted from place to place, avoiding mine and looking, it seemed, for some reason to be elsewhere.

'He should stay here for now. I will attend to everything as soon as I have the opportunity, but for now I have business to deal with.'

He turned to go but I put my hand on his arm to detain him. 'I am happy to buy your time.'

I started to reach for some coins but he shook his head. 'You have paid me already and I will do what you have paid me for. I will make sure your friend is safe.'

At that, he positively scurried away, leaving me wondering what was worrying him so much that he would not even take my money.

I rode on, heading up the Course toward the European settlement. All around me, I saw rebel soldiers and civilians strolling aimlessly in the sun, smiling, laughing in groups. All was as it should be in the hour of their victory – so why was I so uneasy?

Here and there, as I neared the river, I saw small groups of soldiers who seemed more earnest than the others. When I reached the ravine that ran down to the ghat, there were half a dozen men squatting beside the burned out ruins of a bungalow and cleaning their muskets. This surprised me, as native troops were never that careful of their weapons and I thought they would hardly bother to clean them if they did not expect to have immediate need of them. They looked up at the sound of my horse's hooves and waved cheerfully. I waved back with a smile on my face but a growing sense of unease.

I eased Kuching carefully down the steep path. When the rains came, there would be a stream rushing down to the Ganges, but now the bottom of the ravine was baked dry in the heat, though the steep sides provided a little protection from the sun.

When I reached the foot of the path, I found myself still a hundred yards or more from the water. Between the bank and the line of boats, presumably intended for the evacuation, was a noisome stretch of mud, strewn with filth. The bodies of two or three dead dogs were visible within a few paces of the platform where I now stood. The stench made it all too clear how the sewage from Sati Chowra was disposed of.

I snapped a branch from one of the neem trees that lined the bank and, standing on the platform, I cautiously prodded at the mud below me. To my relief, it was not particularly deep and I reckoned that the men of the garrison would have no difficulty in crossing it. The women would find it unpleasant but not impossible and the children could be carried to the boats.

Shading my eyes from the sun, which turned the filthy water into a dazzling ribbon of light, I squinted out to those boats. There were around two dozen of them. Some had thatched roofs to protect from the sun but others had only the framework where thatch should be but no sign yet of any covering. The boats were moored on the edge of the deeper water, a few bobbing freely in the current, but most grounded on the mud. Even from here, I could see that they were old and battered. At least – as far as I could tell from the shore – none was actually sinking. I had seen boats like these on the Ganges before – ungainly things around ten yards long and ten feet wide. They were difficult to steer and each would need a crew of four or five men, but I saw far fewer than that scrambling about the vessels, apparently trying to make them ready to sail.

While I watched their preparations, I heard the sound of naked feet slapping on the stone steps behind me. Turning, I saw a group of porters carrying baskets on their heads. Arriving on the platform, they stepped unhesitatingly into the mud and waited across to the line of boats. I was relieved to see that I had been right – they made the journey with little difficulty, though one spilled some of his load, rice flour pouring down his shoulders and into the mud.

I would have stayed longer, but at the end of the line of porters was one of the Nana's officers who, seeing me there, told me brusquely at I should make myself useful on the other bank. I had no idea what he meant, but it was clear that he expected me to make my way there. It seemed wisest to avoid suspicion and I set off immediately up the ravine.

Back on the road again, I puzzled over the order I had just been given. All the time I had ridden under the Nana's colours my duties, and those of all the sowars I had spoken with, had been confined to this side of the river. Why should the Nana now be deploying cavalry on the Oudh bank? Although the garrison had hoped for relief from Lucknow, the rebels' scouts were confident that there were no troops on the way and I could think of no other threat from the East.

I decided that rather than return directly to the Entrenchment, I would ride North along the river to the bridge of boats which connected Cawnpore to the Lucknow shore.

The bridge had not been cut and, indeed, was barely guarded. This made sense in view of the absence of any threat from this direction, but it made me even more confused as to why cavalry was being dispatched to the Eastern bank.

There was no equivalent city to Cawnpore on the Oudh side of the river, so there was no proper road along its bank. There was a track, though, used by boatmen and the people who lived in the little villages which one came across every mile or so. There were bushes and some small trees growing between the bank and the river. This close to the Ganges, they remained in leaf even in the dry season, sucking river water from deep beneath the ground. Even the grass grew lush and tall. The greenery was a welcome change from the arid ground around the Entrenchment, where the trees on the Course were the only growing things above the height of a dandelion. Through the leaves, I could see the sunlight shining on the river. After Cawnpore, it was close to a rural idyll.

I relaxed, enjoying the comparative cool of the morning, the heat tempered further by the faintest whisper of a breeze off the water.

I rode on for a mile or two until I saw, through a gap in the vegetation, the Sati Chowra ghat. It was a little downstream of my position but I could make it out quite clearly with the boatmen still busying themselves about the line of craft in the stream. I turned my gaze back to the path ahead. At first, I saw nothing untoward, but then a glimpse of scarlet caught my eye. There, concealed amongst the bushes, was a group of rebel soldiers.

I hesitated for a moment. The men ahead were clearly trying to hide from sight and I wondered if it might be best to turn back. But I was wearing the Nana's uniform and I had been ordered to this point. On balance, it seemed best to ride on and see how matters would develop.

As soon as the rebels were sure that I had seen them, they stood up from cover and I found myself facing a score or more of men clustered around two cannon. A dozen muskets pointed at my chest. They were clearly not pleased to see me.

One man, who appeared to be in charge, though he wore no rank badge, stepped forward to challenge me. 'Who are you and what are you doing here?'

'I am Anjoor Tewaree,' I replied, giving the name I used in my native guise. 'I am a rider in the Peshwa's own cavalry and I was ordered here by an officer at the ghat.' I gestured through the grass and bushes at the platform, which lay directly opposite the guns.

The man looked at me as if I were some low-caste beggar. 'Whoever told you to come here is a fool. We have no need of horsemen on this side of the river.'

'My apologies.' I had nearly said, 'My apologies, sir,' but I choked on the honorific. Clearly, this was an officer of some importance on a special mission for his Peshwa, but I was still dressed as one of the Peshwa's own sowars and I would never willingly acknowledge the superiority of any lesser type of soldier. 'If you are sure you have no need of me, I will return to Cawnpore where there may yet be fighting to be done.'

The fellow sneered at me. 'Yes, it's probably best you return to the city. After all, when we have finished our work, the Peshwa may still have some small requirement for your services.'

I decided not to linger, but to turn at once and ride back the way that I had come. Not for the first time, I blessed the rebels' poor communications and inept officering which had turned so many of their attacks into chaos.

Still, whatever their military inadequacies, these men were quite able to fire a cannon and the sight of their artillery had unnerved me. I struggled to find an innocent reason for its being in that position and aimed so squarely at the line of boats that was to be used in the evacuation. Yet, it was difficult for me to believe that Nana Sahib, for all his faults, intended treachery. Clearly, the men that I had seen relaxing around the rebel camp did not anticipate anything untoward. At the same time, a secret plan to attack the British boats would explain the nervousness of the jailer and the sight of soldiers apparently preparing for action.

Perhaps, I thought, some elements amongst the various factions that made up the rebel forces had decided to act independently, carrying on their attacks on the British after Nana Sahib had promised an armistice. Certainly, the men I had just seen looked to be Musalmans. The followers of the Prophet had shown themselves much more ruthless in their hatred of the Europeans than had the Hindoos.

If there were a plan to attack the British and if this was

a conspiracy amongst just some of the rebel soldiery, then perhaps the best course was to go to the Nana and warn him of what was afoot. But if the Nana knew of the plan, then going to him would achieve nothing and might, by exposing me to questioning, result in the discovery of my true identity. Perhaps, instead, I should warn the British they might be walking into a trap. But, even forewarned, what could they do? The terms of the surrender meant that their artillery had already been handed over to the rebels. Rebel soldiers had entered the Entrenchment to take possession of the guns and any pretence that the Europeans were in any condition to maintain their defence was now exposed as a lie. They were now entirely at the mercy of the rebels. Indeed, it was their very helplessness that made me question whether treachery was really planned. For why commit an act of such barbarity that it would be bound to lead to future reprisals when the Entrenchment would inevitably fall in the next few days anyway?

By the time I reached the bridge of boats and my horse's hooves were clattering across to the Cawnpore bank, I had decided that the first thing was to rejoin my fellow sowars to see if they had any intimation of treachery.

I returned by the road that I had come. I noticed in passing that the jail was firmly shut and a guard stood with his musket at ready at the door. It seemed that whatever the jailer did or didn't know, he had decided to watch his charges more carefully than he had in the past.

By now, I was seeing threats everywhere and I could not judge what was real and what my imagination. It seemed that there were somewhat fewer men on the road, though, as ever, the place was still busy. And it may be that those that were about were less careless in their manner than they had been only a few hours earlier.

Yet when I rejoined my fellows, they were as relaxed as ever. I was sure they did not suspect me of being anything other than I claimed for, if they had, my life would have been forfeit. So when they suggested riding down to the Entrenchment to see the Nana's men bring away the treasure that Wheeler was handing over, I was confident that they knew nothing of any plans other than for an orderly surrender.

As had been the case even at a height of the conflict, we sowars passed the midday hours taking a leisurely tiffin in the shade. It was late in the afternoon before we made our way down past the ruins of the half-built barracks and over the crumbling defences into the European camp. The Nana's men had yet to arrive to take away the treasure but we were not the only rebel soldiers to visit the camp. Natives were coming and going with impunity. Some were there to gloat but others had come to see if old friends had survived the siege and to offer them such comfort as they could. Many of the officers' servants had remained in the city, trying to protect their masters' property and now appeared to report what had been saved and what was lost.

The Company's European soldiers watched with their muskets at the ready. From here and there came the sound of bayonets being sharpened on grindstones. Clearly, many there were not convinced the fighting was over. The sight of the skeletal figures of their womenfolk, in their ragged clothes and bare feet, showed that however brave the fighting men, there could be no more serious resistance while they were encumbered with so many civilians.

A boy of no more than five or six ran up to where we sat, still mounted. He stared at me. I feared he might recognise me, but he just stared at each of us in turn and then asked, 'Did you kill my Daddy?'

Before any one of us thought to answer his mother, seeing where he stood, called urgently for him to come and he turned and ran to her. But for every child boldly searching the ruins for wood for the cooking fires or grabbing at the arms of natives they recognised among the visitors, three or four others would be clinging to their mothers, looking nervously at the world from behind what remained of their dresses.

'It is a bad thing,' said one of the sowars, 'when men make war on children and their mothers.'

'It is truly a bad thing.' I looked around and realised that almost all those I could see were, indeed, women and children or enlisted men. I called to one of the soldiers watching us.

'Where are your officers?'

'Lieutenant Bridges is in the Main Guard, sir.'

The 'sir' had slipped out before he could stop himself and I saw him blush with shame. It was the natural deference of the defeated foot soldier toward the mounted victor, yet it marked, I knew, a change in the relations between the races in India. Things would never be quite the same again.

'I don't ask for your lieutenant, man. I want to know of your captains.' I hoped that if Captain Moore were at hand, I might yet make an opportunity to talk secretly with him about my fears.

'All the officers of rank that are fit have gone to the river to inspect the boats.'

I turned to my companions.

'Would you like to see the boats that will carry our enemies from Cawnpore?'

There was some shrugging of shoulders and they decided they would not bother. 'We will see them go soon enough. There is nothing to be gained by looking at boats now.'

I shrugged in my turn. 'I am curious to see how this will be managed, and if there will be any role for us sowars. I shall ride down to the river to see.'

I set off, leaving the others to return to the Nana's camp. I took the metalled road that ran North from the Entrenchment and carried on past the ruins of St John's

Church and the Artillery Bazaar until I found myself back on the road I had followed that morning. The soldiers I had seen cleaning their weapons were no longer there. Indeed, the place seemed strangely empty.

Before I reached the ravine, the unnatural quiet was broken by the sound of men and beasts waiting on the road. A few of the Nana's sowars who had been absent from our camp that morning stood with their horses, alongside two elephants and their mahouts. The first of the sowars to see me was young Appa, who greeted me with a laugh. 'So you've decided to join us and do some work, have you?'

'This is work? A trip to the Ganges? And then you can't even be bothered to climb down to the river.'

'The Peshwa has sent some fine gentlemen to show the English their transport. They're down at the river now. But we know our place. It's up here with the beasts.'

I laughed. The idea of a sowar knowing his place was absurd.

Appa joined in my laughter. 'Truth to tell, the path is steep and the company uncongenial. The British are insisting that they will not leave today and that we should provide proper transport to bring them to the river. I am sure that they will complain about the state of the boats, too. The Peshwa's courtiers are the right people to soothe them.' He spat on the ground. 'If it were up to me, I'd have them walk to Allahabad or stay in their wretched fort and die.'

'But you are content that they should have safe passage to Allahabad?'

He shrugged. 'So long as they leave Cawnpore and do not return, I care not where they go.'

I was relieved to hear him say so. Some troops may be planning treachery but it was clear that most of the sowars expected the rebels to hold to their word.

We waited, exchanging tall tales of our exploits during

the siege. After about twenty minutes, we heard the sounds of the British returning up the ravine. Even before we could see them, it was clear that Appa was right: the British were unhappy with the arrangements. Raised voices echoed off the rocks. '… disgraceful … inadequate … deceived…' Occasionally, as the British voices paused for breath, I caught the soothing tones of the Nana's courtiers.

They were still complaining when they arrived at the top and continued to grumble as the mahouts ordered the elephants to kneel so that the officers could scramble up to the howdahs on their backs. There was not enough room for them all and a few walked beside the elephants where they continued to wrangle with the Nana's men. Captain Moore was one of those who walked and I heard him complaining that the boats were not ready to sail and the provisions were inadequate.

Beside him, a courtier continued his attempts to reassure. 'You can see the boatmen are working to get everything ready and more provisions will be loaded. Not only flour, but sheep and goats also.'

It was clear from his face the Moore did not believe him but, though he continued to complain, he had the appearance of a beaten man. The dashing soldier I had met in the half-finished barracks was gone. The captain now was gaunt, his features worn with fatigue. The battle had been lost and I could see that in the end he would accept whatever the Nana would give him.

I pushed my horse alongside him as he walked. I had hoped to catch his eye but when he was not looking at the man he was talking to, his gaze was fixed morosely on the ground. With his cavalry escort all around and the Nana's agents in our midst, I had no chance of a private word. The best I could do was when one of the other officers started his own complaints and Moore was left alone for a few moments. Bending in my saddle, I had just time to whisper a few words. 'There may be treachery. They have cannon aimed at the boats.' Then the Nana's man turned back to Moore and I had no chance to say anything further.

I watched Moore's expression to see how he responded to my news but, though he looked up at me, his face registered no recognition. He seemed past the point where he could respond any further to the blows that fate was dealing him.

As the sad little procession made its way back to the Entrenchment, I discussed loudly with the other riders whether there was any possibility that the British might be attacked as they tried to leave. As I had expected, they expressed shock at the very idea but I hoped that at least some of the officers might hear the word 'treachery' and be alerted to the possibility that all was not as it appeared.

By now, I was almost certain that at least some of the rebels planned to violate the terms of the surrender. The attractions of my present guise were growing greater. I could remain as a sowar and, if the evacuation proceeded safely, slip away from the rebel army later. I feared that if I revealed myself now, I could find myself with the other Europeans walking into a trap as they boarded the boats.

As soon as we arrived back at the Entrenchment, Moore was away to consult with Wheeler, who even the natives knew was by now so broken that he remained commander in name only. The Nana's cavalry had no reason to linger and obviously expected me to return with them, so I had no opportunity to pass any private messages, even if there were faces I recognised to pass them too. I had to content myself with uttering bloodthirsty threats to every white face we passed, in the hope that they would at least realise that the armistice was not as secure as they might imagine. I did notice several of the men responded with suspicious glares but, as I passed for the last time through the devastation of Wheeler's defences, I found myself wondering, yet again, what choice they had. The British would trust Nana Sahib to keep his word because the alternative was annihilation.

At least, I thought, I could make sure that one man escaped. As we drew back to the rebel lines, I told my companions that I had a cousin in the jail and I must go and enquire after his health. It says much for the state of lawlessness that by now prevailed in the region that it was accepted without question that one of their leader's own cavalry might be related to a felon. Indeed, by now I doubt that there were many native families left where at least one person had not fallen foul of one faction or another amongst the new rulers.

The door to the jail was still barred, now with two guards on duty. One went and got the old subadar. I bowed to him, my palms pressed together in front of me.

He gave me a small smile, grim but not unfriendly. 'Each new day gives us the possibility of wisdom. Are you wiser than you were this morning?'

I returned his smile. 'I know you have my friend's interests at heart.'

He nodded and, as he did so, moved casually away from the door and out of earshot of the guards.

'I do, though he does not know it. He heard this afternoon that the fort is to be evacuated and he claims he is not Budloo but Mr Shepherd and one of those who have been fighting against us. He would have me tell the Peshwa of this, so that he might rejoin his friends.' There was a long pause. 'I have told him that I am too busy to run such an errand.'

I bowed again. 'I am sorry that your duties keep you so busy but perhaps all will be for the best.'

'I pray every day that it might be so.' He cocked his head on one side and looked quizzically at me. 'It's strange, isn't it, that you should have known him as Budloo, if that is not truly his name?'

'Perhaps his name really is Budloo and now he lies in

the hope of his release.'

'It is possible. But, there again, in these days it may be that many people are not who they claim they are.'

His old eyes glinted with amusement and I knew he sensed my discomfiture.

'Do not worry,' he said. 'Enough people have died, both the innocent and the guilty. And I fear there will be more blood spilt yet. I would not add to the deaths if I can avoid it.'

I reached again for the money I kept in the pouch on my belt but he shook his head. 'I will not have you think I acted for money. I am an old man and it is time I think of gaining some merit before I die.'

I bowed a third time. 'I am sure that the gods will look kindly on you for what you do now.'

'Well …' He chuckled. 'I hope some of them will.'

I watched him walk back to the jail and vanish within. I was sure I had just been talking to a good and honest man. But I was now certain that there were those in authority who were neither good nor honest.

The day was drawing late. Wheeler would evacuate the next morning. Until then, there was nothing further I could do.

Mounting, I set off back to spend another night camped with the horses. As I rode, I looked across the plain at the shattered remnants of the Entrenchment, and the rebel piquets, keeping up their half-hearted guard. I tried to fix it all in my mind. Whatever happened, tomorrow the garrison would leave and things would never be the same again.

Chapter Nine

The next morning we were awake before dawn. Looking from the low hill over toward the Entrenchment, we saw the lights of a dozen or more little fires. I imagined the women I had seen in the past dining on banquets prepared by an army of native servants, now crouched over their cooking fires, making chapattis for the journey ahead of them.

By dawn, the Nana's transport had arrived in Wheeler's camp. We watched from above while a motley array of elephants, palanquins, and carts started to take on board their human cargo. A line of rebel troops stood sentry around the convoy, supposedly offering some security to their defeated foe. However, as we watched hundreds, perhaps thousands, of the rebels who had been surrounding the camp entered into the Entrenchment to see the British leave and to mock them in the hour of their humiliation.

'Shall we ride down there?' Appa asked.

'No.' Chimnaji's voice was definite. 'We are men of honour. We have no business there.'

So we stood watching the spectacle as the weary defenders, some so wounded that they had to be carried to the carts, gathered in dreary procession. There must have been about four hundred men, women, and children who set off to the ghat that morning. At the front came the elephants carrying the officers and these made a fine show. Looking at them, it was possible to believe that I was watching an army leaving with the honours of war. Behind them, came the palanquins, mostly carrying women and children. The common soldiers and those whose position in society could not obtain them a place in the palanquins followed behind in the carts. Even then, there were those left who could not be accommodated in any of this transport and they followed the rest on foot. They dragged themselves along as best they could while the mob drew close about them, yelling insults and striking at them with their fists.

I watched with the others for almost an hour, and still the stragglers had not left the Entrenchment. I turned to Chimnaji, saying that I would watch no longer. He nodded his understanding and I mounted my horse and rode off in the direction of the jail.

Most people were in the Entrenchment, either to watch the British depart or in the hope of finding loot – although I could not imagine what might be left there to steal. This left the roads quiet and, once clear of the Nana's camp, I was able to gallop my horse toward the ghat.

I was not sure exactly what I intended to do, but if treachery were planned, then at least I would be at the riverside to take such action as I could. There was no point in my taking the path to the ghat that I had followed the previous day. The road would be packed with Wheeler's people and the natives who had come to watch them pass. I decided instead to head for the river slightly to the North, by way of the village of Sati Chowra itself.

I misjudged my path and arrived at the river a little upstream of the village, which announced its presence with a noisome stink of fish and filth, though the place was a quarter of a mile away from where I stood. The line of boats stretched upriver from the ghat to level with Sati Chowra and I had a clear view of them without moving any closer to the ravine. The vanguard of the evacuation had already arrived at the river and British officers were splashing through the mud, trying to get the boats into the water. Whether the river had dropped overnight or the boats had been pulled further toward the shore, I could not say, but almost all were beached.

At the first of the boats, I could make out a small figure in gold braid that I recognised even at this distance as General Wheeler. The elephant that had brought him to the river had waded out to the boat and the mahout was now guiding it against the vessel which it pushed gently away from the shore until it was bobbing safely in the stream. The officers in the other boats were not so fortunate as to have pachydermous assistance and they were still struggling to get their vessels afloat. More officers and men were pushing through the mud from the ravine. A few women had already joined them, though they were slower than the men, hampered by what remained of their dresses. All was chaos and confusion but there was no sign of any attack.

I dismounted and stood beside the river. Looking at the height of the sun in the sky, I judged it almost nine in the morning. It would take an hour or more to load all the boats and get everyone into the stream. I could watch the progress of the evacuation from where I was – close enough to act if action was required but far enough away to be inconspicuous.

I looked across to the Oudh bank. There was no sign of the gun crews that I had seen there the day before but anything could be lurking in the greenery.

On this side of the river, my view of the bank was obstructed by the huts of the village. The ravine and its little platform were entirely hidden from view but I could see the temple that was perched just a little higher on the bank above the ghat. I could see some natives sat there, the sun catching red cloth and gold braid. I imagined the Nana's generals and officials there to gloat.

A movement just beyond the village caught my eye. For a second I thought I saw a glimpse of red there too, but I looked again and it was gone.

My horse sensed my nervousness and whinnied softly. I

imagined another whinny from further along the bank but then a group of monkeys, disturbed from their rest in the ravine, came bounding along the higher ground behind me, chattering and screaming.

Every sound had me jumping. I looked out again at the boats. Two had been pushed clear of the mud and men were climbing aboard. All was proceeding according to plan. I willed myself to relax. I thought of Mungo and his smile, the green of the gardens at Saturday House. Out on the river, the men continued to clamber aboard the boats, some were helping wounded comrades to clamber aboard. The first of the women were pulling themselves clear of the mud, dresses hanging heavy with filth.

I began to think I had been imagining the danger. Everything would go smoothly. No one else need die.

I had just convinced myself that my fears were groundless when, from somewhere in the direction of the temple, came the sound of cannon fire. I started forward and, seizing my reins, I mounted. Yet there was no sign of artillery falling on the boats. No water spouted in the air. There were cries of alarm, certainly, but no screams of pain.

Aboard the boats, though, all was confusion. The native boatmen, who had so far taken little part in proceedings, suddenly threw their oars into the water and leapt from the craft to splash through the mud toward the shore. In the panic and uncertainty that immediately gripped those trying to board, it took a few moments before people noticed the smoke pouring from the thatch of several of the boats which the boatmen must have fired before fleeing.

Hardly had I realised that the initial cannon blasts had been a signal, than the rebels opened fire in earnest. Grapeshot and cannonballs fell around the boats, mud and spray drenching the vessels and their occupants.

Now I saw that my eyes had not deceived me. From

where they had been concealed the other side of the village, scores of sepoys rose and ran toward the temple, firing their muskets. At the same time the sound of shots and screaming made me realise that more were attacking down the ravine itself.

Although the cannon fire had caused terror on the river, I had seen no one hit. By contrast, the sepoys' attack was immediately effective. As their musket balls struck home, I saw men fall on the boats. For a moment, all I heard was screams and the sound of firing, but then British voices shouted over the din as the officers rallied their men. Some of those on board were set to beating at the burning thatch with their coats while others returned fire. The British musketry brought down several of the sepoys who were forced to concentrate their efforts on the men shooting from the boats, allowing the soldiers who were still in the water to keep pushing at the vessels in their desperate efforts to get them afloat.

Now another cannon came into action. Shot was falling from four separate places and the rebels had found their range. Boat after boat was struck and this, combined with the flames billowing from the roofs, made escape impossible. The men and women who had so recently clambered aboard now threw themselves over the sides. The wounded, who had been painstakingly lifted into the boats, were abandoned and, as the vessels blazed, I could hear the screams of those trapped aboard.

Most of those fleeing the wrecks jumped out on the side furthest from the shore, hoping thus to shield themselves from attack. Alas, the flimsy vessels provided scant protection from cannon ball and grapeshot.

The rebels had by now formed themselves into a long line along the bank, firing repeatedly into the smoke. I looked on helplessly. I wondered whether to make a charge along the line. It might be possible, I supposed, to kill one or perhaps even two before they turned their muskets on me and I joined the English dead.

By now, a few of the boats had floated free and the sepoys were following them down river. Almost all the other vessels had been abandoned and their passengers floundered in the mud between boats and riverbank. With the boats out of action, the cannons ceased to fire and it seemed for a moment that the survivors were to be left to make their way to dry ground as best they might. Anticipating this, I started forward to assist them to the shore but, as I did so, I saw rebel horsemen start out from the other side of the village where the sepoys had concealed themselves before their own attack. While I hesitated, they rode into the shallows and, leaning low in their saddles, began to hack at the people struggling in the mud. Desperately, the survivors from the boats who, as the sepoys drew off, had started to struggle toward the shore, now turned back to the river, hoping to hide themselves in the smoke. Their attempts at escape were unavailing. The horses were coming at a canter and, one after another, they were struck down. Watching, and listening to their screams, it seemed to me that many of the riders had allowed their blades to lose their edge for some people were struck four or five times and fell back, still living, to drown in the muddy water.

I could watch and wait no longer. Urging my own horse forward I joined the fray. Busy at their bloody work, I doubt any of the rebels noticed an extra rider.

My plan, such as it was, relied on the notion that any rabble of men engaged in attacking a body of women would be sure to include a few who would seize some of the females for their private pleasure. I therefore hoped that I might be able to bear off at least one of the young women without it being seen as anything other than an undisciplined attempt to satisfy my lust. Indeed, as I splashed into the mud, I saw one or two of the men in the melee ahead of me sheath their swords and reach down to seize one of the struggling creatures in the water.

Those boats that had not been destroyed or pushed free into the river were now being systematically pillaged by rebels. On the vessel nearest to me, I saw men shoot down two children no more than eight years old before turning on the adults who they were robbing even as I approached. By now the water was almost at the height of my saddle and my horse was struggling to keep moving through the mud, but I came right up to the boat just as the ruffians were attacking the last of the survivors – a young, dark-complexioned girl who was trembling with terror. They were searching her roughly, tearing at what was left of her gown, and I was sure that once they had robbed her of whatever money or valuables she had secreted about her person they would kill her as they had all the others aboard.

Drawing my sabre, I shouted to the nearest rebel that the girl was mine and that he should throw her to me. For a moment, he hesitated but there is always something commanding about the presence of an armed man on horseback, especially as he is holding his weapon within an easy arm's reach of your throat. I think, too, that the man was also responding to authority in the way that Indians of lower caste will do. Whatever his reasons, he obeyed, seizing her around the waist and tossing her into the river. Caught by surprise, she was unable to find her feet and was carried along in the water while I pushed my horse to catch up with her, finally grabbing her and pulling her over my saddle as she reached dry ground and tried to stand.

I now found myself with a frightened and angry girl trying desperately to wriggle free and landing several blows about my person with her fists and her feet. I had, unthinkingly, imagined that I could simply tell her in English that I was a friend and that she would then trust me to save her. Foolishly, I had failed to take account of her fear and confusion and the natural terror my appearance roused in her. Her struggles, though, were ineffective, for she was lightly built and the privations of the siege had reduced her strength to the point where her blows caused me no harm.

By now, we were almost level with the ghat. The platform and the steps were covered with bodies and soldiers were searching the clothing of the dead for any loot they might still be able to recover. I turned my horse away, having no desire to push through either the living or the dead. The looters were shouting and cursing as they tore at clothes where jewels might be sewn into the hem or concealed in undergarments and they had attained the degree of excitement where they might well turn on the girl even though she was notionally under my protection.

I turned instead back toward the village. None of the other sowars tried to stop me or even seemed to think my behaviour unusual. Indeed, one or two grinned broadly when they saw the young woman struggling in my grip and made imaginatively obscene suggestions as to what I might do with her.

What I actually did with her was to carry her beyond the village and, once we were alone on the track back to Cawnpore, to put her on her feet on the ground and try to explain the situation she found herself in.

'I'm trying to help you. If you don't want to be helped, I can leave you here. The first man to find you will kill you. He may dishonour you first or he may be merciful and kill you quickly but you will die. I'm British. You have to trust me if you want to live.'

I had to say this several times, for the poor girl was in a terrible state of shock. She had survived the Entrenchment and had believed herself saved when the rebels' treacherous attack brought her again to the edge of death. Her friends and her family were being cut down around her and she herself was about to join them when she was carried off by a mounted ruffian. No wonder she struggled to take in what I was trying to tell her. I was only surprised that she had not entirely lost her reason.

Once I had made myself understood, the girl's first reaction was to break down in hysterical weeping. I stood beside her, quite uncertain as to what to do, nothing in my experience having prepared me for such a circumstance. At length, though, she recovered herself and I was surprised by how calmly she seemed to accept her situation. She told me that her name was Amy Horne and that she had seen all of her family slaughtered. She said she would place herself entirely in my hands and asked what I intended to do.

At least I was no longer in the situation I had found myself with Mr Ashley for I had a plan ready. 'I will take you to a place of safety,' I said. 'There you will be concealed until this revolt is over and the British have returned.'

She looked at me with deep brown eyes that had seen too much suffering but now showed, not fear, but a calm calculation of the possibilities for the future. 'And what if that day should never come?'

'It will come,' I said. 'I'm sure of it.

She made no reply but appraised me with another look and I knew that she recognised my words to be a lie.

I lifted her from the ground. We had a long way to ride and I suggested that she sit astride the horse. Perhaps once maidenly modesty would have caused her to object but women who had survived the siege had lost their concern for superficial propriety. The rags she wore did not constrict her legs and, emaciated as she was, she was easily able to sit before me on the saddle.

We had been riding for an hour when she began to sway dangerously from side to side. Fortunately, we were not far from a grove of mango trees and I rode toward them and dismounted, lifting her gently down from the saddle. As I put her on the ground, her legs buckled and I had to catch her before she fell. I cursed myself for my stupidity. The poor girl was exhausted and in no state to ride further without food and drink. I would have liked her to have a chance to rest as well, but I feared to stop for more than half an hour, so I had to be content with giving her water from my flask and dried beef that was carried in my saddlebag.

She sat, pulling her rags around her to maintain her decency and, while she sipped from my flask and chewed at her meat, I encouraged her to talk about herself, for it seemed to me that she would recover from her ordeal more easily if she could share her story with another.

'What brought you to Cawnpore?'

She started to laugh and I feared that she would fall prey to hysteria but, swallowing, she controlled herself.

'Would you believe that my father brought us here from Lucknow because he thought it would be safer? We arrived only in April.' She began to sob. 'He's dead now. And my mother. There were five children beside me and now ...'

She was weeping uncontrollably by now and for a while she could not speak. I sat beside her on the ground, not knowing what to say or do. At last, I put one clumsy arm around her shoulders and she leaned against me and, slowly, the sobbing eased.

Amy and her family had been billeted in a bungalow near the St John's Church and had only moved into the Entrenchment when the mutiny broke out. There she and her family had sheltered under a veranda, which had been their home for three weeks.

'They died every day.' She was shaking with the horror of it. 'One day an officer rested from the sun next to us when a shot struck him full in the face, taking his head clean off. His body just stayed sitting there, his hands falling by his sides, the blood gushing from between his shoulders like a fountain.' She described how those around her had died one after another. Sometimes whole families would be found lying dead side-by-side. 'I tried not to look at it, but the smell! My God, the smell! And the flies. Flies everywhere.'

Both Amy and her mother had been wounded in the head and her five-year-old sister had her leg fractured by a falling block of masonry. They were so hungry that the children had been reduced to eating a horse that had died outside the Entrenchment and been dragged in by the troops. Her mother had gone mad. That Amy herself had remained sane seemed little short of a miracle and I was determined to see her safe.

As soon as she was recovered enough in mind and body for us to remount, I rode on. We headed North, skirting Bithur and making directly for the shelter we had been promised we could find with Mungo's cousin, Dara. I had met him only once, when he first volunteered his house as a place of refuge, but I had trusted him immediately.

My confidence in him was repaid. His gatekeeper may have looked askance at the sight of one of the Nana's riders arriving at the compound with a half-naked young woman mounted before him, but he clearly had orders to admit me without question. The gate swung open and, moments later, Dara came bustling out to greet me. 'I am glad that you have need of me, for it means that you have saved at least one person from this disaster. Our gods teach us that, though there are times we must kill, life is sacred and we have a duty to protect it whenever we can.'

As a respectable householder, Dara had Amy whisked away to the women's quarters as soon as he set eyes on her. I was not entirely comfortable at the idea of abandoning her but Dara was firm that I could not penetrate his zenana. 'It is a place reserved to women and your friend will be safe there. It would be quite improper for you to enter. Beside,' he smiled, 'judging from her appearance, I think the first thing that the ladies will do is to bathe her and provide her with new clothing. I am sure you would not wish to intrude on that.'

I had to accept his argument. In any case, I felt it was best not to linger. I did not want curious minds to wonder where I was spending my time. So I drank the tea I was offered, nibbled at some sweets presented on golden trays and, as soon as was decently possible, I was back on my horse and headed South.

It was less than a week since I had left Bithur, but when I opened the door to find Mungo waiting in his room, I fell upon him as if we had been parted for many months. Holding him in my arms, I felt somehow cleansed, as if his presence washed away some of the horror of what I had just witnessed. The eagerness with which Mungo pressed his body against mine suggested that he too had felt my absence.

'You should have come back after the battle or at least sent me word. I heard that the cavalry were driven back. Can't you imagine how worried I have been?'

'I'm here now. I'm safe.'

He pulled me tighter to him, his fingers tracing the line of my spine as if he thought it might have changed since last he saw me. 'You're safe and the fighting is over.'

'For now, at least.'

Mungo pulled away, searching my face for my meaning. 'How can it not be over? The Peshwa is to review his troops in Cawnpore tonight, in celebration of his victory.'

'And do you know how that victory was achieved?'

Mungo could tell from my voice that there was something amiss but his honest face showed he had no idea of what had happened on the river.

'The Europeans must have realised that they could not beat off the cavalry again, so they surrendered.' He tried a smile. 'You see, your efforts won the day after all.'

I could not smile back and his face turned serious. 'In any case, I suppose you should be at the review.'

He was right. I was supposed to be a soldier of the Nana and, after what I had seen, I had no illusions as to my fate if my true identity were discovered. Nor was I the only one with an identity to protect. Shepherd must be in more danger than ever. I could only pray that the old subadar had kept faith.

'Yes, I need to be there. I must show myself with the others – and I have someone under my protection and I must see that he is well.'

Mungo obviously wanted to know about his person and I told him in as few words as possible of Mr Shepherd's disguise and my efforts to buy his safety. I was undressing as I spoke, for I wanted to get myself clean before I rode back to Cawnpore and it was already afternoon. I had little time to waste if I were to take my place in the Nana's victory parade.

Mungo insisted on 'helping' me bathe, so I spent much, much longer than I had intended being cleaned and scented and generally cosseted before I was allowed to put on a clean uniform (Mungo having secreted one away while I was in Cawnpore) and presented myself at the stables to find my horse, too, had been pampered. At least, as the two of us set out on the weary road back to the battlefield, we started with the benefit of cleaned and rested bodies.

Even so, by the time I rejoined my fellow sowars I was weary in the extreme. My fatigue meant that I did not find the grand review as impressive as I otherwise might have for all of the Nana's troops were arrayed on the plain, which now took on its original purpose as a great parade ground. There were mutineers from Cawnpore, Lucknow, Allahabad, Azimgurh, and Nowgong; Benghalis, Golundazes, and Nawabees as well as a great mob of zemindars – landowners who had pretended loyalty to the

244

British but who had turned up with gangs of armed followers once they thought the Nana's cause would be triumphant. In all, there were some tens of thousands of men parading. A twenty-one-gun salute was fired for the Nana after which he made a mercifully short speech, praising us for our great courage and bravery and promising us a lac of rupees apiece as a reward for our labours (although I was not alone in doubting that we would ever see the money).

We woke late the next morning and took our ease. We talked, of course, of what had happened the previous day. The others in my company had been as shocked as I by the massacre. Chimnaji was especially upset.

'I have ridden for the Peshwa for many years and I can scarcely believe that he could be involved with such a thing. To promise safe passage and then to strike down your enemy when he is defenceless. It is not an honourable way to wage war.' He shook his head and there was a murmur of agreement from our little assembly. 'At least the women and children were spared.'

This news caused me not only astonishment but some indignation, for I had seen them being cut down, but I did not want to admit that I had been present at the massacre so I simply asked if he was sure that it was true.

'Certainly it is, for I saw them brought up here and locked into Savada House with the other European prisoners.'

The news that at least some of the women and children had escaped filled me with joy. I decided that I would try to visit all the prisoners that afternoon and I set off with high hopes of being able to bring some succour to them but, alas, I was to be disappointed. Savada House was, as ever, well guarded and I was told in no uncertain terms that the prisoners were allowed to see no one.

'But one of the ladies employed my sister's nephew as her houseboy and when she went into the fort, he was left without his wages. I would see her to ensure that arrangements are made to pay him.'

The guard laughed. 'No one here will be paying any of their debts. They have nothing but the clothes they stand in – and those are little better than rags. Tell your cousin to help himself to anything he wants in the house and take that for his wages. Not that I doubt he has stolen from them already.'

Rebuffed, I made my way to the cavalry hospital where Jonah Shepherd was still a prisoner. When I arrived, though, the old subadar was not at his post and I was rebuffed there too. A young guard I had not seen before claimed to be in charge and refused me entry.

'The old man is too soft on them.' He spat on the ground between us. 'I've ordered your cousin chained up. He's a dirty traitor to the Peshwa and he'll have no visitors while I'm in charge.'

He spoke with the arrogance of a young man revelling in his first taste of authority. I could see that bribery would not help me here. The guard was enjoying his moment of power and the control it gave him over the lives of his prisoners. All I could do was return to my place with the other sowars and trust that the old subadar would return soon.

We had been told that Nana Sahib would return to Saturday House the following evening, when there was to be a great ceremony acknowledging him as Peshwa. Until then we had no duties and we were all grateful for a day of rest after the excitement of the last week. I took the opportunity to explore the remains of the European Quarter. One or two of the houses had escaped looting. I think these were where servants loyal to their old masters had remained in their homes. Now, with the Europeans gone, the servants had fled too. Everywhere was desolation.

Near my old home a Labrador, someone's favourite

gun-dog I guessed, trotted hopefully toward me. Its coat was glossy and it looked well fed. Again, the work of loyal servants was evident. Now, it had been abandoned like the homes. I threw a stick and, as it ran to catch it, I turned my horse and rode away.

I returned to camp with some delicacies pillaged from abandoned kitchens. There was tinned fish, a jar of marmalade, a tin of Bath Oliver biscuits, and even a jar of Gentleman's Relish. The other sowars thought my taste eccentric but all were happy to sample the food with me, though some claimed the flavours (especially the Gentleman's Relish) too alien to be enjoyable. I welcomed the feast as a reminder of what seemed a long-lost life, but I had to be careful not to seem too familiar with the food, lest I rouse my comrades' suspicions.

The next day, to my relief, I found the old subadar back on duty.

'I am sorry I was away. A family matter.'

'I hope it is resolved now.'

'All is well now. At least, all is well with my family. As for your friend here …' He gestured toward the jail. 'I must confess that he is becoming a thorough nuisance. He's heard that there were Europeans who escaped the killing and he wants to be put with them.'

'Is that why he has been put in chains?'

'Not really. I am afraid that while I was away my young colleague became rather – shall we say, overenthusiastic. Don't worry. I will ensure that they are removed today.'

I thanked him.

'You have been generous to me and I am generous to your friend. But he thinks I am cruel in keeping him a prisoner here. He still insists he is a European and should be at Savada House with the others.'

I had seen how the Nana had dealt with the Europeans who had fallen into his hands at Sati Chowra. I understood that if Shepherd thought his family might have survived he would be desperate to join them but, like the subadar, I thought he was safer kept in jail as Budloo. 'He is no more a European than I am.' We both smiled at this. 'He should stay here. And, if he is to stay longer with you, it is only right that you are rewarded for your care of him.'

Gold passed from my hand to his. The subadar bowed his gratitude and I returned to camp believing that I had at least been able to assist one prisoner, even if I had not been able to reach the others.

In mid-afternoon, when the worst of the heat was over, we mustered to escort Nana Sahib back to Saturday House for his inauguration as Peshwa. He moved in state, sitting in a gilded howdah, while we cavalry formed an escort around his elephant. Following us came many of the troops who had marched in his victory parade. By no means all the troops left Cawnpore, though. The most enthusiastic rebels remained and I noticed the green flags of the Musalmans conspicuous among those who stood and watched our departure rather than ride with us. Even without them, though, our train was miles long. I did wonder if the tail had left Cawnpore by the time we arrived at Bithur. Riding at the front, as I was, I never saw the back of the procession.

Once the Nana was safely deposited at his home, we sowars were dismissed, allowing us time to smarten ourselves up for the ceremony. I prepared alongside Mungo, who was bubbling with more than his usual enthusiasm.

'It will be a splendid ceremony. To think that I will be one of those who see him finally made Peshwa.'

Tired from my journey and having sat through one evening of ceremonial already that week, I could not summon up the same enthusiasm. 'He's been telling everybody that he's the Peshwa already.'

'And he is!' Mungo's face flushed and I had to remind myself that it was his own family honour he was defending. 'But he said he would lay formal claim to the title only once he had won it in battle. And this night his reign will be inaugurated. How can you say that the fighting is not over?'

'I know the British. They will not let this pass.'

'But they are few and we are many. They have left Cawnpore. Surely they would not be such fools as to return?'

I tried to reassure him with a smile but I had broken the mood.

'Anyway, we should not linger here.' Mungo was all business now. 'I must be seen at the celebration, honouring my master's new role. And you should tidy yourself up and be there too.'

We did not speak again of whether the fighting was over or of whether the British would return. I bathed and Mungo and I both scented our bodies. He relaxed enough to laugh at this, rubbing scented oil into my hair and then massaging me in my private places, and I laughed too and pretended that the events of the past days had not come between us.

As night fell, we went out into the gardens. I think every servant in the place must have been pressed into working there. I wondered how Mungo had escaped fetching and carrying but I supposed that a Peshwa has more than enough people to do that sort of thing. Two great pavilions had been set up. One already housed the ladies of the court, so that they could see the celebrations through a screen without exposing themselves to the gaze of men. I glanced at it curiously. Hidden in there were the late Peshwa's widows, whose disinclination to see any sister slain had saved at least some European lives. I remarked to Mungo that they may have been unhappy to hear of the massacre of women and children at the ghat.

'I have heard a few were killed in the fighting, but when the Peshwa heard that there were women and children there, he ordered them spared.'

'Only after a score or more had died.'

Mungo bridled as he had in his room. 'I tell you that the Peshwa has shown mercy. The women and children are kept prisoner and no harm should come to them.'

I could not bear another argument. 'I'm sorry. It's difficult in the heat of battle. I'm sure the Peshwa was as merciful as he could be. '

At once, Mungo's tension was gone and he smiled at me with the smile of the innocent boy that he was. 'You see, you need not have worried. Really, you could send that girl you carried away back to Cawnpore. She'd probably be better off with the others.'

I tried to keep my face from showing the horror that I felt at this suggestion. I had seen the Nana's treachery at first hand and I did not intend to trust Amy to his uncertain mercy. Fortunately, the sight before us made it easy to change the subject to something less likely to generate discord.

'I had thought the Peshwa's pavilion at Cawnpore was splendid but this is even more amazing.'

Mungo beamed as if the pavilions before us were his own property. 'It is as it should be for the inauguration of the Peshwa. It will truly be a wonderful thing. You'll see.'

The gardens were already filling with people. There must have been several thousand there. Mungo pushed through with the easy authority of a courtier. I always thought of him as my friend – a young man easy in his manners and pleasant to know. It was always a shock to me when I saw him in situations like this, where others quickly deferred to his rank.

Thanks to him, I was seated in one of the best positions when Nana Sahib's procession entered. It was led by elephants in crimson and gold trappings. Behind them followed bullock carts, palanquins, and led horses. Mixed in amongst the animals were men dressed up as horses who pranced about, kicking and playing antics. The most curious part of the procession was the platforms for the dancing girls. These were made of bamboo over which was spread an awning ornamented with crimson and gold and silver. On each travelling throne sat a native musician playing on a kettledrum and before him danced two girls, swirling with all their might and skill. The platforms were carried on the heads of men in the procession and had a curious and singular effect. The situation was a very unsteady one for the dancing girls, one of whom became giddy and tumbled down upon the heads of the crowd of people below.

The Nana himself was, of course, riding on the state elephant. He sat in a howdah covered in red cloth and liberally decorated with gold. Arriving at the pavilion, he dismounted and was carried the short distance to his throne on a litter. He sat while Hindoo priests charted and anointed him with oil. Representatives of the Musalman community were present too. They watched the Hindoo ceremonies without enthusiasm but, just by being there, they endorsed Nana Sahib as a ruler acceptable to both of the faiths.

The ceremony lasted an hour or more. At its conclusion, the new Peshwa rose from his throne and raised his arms in benediction to the crowd. The noise of cheering from the thousands of men assembled there was such as to render thought, let alone conversation, almost impossible. It went on for several minutes and as soon as the cacophony started to diminish, fireworks burst into the air from all around the garden supplementing the noise of the crowd with their own bangs and whistles.

Mungo turned to me, his face lit by the flashes of red and blue in the night sky.

'You see, John. It is a new beginning. The British have

gone. Everything is going to be all right.'

The British hadn't gone, of course. In fact, the news from Allahabad was that the British now controlled the town. They had assembled an army there and were marching toward Cawnpore. The new Peshwa had to leave his palace and hurry back to lead his troops again. From his headquarters, set up in the Old Cawnpore Hotel, he sent out orders, passed laws, appointed officers, and generally conducted all the business of state associated with his elevated title, though in the chaos of those times his writ did not run more than a day's ride from the city.

The women and children from Savada House were moved to a small house near the Nana's headquarters, as if he felt more secure with his hostages nearby. I went to see the building for myself. It was pleasant enough, having been the home of some European's mistress in the days when such liaisons were more public than they are now. But it was small – only about forty feet by fifty feet – and quite inadequate for the one hundred and eighty or more souls now crammed into it. I know that the Nana had the prisoners fed, for I saw servants going and coming with food, but I think they must have been hungry. Sometimes they were allowed to take the air, outside the house and I saw some of the women once. They were a pathetic spectacle, thin to the point of emaciation and clad in rags. They limped pitifully up and down the patch of ground allowed them, for most had no shoes and several had obviously been wounded, either in the Entrenchment or at Sati Chowra. I would have approached them to offer comfort, or treats of food and drink, but they were carefully watched and no one, not even soldiers of the Nana's guard, was allowed to draw near to them.

There were still vast numbers of rebel troops in Cawnpore. Some were waiting for their pay, some were waiting for orders, and some had just decided that staying where they were and looting the remains of the city was preferable to marching off to somewhere like Delhi where there was fighting to be done. Now, ten days after the celebration of the driving out of the *feringees*, the shirkers and the idlers were gathered up with the remnants of the mutinous regiments. The Nana's generals had recognised the danger and I was kept busy with my fellow sowars, carrying despatches from the hotel here and there about the city as the rabble of the Nana's followers was shaped into an army that might resist a British advance.

After almost a week of frantic activity, the Nana had eight thousand men under arms in something approaching a disciplined force. By now, the British were reported to be closing on Cawnpore so, on July 14th (my commonplace book tells me it was a Tuesday) we were told that the next day we were to march out to meet the enemy on the road to Allahabad.

With everyone on the lookout for deserters, there was no question of my not rejoining Chimnaji and the other sowars to head South with the rest of the troops. I sought my erstwhile comrades out that evening, and we camped together overnight. Some of our company were in a sombre mood. They remembered the struggle that the garrison had put up when hopelessly outnumbered and outgunned and they were not looking forward to meeting a British column that was well prepared for battle. Chimnaji worked hard to raise the mood, though, with tales of great victories in the past and a store of jokes and anecdotes about the life of a sowar. By the time we were lying on the ground, waiting for sleep, we were all, if not happy, at least prepared for the day ahead.

In the morning, Chimnaji suggested that we leave ahead of the main force. It would take hours for the army to muster together and, he pointed out, if we set off to scout ahead of the troops, we could ride out in the cool of early morning, rather than wait in the sun while everyone else was organised. We were all happy with the idea so, early on the Wednesday morning, we rode a way out of the town and then camped in the shade.

It was not until the middle of the afternoon that we saw clouds of dust advertising that the Nana's army was on the move. We scouted quickly to make sure that the British army had not arrived while we were dozing and then we rode back along the road until we met the rebel force. Salutes were exchanged, we reported the way ahead clear and took up our rightful position as the advance guard of the column.

We led the way for about ten miles to a place called Aherwa. It was a village of no importance but it was well situated beside the road, allowing a force placed there to prevent the movement of troops Northward. Accordingly, it was here that the Nana decided to make his stand.

The cavalry were to be held back in reserve, so I was not at first clear how our force was to be deployed. Only as I saw the troops spread out ahead of us did I realise that the Nana's generals were finally getting to grips with the basics of proper strategy. Apart from us in his cavalry, Nana Sahib deployed all his troops in a wide arc across the road, with one end of his line anchored on the Ganges so that he couldn't be outflanked on that side. The whole army was screened by mango groves and five mud-walled villages that hid his artillery.

It was an impressive plan. The land here was lower than the country further South so the army was concealed in a dip in the landscape. The British would not see the rebel force until they were practically on top of it. Having fought their way so far, they would be unlikely to retreat but would attack straight down the road. When they were within the curved line of the rebels' army, the Nana's force could open up with their artillery, wreaking havoc on the British ranks. It was a simple trap but nonetheless likely to be effective.

Now, at last, I had some information of real value to the British. As importantly, the confusion of movement inevitable when inexperienced commanders tried to position that number of troops, gave me an excellent opportunity to carry that intelligence to them.

I did not try to slip away unnoticed. Rather I rode openly from place to place, as if carrying despatches from one part of the army to another. I was able in this way to reconnoitre the whole of the line, confirming my view that the Nana's strategy was sound. Once I reached the end of the line, I simply carried on until one of the mango groves that were so useful in concealing the rebels from the British now served to conceal me from them.

The delays in leaving Cawnpore, the inevitably slow progress of a large body of men, and the time I had spent scouting the rebel positions all meant that by now dusk was falling. I waited an hour until full dark and then eased my way in a wide loop back to the Allahabad road.

Once safely away from the rebel lines, I settled to a night of fitful sleep and, as soon as there was light enough to ride, I headed on to meet the British.

I had removed my turban and made a bundle of my uniform jacket, so when I ran into General Havelock's scouts, they did not shoot me before I had time to greet them as friends and tell them that I had urgent information for their general.

'Have you, indeed? And who the hell are you, when you're at home.'

I opened my mouth to give my name and then I hesitated. As soon as I was known as John Williamson, I would be gathered back into the bosom of the European community. What then of Mungo, waiting trustingly for me to return to him? What of Amy Horne? Even Jonah Shepherd's life was safer for as long as I could pay his jailer to make sure he came to no harm.

I had a whole life as Anjoor Tewaree. I had friends and

responsibilities. I had someone who loved me. It was, I knew, a life that couldn't last. One day I would have to return to the world I had known before Mungo, but not today. When Anjoor Tewaree departed this earth, he would not be sacrificed to a brutal trooper like this fellow.

'I am Anjoor Tewaree,' I said. 'I have intelligence of the enemy's position and it is vital that I give it to the General as soon as may be.'

While we were talking, an officer had ridden over and now demanded to know what was going on. I gave him a quick summary of my news and he recognised its importance immediately. Ten minutes later, I was standing before General Havelock.

The British were making a quick breakfast of biscuit and beer, anxious to be on the march. The General must have eaten already, for he was on his feet when I was brought before him. Short, like Wheeler, he seemed to stand constantly at attention, brimming with an energy that belied his white hair and the evidence of age in his craggy features. He scarcely deigned to look at me, but barked questions about the exact placement of artillery, the numbers in each of the units and the morale of the men. He asked about fodder for the horses (we had none but that close to the Ganges would have no trouble foraging) and the condition of the ground (firmer where it drained into the river, marshier on the other flank). There was question after question and I was not sure that he really attended to my answers until he bent down and, with a stick, sketched an astonishingly accurate map of the rebel positions in the dust at his feet.

'Is that right?'

'Yes, sir, you've got it exactly.'

'Good man. Well done.' And he just turned away.

I hesitated for a moment and the trooper who had escorted me hissed in my ear. 'You're dismissed, you little runt. Now bugger off.'

So that was my meeting with Old Phlos, as the soldiers called him. I could see why he wasn't popular with his men. He was a brilliant general, though. He led an attack right down the edge of the Ganges, so that he could flank Nana Sahib, for all the rebel strategy. It was a huge risk, relying on my assurance that the ground was firm close to the water and pushing his men into a space where there was no room to manoeuvre if things went wrong.

Perhaps it was not really such a risk. Havelock's men knew about the massacre. They knew that there were still women and children held by Nana Sahib in Cawnpore.

I had to ride back to the rebel lines, galloping my horse, apparently fleeing from the British. I rejoined my fellow sowars and said I had been out scouting and the British were coming. With all the confusion of the night before, no one suspected anything.

Then the British came. They charged at us with a fury that we had never seen before, never even imagined possible. The charge was led by the Highlanders, their kilts incongruous against the Indian landscape. They came with artillery and they came with musket fire but it was their bayonets that carried the day. Seventeen inches of cold steel in the hands of an angry Scotsman is not to be taken lightly. One village after another fell and our infantry were in retreat.

We sowars were ordered to cover the sepoys as they fell back toward Cawnpore. We formed up in a block but the British cavalry came on us like madmen. I heard their captain shouting his orders: 'Point, point, no cuts!' and then we were fleeing to the jeers of the soldiers behind us.

We made one more attempt at a stand around a 24-pounder that had been held in reserve on the Cawnpore Road. Nana Sahib himself rode among us, followed by musicians beating drums, clashing cymbals, and blowing bugles. I was on the flank with Chimnaji, determined to redeem ourselves after the last rout. It seems odd, looking back, but, at the time, my determination to stand up to the British in battle seemed quite normal. I had been in their camp at breakfast, telling them how best to defeat the rebels and now here I was with the rebels, doing my best to defeat them. I can see that it's absurd now, but at the time, riding alongside men I had come to like and trust, it seemed perfectly natural. In any case, I think that most men have an understandable desire to fight back when someone is trying to kill them. And the British were certainly trying to kill me.

At first, we were successful, pushing forward with our artillery smashing into the British and the rebel fighters taking heart at seeing the Nana himself fighting with them. Soon, though, our attack lost momentum. Our guns were pouring grapeshot into the enemy ranks but they just kept coming. They were like men possessed. It seemed that however many we killed, more came at us. After a quarter of an hour of this, we were losing heart. Then the British sent up a sudden cheer and charged for our 24-pounder. Minutes later, we saw Nana Sahib flee the field, riding hell-for-leather on the Cawnpore road.

That was the end of the battle. We all broke for Cawnpore.

I made sure that I rode back to Cawnpore more slowly than my comrades of the Nana's cavalry. Now I had shown myself as a good soldier I had bought some time to deal with my private business.

Cawnpore was in an uproar. The streets had always been busy, but now I could hardly move for people rushing about in a panic. As soon as the first of the retreating rebels had reached the town, the whole population realised that the British could not be that far behind. Everyone was trying to flee. The streets were jammed with every kind of cart. Horses, camels, and mules were everywhere, kicking passersby and each other, adding their cries to the din and contributing more than their share to the stench that pervaded the place. Some enterprising soul had even found an elephant to press into service, though how he intended to use it as a pack animal, I have no idea.

At first, I was quite amused by all the panic. After all, I had nothing to fear from the British and the rebels had surely brought their trouble on themselves. Then I saw among the crowds babus who had been hiding from the rebels for weeks, a shopkeeper who I knew had been loyal, even some of those servants who had come to bid their masters farewell when the Entrenchment was abandoned. What had these people to fear from the British? I knew the troops might be out of hand when they first arrived. There would, doubtless, be looting and some wanton destruction. But those natives who had stayed loyal were in less danger from the Company than they were from the Peshwa. Trapped between the two camps, they nonetheless stood a better chance if they stayed where they were.

I stopped one man who was struggling under the weight of the bundle on his back. I recognised him as one of the Company's babus, but I was confident that he would not recognise me.

'Why are you fleeing? Do you think you have anything to fear from the British?'

He looked at me as if I were mad 'They will surely kill every one of us.'

'Because of the massacre at the river?'

'No, you fool. Because of the killing of the women.'

Despite the heat, I felt a chill shiver across my body.

'What killing?'

'How can you not know? The killing that the Peshwa ordered yesterday.'

Yesterday. While I was camped with Chimnaji and the others, relaxing in the countryside. I turned to the babu in a fury, demanding to know what had happened.

I drew the story from him, with much stuttering and

hesitation. I think he saw madness in my eyes and thought that I might turn on him and destroy him.

The previous morning, he said, orders had come to the guards to destroy all the European prisoners. No one seemed entirely sure where the order had come from originally, though the soldiers were told it was a direct command from one of their generals, who went by the name of Tatya Tope.

'The soldiers said they would not do it and Tatya Tope came to the house himself and said it was their duty but still they said it was unmanly to cut down women and children and they refused. So they brought in men from the bazaars who went into the house with tulwars.'

The screaming had gone on for an hour. The leader of the five swordsmen had twice had to emerge for new weapons as his blades shattered.

In the dawn of the day I had arrived back at Cawnpore, men had entered that dreadful charnel house and cast the bodies down the well that lay beneath a banyan tree. According to the babu telling me the tale, not all those inside the house were dead but, dead or dying, all were thrown together into the well.

'There were some children who lived and ran about trying to find any person who might save them but no one came to their aid and, in time, they were cut down and thrown into the well with the others.'

He was crying when he finished his tale, though whether in sympathy with the victims of the rebels' treachery or for fear of what would befall him, I could not tell. Certainly, he was right to be afraid, for, like him, I knew that the British would be merciless. The massacre at Sati Chowra had been bad enough but at least some of the victims had been under arms, even if they had slaughtered the innocents alongside them. But the women and children who had been held prisoner were just that. They were prisoners, unarmed, helpless, and harmless. I thanked the

Lord that I had not listened to Mungo and that Amy Horne was still safe in the countryside.

'What of the Indian prisoners?'

'What Indian prisoners?'

'There are prisoners in the old cavalry hospital. What of them?'

The babu shrugged. 'They will still be there. It was only the Europeans who were killed.'

I tossed the man a few annas, as much because I was relieved as for any service he had rendered me. Then I headed off, as quickly as I might through the mob in the streets, to see that Jonah Shepherd was still safe where I had left him.

There were fewer people about near the makeshift jail. It was not that people there were calmer, but on the outskirts of the town there were not so many houses and most of those there were had already been evacuated. Outside the old cavalry hospital, though, men were hurrying back and forth, throwing their belongings onto a cart. I saw the old subadar supervising and went to greet him.

'You are leaving as well?'

Some of his usual friendliness had gone but he answered me politely. 'I don't think we want to be here when the British arrive.'

'What of the prisoners?'

He spread his hands in the universal gesture of a man helpless to change the situation.

'I cannot release them. I have my orders and if I release them I could lose my life.'

'Then surely you should stay to guard them.'

This time, as he spread his hands he shrugged as well. 'We are leaving now. If the British arrive, then these men will be released by the British. There is nothing that I can do to stop that and I will not be blamed.'

There was some truth in this idea, but it could be days

before the British came across this jail and paid any attention to the men inside. Days when they would be without food or water and at the mercy of anyone who happened by them. The British would not be able to restore order to Cawnpore overnight. It was likely to be a very dangerous place for a while. The jailer, though, was not going to be concerned about this. Once the British had entered Cawnpore, the prisoners would no longer be his concern. Until then, he was going to keep them locked in.

I tried another tack. 'What if the British do not come?'

The subadar had been struggling to remain polite but now he allowed his irritation to show. 'Do not take me for a fool. The Peshwa's forces have been defeated. Nothing lies between the British and Cawnpore. They will be seeking revenge for all they have suffered here. They will surely come.'

'They could delay. They may not find the prisoners until too late.'

The subadar nodded. 'That is possible. But if they do not come, I will return to my post and the prisoners will still be here.'

I produced ten rupees – a fortune for a man like him. 'Just let them go before you leave.'

He hesitated and I could see the indecision on his face. Then he shook his head. 'I cannot do it. I cannot betray my trust.'

'But if you can't return, then you would be happy for the prisoners to be freed?'

'If I can't return, they can no longer be my responsibility.'

'Suppose you do not return today. Can the prisoners be freed tomorrow?'

'If I am not here tomorrow, I am sure they will be freed.'

I counted out another five rupees. 'Leave me the keys. You have my word of honour that the prisoners will not be released until tomorrow. I will wait here and, if you return, I will yield the keys back to you.'

It was a compromise that allowed the old man to retain his honour.

Five minutes later, he was gone. My purse was fifteen rupees lighter, but I held the keys in my hand.

I rested in one of the houses abandoned in the rebels' flight. It had high ceilings and offered some comfort and shade.

As I waited, I was sorely tempted just to open the jail and release everyone straightaway, but I decided I should keep my word. There had been too many broken promises in Cawnpore. But I did allow myself a liberal interpretation of 'tomorrow' and it was still dark when I set off back to the jail.

I had taken a candle from the house. I doubted that the owners would need it again. By its fitful light, I traced my way to the cavalry hospital and unlocked the door.

Inside was one large room, undivided by any partition. The sound of the door opening had awakened the prisoners who appeared agitated and cried out for food and water. In the dark, I could not see how many men were held there, but it seemed a great number of voices cried out to me from the blackness.

For a moment, I stood in the doorway. The candle flickered in the foetid air and it was as if the wavering light brought the prisoners a realisation that the door was open and that I was all that stood between them and their freedom. A moment later, with cries of joy, they were running out of the building. I had barely time to move from the doorway or I would have been trampled as hundreds of men pushed their way through.

I called over and over again as they ran by. 'Budloo! Budloo from the Entrenchment!' No one paused. I began to think he might have passed without hearing me. In desperation, I even risked shouting his true name. 'Jonah Shepherd!'

I had almost given up hope when, amongst the last to leave that miserable place, hobbled a figure that I recognised from his questioning at Savada House.

'Jonah Shepherd.'

He stared at me in the candlelight, his face blank, his eyes on the edge of madness.

'I'm English, Mr Shepherd. And I've come to save you.'

I gave him water and a little food and warned him to move away from the town as quickly as he could.

'I think our army will arrive today, but until they take control, this is a dangerous place to be. You are weak and in no position to defend yourself. You need to move away from the town. Head toward the British. They are coming on the road from Allahabad. Make your way in that direction.'

Shepherd looked at me in confusion. 'But aren't you coming with me?'

I admit I hesitated. But I was still responsible for Amy Horne. And when the British moved Northward – as I was sure they would – Mungo would need my protection, as he had protected me.

'No. I must stay here. But I will be safe. I fear that my capacity for deceit is greater than yours.' And I have a friend who has assisted me in that deceit, I thought to myself, but I did not share this with Shepherd.

It was still almost full dark but there was starlight and the faintest glimmerings from the rising sun in the East. Perilous as the road might be by night, I wanted to be away as soon as may be. With the Nana's armies gone, any small pretence of law and order would already be breaking down. And though I hoped the British would bring some sort of peace, I thought that any business to be conducted at Saturday House was best done with before their arrival.

I set off, for what I suspected would be the last time, on the road to Bithur. Fortunately, by now I knew the way well enough to find my route in the darkness. The streets were littered with more than the usual amount of detritus. An army in retreat abandons much of its gear and all but the most valuable of its plunder. Still, my horse found a clear path through the rubbish and we moved slowly but surely through the town. There were no people about to disturb us at that hour, although the occasional sound of splintering timber and more than one or two screams in the distance suggested that there was still loot to be stolen and scores to be settled now that the rebel army was no longer there.

Once out of the town and clear of the shadows of the houses, the path was easier to see. By now, too, the glimmerings in the East were already growing brighter. The dawn would soon be on us. I pressed my heels to my horse's flanks and we were soon moving along the highway at a brisk trot.

Dawn comes quickly in the Orient and I was not halfway to Bithur before it was full daylight. Before the revolt, the road here had usually been quiet as it passed through the countryside, but there would be farmers in the fields and the smoke from breakfast fires rising from villages in the distance. Today, though, the countryside as far as I could see was still and silent. Everyone would have seen the Nana's army fleeing North and would know by now that they were on the cusp of change. So they hid in their homes to wait and see what their fate would be.

I pressed on. I had some vague hope that I might catch up with the rebel army. I did pass the odd straggler – men whose wounds slowed them and who had been abandoned in the Nana's flight – but it was clear that the main body of the rebels had pushed on as fast as they could. Well before I reached Saturday House, I knew that they had already abandoned Bithur.

At first sight, everything at Saturday House seemed normal. There was the slightest of breezes and the leaves on the trees lining the avenue that led to the house rustled a little. Otherwise, there was silence and it took a few minutes to realise that the little sounds that you might expect to hear weren't there. The faint clack of hoof on stable stone was missing. There came no whispers of conversation on the breeze. There was no sound of shouted orders or the footsteps of servants hurrying to obey them. There was the occasional cry of a peacock and, as I came nearer, the gentle splashing of fountains, but otherwise there was nothing.

The gates of the compound were open and no sentry challenged me. The sound of my horse's hooves seemed unnaturally loud as we clattered toward the stables.

The stables were quiet too. Every horse had gone. I had never seen them empty before. It seemed that the Nana's army had taken every beast that might carry a fleeing soldier.

At first, I had thought that the stable lads had fled with the army but after I had called two or three times, a nervous boy of thirteen or fourteen appeared from the corner where he had been sheltering and took the bridle from my hands and led my horse away.

'Take care of him!' I called. 'I will not have him stolen by some ragamuffin who would flee after the others and who wants to spare their legs.'

The boy looked at me as if he were about to burst into tears. 'There's none left that would steal your horse, sir. All have fled.'

'All?'

'All the men, sir.'

I turned, leaving him still standing at my bridle, and hurried into Saturday House. Down corridor after corridor, my feet echoing on marble floors. The hour struck as I was near the corridor of clocks and the sudden din in all that silence near unmanned me. I carried on through the maze, which was now as familiar as any place I'd lived, and soon I was at the door of Mungo's apartments. I opened without knocking, sure that I would see naught inside but the evidence of hurried packing.

Instead, I saw Mungo.

He was sitting cross-legged on a carpet placed in front of the door. He held no book or paper for writing. No painting occupied his eyes and there was no little sculpture for those long fingers to play with. He just sat, waiting. And when I opened the door, he raised his eyes to my face and his eyes were filled with tears.

'I thought you might not come,' he said.

Then, after a while, he said, 'I should have known that I could trust you.'

Chapter Ten

Mungo described the panic of the previous day. The army had swept past Saturday House, pausing only long enough for Nana Sahib to collect up his treasure and have it loaded onto barges on the Ganges. He and his closest family had set sail upriver with about a hundred soldiers to escort him. The rest of the army had vanished Northward and Westward. Saturday House had been gripped by panic. The guards at the gates had joined the army's flight. The courtiers had commandeered every horse, cart, elephant, and camel in the place and had set off in pursuit.

'It is because they killed the women,' Mungo said. 'They say Azimullah and the generals made the Peshwa do it so that he could not surrender to the British. They thought it would make him strong. But now they are all weak and fly, as children do who have stolen into their father's rooms and broken the ornaments there and now hear their father returning. They know the British will be merciless.'

'But you stayed.'

'I knew you would return here. And where you are, there I belong. How could I flee and leave you? Where could I live if not with you?'

I held him then, for I do not know how long. I held him as a drowning man clings to the rope that holds him to the shore. I had loved before but I had never been so needed.

At last, I broke off from our embrace to address the practicalities of our situation.

'People have been wise to flee. The British will come here and, when they do, their vengeance will be terrible.

We must leave.'

Mungo nodded enthusiastically. Now that I was with him, he seemed happy for us to leave together.

'The girl I saved is still with your cousin. We should go there. It is far enough from Bithur that it may well be spared. In any case, the worst of the violence should be over by the time the troops have finished with Saturday House.'

'How will we get there? All the horses are gone.'

I looked at his lithe figure. I had always loved the way he looked. Now I could see a practical advantage to his slimness. 'I have a horse. We'll both ride that.'

Relief flooded Mungo's features. 'Very well, I'll pack.'

'No. We shouldn't waste the time and we won't be able to carry much anyway. Your cousin will have enough for us to cope. We shouldn't be there long.'

'Just a few things.'

I started to argue but realised after a couple of minutes that it would be quicker to let him take a favourite tunic and a book he treasured than to waste the time disputing.

'And then there are these.' Mungo was leaning over a chest on the floor where he kept some clothes and a few gold bangles.

I imagined the clocks ticking in the corridor. 'We don't have time for these trifles, Mungo.'

'These are no trifles.'

I looked over his shoulder. The bangles were narrow and the work, to my inexpert eye, of no great value.

'They aren't worth anything, Mungo. Leave them.'

But then I heard a click and Mungo's hand was darting into a cavity in the base of the chest. It came out holding a small bag, from which he shook three diamonds, each about a quarter of an inch across and a ruby of a similar size.

He grinned up at me. 'Perhaps these are worth taking?' He slipped them back into the bag, pulled the drawstring tight and slung it from his neck under his tunic. 'Now we go, yes?'

We hurried to the stables, Mungo almost skipping ahead, as if convinced that he was out of danger now I was here. I was less confident, but the same scared stable boy was quick to return my horse. Though the beast was tired, he had benefited from the brief rest, food, water, and a rub down. Refreshed, Kuching was easily able to carry Mungo's weight along with mine and, as we set off slowly Northward, I began to share his optimism.

It was early afternoon, the hottest time of the day at the hottest time of year. We rode at an easy pace but, even so, our horse was struggling after the first half hour and I was worried that, although I was by now well used to the climate, I could be struck down by the heat, which killed so many Europeans exposed to the midday sun. I decided it would be wise to shelter in one of the occasional groves of trees that broke up the landscape. If the British did send scouts North immediately, they would surely spend some time in searching Saturday House. Now we were clear of Nana Sahib's palace, I thought that there was less urgency to our flight.

We left the horse loose to forage for grass in the shade. There was no danger of it wandering into the open country in the heat of the day. We lay down and rested.

After a few minutes, Mungo rolled against me and I held him in my arms.

'John, now that the British are back, what do you intend to do?'

I did not answer at once. A few weeks ago, my flight to Saturday House and Mungo's protection had seemed just a precaution while we waited for the situation in Cawnpore to settle down. But these past few weeks had seen my life so changed I could hardly believe that once I had breakfasted in the Club, worked in my office with Hillersdon and Simkin, and dined in the evening with the ladies of the Station. All these people were dead now. With them, it seemed to me, a way of life had died and, perhaps, a part of me had died with it. Could I ever return to that world?

'I don't know, Mungo. I really don't know.'

He lay still against me and I knew it was not the answer he had wanted to hear.

'And what of you?'

He forced a smile. 'You have seen the diamonds.'

I could hardly have forgotten them. Since he left Saturday House, they were the sum total of his wealth and he wore the little bag around his neck almost all the time.

'And I have my family. Dara will give me shelter for as long as I need.' He paused and his expression grew more optimistic. 'And you, too. You can stay there with me. You will be welcomed as one of my family.'

I knew that what he said was true. Family ties were close and I knew that Dara would offer me the same protection as he would Mungo. Perhaps it would be for the best. Perhaps I should settle down as a zemindar – just another of those thousands of landlords whose livelihoods I had been so busy trying to tax away while I worked for the Company.

It was an idea not without its attractions. The attractions grew when we finally rose from our rest and completed our journey. We were welcomed into the compound where Dara lived with his extended family. The main building, with its separate wing for the women, housed him, his two brothers, and their sons. I don't think I ever worked out exactly how many sons there were. Around a score of boys and young men, ranging from a toddler to a strapping youth in his early twenties, were forever coming and going about the place. Another son had his own separate house in the compound where he lived with his wife. There were separate, smaller houses for the servants and the farmers and their servants who farmed the fields closest to Dara's home. Mungo explained that a zemindar like Dara would never take direct responsibility for his land but that the farming would be left to the tenants. Many of these people were not relatives, but the man who farmed closest to the compound was another of the network of cousins that bound these families together.

Mungo and I were given a room in the main house. Dara did not seem concerned about our relationship. He was much more worried about my request for a private interview with Miss Horne. It was not until we had been there for two days that Mungo was able to convince him that, as Europeans, it would be acceptable for the two of us to meet and then Dara only allowed it on condition that Mungo acted as chaperone.

When I finally did meet Amy Horne, I scarcely recognised her. The frightened, starved, half-naked girl I had rescued has been replaced by a calm and assured young lady, dressed in native clothing beneath which, as far as I could judge, was a well-fed and healthy body.

'I find you in better health than when last we met, I hope.'

'Thank you, sir, you do.'

'And you are happy here?'

Her face, unremarkable in repose, was beautiful when she smiled, as she did now.

'Very happy, sir. Everyone has been most kind.'

'You know that the British are back in Cawnpore?'

The smile vanished. 'I did not know. There has been talk, of course.' She paused, chewing her lower lip. 'I think that the others must have known but have kept this from me.'

'I imagine that this must be good news for you.'

She rallied, trying hard to summon an appearance of delight to her features, but she was too palpably honest a girl to succeed.

'We think it will soon be safe to carry you to Cawnpore to rejoin your people.'

At this, all attempt at dissemblance was abandoned. Indeed, I fcared she might burst into tears. 'Please do not send me away. What would I go back to? I have no people. My father was neither a Company servant nor a soldier. No one will care that he has died and I have no family living.'

I endeavoured to set her mind at rest . 'You are a pretty girl, Amy. I am sure that someone will take care of you.'

She blushed. 'Sir, it will be known that I have been living with the natives. It will be assumed that I have been dishonoured.' She must have seen something in my face for she hastened to reassure me. 'No such thing has happened, sir. I have been treated with every kindness and I believe that the women here love me as my sisters did when they were living. I would be protected from any insult. But you must understand, sir, that no one in Cawnpore will believe this. No man will have me now.'

I did my best to reassure her that this could not be the case. All I achieved, though, was more tears. In the end, I released her back to the women's quarters.

'It's a poor show, Mungo,' I said, once she was safely out of earshot. 'For I fear that she is right.'

Mungo shook his head in astonishment. 'But she is young and very beautiful. I am sure that one of Dara's people would be happy to marry her.'

'But not any of her own people, I'm afraid. I don't know what we are to do, for with no family, no income, and no prospect of marriage, her condition once she leaves here will be pitiable.'

'Then she must not leave here.'

I was surprised by Mungo's comment. It was one thing for me, a man, to have chosen to live among the natives, but it was unseemly to see this imposed on an English girl. My irritation at his suggestion must have shown and

Mungo resented it.

We ended up arguing for some time. By the end of our altercation, both of us were in an ill humour and all that had been agreed was that the girl would have to stay for the time being. That was hardly a concession on my part for with neither rebel nor European army clearly established in the countryside, transporting Miss Horne to Cawnpore would have been, in my view, too much of a risk to expose her to.

So life continued, with we three refugees enjoying Dara's hospitality. I had occasional interviews with Amy. She was by now physically recovered from her ordeal, but Dara said that the women told him that she would often wake screaming. They had all grown to love her and had coaxed out more details of her life in the Entrenchment. It seemed that, young as she was, she had done everything she could to help the men and women around her, looking after her younger brothers and sisters while her mother descended into madness, and always willing to assist with the nursing of the wounded soldiers.

'I think,' said Dara, 'that European women can be braver than their men.'

For Mungo and me, our stay was, in many ways, a simple holiday. I did worry, from time to time, that our idling might eventually cause offence within the household but then I observed that idleness was endemic amongst the zemindar class. The day-to-day running of the farms was the responsibility of the tenants though they, of course, did no actual labour themselves. The work was done by labourers who lived on a few annas a day. The tenants lived quite well themselves but the majority of the profits came to Dara, whose efforts consisted mainly of attending to his accounts and adjudicating on the odd dispute amongst his various tenants and sub-tenants.

'You are unfair, John,' Mungo argued when I remarked on this to him. 'When you worked for the Company, did you tend the fields?'

'Well, no. But the Company administered the whole country. We made laws and enforced them. We built roads and kept order. We did our best to protect the weak from exploitation.'

'And Dara and the other zemindars do the same. Do you think there were no roads in India before you came? Did we not have laws and were they not observed? The zemindar acts as your magistrate did, adjudicating disputes. When men are needed to guard the country or keep the peace, the zemindar provides them.'

I thought of the landlords who had joined the Nana's army, each bringing their own followers to swell the ranks. I thought of the beggars I had seen fed, the bloated household of the Nana Sahib with all the retainers whose survival depended on his generosity. I thought of myself and Mungo, fed and cared for because Dara had a responsibility for his family.

Mungo watched the working of my face while I thought these things.

'You see, John. You think the Company changed so much. But really, we Indians just exchanged one zemindar for another.'

It was a few days after this that the British sent a force North from Cawnpore on the road to Bithur. Word spread from village to village, through that network of family connections and casual gossip that has served the Indians for their news for longer than there have been Europeans in the country. One of the first acts of the rebels had been the destruction of the telegraph, but I believe that, even had the wires still been in place, news would spread on the native grapevine faster than it could ever be transmitted officially from Company outpost to Company outpost. In any case, before we took our tiffin at midday, we knew that the British had marched out that morning.

It will have taken them hours to reach Bithur. A military expedition moves slowly, even in the absence of organised resistance. Even so, by that evening we were being told that the soldiers had got to Saturday House. By then such servants as remained had evacuated the building so we had no news of what occurred inside, but I could imagine the destruction. Still thirsting for vengeance, the troops will have rampaged through the place, stealing anything they thought of value and, as often as not, destroying all they could not steal. I imagined the mirrors smashed, the idols desecrated, the books in the library torn and scattered on the floor. The corridor of clocks would not be disturbed by their din again.

That night neither Mungo nor I could sleep. The British would have rested at Bithur. The question that kept us awake through the night was whether would they turn back to Cawnpore or press on Northward?

An hour after dawn, the word from the field hands – who had it from a farmer's son who had it from a beggar who had it from who knows where – was that the British were making their way back South. Our relief was short lived, though. Soon after came news that, while the main force had headed South, a small column was pushing on Northward.

By mid morning, we did not need news to tell us where the British were. Smoke from burning buildings on the horizon made all too clear the direction of their advance – and they were heading directly toward us.

Tired as we were after our restless night, we could not sleep through the heat of midday. We knew that the British would rest at noon and march again as the afternoon cooled. What we did not know was whether they would continue Northward or turn to rejoin the rest of the army.

Labourers working on Dara's land watched the soldiers, ready to bring news as soon as they moved. Meanwhile, we could do nothing but wait.

The first of them returned at around three in the afternoon. The soldiers were making North.

Dara gathered his household together (by which I mean the men, for the women remained secluded) and announced his intention to abandon his home. 'If we flee now, we will stay well ahead of the British. They may burn and pillage for another day, maybe two, but then we can return.'

It was Mungo who objected to the plan. 'Cousin, you do not have to abandon your home and expose your women to the dangers of the countryside. The British are not barbarians, killing and destroying without reason.'

'Mungo, we can see the burning from here. They are destroying the farms. Burning the villages.'

'But we are not their enemies.'

'You are of the Peshwa's household. I am your cousin. How can we not be their enemies?'

I had remained silent, leaving Mungo to debate with Dara, but now Mungo turned to draw me into this argument.

'We have John here with us. He can speak to them and tell them that we have not fought against the British but rather that we have protected him.'

'Can you do this?' Dara asked.

'I can speak to them. I will do my best.'

'They will listen to John,' Mungo assured his cousin, 'and we will be spared.'

'Is Mungo right?'

I hesitated. I remembered seeing British sailors in Borneo killing without compunction or mercy. The troops that were heading in our direction would know all about the massacre. They would be angry and looking for revenge.

Dara spoke again. 'Is Mungo right?'

It would be all right. I would speak to their officer. They would listen and leave the place unharmed.

'Will we be safe?'

'Yes,' I said. 'You will be safe.'

It was late in the afternoon and the day was beginning to cool when the troops arrived. There were about thirty of them, marching slowly but steadily in a neat block with a young lieutenant riding beside them.

As they approached the compound, I walked out to meet them with more trepidation than I allowed to show. My European clothes had been abandoned, so I was dressed as an Indian, though I left my head uncovered. I had given up using walnut juice some weeks earlier but my skin still carried the stain and my constant exposure to the sun had left me well tanned. Given my natural dark colouring, it was not immediately obvious that I was a European.

I walked slowly toward them, my arms raised, shouting, 'I'm British,' over and over again, as loudly as I could. Even so, the platoon halted and rifles were pointed in my direction before two men were detached to bring me to the officer.

As soon as my escort had me in hand, the rest of the men started to move forward again. I was led forward by the arm and the soldiers seemed to think of me as much as a prisoner as a free citizen of Great Britain.

As soon as I had been secured the platoon moved forward and, by the time I had been brought before the officer, the front rank was already pushing into the compound.

The young man looked down from his horse. 'You say you're British.'

'I am British. I'm John Williamson.'

He looked at me blankly and I realised that, with the European community in Cawnpore all dead, there was no reason why the name should mean anything to him.

'I'm the Deputy Collector.'

The lieutenant snapped a salute and dismounted.

'I'm happy to see you well, sir. My understanding was that all the Company's officers in Cawnpore were killed.'

'Well, as you see, I survived. Thanks largely to the protection offered to me by the men in that compound that your soldiers are forcing their way into now.'

He turned to see the last of the platoon vanishing inside the compound walls.

'I will ensure that they are gentle, sir.'

He pushed his horse forward to follow the men but, before he reached the gate, I heard the sound of shots from inside. He kicked his horse to a trot and I started to run after him. There were more shots and then I heard him cry out, 'Cease your firing! Sergeant, rally the men.'

By the time I arrived, some sort of order had been restored. The doors to the main house hung off their hinges. In front of them, a line of troops, bayonets fixed, stood on guard. Two bodies lay on the ground in front of them. Servants clustered sullenly in front of their homes. It looked as if they had run out to protect their master when the troops forced the doors of the house and had paid the price. Looking at them as they faced the troops, I feared that they might rush forward again.

'Wait!' I shouted in Hindoo. 'All will be well if you wait.'

The men shifted and muttered amongst themselves. They clearly remained unhappy and suspicious, but by now they knew me and I felt my words might have some effect. I had no time to wait to be sure, though. The lieutenant had left his horse at the entrance to the house and I hurried catch up with him.

Inside was chaos. Doors were open, the low tables had been kicked over, soldiers seemed to be everywhere and I could hear shouts and screams. The worst of the noise seemed to be coming from the direction of the women's quarters so I made my way toward them.

I have explained that the women's quarters were separate from the rest of the building and that the men, except for Dara, did not enter unless special permission had been given. There was but one door that linked these rooms to the rest of the house and that was generally guarded by a servant. It was not that Dara thought anyone might enter without permission but more that the proprieties might be observed. Unfortunately, faced with British soldiers demanding entrance, the servant had elected to stand his ground and he had been struck down. As I arrived, the lieutenant was crouched over him. He looked up as he saw me approaching.

'He'll live.' Then, gesturing toward the door. 'What's through here?'

'The women's quarters. For God's sake get your men out.'

The poor lad was really very young. He looked around as if hoping to find inspiration in the corridor where we stood, but before he could do anything there was the sound of women's screams from the zenana, followed by European oaths and the noise of booted feet running back toward the door.

Four soldiers appeared, coming full tilt toward us. Their faces were blotched red with fury.

'He's got one of our women in there. A British girl in his bloody harem!'

The lieutenant gawped at the man, who ran on into the house.

'You need to stop them!'

'But ...' He looked puzzled. 'I say, what do they mean about an English girl?'

'I saved her. She's been sheltering here with me.'

He was still gawping. He was obviously new to India. Brought up on stories of the exotic East, he saw no difference between the careful propriety of the zenana and the erotic fantasy of the harem. The idea that Amy Horne's most exotic activity in the past weeks was a little embroidery work would have been utterly incomprehensible to him.

'Get your men under control!'

It was too late. He was too inexperienced and the men had their blood up. If he did not understand the finer points of the position of women in the household, his men knew nothing and cared less. They had found a pure English lass at the mercy of the foul Indian fiend and the rage that they would have been nursing since they learned of the massacre was now allowed full rein.

I heard shouts from room to room and the sound of splintering doors and breaking furniture.

'Avenge our women!' was the cry which swept through the platoon. I started to follow the noise but the lieutenant grabbed my sleeve.

'Don't try. They'll kill you too. There's no stopping them when they're like this.'

His face was white but I think he was no coward. He might have been young and inexperienced but he knew the temper of the British soldier. He had allowed himself to lose control. Now all that could be done was to wait for their fury to burn itself out.

It was probably only about ten minutes before his sergeant began to drive the men to the door but it felt much longer. Two corporals were sent back to the zenana to escort Amy Horne back to what they doubtless thought of as civilisation. I watched as she was brought out. Tears were pouring down her cheeks and she was screaming at the men to let her go. Behind her, I could hear the keening of the women.

They dragged her past the bodies that lay in the entrance hall. I recognised Dara and two of his sons. The others had been beaten so badly they could have been anyone.

There was no sign of Mungo.

'Best if you leave with us, sir.'

'I can't. I have to ...'

I had to find Mungo, was what I wanted to say, but I didn't feel I could explain.

'We'll wait a few minutes, sir, but then you'll have to come with us. I'm sorry about the way things turned out but I can't leave you here.' He tried to smile. 'I can't have them say I found the Deputy Collector and then lost him again.'

I started back to the room I had shared with Mungo. I tried to ignore wreckage all around, the smeared blood on the floors, the last of the soldiers pocketing such small valuables as they could loot before their sergeant rounded them all up. One was hacking a sapphire from a statue of Ganesh that sat in a niche in the wall. Another was holding a drawstring bag. He grinned at me. 'Diamonds,' he said. 'And a ruby.'

I was on him before I had time to think, my hands at his throat. His comrade seized my coat and tried to pull me off but I was a man possessed. Now the soldier behind me was striking at my head and shouting for help, but I scarce felt his blows. All that mattered was my fingers, tightening on the throat of the man below me.

There was the sound of running feet. Men pulled at my arms but still I did not release my grip. The face below me was purple. The eyes bulged. The lips were turning blue.

'Mr Williamson! Williamson! Let him go!'

Gradually the lieutenant's voice penetrated my brain. Suddenly I felt the pain where my head had been struck and the force of the men pulling at me. My fingers released his throat and I was pulled to my feet.

The sergeant was kneeling beside his man.

'He's alive. Just.'

The lieutenant started to speak but something in my face stopped him.

I shook the men off and turned to walk away. No one tried to stop me.

As I walked, I became aware of the lieutenant walking with me. I let him be. It seemed easiest.

I knew what I would find. I didn't know the details, of course, but I knew that Mungo would have been wearing that bag round his neck. No one would have searched his body while he was alive.

He was lying on the floor. There was no blood. I was glad of that. I think his neck had been broken. He lay there, as if he had just fallen asleep. His shirt had been ripped open and the skin still glowed as it had when he was alive.

He was so beautiful. I knelt and lifted him to me and kissed his lips. I did not care that I was watched.

The lieutenant said nothing. He waited and when I laid the body down, he took me gently by the arm and guided me out.

I did not cry. I wanted to but I did not.

Someone had found me a horse. It was not mine but I didn't care. They helped me mount.

The platoon moved off. South, toward Cawnpore.

'It's all right,' said the lieutenant. 'We're taking you home.'

Chapter Eleven

The next few weeks passed in a daze. Cawnpore was still at the forefront of the fighting with the rebels expected to counterattack at any time. It was no place for a civilian. I was evacuated to Allahabad. Amy Horne was whisked away somewhere. I don't know what happened to her, though I heard she eventually arrived in Allahabad too.

Physically, I was in good shape but the doctors said I was suffering from nervous exhaustion and the effects of the heat. I suppose that sounds better than to say I had a broken heart.

The British won the war, of course. Looking back, it seems inevitable that they would have, but it didn't seem inevitable at the time. For a few weeks in Cawnpore, it seemed that the world was about to change. Maybe in some ways it did. The East India Company was wound up and India became part of the British Empire. The same officials remained in charge but the British Government was able to maintain a tighter control on how things were done. There was some liberalisation of the way that the natives were treated. Annexations were to end. The Government recognised that the best way to maintain control in India was to develop an Indian middle class which would act as a cushion between the bulk of the native population and their European rulers.

The babus, like Mr Shepherd, many of whom had risked everything by their loyalty to the British, were among the principal beneficiaries of this policy. At last they were to have the chance to rise up the ranks of what was to become the Indian Civil Service, instead of being condemned to toil always at the lowest levels.

These changes, though, were all to take time to implement and, meanwhile, with the fighting over, there was still a country to run. And though the Company men were now servants of the Crown, we still had to do the same old work. The Summer of 1858 found me back in Cawnpore. The Company offices had been much damaged during the revolt, but repairs had been effected and the place was still familiar. I was not to sit in my old room, though. Mr Hillersdon's death had left a vacancy for Collector and, once I was judged recovered, it was felt that I should be allowed a run at the job.

The press of work required in the rebuilding of the country can easily be imagined. The late starts, long lunches, and early ends to the day, which had so characterised the office when I first arrived, were no more. Indeed, we were under the necessity of holding office for eight or ten hours daily, inclusive of Sundays, and such a thing as a holiday was never heard of. At first I welcomed the work as distraction from my grief, but as the months passed I began to find concentration difficult. A phrase in Hindi, a glimpse of a young man whose face brought to mind that of my beloved Mungo, the smell of herbs in a cooking pot: all these things might suddenly bring to mind my time in Saturday House and I would be lost in reverie until an anxious colleague would bring me back to the business in hand with enquiries as to my health. Sometimes, I sat at my desk, unmanned, tears streaming down my cheeks. No one ever referred to these incidents but I know they talked about me behind my back. I do not think they were cruel, but I know the gulf that had always separated me from them had grown wider.

I could not remain as Collector, of course. A new man arrived as the worst of the summer heat gave way to the more bearable weather that presaged the bliss of the winter cool. He was very kind. I should not really have remained as Deputy Collector, but there was much to do and he felt that the work helped me by keeping me from dwelling on what had passed. In fact, everyone was very kind, as one is kind to a dog that has been beaten. Their kindness was distant. I cannot blame them for, of course, they did not know the one unbearable truth that was at the centre of my distress. I had loved Mungo more than I realised and his death had left me diminished. I had thought that leaving Borneo and the love I had known there was hard but this was a thousand times worse. I had loved him with the passion of an older man for a younger lover. It was the flowering of a lifetime of experience, intoxicated by the excitement of youth. And, for so long, I had dismissed it as mere lust, denying what I only now realised was the marriage of two souls.

My youth has long departed. Mungo had warmed my middle years and made me feel young again. Now all that was over. I was suddenly an old man.

I struggled on to the end of the year but I was tired. Tired of India, tired of the life I had lived there. It was time to go home.

The Collector was very good about it. I was a survivor of Cawnpore, after all. He spoke a lot about strain and nervous collapse. He said I shouldn't feel guilty. He said that the Company would pay my passage home and arrange a pension for me. He was very generous.

So, almost exactly three years after I had arrived in Cawnpore from Calcutta, I retraced my steps. It was a melancholy journey, for it lacked the sense of excitement and discovery that I had felt on my arrival. The country, too, was melancholy, at least in the early stages of the journey, for the British had not been gentle in their destruction of the rebels and we passed village after village that had been put to the flame. Among the men rebuilding their habitations, almost all were very old or very young. On some trees still hung the remains of the ropes where a vengeful army had hanged all the men of fighting age who could not account for their actions during the rebellion.

At Allahabad, instead of travelling on by road, we took to the river. I travelled in a very fine sixteen-oared pinnace, containing two excellent cabins, fitted up with glazed and venetian windows, pankhas, and two shower-baths. Even on this final journey, the Collector had insisted that I travel with an appropriate number of servants, so there was a separate dinghee for the cook and provisions for the voyage and another for a valet and my baggage. I had been pressed to take another so to carry more servants but I had drawn the line at this. There was, after all, a full crew on the pinnace and they would more than adequately see to my needs on the journey South.

So we flew down the river on a powerful wind. We passed Mirzapur and Patna, Berhampur and Cutwa. I am told the journey is very beautiful but I was in no mood to appreciate it, although I did enjoy the smoothness of carriage in the pinnace, compared to the rigours of travel in a buggy.

By the time we reached Nuddea, the tide was perceptible and I began to brighten at the prospect of arriving in Calcutta and transferring to the vessel that would take me home.

We arrived in Calcutta on February 12th. The view of the shipping was beautiful and I enjoyed it, although the crew dashed among the other vessels with fearful velocity.

I was put ashore in Calcutta and stayed two days in the same hotel where I had rested on my arrival. During this time a Government agent found a vessel with accommodation suitable for my return trip, so, with only the briefest of delays, I was settled aboard the *Earl of Hardwicke*. A steamer towed us down the river on the morning of 15th February, and the pilot quitted us on the 17th, from which moment the voyage actually commenced.

I will say nothing of the passage. It was long, and we

broke our journey at the Cape and at St Helena, arriving in the Channel early on 3rd June 1859. I determined to leave the ship at Plymouth and I, together with a large party of other passengers, was taken off by the pilot vessel.

So it was that, after so many years, I found myself once more in the county where I spent my youth. It was a balmy day and, as I walked up from the port, roses were blooming in the hedges. I breathed in their smell. It was the smell of England.

I was home.

EDITOR'S NOTES

Williamson's account of events at Cawnpore is generally in agreement with other published accounts. There are a few details that do not fit the public record. In some cases, it is clear that the public record was edited to avoid awkward questions. (Amy Horne's account of what happened to her between her capture and her eventual reappearance in Allahabad would be a case in point.) In other cases, it seems people's recollections of what actually happened when they were caught up in these traumatic events may not always be precisely accurate.

The principle facts about Cawnpore would, until the mid-20th Century, have been known to every British schoolchild. Wheeler's force consisted of around sixty European artillerymen with six guns, eighty-four infantrymen, and about two hundred unattached officers and civilians and forty musicians from the native regiments. In addition, he had seventy invalids who were convalescing in the barrack hospital and around three hundred and seventy-five women and children. They were besieged in a wholly inadequate position from 6th June 1857. From 6th to 25th June, the Entrenchment was under continual bombardment by day and sometimes by night. Faced with overwhelming numbers of enemy cavalry and infantry, the tiny defence force nonetheless managed to hold out until they were offered safe passage in return for their surrender. General Wheeler, by then a broken man whose son had been killed during the siege, accepted the terms. Many people think that he was strongly influenced by the views of Captain Moore, who had taken much of the responsibility for the defence as Wheeler's health had deteriorated. Williamson's account confirms the general belief that Moore was a man of exceptional vigour and courage who did much to maintain the spirits of the garrison.

The rebels broke the terms of the surrender and the massacre at the ghat became part of the history of the British Empire. Williamson's description of the massacre is consistent with other accounts. Amy Horne was carried off by a sowar, although she afterward claimed that the man had been a Muslim. Reading Williamson's account, it is easy to see why Miss Horne may have been discouraged from telling the whole truth about the incident.

The massacre of the women and children at a house generally referred to by the English as the Bibighar, happened almost exactly as described to Williamson. The reason why Nana Sahib ordered such an atrocity is not clear. Some people believe that he hoped, by killing the last surviving witnesses, to escape responsibility for the earlier massacre. Others consider that he was trapped into it by hardliners within his court who wanted to make sure that he would not be able to make peace with the British. Nana Sahib's role throughout the events reads strangely to a modern Western onlooker. It may well be best explained in the terms used by Mungo. It is quite likely the Nana Sahib was trying desperately to maintain a position where he could claim to be favouring either side until it was quite clear who was winning. Many local leaders in India at the time changed sides and the British were often prepared to accept as allies people they had every reason to think had been plotting against them when it looked as if they were going to be defeated.

Williamson's depiction of the battle against Havelock fits the known facts. Havelock's victory was in part down to intelligence received from a native spy called Anjoor Tewaree. Williamson's account provides a valuable insight as to who Anjoor Tewaree actually was.

We do not know for certain what became of Williamson after his return to England. In 1861, a John Williamson is recorded as having bought the Grange, a substantial house in the village of Bickleigh, just North of Plymouth. The parish records show no trace of him in the years before that and whether it is the same John Williamson, we have no way of knowing. He seems to have been a well-respected member of the community, as he was churchwarden from 1863 until his death in 1872.

Williamson was obviously not in a position to know exactly what became of all the people that he met at Cawnpore. However, the fate of many of them is a matter of historical record.

CHARLES HILLERSDON was struck by a cannonball in the Entrenchment. Some reports put his death on June 7th, others on June 13th.

LYDIA HILLERSDON survived childbirth but was killed by a cannonball on June 9th.

LADY WHEELER and her daughter ELIZA WHEELER died with the General at the ghat.

MARGARET WHEELER is believed to have been one of the only survivors. She was captured by a Muslim soldier whom she later married. She lived quietly in Cawnpore, finally admitting her identity to a priest shortly before her death early in the 20th century.

CAPTAIN MOORE died at the ghat.

NANA SAHIB returned to Cawnpore to lead a counter-attack on the British but failed. After a succession of military defeats, he fled. It is widely believed that he died in Nepal.

JONAH SHEPHERD survived to publish an account of his adventures. He came close to death on several occasions and was saved more than once because his jailer refused to allow him to plead before the Nana that he was with the Europeans and should be released with them. He ascribed his survival to the direct intervention of God and, as a result, in his later life his enthusiasm for proselytisation verged on religious mania. Williamson's narrative suggests that his survival may have had a more secular explanation.

AMY HORNE survived and, despite the prejudice she feared she would be exposed to, married.

There are several contemporary accounts of the siege of Cawnpore. Captain Mowbray Thomson's book, *The Story of Cawnpore* is available online through Google Books. Jonah Shepherd's book, *A Personal Narrative of the Outbreak and Massacre at Cawnpore: During the Sepoy Revolt of 1857* is available through Nabu Public Domain Reprints.

Sir George Otto Trevelyan's book *Cawnpore*, published in 1866, draws heavily on Thomson's account but does provide other useful background.

Andrew Ward's book, *Our Bones Are Scattered* (1996), provides an astonishingly detailed and comprehensive account of the events in Cawnpore. For a broader discussion of the events in India, I would recommend Julian Spilsbury's *The Indian Mutiny* (2007). For a more accessible account, you could try John Harris, *The Indian Mutiny* (1973).

Williamson's experiences do, at times, show remarkable similarities to the accounts given by Fanny Parkes (*Wanderings of a Pilgrim in Search of the Picturesque*) published in 1850 and now available free through Google Books and Vivian Dering Majendie (*Up Among Pandies)* published in 1859 and recently republished by Leonaur Ltd.

Some readers have complained that Williamson's success in disguising himself as an Indian is not credible. In fact, some British officers used such disguises successfully during the Mutiny. At the siege of Lucknow, Henry Kavanagh, one of the European volunteers in the garrison, offered to pass through the rebel lines to guide in the relief column. He dyed his skin and dressed himself in native clothing before passing around the European camp and ensuring that he was not recognised for what he was.

He escaped from the siege by swimming across a river but soon ran into an enemy sentry.

'I thought it prudent to be the first to speak, and remarked, as we approached, that the night was cold, and after his repeating that it *was* cold, I passed on observing that it would be colder bye-and-bye.'

He passed several other sentries without his disguise being penetrated. At one point, he and his native companion were stopped and questioned. The native became visibly frightened. Kavanagh wrote:

'I drew their attention to his fright, and begged that they would not terrify poor travellers, unaccustomed to being questioned by so many valorous soldiers.'

The sentries were satisfied and let him go.

John Williamson, of course, got away with much more than this, but then he was a devotee of Indian culture and had Mungo to help him.

TCW, London, 2014

Tom Williams

The Williamson Papers

The White Rajah
Cawnpore
Back Home

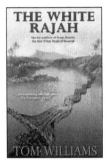

For more information about **Tom Williams**

and other **Accent Press** titles

please visit

www.accentpress.co.uk

Printed in Great Britain
by Amazon